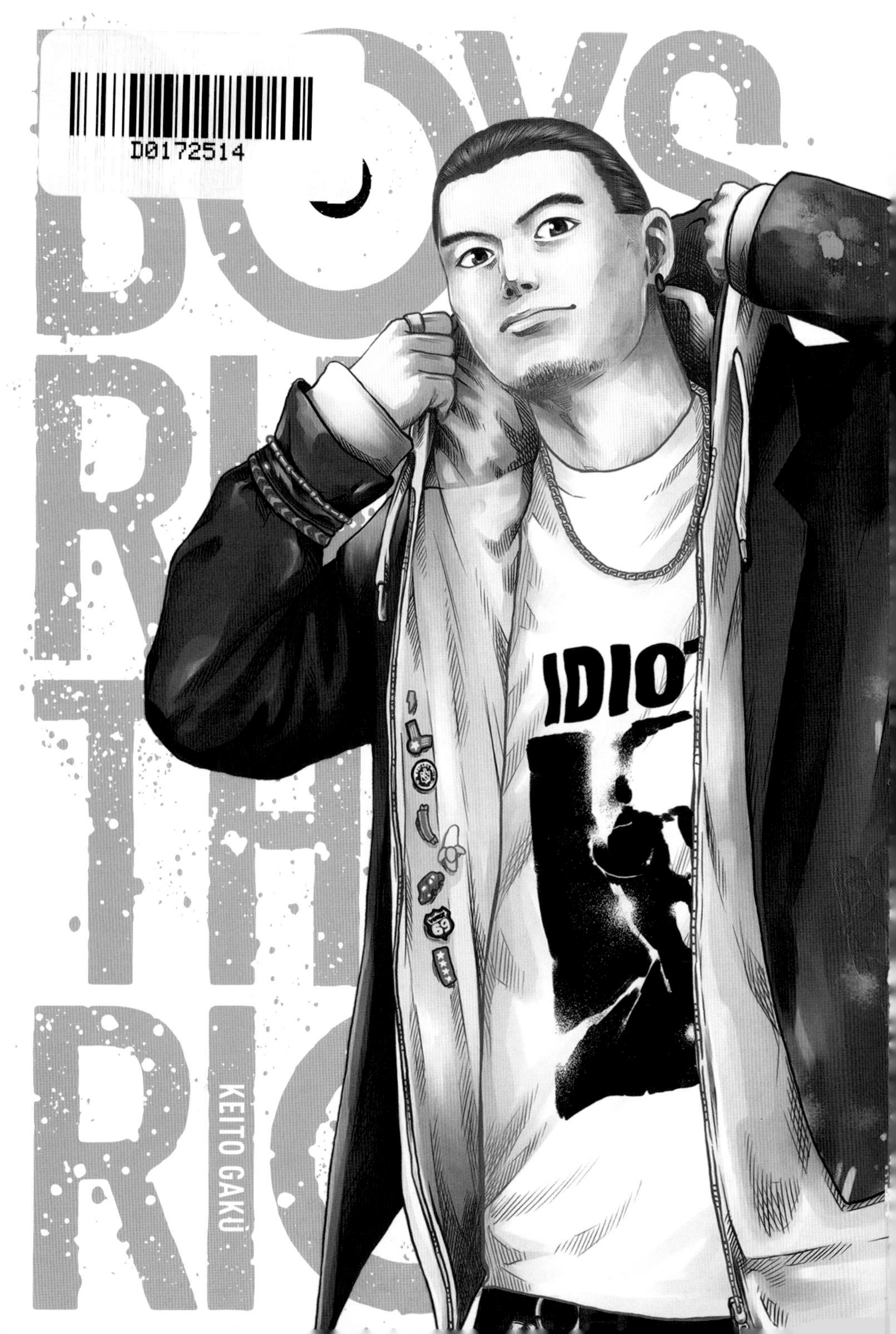
KEITO GAKU
IDIO

CONTENTS

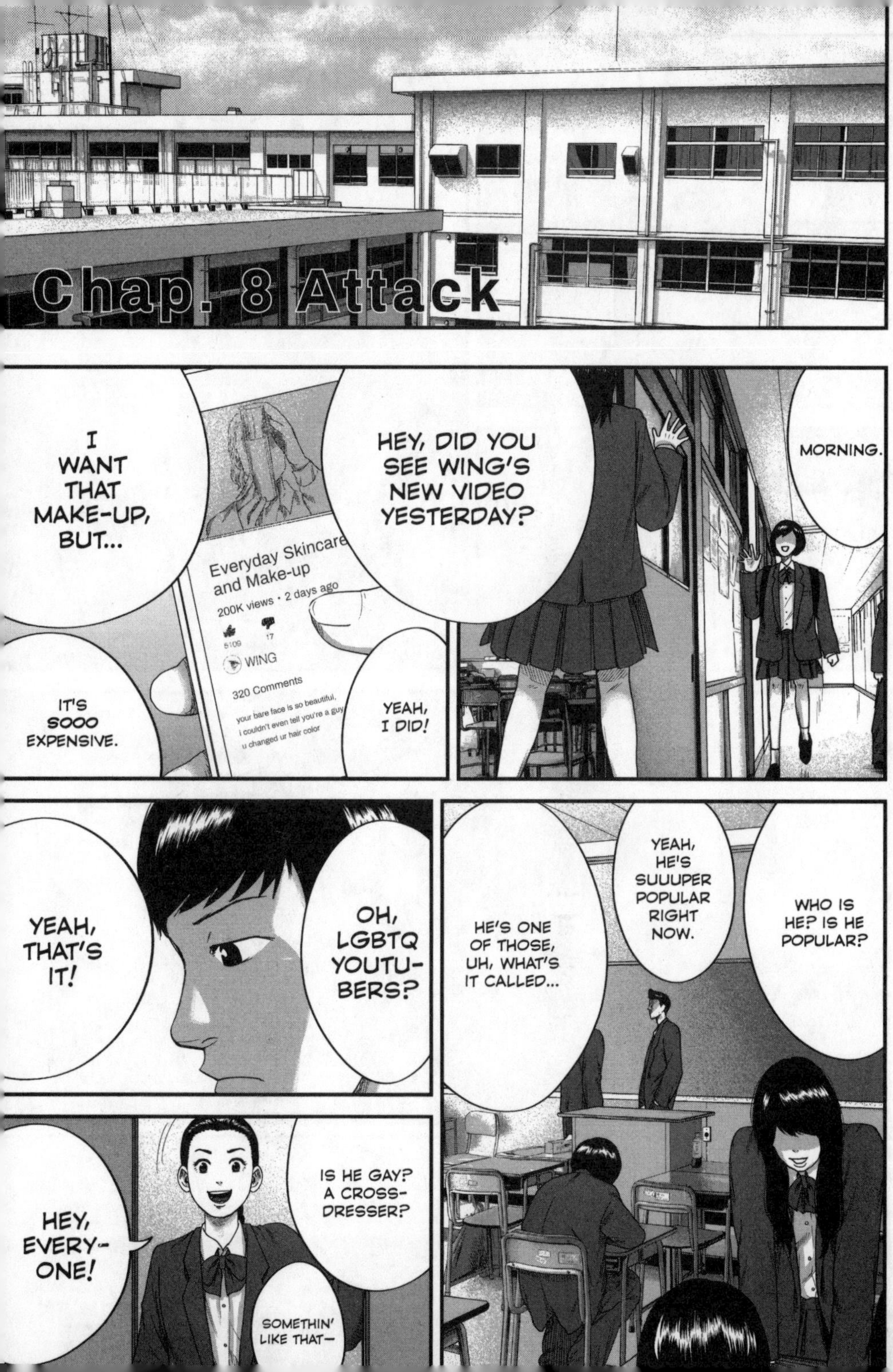
Chap. 8 Attack
MORNING.
HEY, DID YOU SEE WING'S NEW VIDEO YESTERDAY?
YEAH, I DID!
I WANT THAT MAKE-UP, BUT...
Everyday Skincare and Make-up
200K views • 2 days ago
5109
17
WING
320 Comments
your bare face is so beautiful,
i couldn't even tell you're a guy
u changed ur hair color
IT'S SOOO EXPENSIVE.
WHO IS HE? IS HE POPULAR?
YEAH, HE'S SUUUPER POPULAR RIGHT NOW.
HE'S ONE OF THOSE, UH, WHAT'S IT CALLED...
OH, LGBTQ YOUTUBERS?
YEAH, THAT'S IT!
IS HE GAY? A CROSS-DRESSER?
SOMETHIN' LIKE THAT—
HEY, EVERYONE!

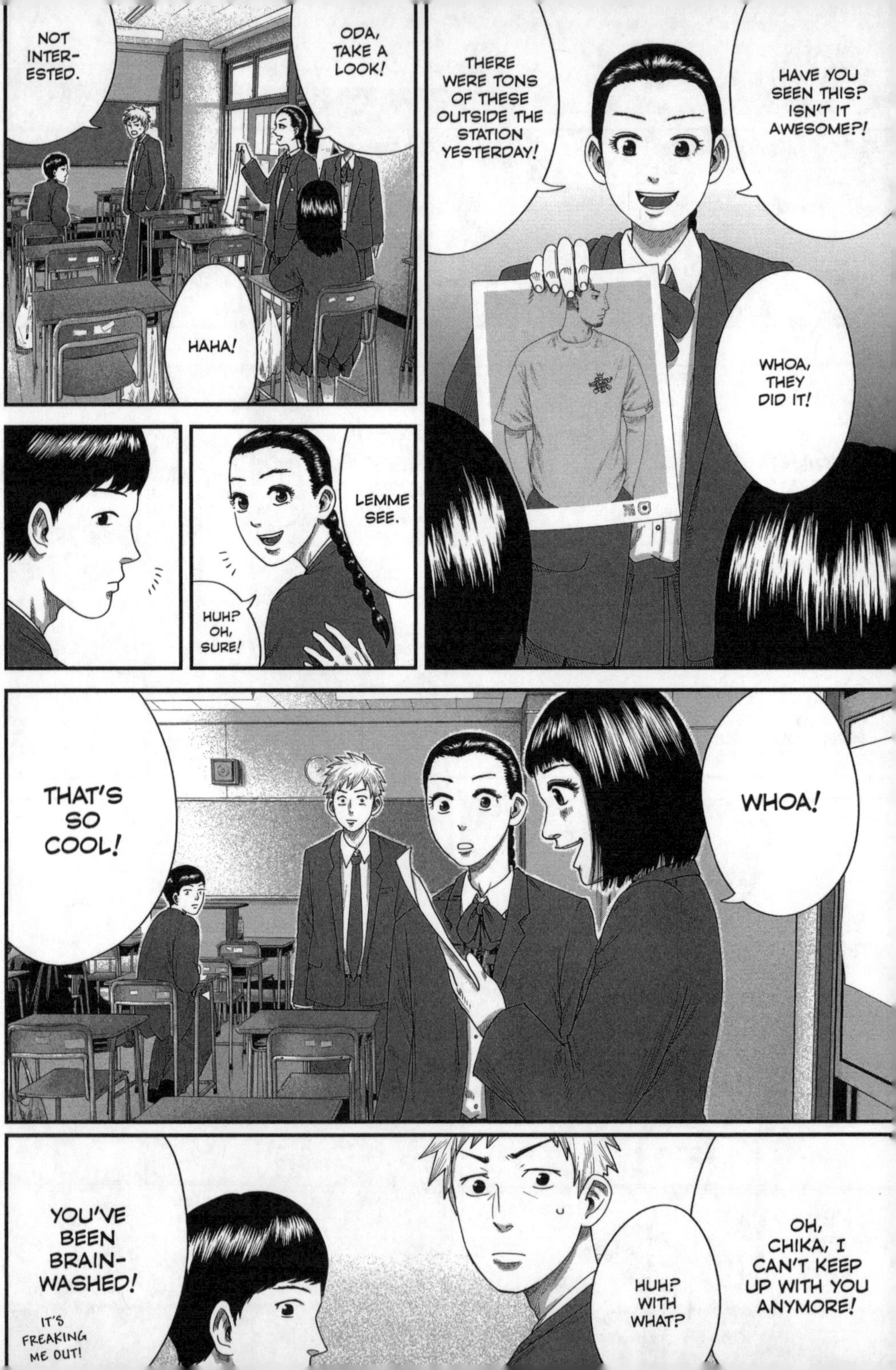
HAVE YOU SEEN THIS? ISN'T IT AWESOME?!
THERE WERE TONS OF THESE OUTSIDE THE STATION YESTERDAY!
WHOA, THEY DID IT!
ODA, TAKE A LOOK!
NOT INTER-ESTED.
HAHA!
LEMME SEE.
HUH? OH, SURE!
WHOA!
THAT'S SO COOL!
OH, CHIKA, I CAN'T KEEP UP WITH YOU ANYMORE!
HUH? WITH WHAT?
YOU'VE BEEN BRAIN-WASHED!
IT'S FREAKING ME OUT!

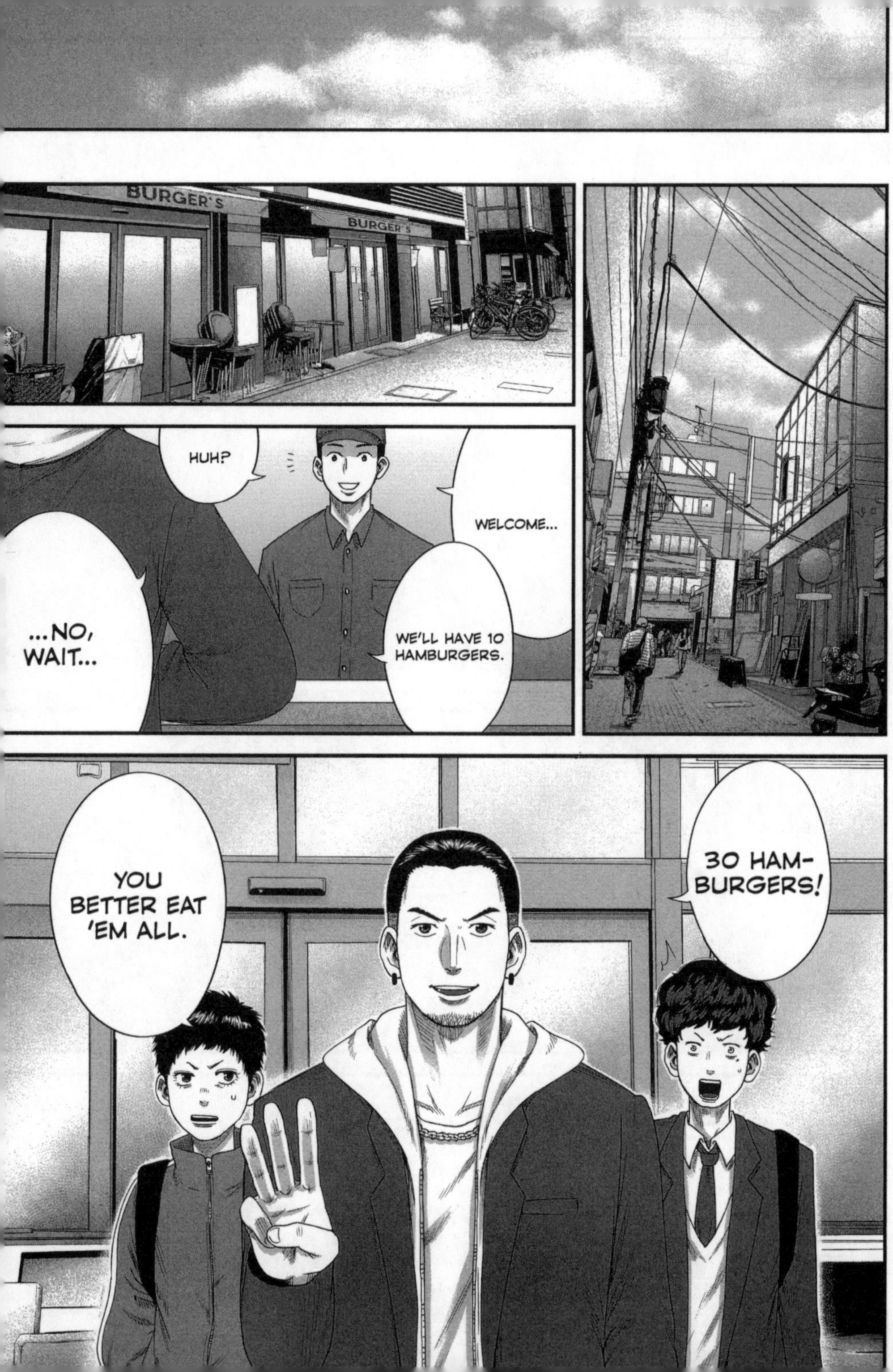
BURGER'S
BURGER'S
WELCOME...
WE'LL HAVE 10 HAMBURGERS.
HUH?
...NO, WAIT...
30 HAM-BURGERS!
YOU BETTER EAT 'EM ALL.

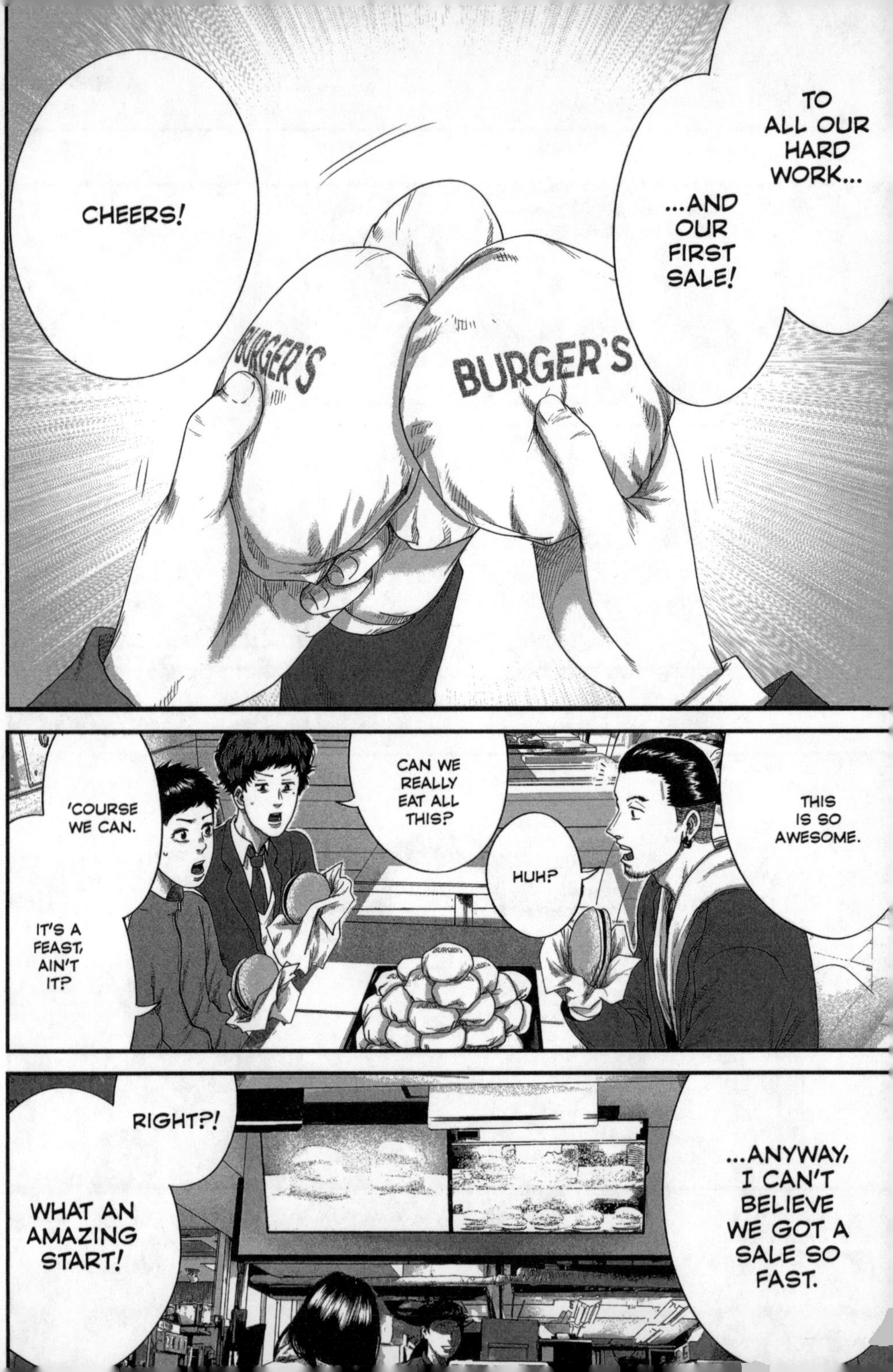
TO ALL OUR HARD WORK...
...AND OUR FIRST SALE!
CHEERS!
THIS IS SO AWESOME.
HUH?
CAN WE REALLY EAT ALL THIS?
'COURSE WE CAN.
IT'S A FEAST, AIN'T IT?
...ANYWAY, I CAN'T BELIEVE WE GOT A SALE SO FAST.
RIGHT?!
WHAT AN AMAZING START!

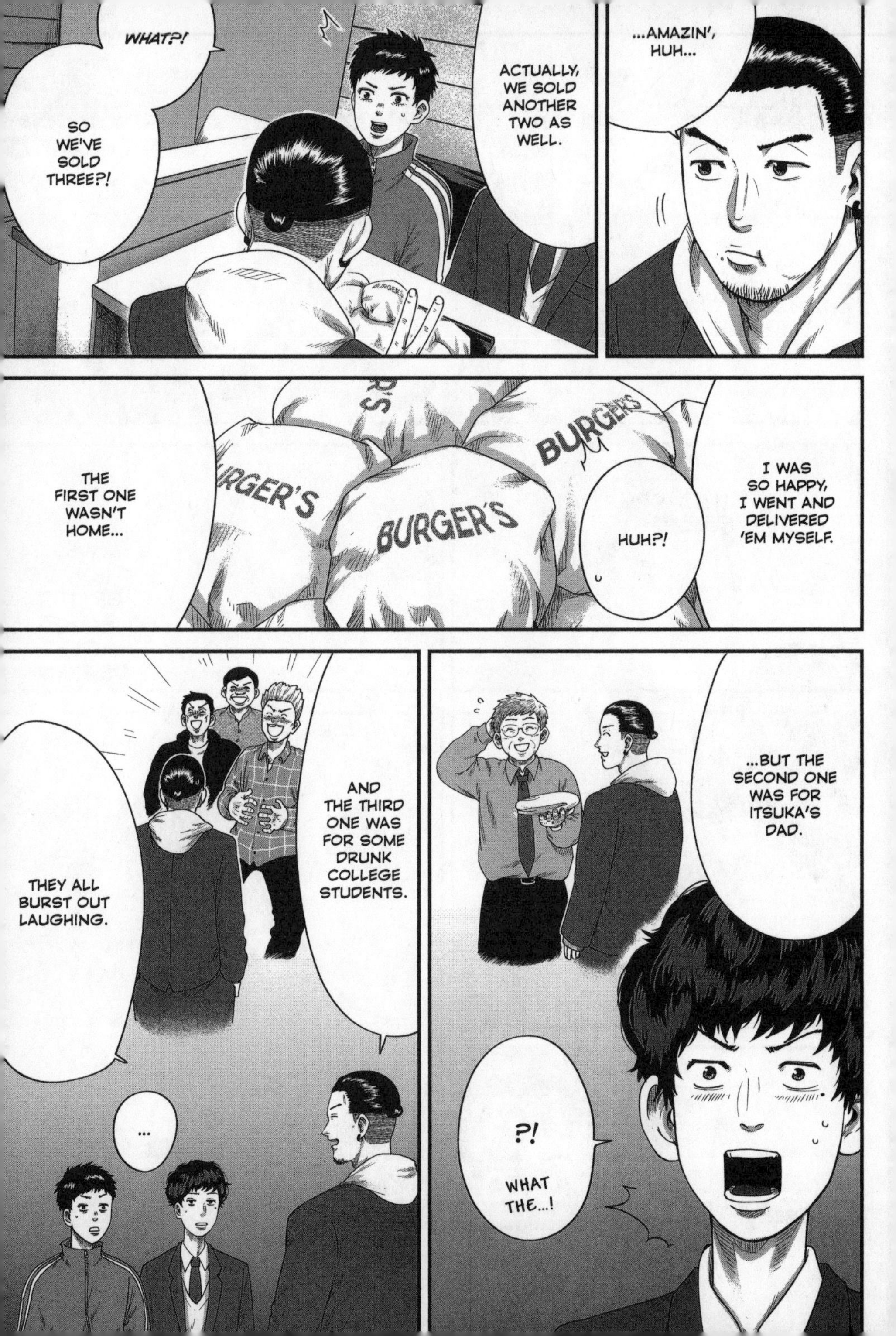
...AMAZIN', HUH...
ACTUALLY, WE SOLD ANOTHER TWO AS WELL.
WHAT?!
SO WE'VE SOLD THREE?!
I WAS SO HAPPY, I WENT AND DELIVERED 'EM MYSELF.
HUH?!
BURGER'S
BURGER'S
THE FIRST ONE WASN'T HOME...
...BUT THE SECOND ONE WAS FOR ITSUKA'S DAD.
?!
WHAT THE...!
AND THE THIRD ONE WAS FOR SOME DRUNK COLLEGE STUDENTS.
THEY ALL BURST OUT LAUGHING.
...

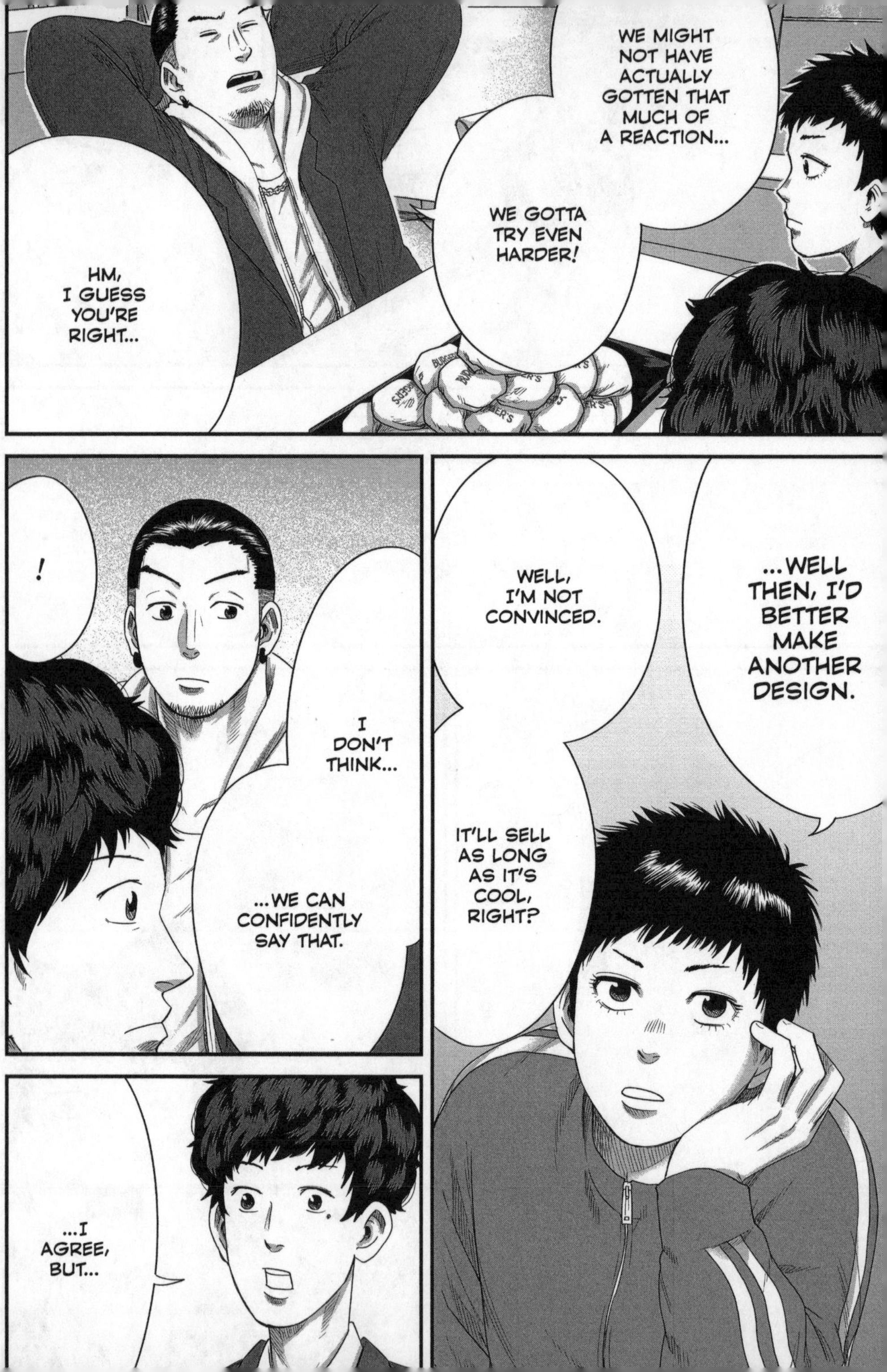
WE MIGHT NOT HAVE ACTUALLY GOTTEN THAT MUCH OF A REACTION...
WE GOTTA TRY EVEN HARDER!
HM, I GUESS YOU'RE RIGHT...
...WELL THEN, I'D BETTER MAKE ANOTHER DESIGN.
WELL, I'M NOT CONVINCED.
IT'LL SELL AS LONG AS IT'S COOL, RIGHT?
!
I DON'T THINK...
...WE CAN CONFIDENTLY SAY THAT.
...I AGREE, BUT...

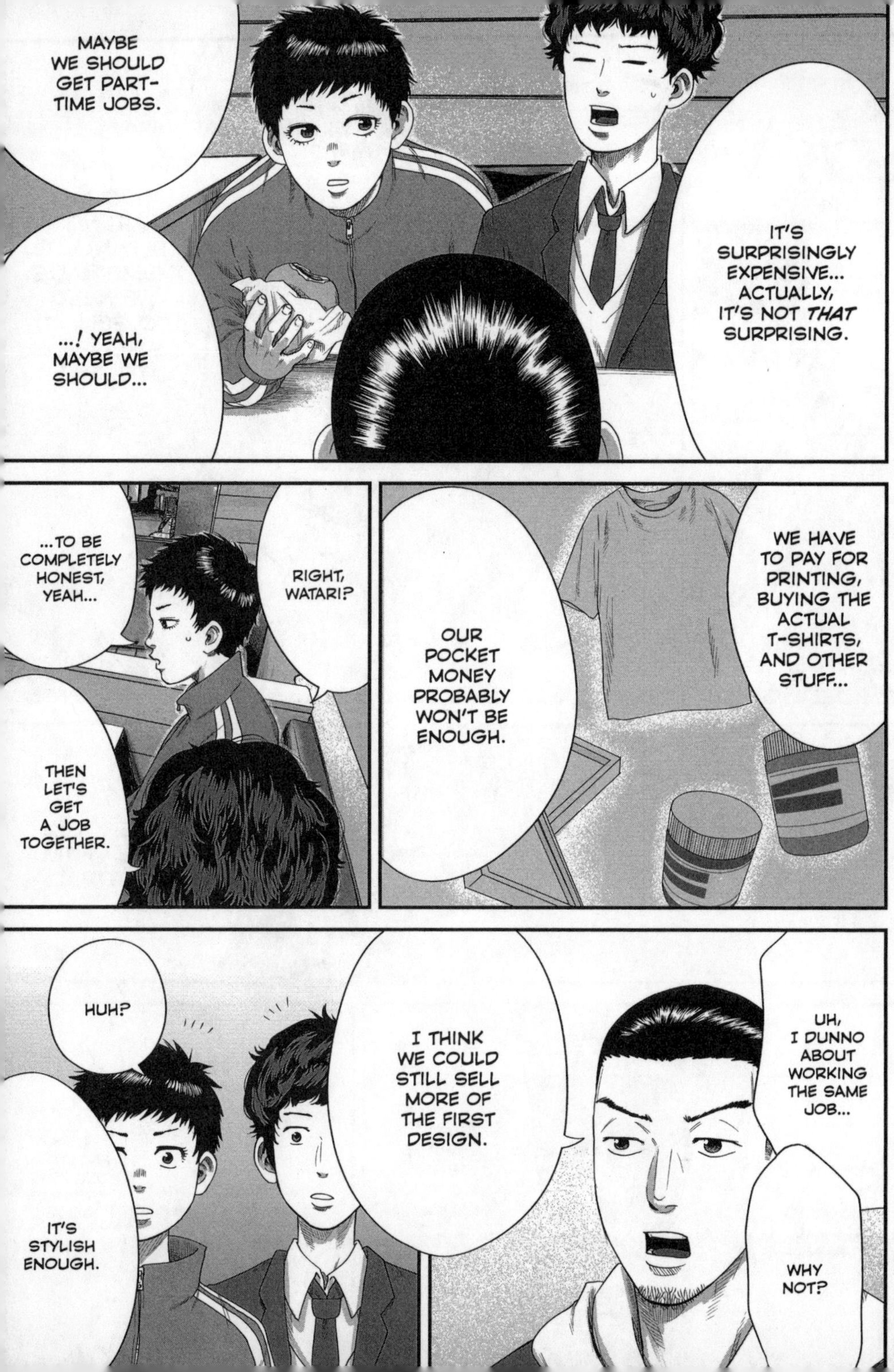
IT'S SURPRISINGLY EXPENSIVE... ACTUALLY, IT'S NOT *THAT* SURPRISING.
MAYBE WE SHOULD GET PART-TIME JOBS.
...! YEAH, MAYBE WE SHOULD...
WE HAVE TO PAY FOR PRINTING, BUYING THE ACTUAL T-SHIRTS, AND OTHER STUFF...
OUR POCKET MONEY PROBABLY WON'T BE ENOUGH.
RIGHT, WATARI?
...TO BE COMPLETELY HONEST, YEAH...
THEN LET'S GET A JOB TOGETHER.
UH, I DUNNO ABOUT WORKING THE SAME JOB...
WHY NOT?
I THINK WE COULD STILL SELL MORE OF THE FIRST DESIGN.
HUH?
IT'S STYLISH ENOUGH.

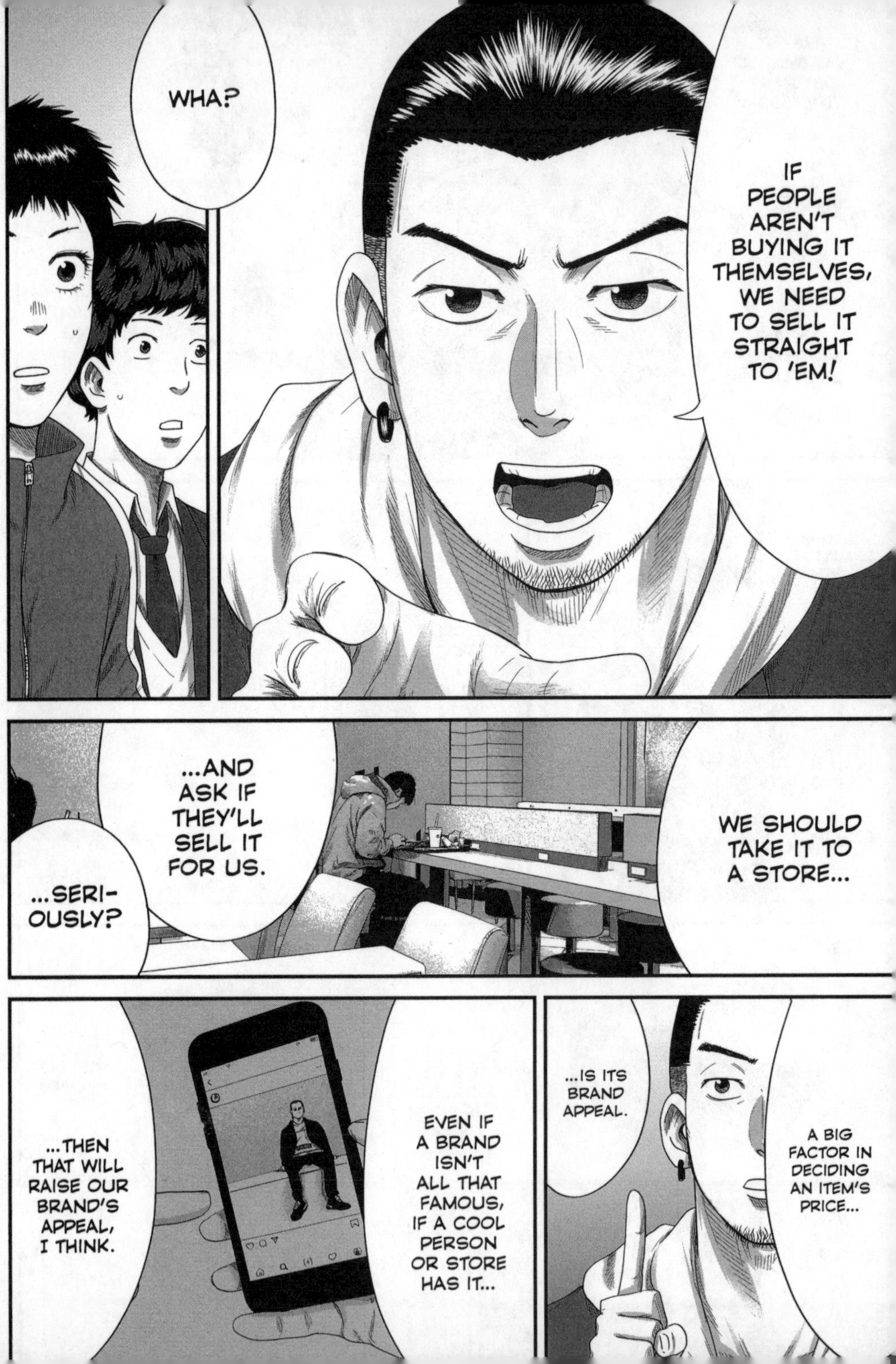
IF PEOPLE AREN'T BUYING IT THEMSELVES, WE NEED TO SELL IT STRAIGHT TO 'EM!
WHA?
WE SHOULD TAKE IT TO A STORE...
...AND ASK IF THEY'LL SELL IT FOR US.
...SERI-OUSLY?
A BIG FACTOR IN DECIDING AN ITEM'S PRICE...
...IS ITS BRAND APPEAL.
EVEN IF A BRAND ISN'T ALL THAT FAMOUS, IF A COOL PERSON OR STORE HAS IT...
...THEN THAT WILL RAISE OUR BRAND'S APPEAL, I THINK.

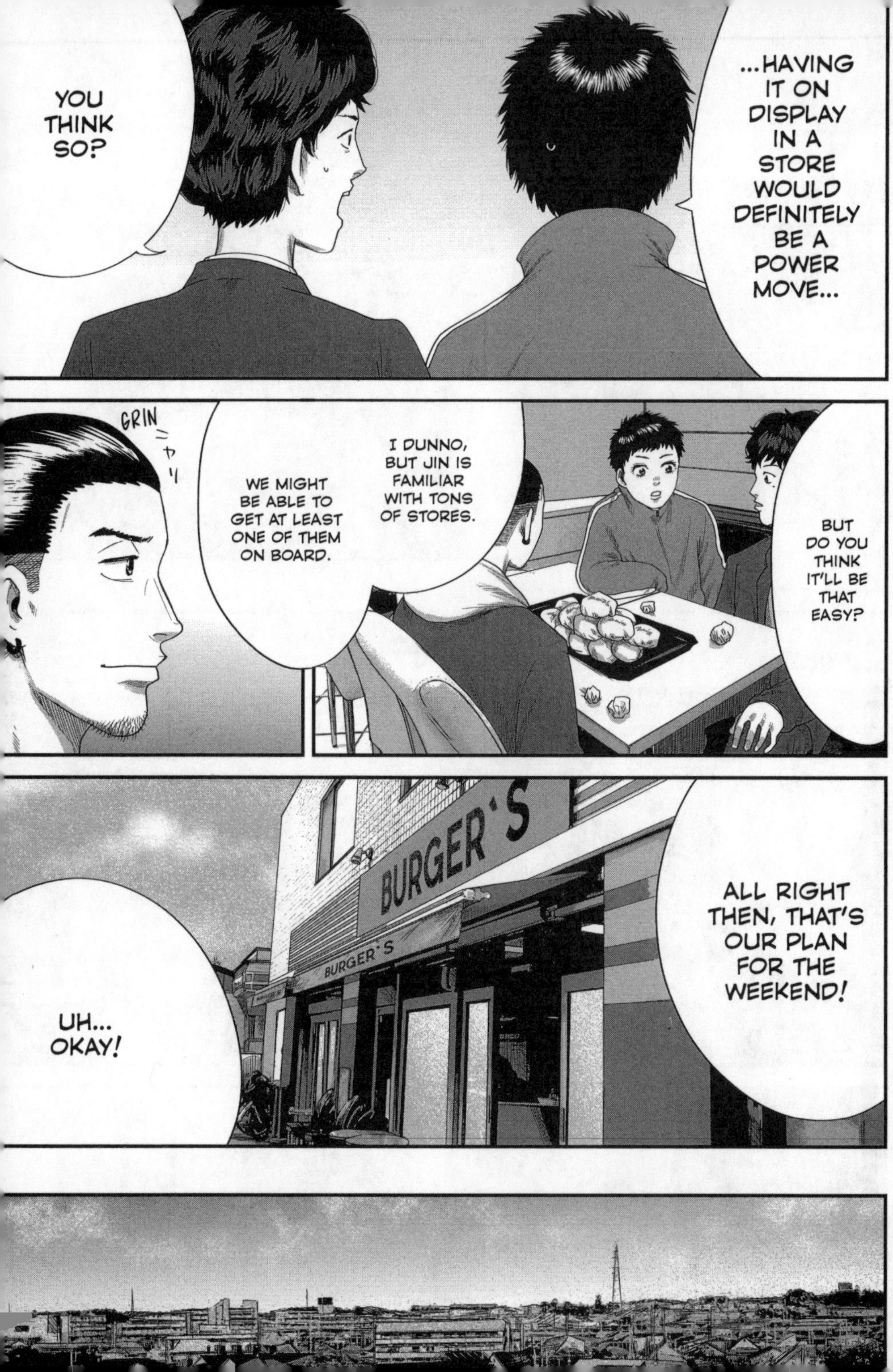
...HAVING IT ON DISPLAY IN A STORE WOULD DEFINITELY BE A POWER MOVE...
YOU THINK SO?
BUT DO YOU THINK IT'LL BE THAT EASY?
I DUNNO, BUT JIN IS FAMILIAR WITH TONS OF STORES.
WE MIGHT BE ABLE TO GET AT LEAST ONE OF THEM ON BOARD.
GRIN
ニヤリ
BURGER'S
BURGER'S
ALL RIGHT THEN, THAT'S OUR PLAN FOR THE WEEKEND!
UH... OKAY!

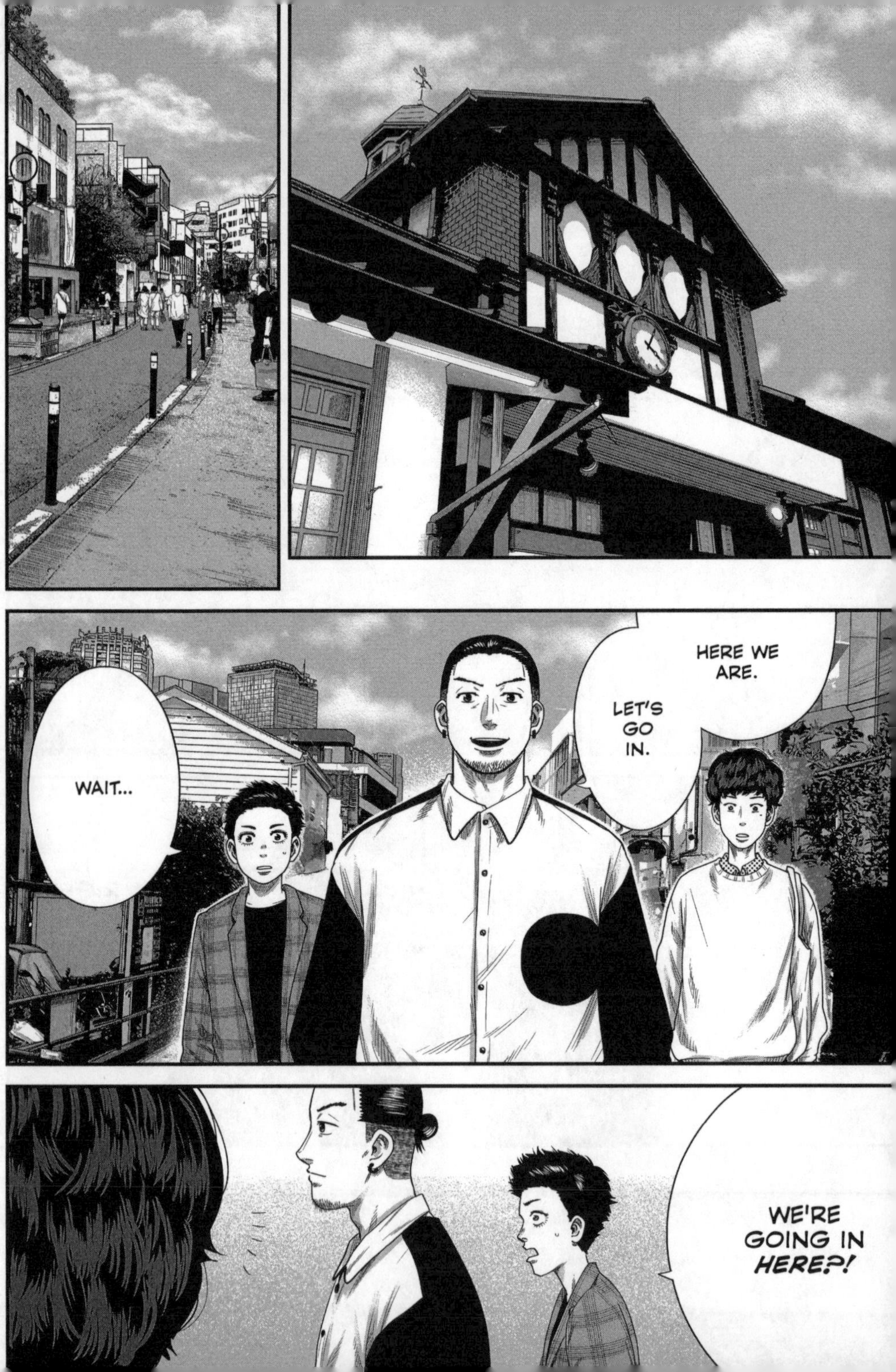
HERE WE ARE.
LET'S GO IN.
WAIT...
WE'RE GOING IN *HERE?!*

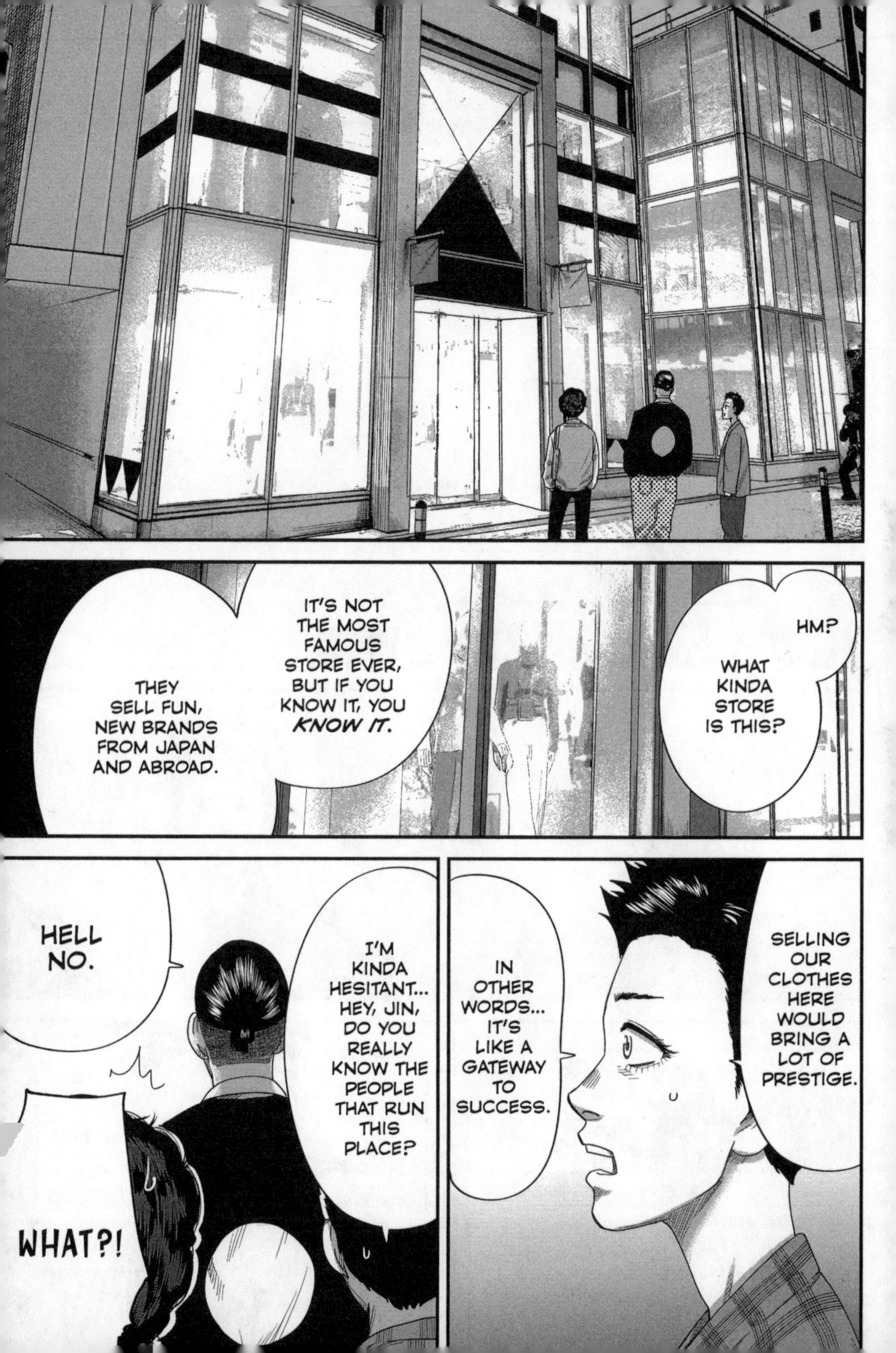
HM? WHAT KINDA STORE IS THIS?
IT'S NOT THE MOST FAMOUS STORE EVER, BUT IF YOU KNOW IT, YOU *KNOW IT*.
THEY SELL FUN, NEW BRANDS FROM JAPAN AND ABROAD.
SELLING OUR CLOTHES HERE WOULD BRING A LOT OF PRESTIGE.
IN OTHER WORDS... IT'S LIKE A GATEWAY TO SUCCESS.
I'M KINDA HESITANT... HEY, JIN, DO YOU REALLY KNOW THE PEOPLE THAT RUN THIS PLACE?
HELL NO.
WHAT?!

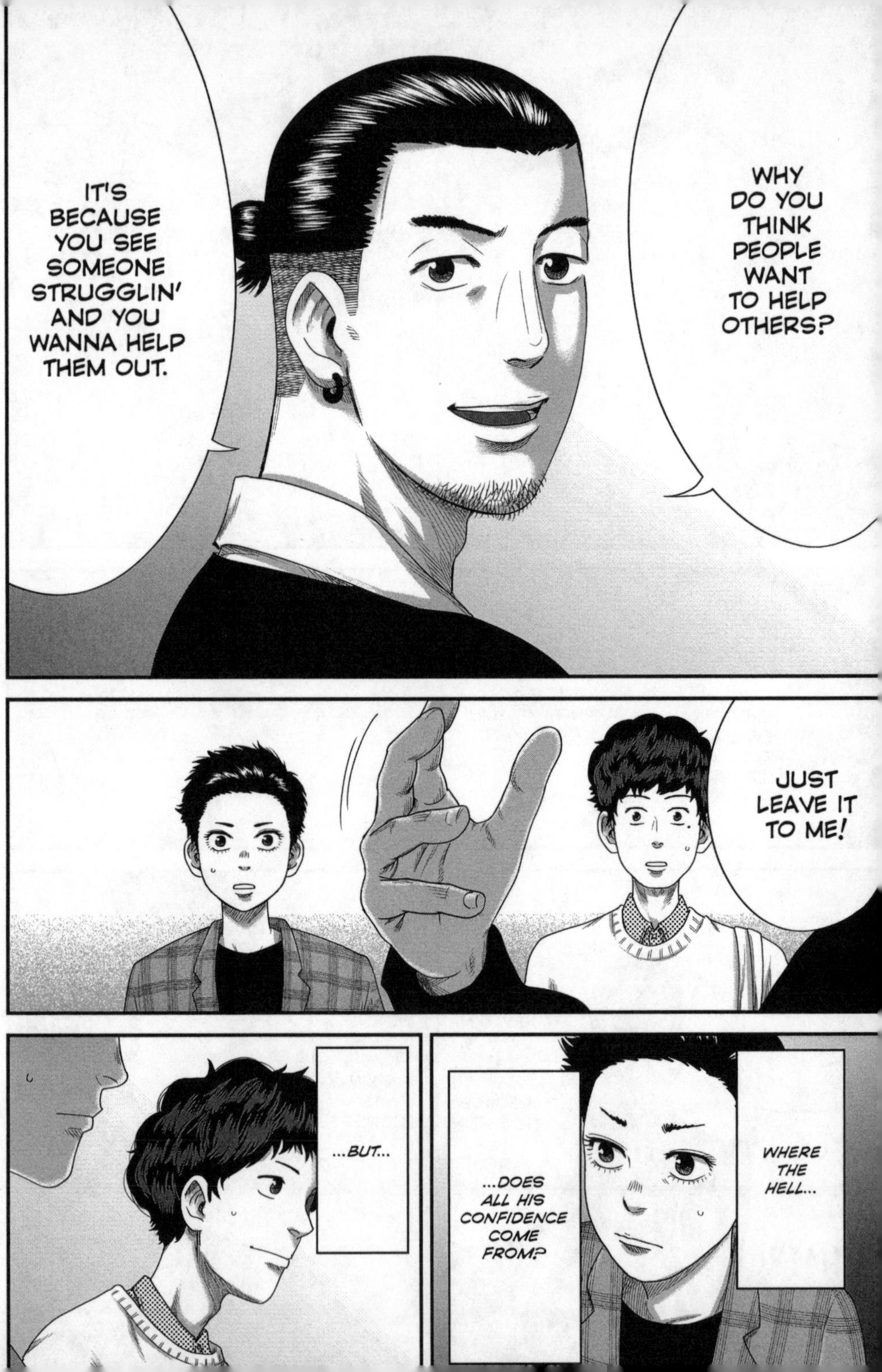
WHY DO YOU THINK PEOPLE WANT TO HELP OTHERS?
IT'S BECAUSE YOU SEE SOMEONE STRUGGLIN' AND YOU WANNA HELP THEM OUT.
JUST LEAVE IT TO ME!
WHERE THE HELL...
...DOES ALL HIS CONFIDENCE COME FROM?
...BUT...

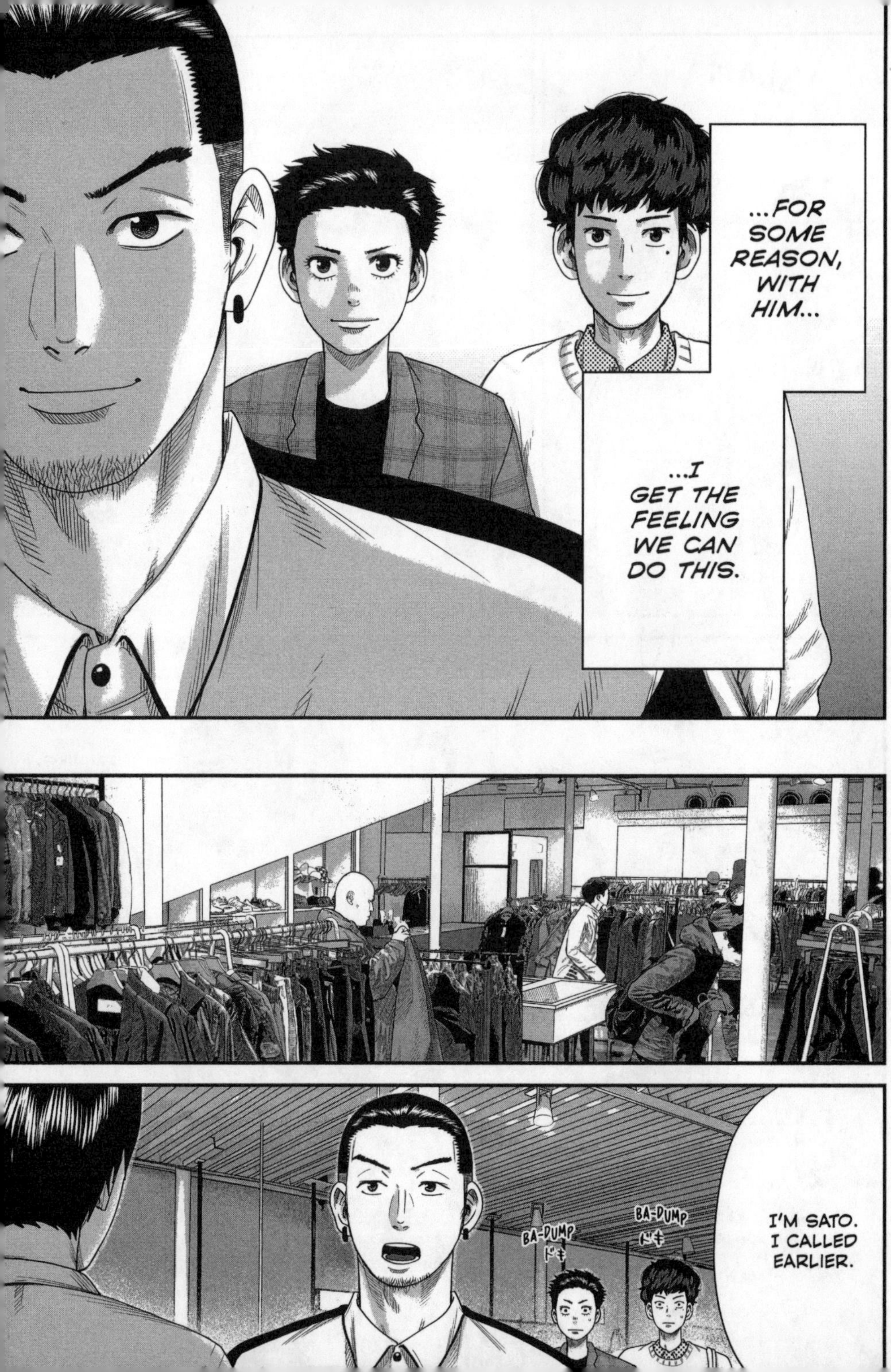
...FOR SOME REASON, WITH HIM...
...I GET THE FEELING WE CAN DO THIS.
I'M SATO. I CALLED EARLIER.
BA-DUMP
ドキ
BA-DUMP
ドキ

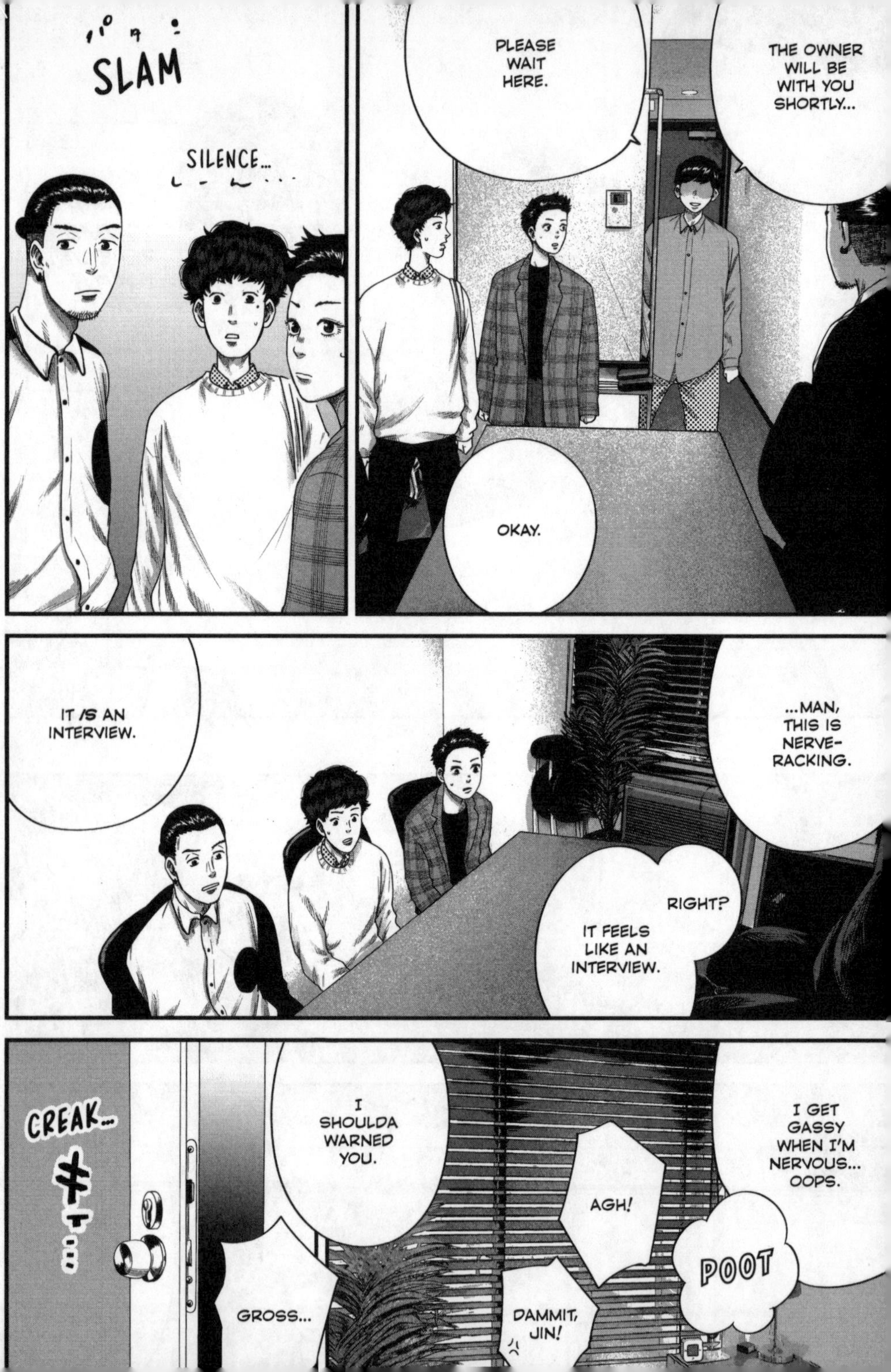
THE OWNER WILL BE WITH YOU SHORTLY...
PLEASE WAIT HERE.
OKAY.
SLAM
SILENCE...
...MAN, THIS IS NERVE-RACKING.
RIGHT?
IT FEELS LIKE AN INTERVIEW.
IT IS AN INTERVIEW.
I GET GASSY WHEN I'M NERVOUS... OOPS.
POOT
I SHOULDA WARNED YOU.
AGH!
DAMMIT, JIN!
GROSS...
CREAK...

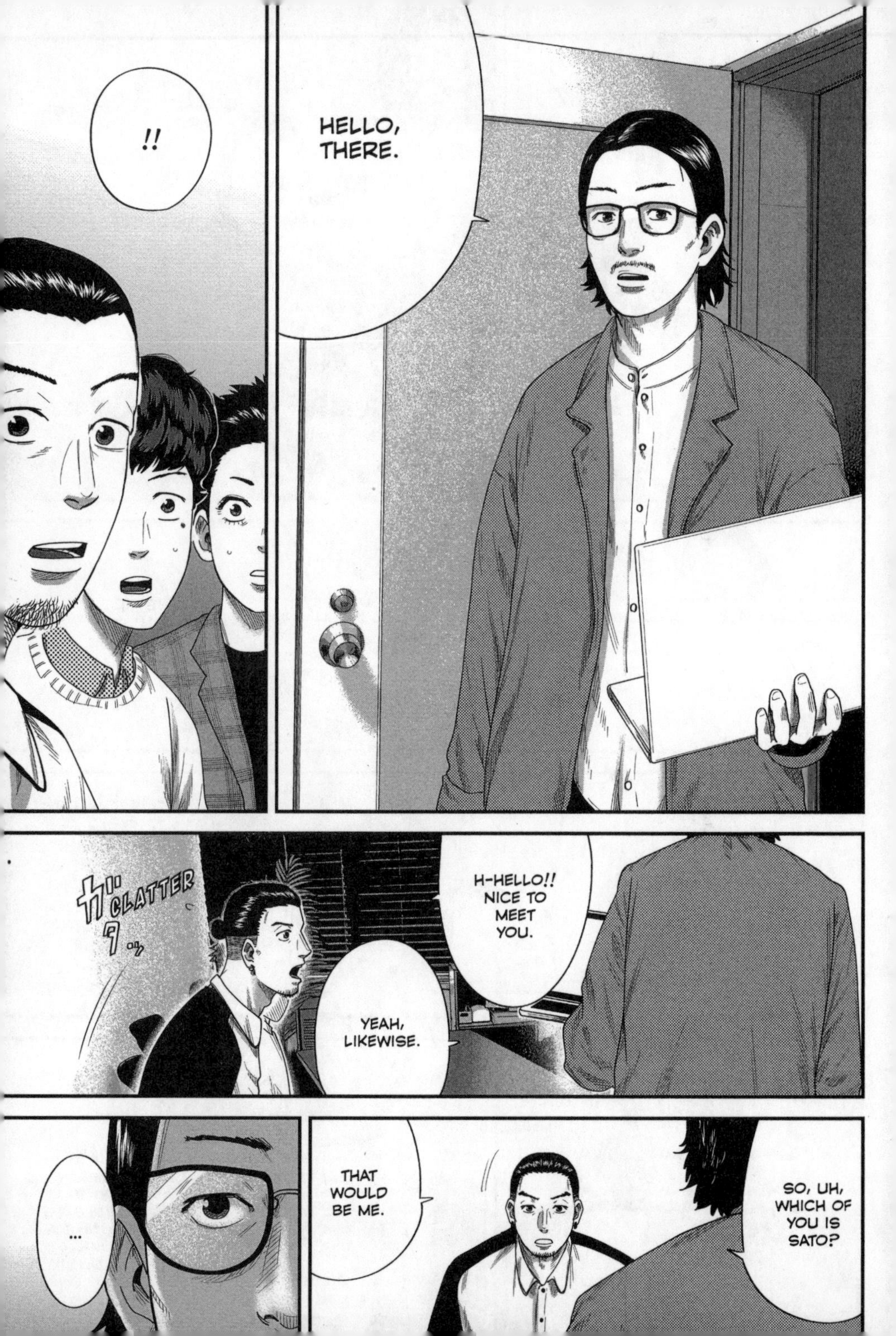
HELLO, THERE.
!!
H-HELLO!! NICE TO MEET YOU.
YEAH, LIKEWISE.
CLATTER
SO, UH, WHICH OF YOU IS SATO?
THAT WOULD BE ME.
...

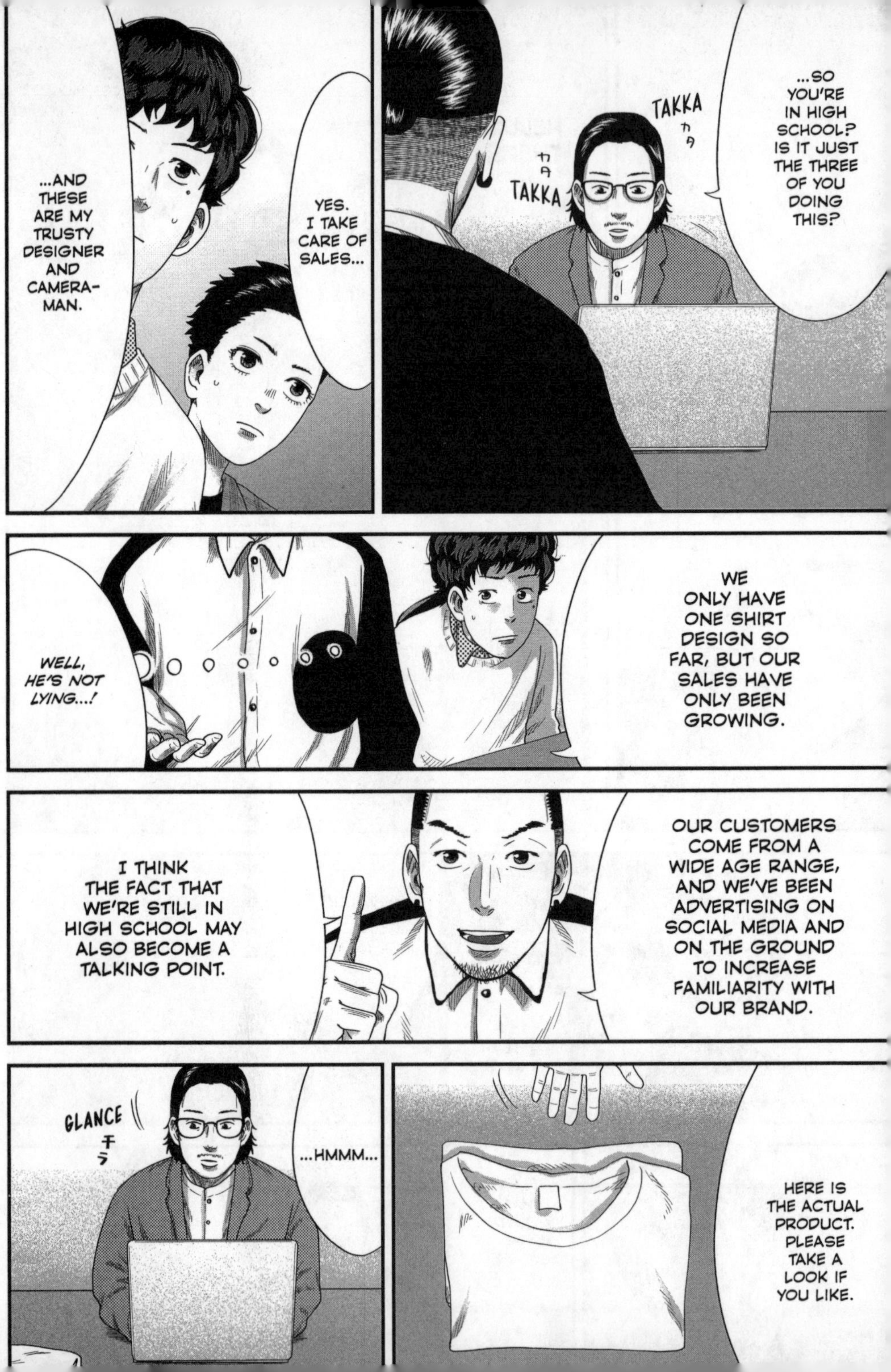
...SO YOU'RE IN HIGH SCHOOL? IS IT JUST THE THREE OF YOU DOING THIS?
TAKKA カタ
カタ TAKKA
YES. I TAKE CARE OF SALES...
...AND THESE ARE MY TRUSTY DESIGNER AND CAMERA-MAN.
WE ONLY HAVE ONE SHIRT DESIGN SO FAR, BUT OUR SALES HAVE ONLY BEEN GROWING.
WELL, HE'S NOT LYING...!
OUR CUSTOMERS COME FROM A WIDE AGE RANGE, AND WE'VE BEEN ADVERTISING ON SOCIAL MEDIA AND ON THE GROUND TO INCREASE FAMILIARITY WITH OUR BRAND.
I THINK THE FACT THAT WE'RE STILL IN HIGH SCHOOL MAY ALSO BECOME A TALKING POINT.
HERE IS THE ACTUAL PRODUCT. PLEASE TAKE A LOOK IF YOU LIKE.
...HMMM...
GLANCE チラ

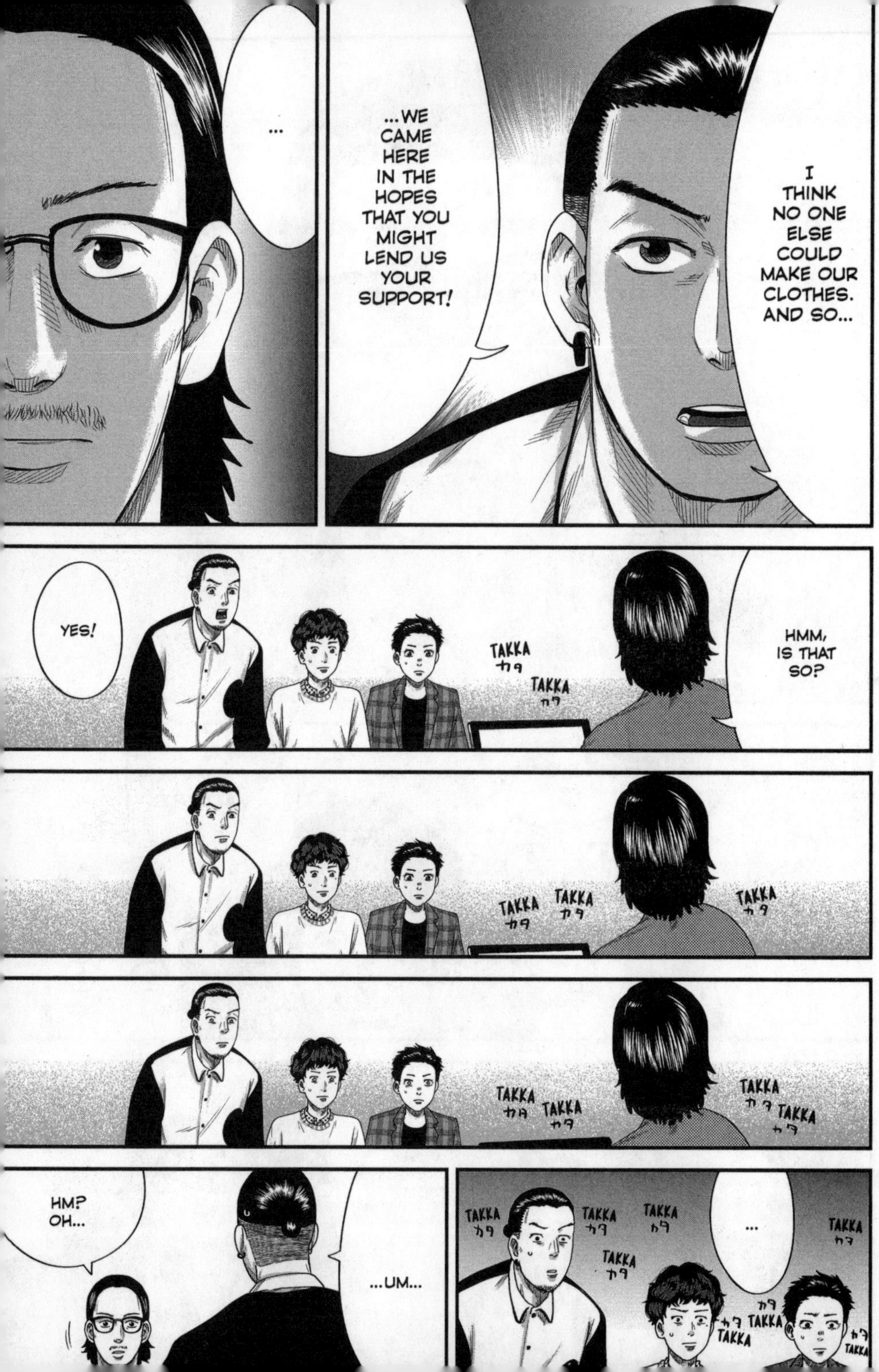
I THINK NO ONE ELSE COULD MAKE OUR CLOTHES. AND SO...
...WE CAME HERE IN THE HOPES THAT YOU MIGHT LEND US YOUR SUPPORT!
...
HMM, IS THAT SO?
TAKKA カタ
TAKKA カタ
YES!
TAKKA カタ
TAKKA カタ
TAKKA カタ
TAKKA カタ
TAKKA カタ
TAKKA カタ
TAKKA カタ
TAKKA カタ
...
TAKKA カタ
TAKKA カタ
TAKKA カタ
TAKKA カタ
TAKKA カタ
TAKKA カタ
TAKKA カタ
...UM...
HM? OH...

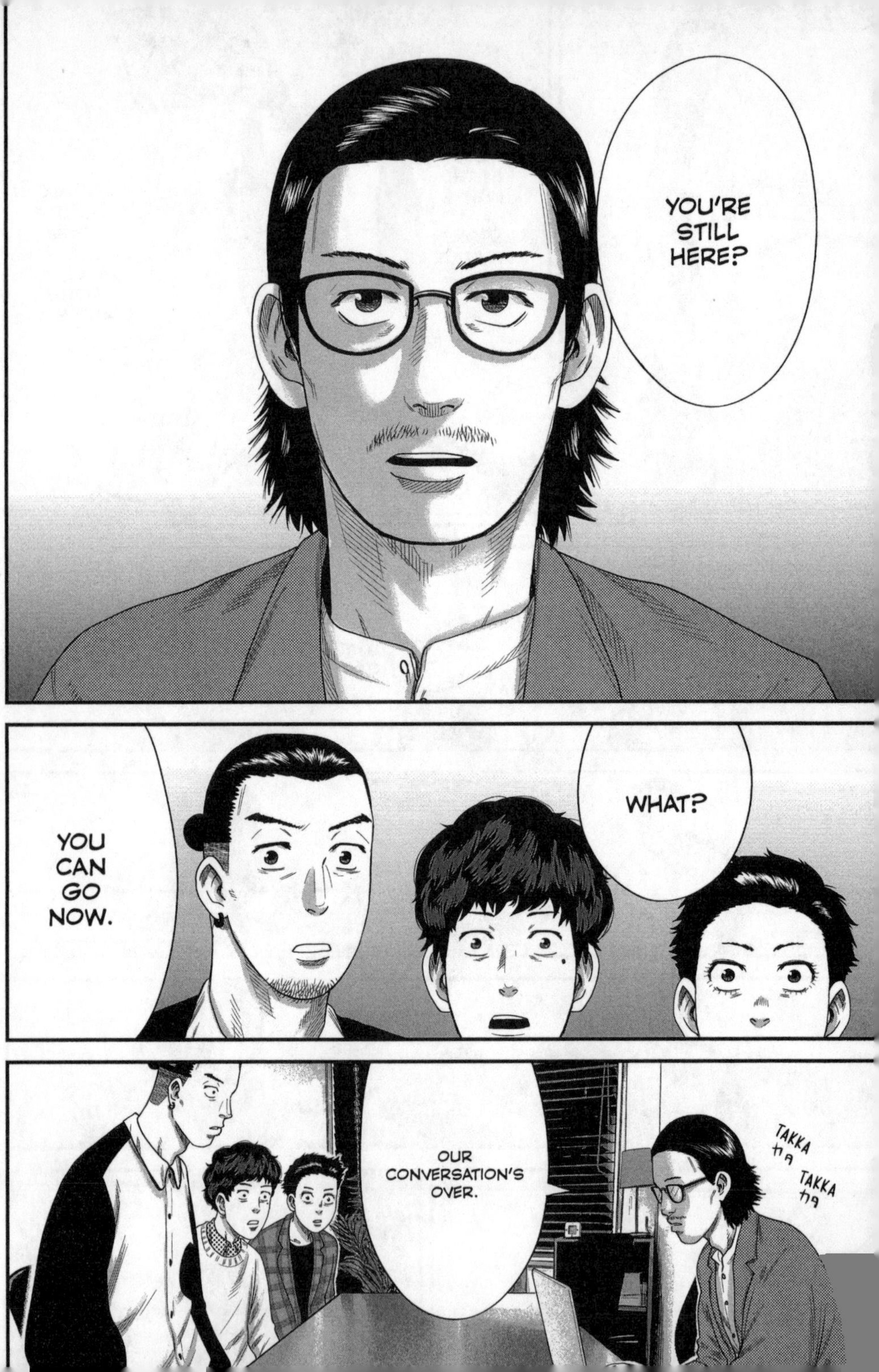
YOU'RE STILL HERE?
WHAT?
YOU CAN GO NOW.
TAKKA カタ
TAKKA カタ
OUR CONVERSATION'S OVER.

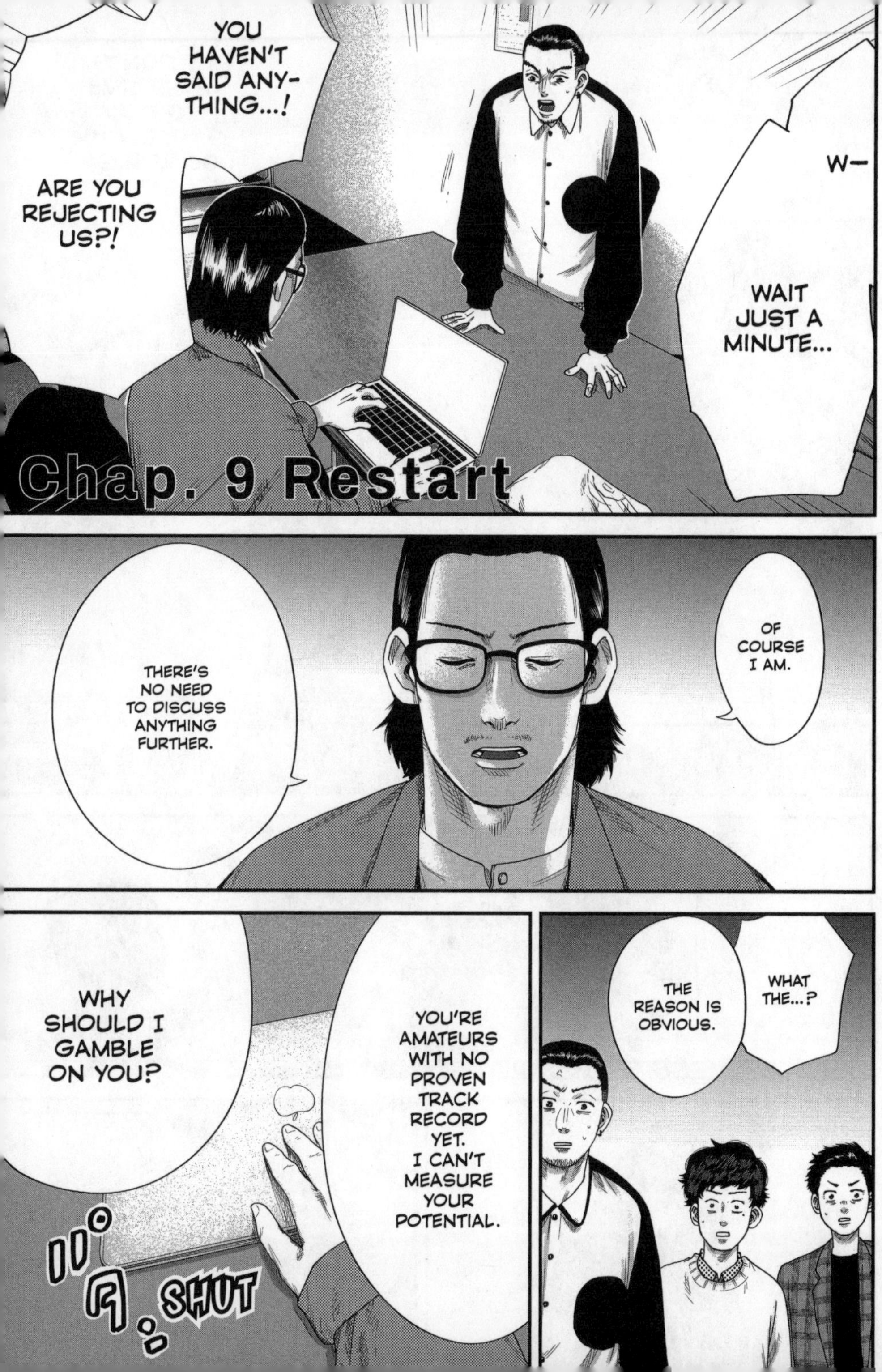
W—
WAIT JUST A MINUTE...
YOU HAVEN'T SAID ANY-THING...!
ARE YOU REJECTING US?!
Chap. 9 Restart
OF COURSE I AM.
THERE'S NO NEED TO DISCUSS ANYTHING FURTHER.
WHAT THE...?
THE REASON IS OBVIOUS.
YOU'RE AMATEURS WITH NO PROVEN TRACK RECORD YET. I CAN'T MEASURE YOUR POTENTIAL.
WHY SHOULD I GAMBLE ON YOU?
SHUT

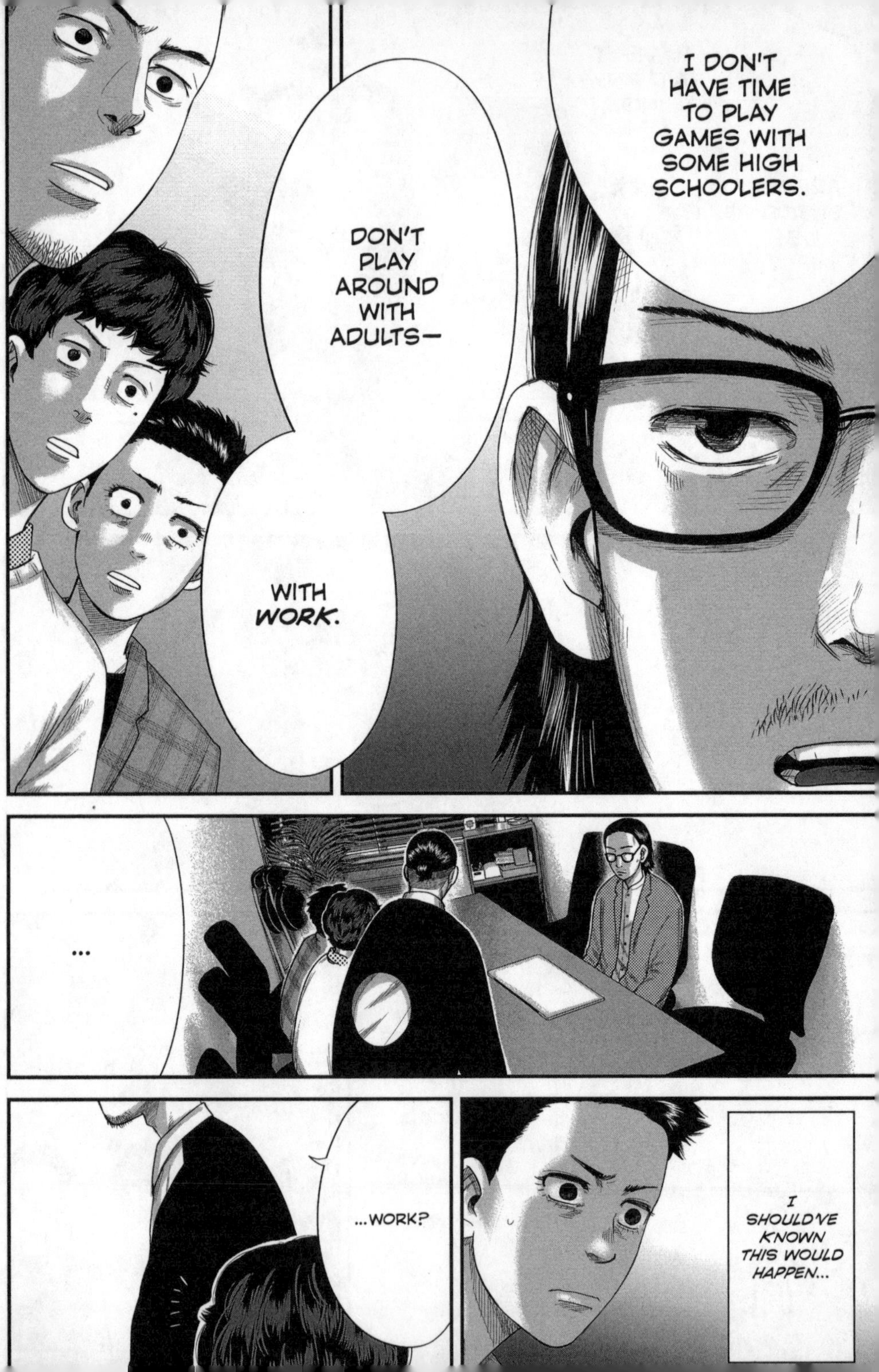
I DON'T HAVE TIME TO PLAY GAMES WITH SOME HIGH SCHOOLERS.
DON'T PLAY AROUND WITH ADULTS—
WITH *WORK*.
...
I SHOULD'VE KNOWN THIS WOULD HAPPEN...
...WORK?

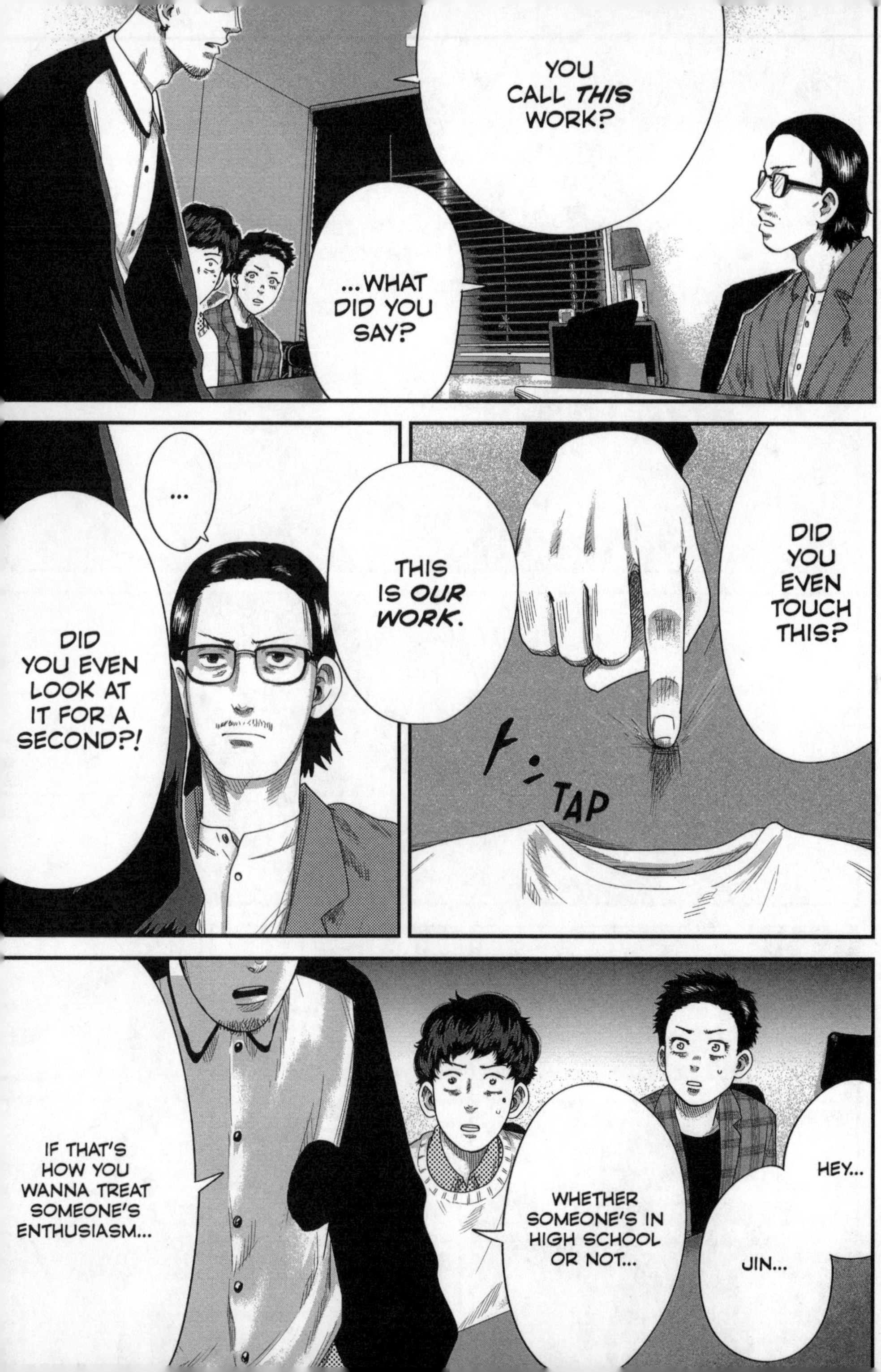
YOU CALL THIS WORK?
...WHAT DID YOU SAY?
DID YOU EVEN TOUCH THIS?
THIS IS OUR WORK.
TAP
...
DID YOU EVEN LOOK AT IT FOR A SECOND?!
HEY...
JIN...
WHETHER SOMEONE'S IN HIGH SCHOOL OR NOT...
IF THAT'S HOW YOU WANNA TREAT SOMEONE'S ENTHUSIASM...

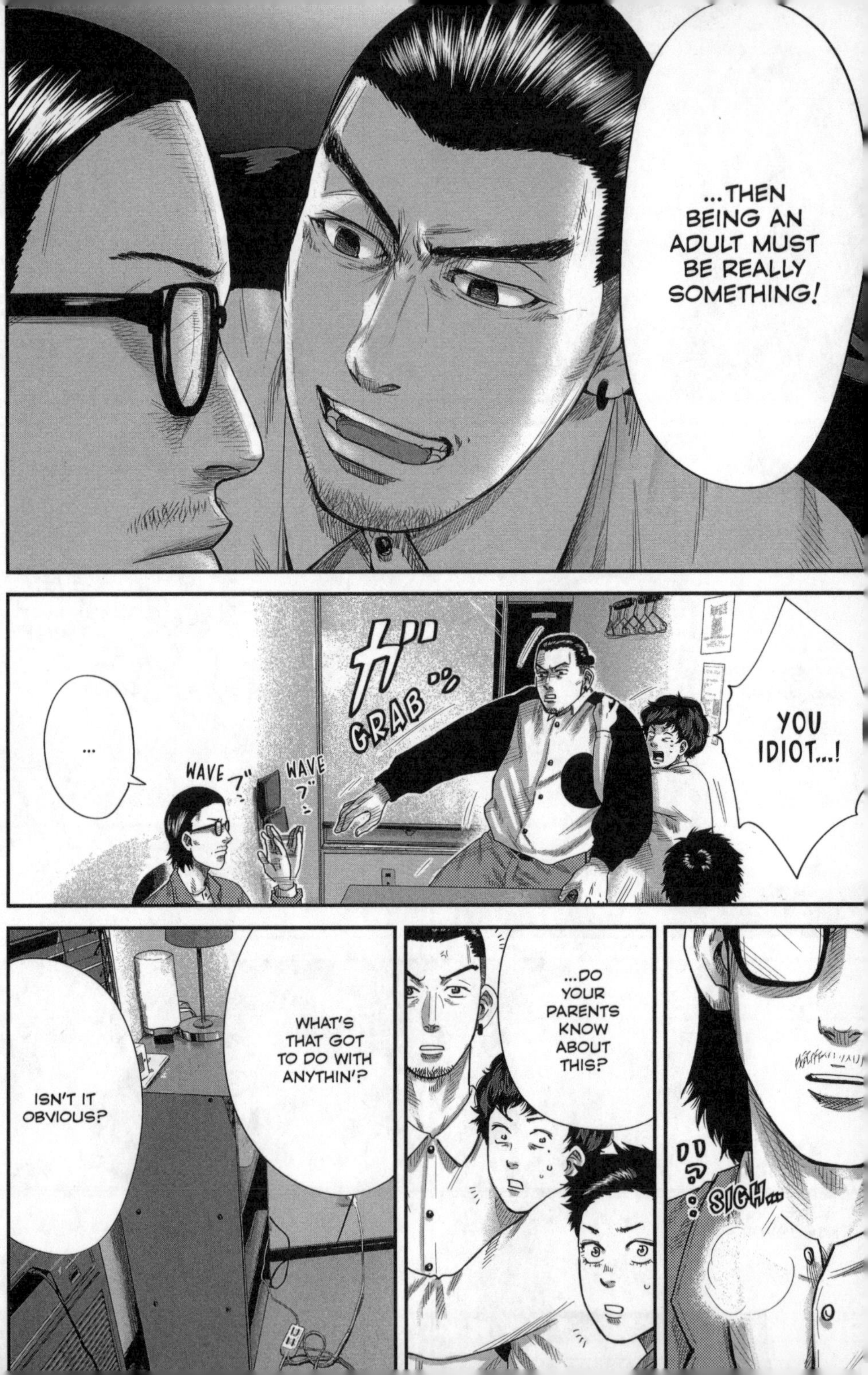
...THEN BEING AN ADULT MUST BE REALLY SOMETHING!
YOU IDIOT...!
GRAB
WAVE
WAVE
...
SIGH...
...DO YOUR PARENTS KNOW ABOUT THIS?
WHAT'S THAT GOT TO DO WITH ANYTHIN'?
ISN'T IT OBVIOUS?

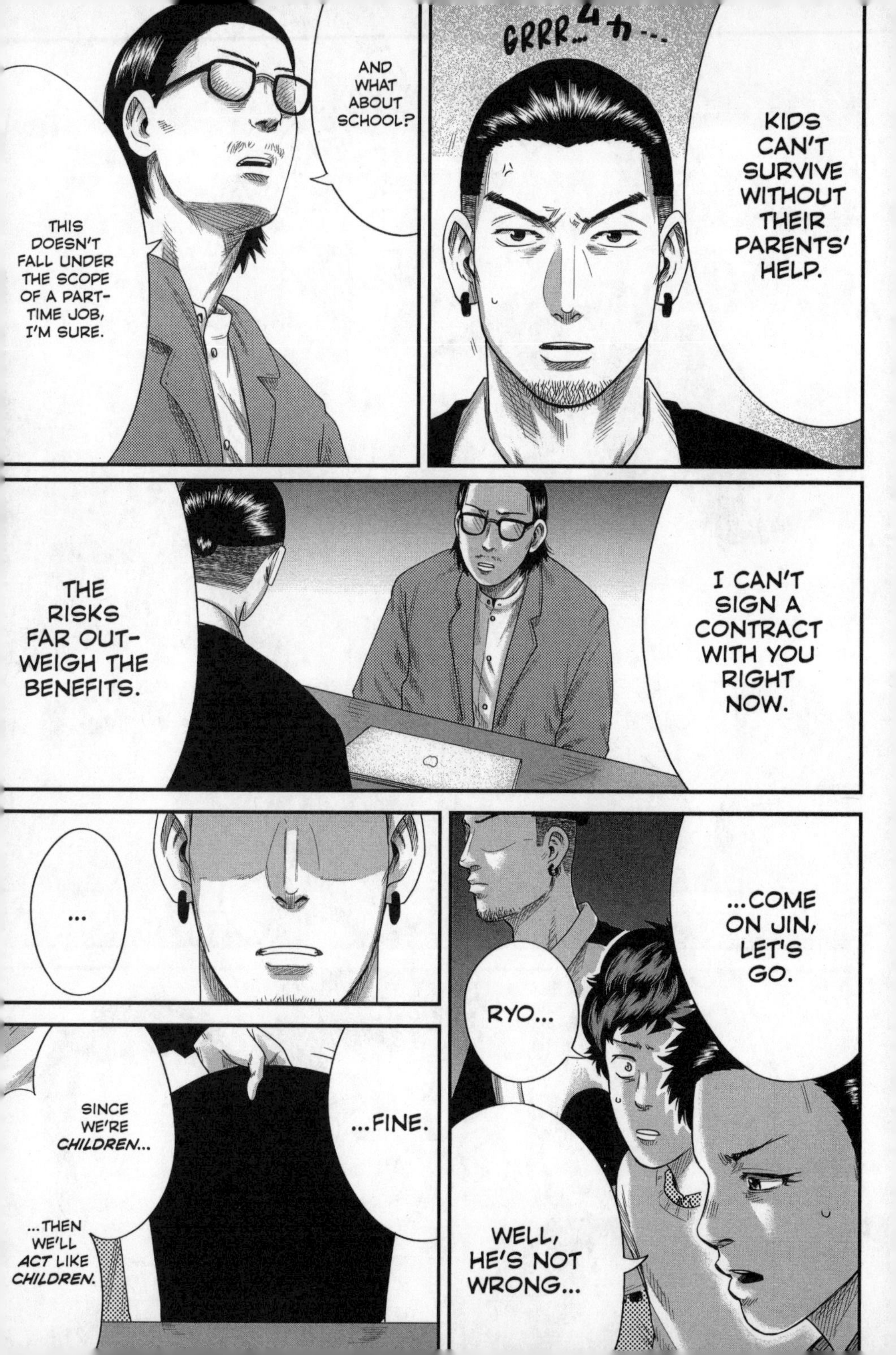
GRRR...
KIDS CAN'T SURVIVE WITHOUT THEIR PARENTS' HELP.
AND WHAT ABOUT SCHOOL?
THIS DOESN'T FALL UNDER THE SCOPE OF A PART-TIME JOB, I'M SURE.
I CAN'T SIGN A CONTRACT WITH YOU RIGHT NOW.
THE RISKS FAR OUT-WEIGH THE BENEFITS.
...COME ON JIN, LET'S GO.
RYO...
WELL, HE'S NOT WRONG...
...
...FINE.
SINCE WE'RE *CHILDREN*...
...THEN WE'LL *ACT* LIKE *CHILDREN*.

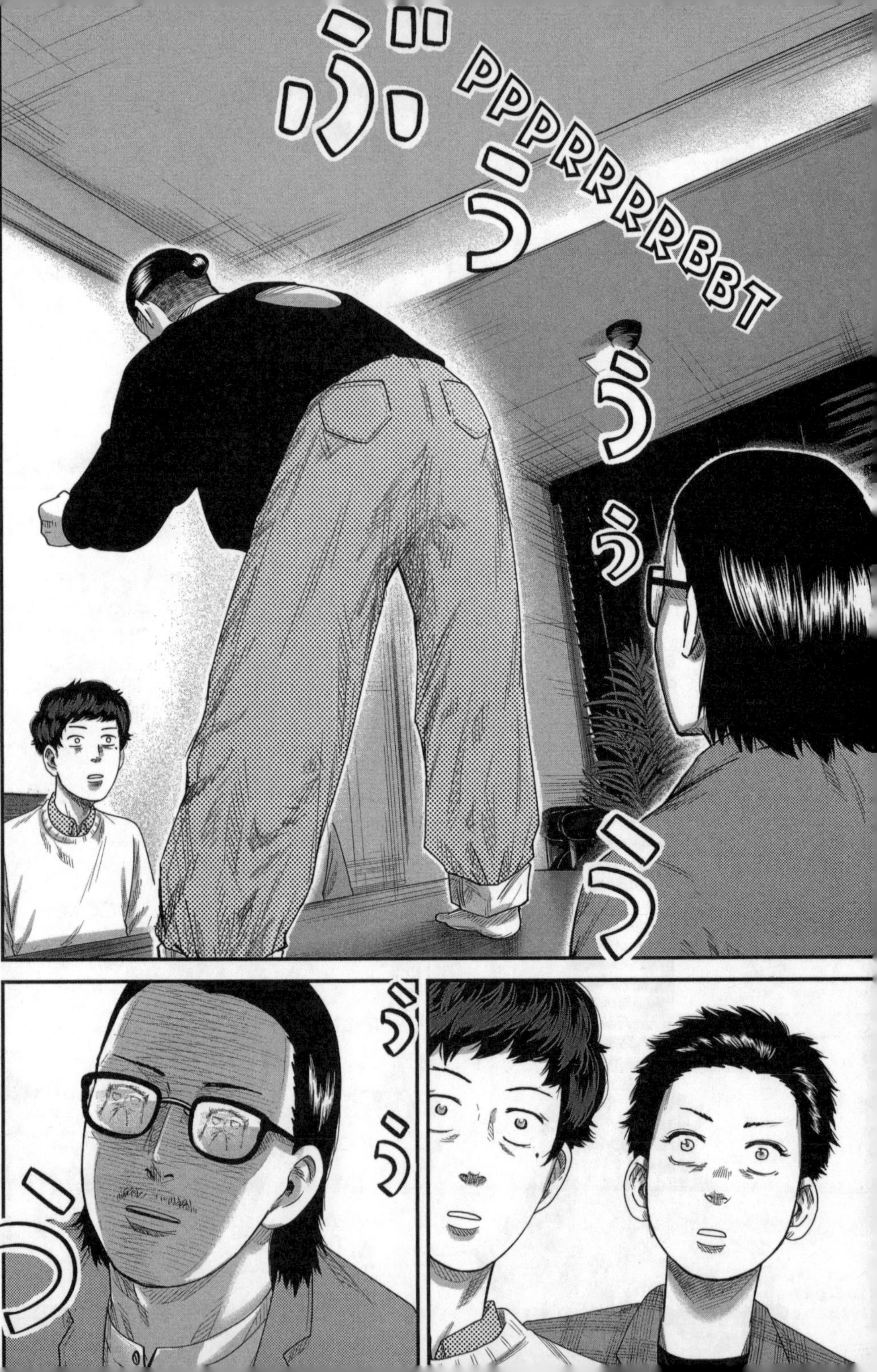
ぶうううう
PPPRRRRRBBT
ううう
う

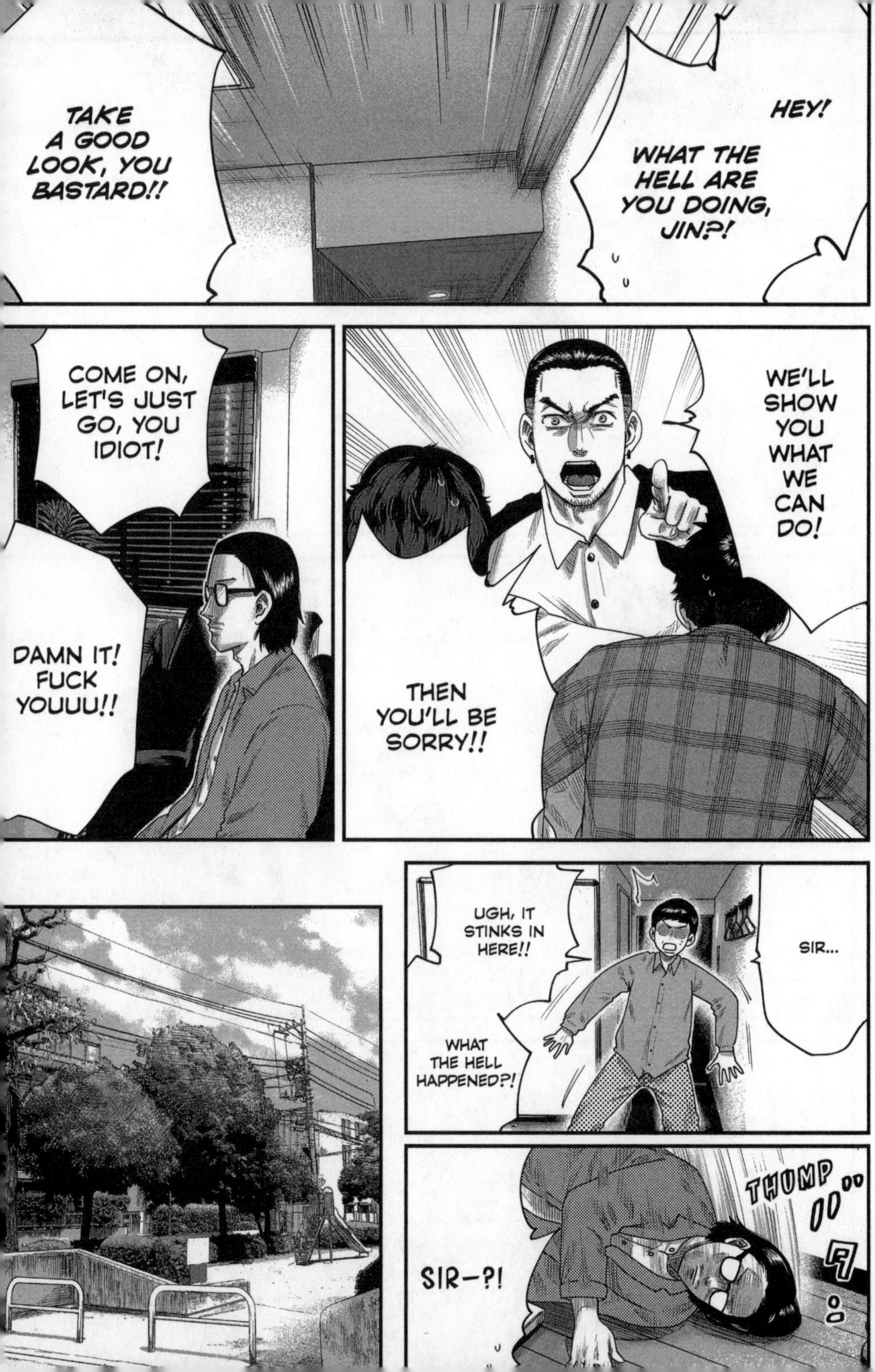
HEY!
WHAT THE HELL ARE YOU DOING, JIN?!
TAKE A GOOD LOOK, YOU BASTARD!!
WE'LL SHOW YOU WHAT WE CAN DO!
THEN YOU'LL BE SORRY!!
COME ON, LET'S JUST GO, YOU IDIOT!
DAMN IT! FUCK YOUUU!!
SIR...
UGH, IT STINKS IN HERE!!
WHAT THE HELL HAPPENED?!
THUMP
SIR-?!

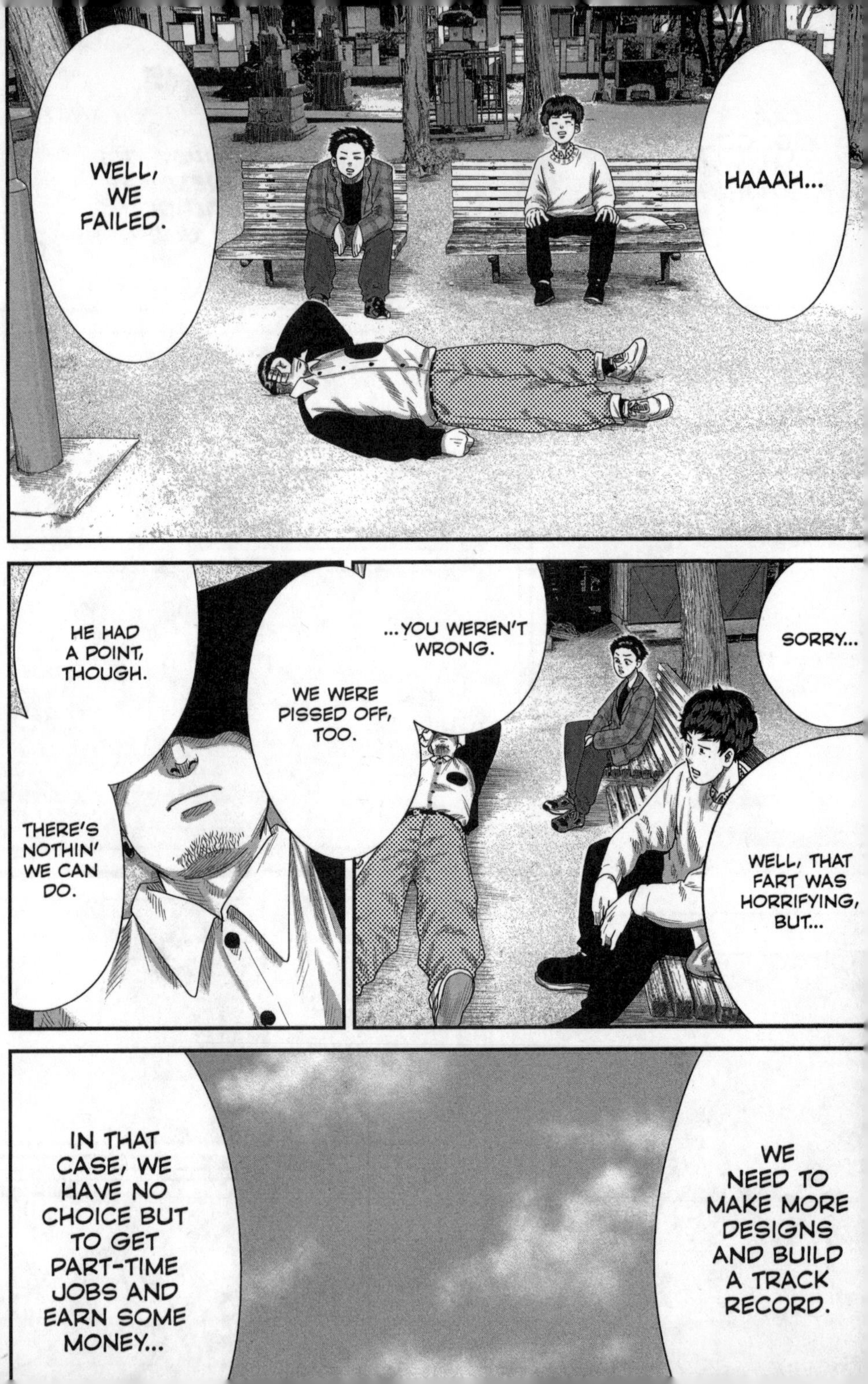
HAAAH...
WELL, WE FAILED.
SORRY...
WELL, THAT FART WAS HORRIFYING, BUT...
...YOU WEREN'T WRONG.
WE WERE PISSED OFF, TOO.
HE HAD A POINT, THOUGH.
THERE'S NOTHIN' WE CAN DO.
WE NEED TO MAKE MORE DESIGNS AND BUILD A TRACK RECORD.
IN THAT CASE, WE HAVE NO CHOICE BUT TO GET PART-TIME JOBS AND EARN SOME MONEY...

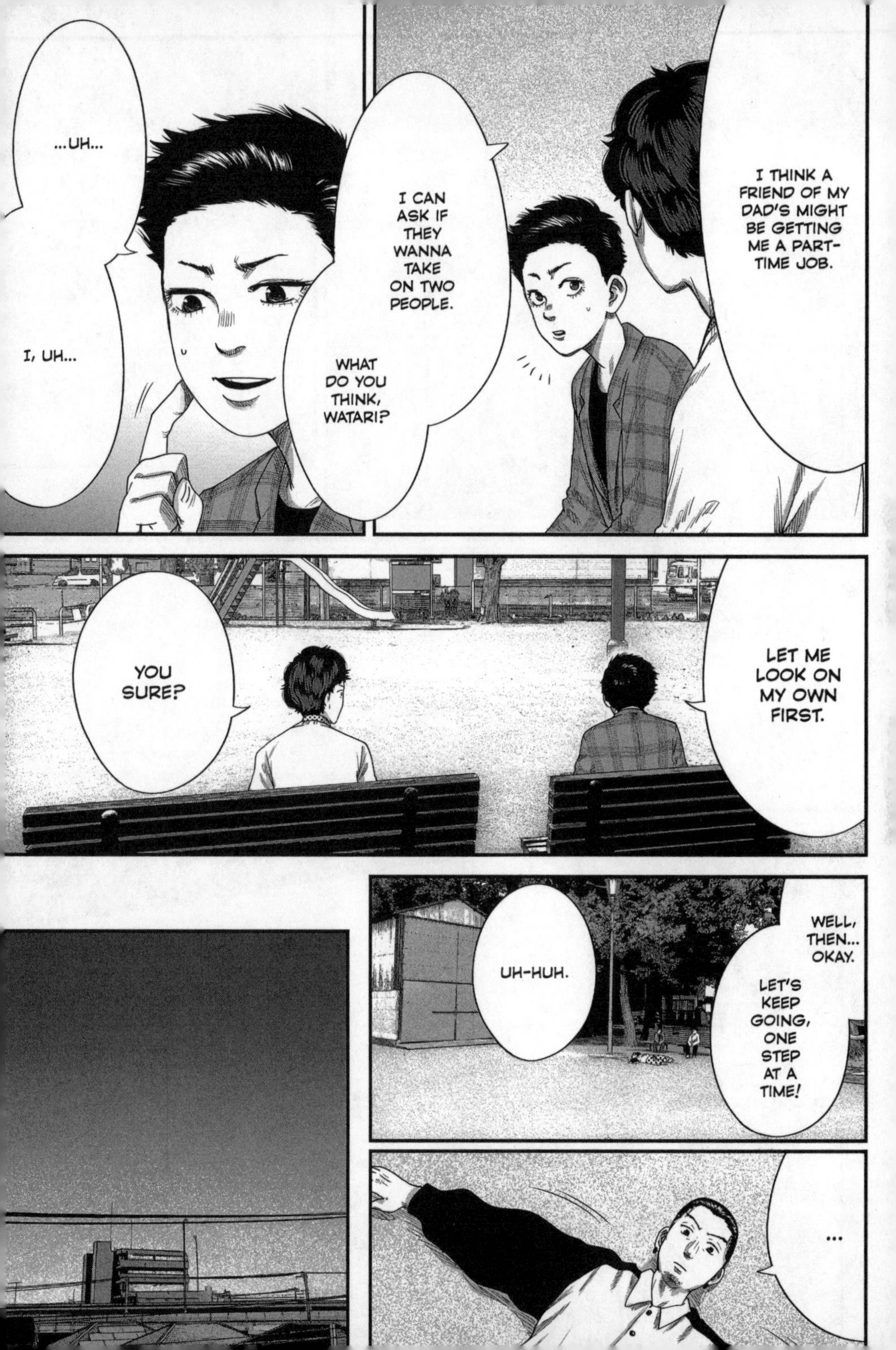
I THINK A FRIEND OF MY DAD'S MIGHT BE GETTING ME A PART-TIME JOB.
I CAN ASK IF THEY WANNA TAKE ON TWO PEOPLE.
WHAT DO YOU THINK, WATARI?
...UH...
I, UH...
LET ME LOOK ON MY OWN FIRST.
YOU SURE?
WELL, THEN... OKAY.
LET'S KEEP GOING, ONE STEP AT A TIME!
UH-HUH.
...

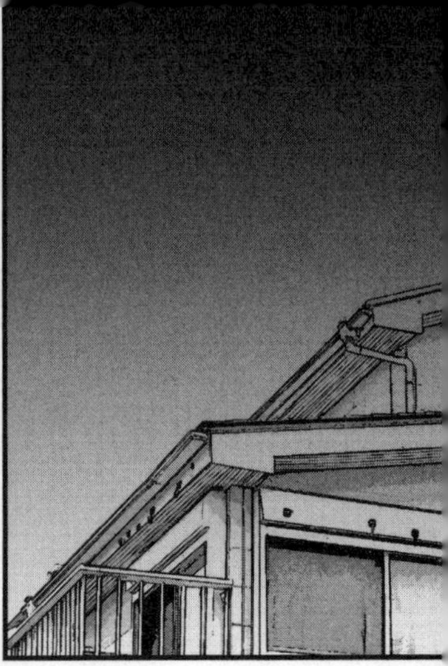

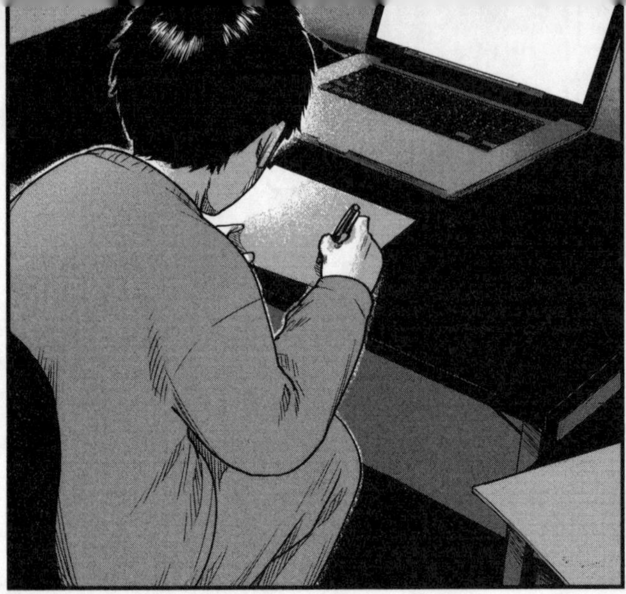

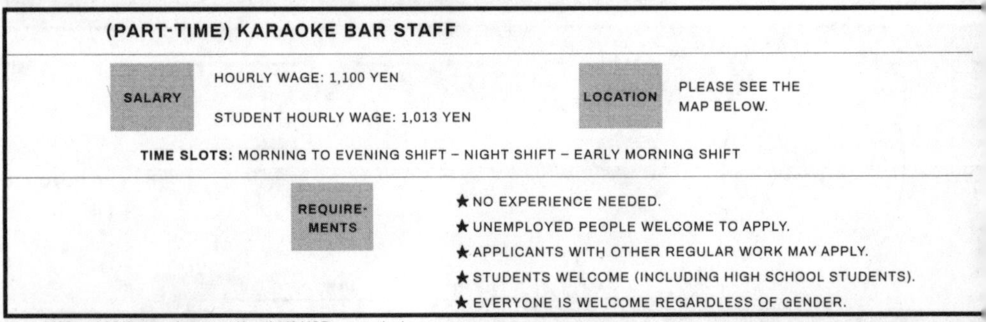
(PART-TIME) KARAOKE BAR STAFF
SALARY
HOURLY WAGE: 1,100 YEN
STUDENT HOURLY WAGE: 1,013 YEN
LOCATION
PLEASE SEE THE MAP BELOW.
TIME SLOTS: MORNING TO EVENING SHIFT – NIGHT SHIFT – EARLY MORNING SHIFT
REQUIRE-MENTS
★NO EXPERIENCE NEEDED.
★UNEMPLOYED PEOPLE WELCOME TO APPLY.
★APPLICANTS WITH OTHER REGULAR WORK MAY APPLY.
★STUDENTS WELCOME (INCLUDING HIGH SCHOOL STUDENTS).
★EVERYONE IS WELCOME REGARDLESS OF GENDER.

1,100 and 1,013 yen = Approx. $11 and $10 USD respectively

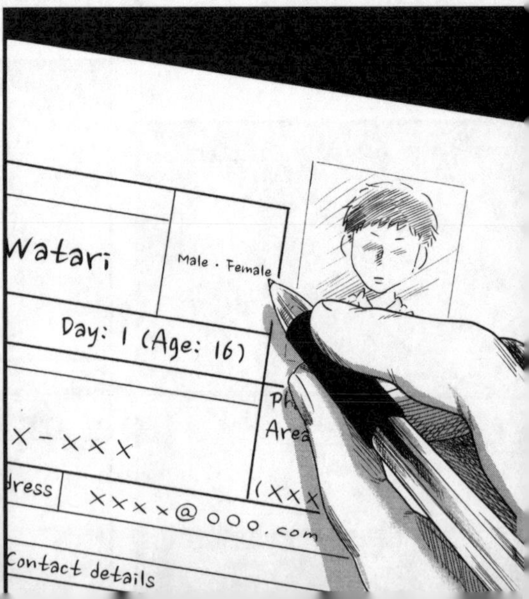
Watari
Male · Female
Day: 1 (Age: 16)
Ph
Area
X-XXX
dress
xxxx@ooo.com
(XXX
Contact details

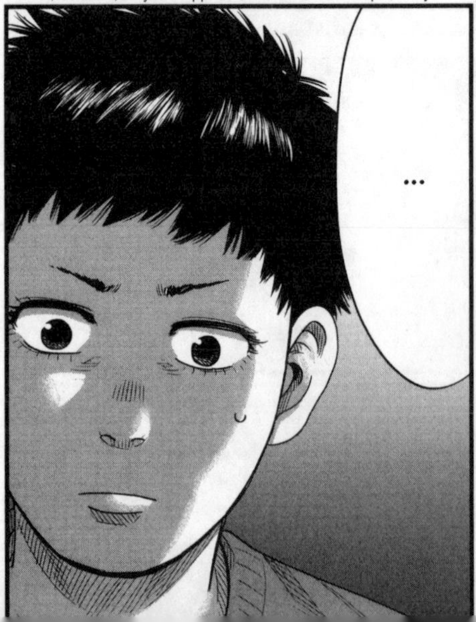
...

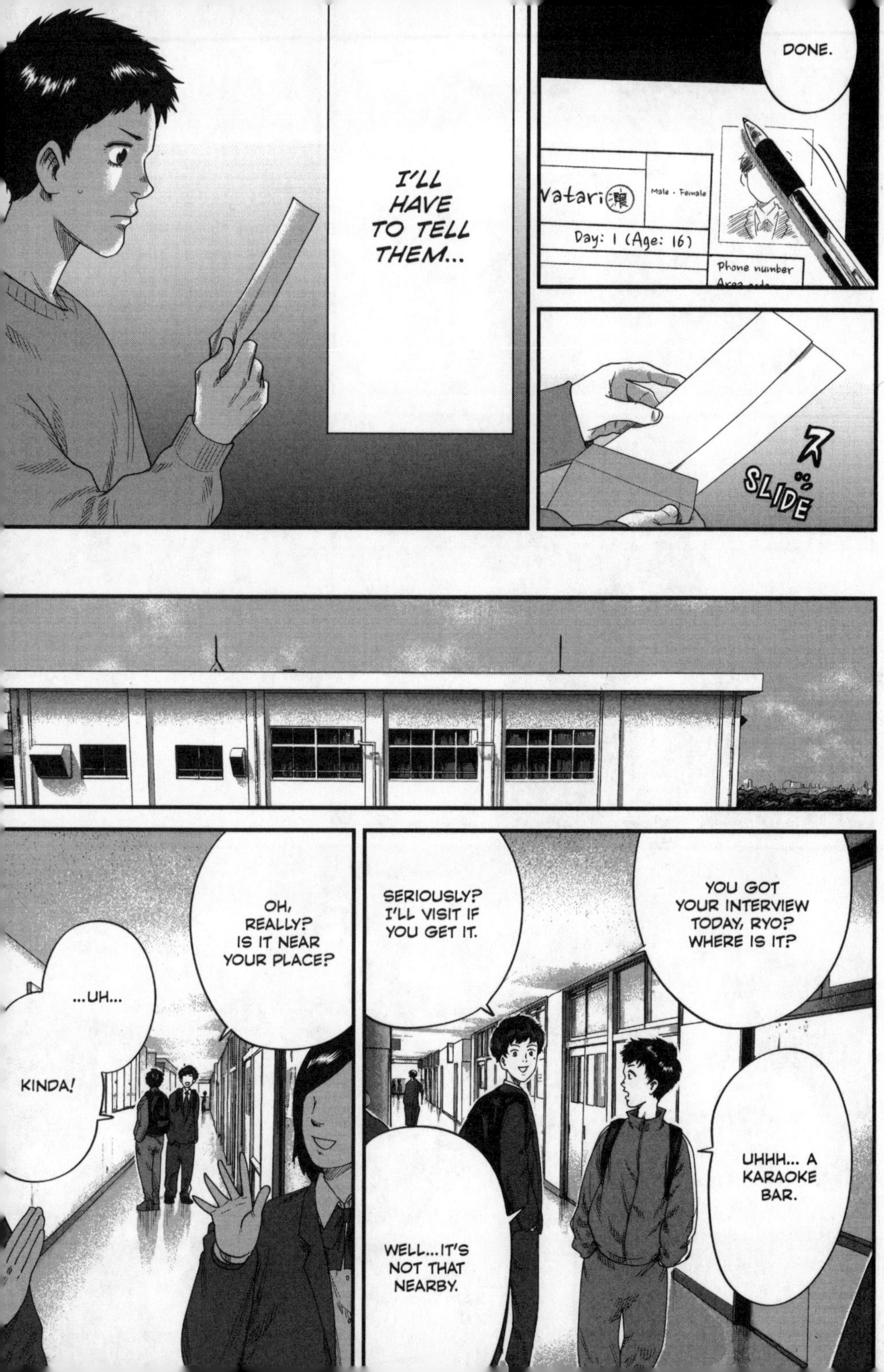
DONE.
vatari
Male · Female
Day: 1 (Age: 16)
Phone number
ス
SLIDE
I'LL HAVE TO TELL THEM...
YOU GOT YOUR INTERVIEW TODAY, RYO? WHERE IS IT?
UHHH... A KARAOKE BAR.
SERIOUSLY? I'LL VISIT IF YOU GET IT.
WELL...IT'S NOT THAT NEARBY.
OH, REALLY? IS IT NEAR YOUR PLACE?
...UH...
KINDA!

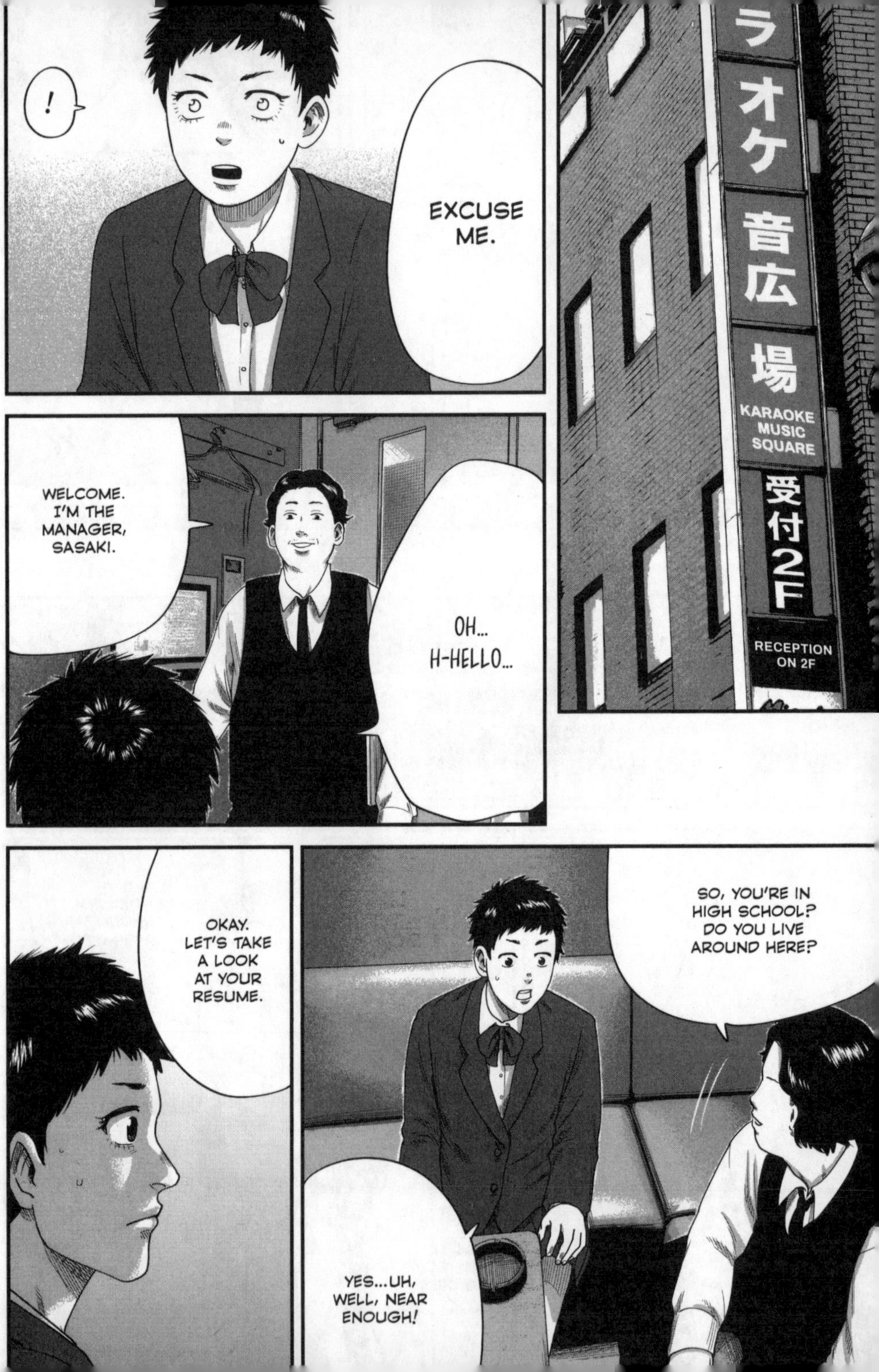

ラオケ
音広場
KARAOKE MUSIC SQUARE
受付2F
RECEPTION ON 2F
EXCUSE ME.
!
WELCOME. I'M THE MANAGER, SASAKI.
OH... H-HELLO...
SO, YOU'RE IN HIGH SCHOOL? DO YOU LIVE AROUND HERE?
YES...UH, WELL, NEAR ENOUGH!
OKAY. LET'S TAKE A LOOK AT YOUR RESUME.

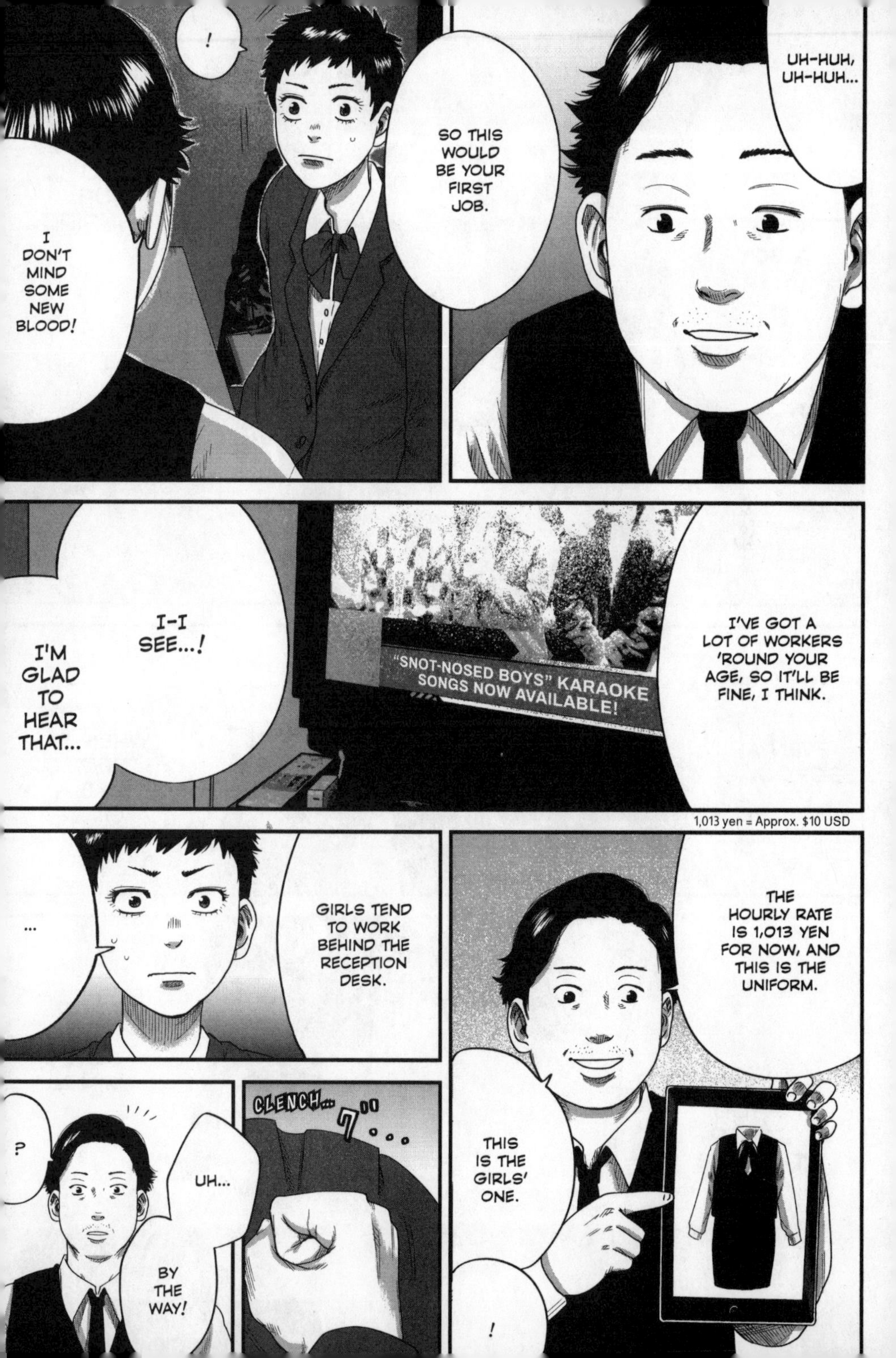
UH-HUH, UH-HUH...
SO THIS WOULD BE YOUR FIRST JOB.
!
I DON'T MIND SOME NEW BLOOD!
I'VE GOT A LOT OF WORKERS 'ROUND YOUR AGE, SO IT'LL BE FINE, I THINK.
"SNOT-NOSED BOYS" KARAOKE SONGS NOW AVAILABLE!
I-I SEE...!
I'M GLAD TO HEAR THAT...
THE HOURLY RATE IS 1,013 YEN FOR NOW, AND THIS IS THE UNIFORM.
THIS IS THE GIRLS' ONE.
!
GIRLS TEND TO WORK BEHIND THE RECEPTION DESK.
...
CLENCH...
UH...
?
BY THE WAY!
1,013 yen = Approx. $10 USD

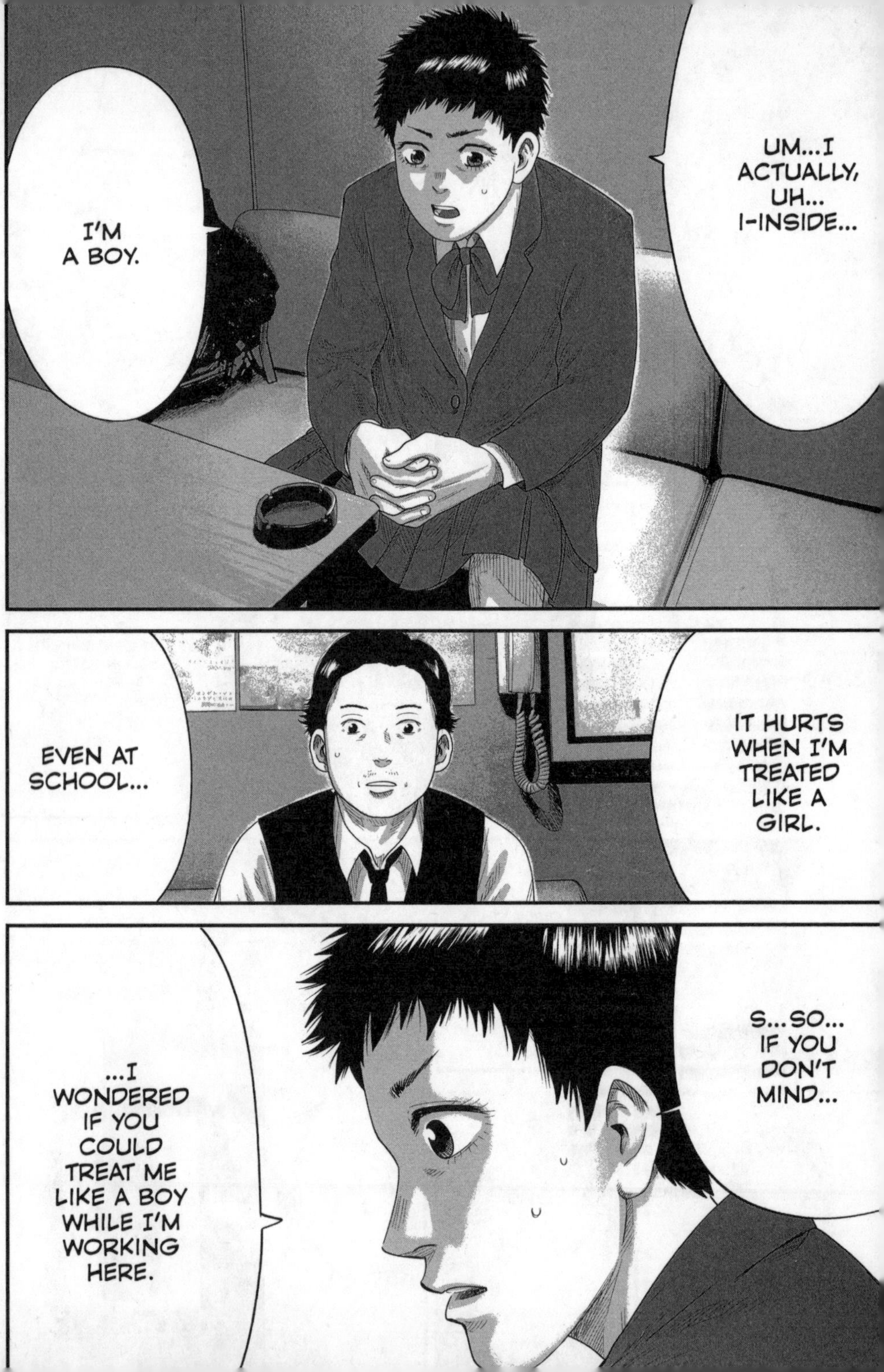
UM...I ACTUALLY, UH... I-INSIDE...
I'M A BOY.
IT HURTS WHEN I'M TREATED LIKE A GIRL.
EVEN AT SCHOOL...
S...SO... IF YOU DON'T MIND...
...I WONDERED IF YOU COULD TREAT ME LIKE A BOY WHILE I'M WORKING HERE.

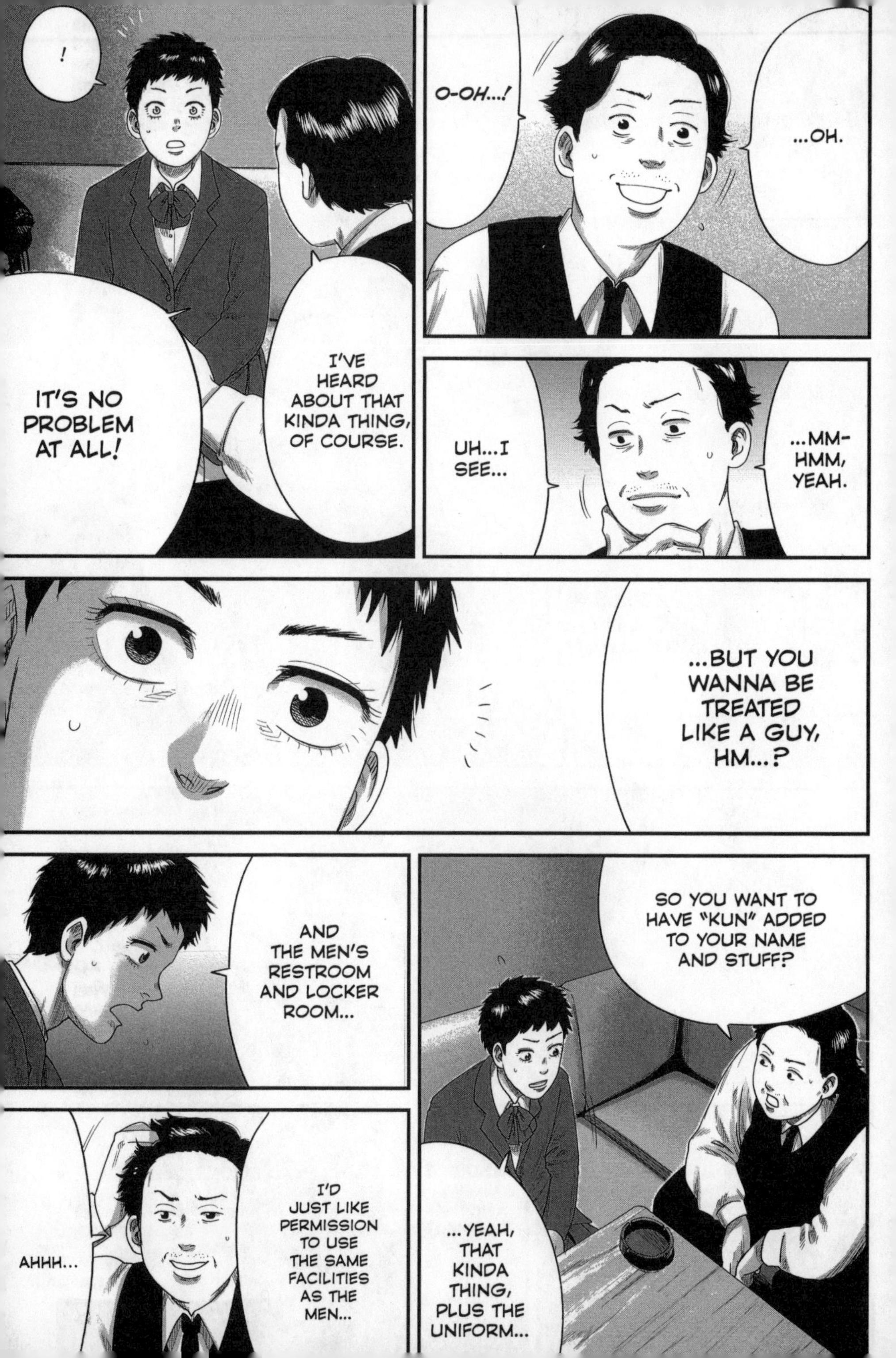
...OH.
O-OH...!
...MM-HMM, YEAH.
UH...I SEE...
!
I'VE HEARD ABOUT THAT KINDA THING, OF COURSE.
IT'S NO PROBLEM AT ALL!
...BUT YOU WANNA BE TREATED LIKE A GUY, HM...?
SO YOU WANT TO HAVE "KUN" ADDED TO YOUR NAME AND STUFF?
...YEAH, THAT KINDA THING, PLUS THE UNIFORM...
AND THE MEN'S RESTROOM AND LOCKER ROOM...
I'D JUST LIKE PERMISSION TO USE THE SAME FACILITIES AS THE MEN...
AHHH...

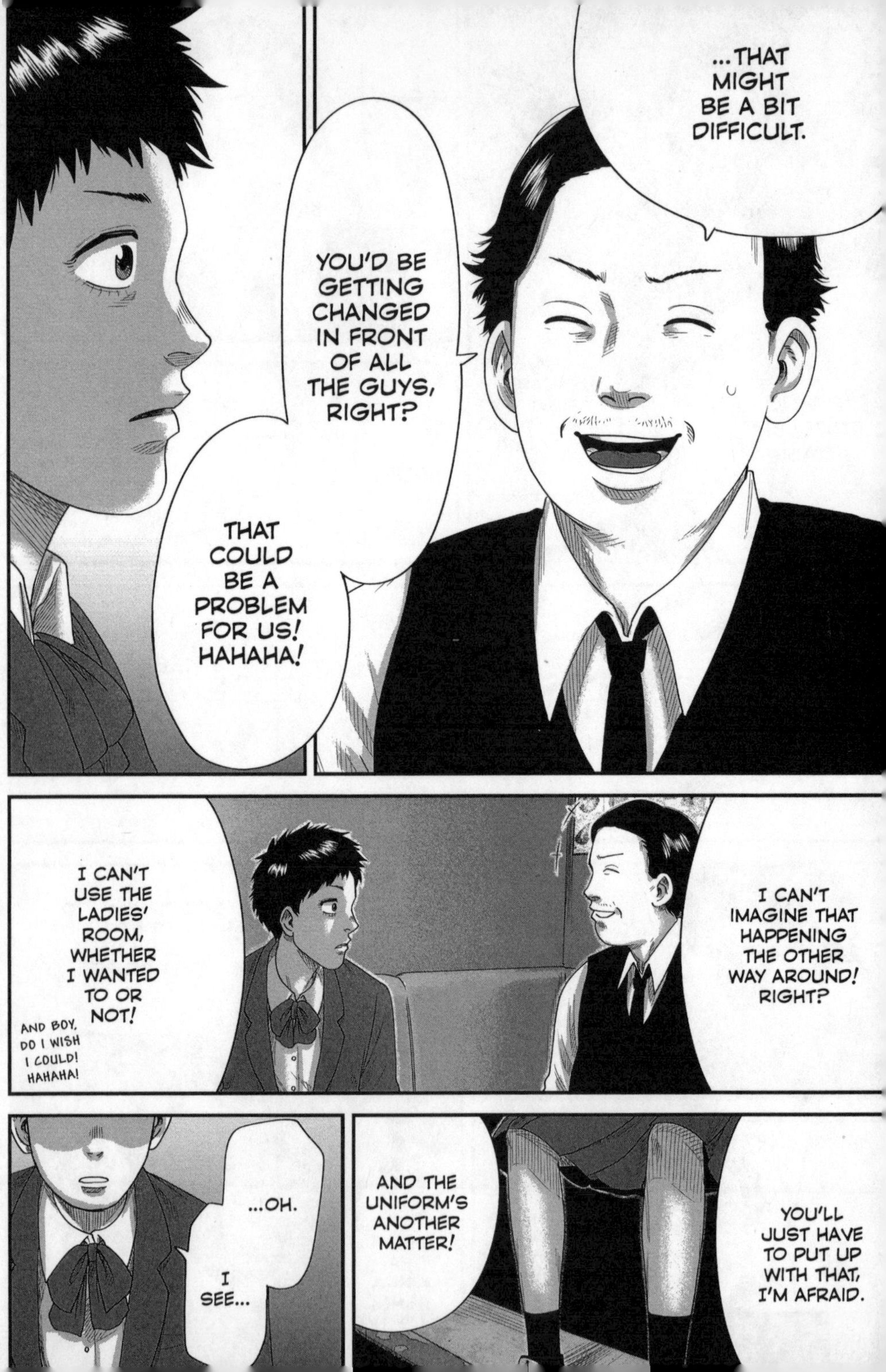
...THAT MIGHT BE A BIT DIFFICULT.
YOU'D BE GETTING CHANGED IN FRONT OF ALL THE GUYS, RIGHT?
THAT COULD BE A PROBLEM FOR US! HAHAHA!
I CAN'T IMAGINE THAT HAPPENING THE OTHER WAY AROUND! RIGHT?
I CAN'T USE THE LADIES' ROOM, WHETHER I WANTED TO OR NOT!
AND BOY, DO I WISH I COULD! HAHAHA!
YOU'LL JUST HAVE TO PUT UP WITH THAT, I'M AFRAID.
AND THE UNIFORM'S ANOTHER MATTER!
...OH.
I SEE...

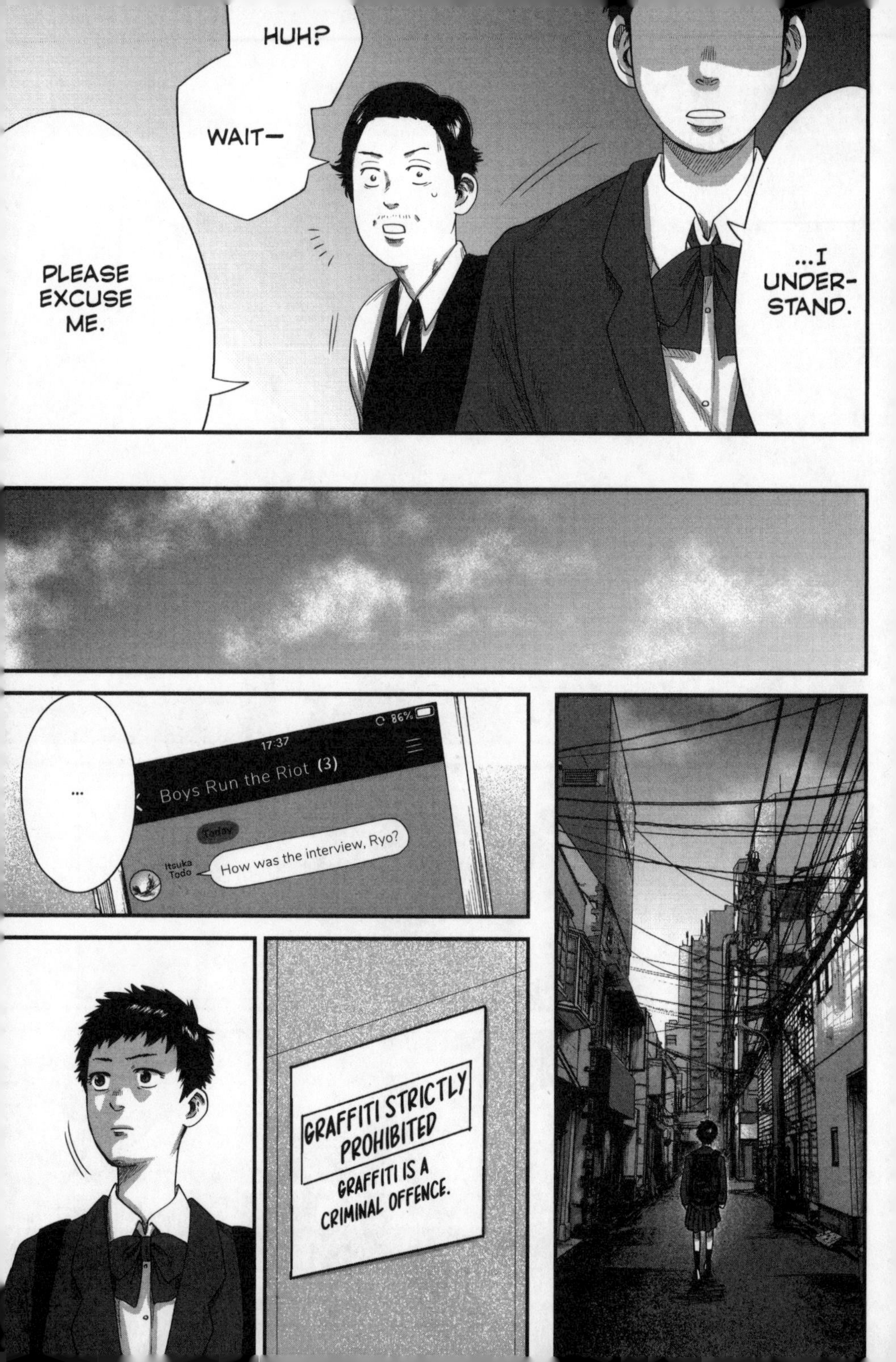
...I UNDER-STAND.
PLEASE EXCUSE ME.
HUH?
WAIT—
17:37
86%
Boys Run the Riot (3)
Today
Itsuka Todo
How was the interview, Ryo?
...
GRAFFITI STRICTLY PROHIBITED
GRAFFITI IS A CRIMINAL OFFENCE.

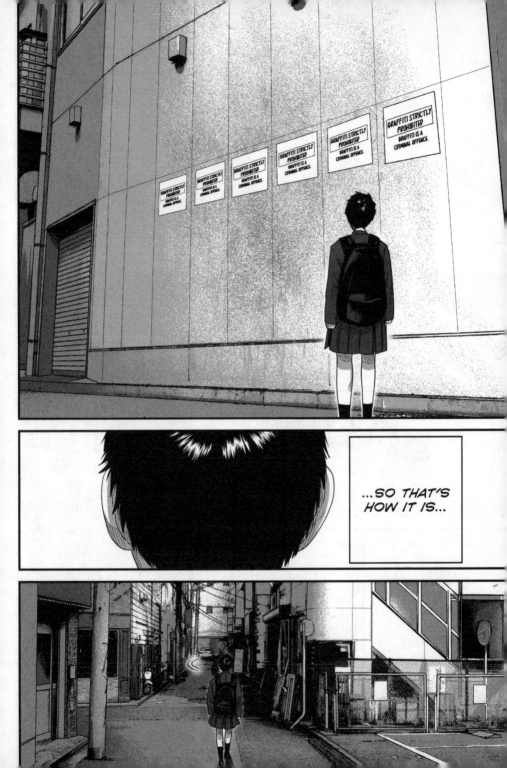

...SO THAT'S
HOW IT IS...

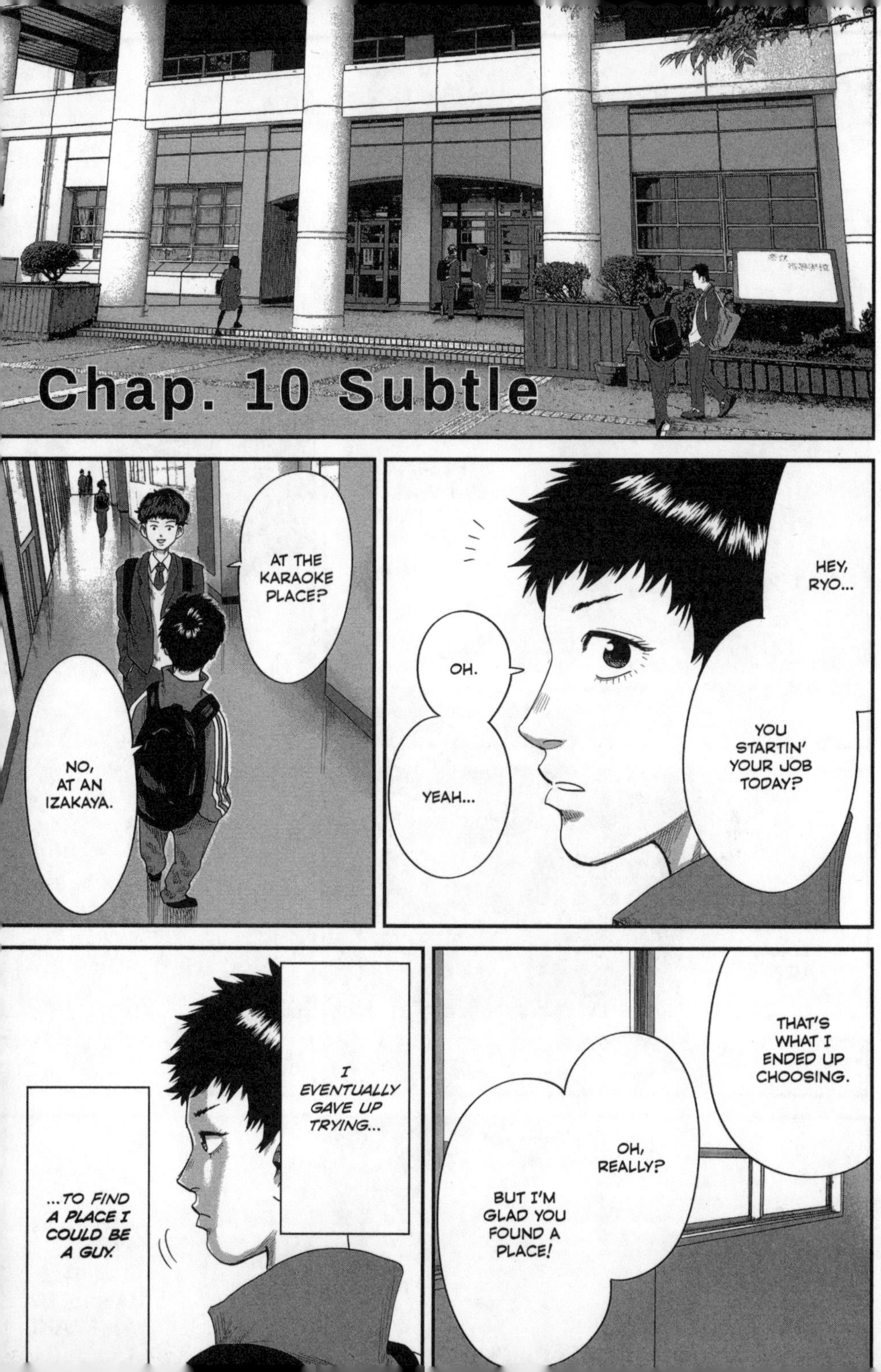

Chap. 10 Subtle
HEY, RYO...
YOU STARTIN' YOUR JOB TODAY?
OH.
YEAH...
AT THE KARAOKE PLACE?
NO, AT AN IZAKAYA.
THAT'S WHAT I ENDED UP CHOOSING.
OH, REALLY?
BUT I'M GLAD YOU FOUND A PLACE!
I EVENTUALLY GAVE UP TRYING...
...TO FIND A PLACE I COULD BE A GUY.

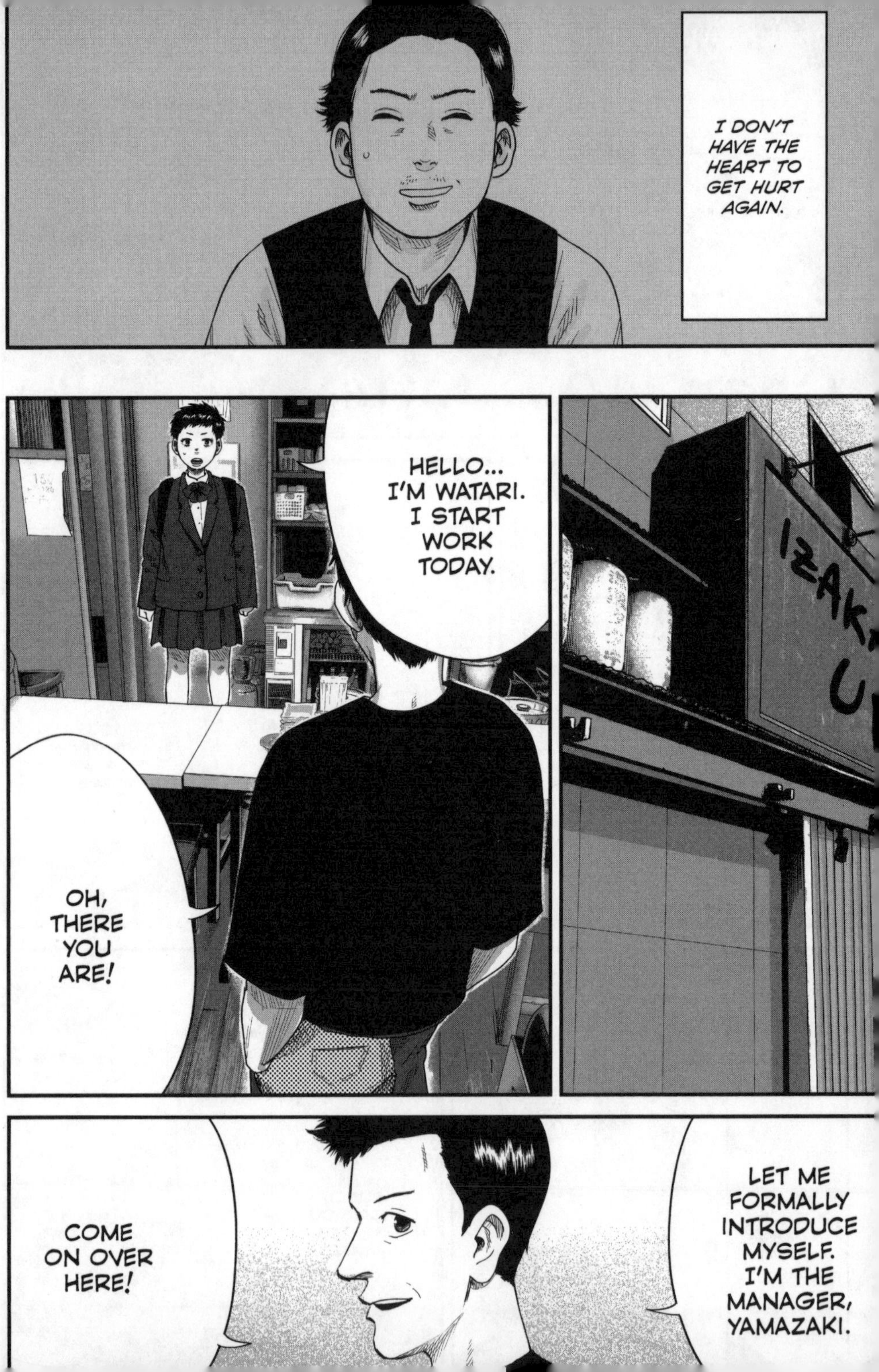
I DON'T HAVE THE HEART TO GET HURT AGAIN.
HELLO... I'M WATARI. I START WORK TODAY.
OH, THERE YOU ARE!
LET ME FORMALLY INTRODUCE MYSELF. I'M THE MANAGER, YAMAZAKI.
COME ON OVER HERE!

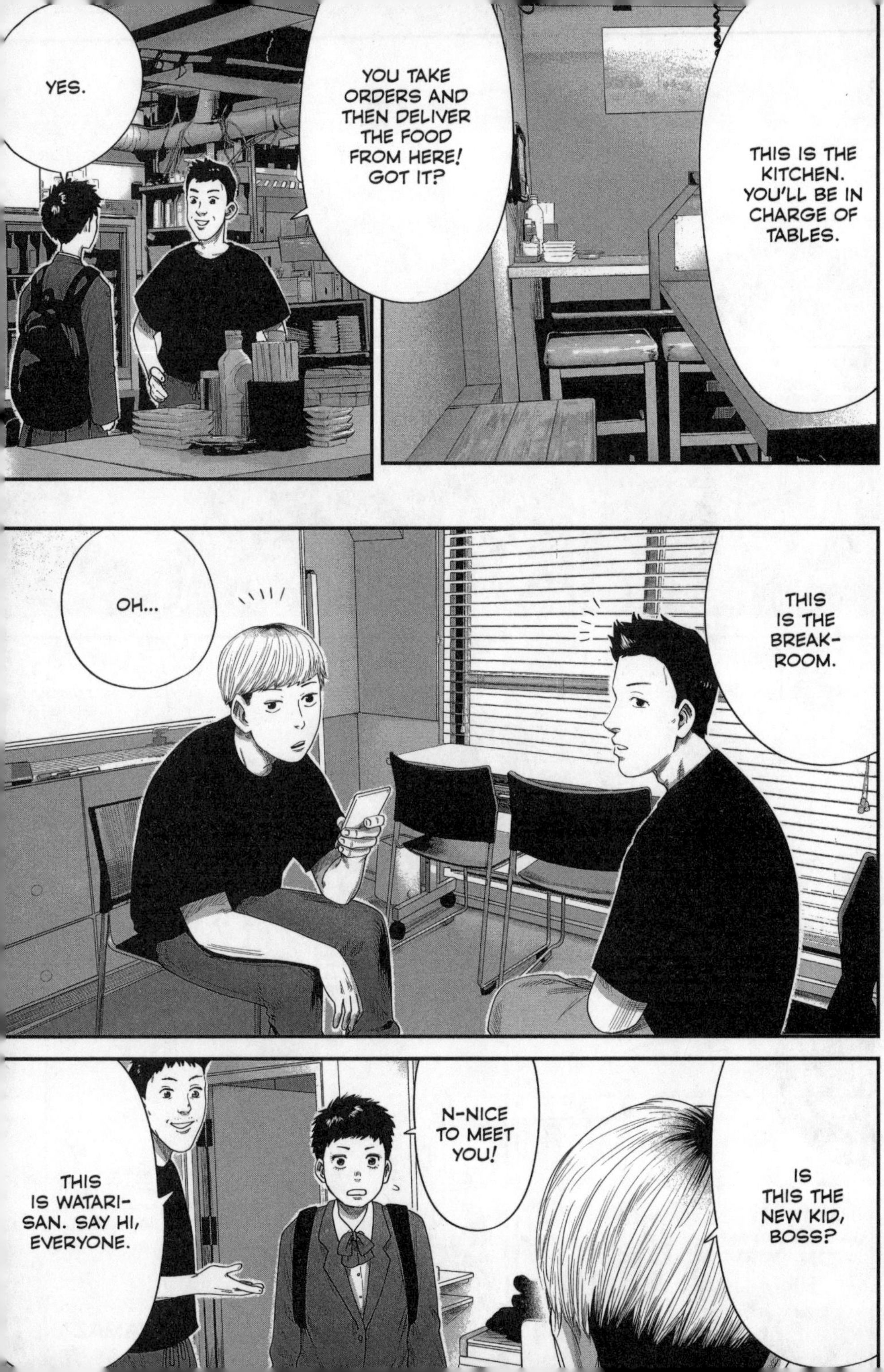

THIS IS THE KITCHEN. YOU'LL BE IN CHARGE OF TABLES.
YOU TAKE ORDERS AND THEN DELIVER THE FOOD FROM HERE! GOT IT?
YES.
THIS IS THE BREAK-ROOM.
OH...
IS THIS THE NEW KID, BOSS?
N-NICE TO MEET YOU!
THIS IS WATARI-SAN. SAY HI, EVERYONE.

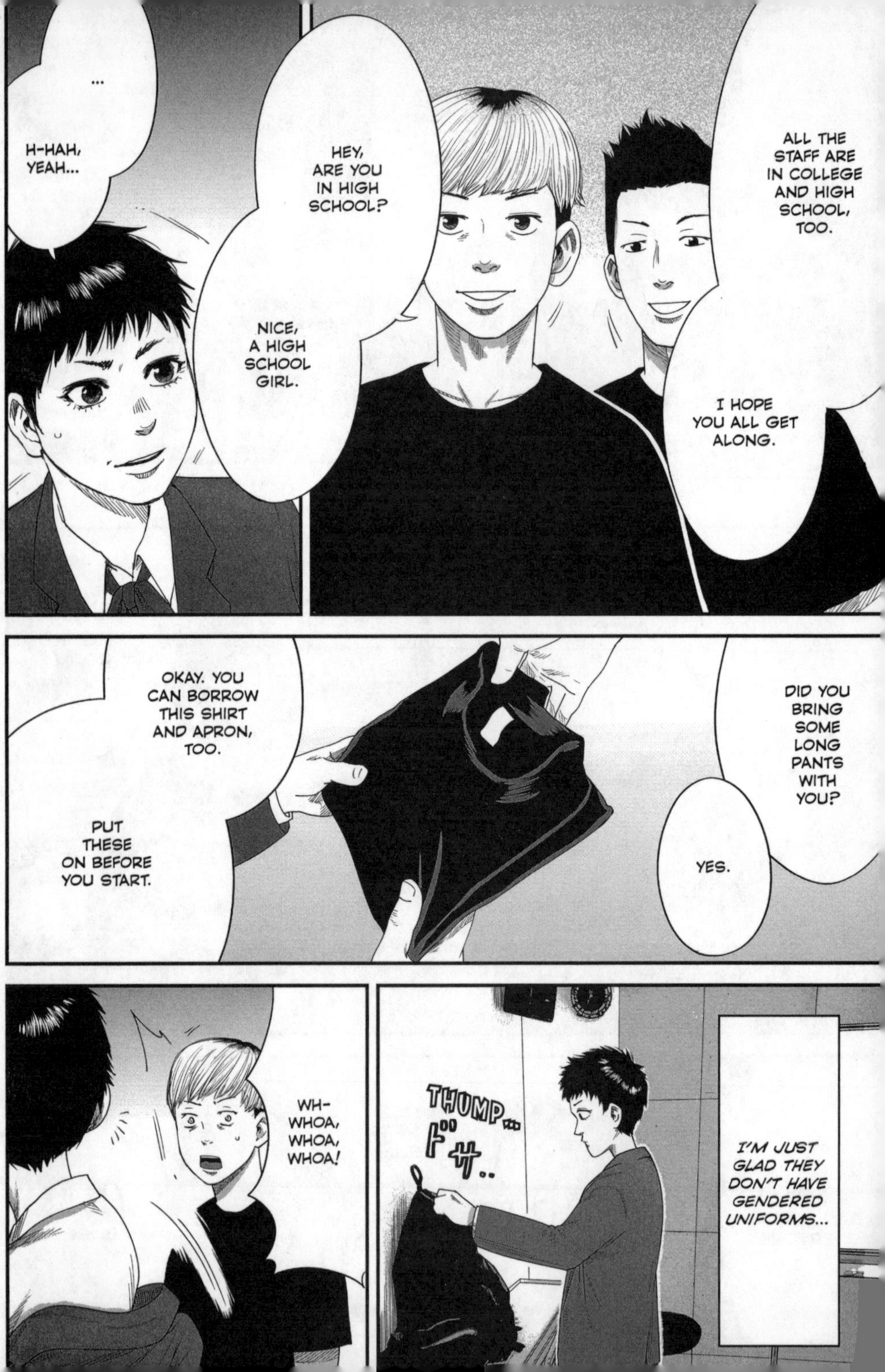
ALL THE STAFF ARE IN COLLEGE AND HIGH SCHOOL, TOO.
I HOPE YOU ALL GET ALONG.
HEY, ARE YOU IN HIGH SCHOOL?
NICE, A HIGH SCHOOL GIRL.
...
H-HAH, YEAH...
DID YOU BRING SOME LONG PANTS WITH YOU?
YES.
OKAY. YOU CAN BORROW THIS SHIRT AND APRON, TOO.
PUT THESE ON BEFORE YOU START.
I'M JUST GLAD THEY DON'T HAVE GENDERED UNIFORMS...
THUMP...
ドサ..
WH- WHOA, WHOA, WHOA!

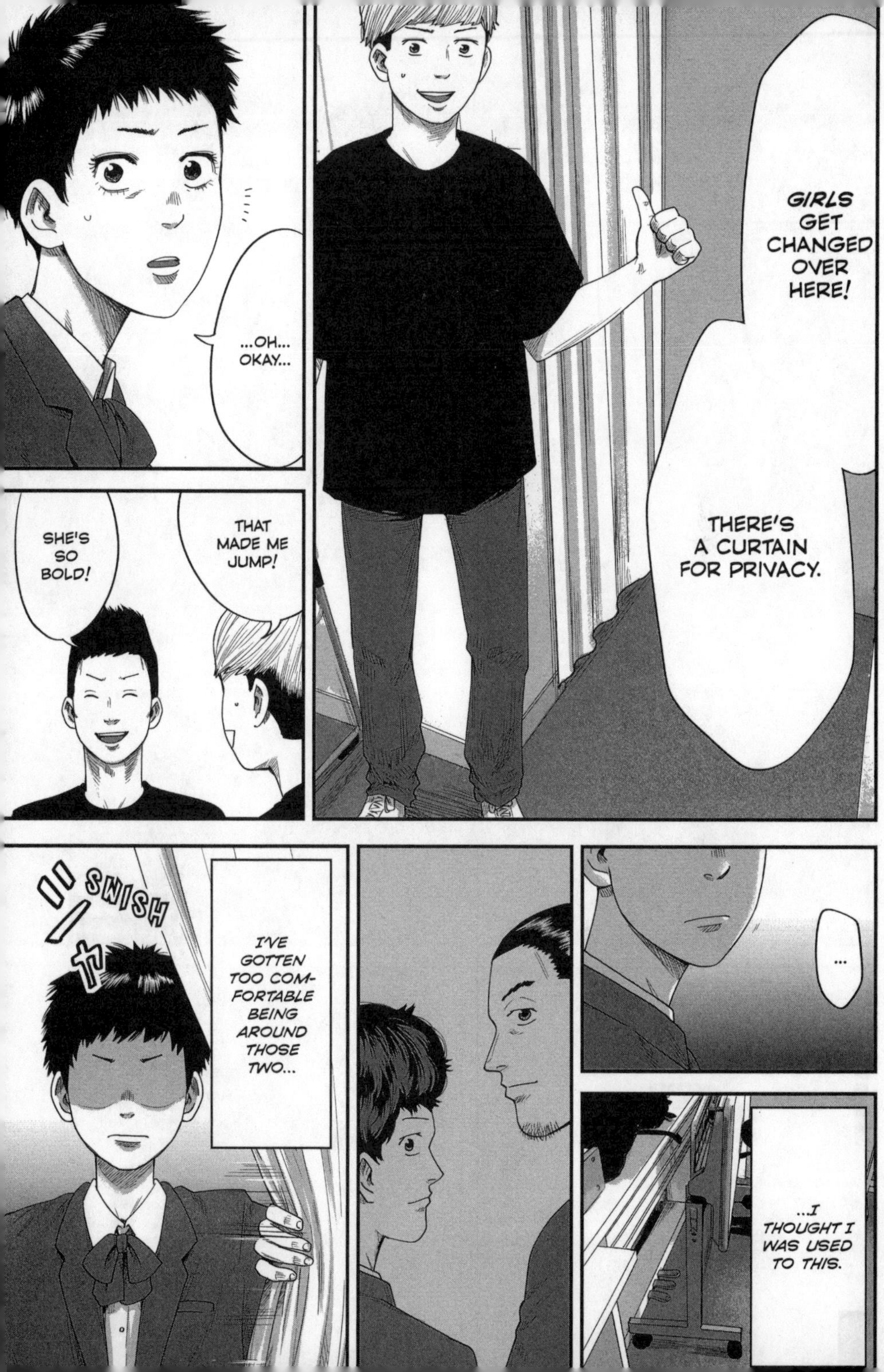
GIRLS GET CHANGED OVER HERE!
THERE'S A CURTAIN FOR PRIVACY.
...OH... OKAY...
THAT MADE ME JUMP!
SHE'S SO BOLD!
...
...I THOUGHT I WAS USED TO THIS.
SWISH
I'VE GOTTEN TOO COMFORTABLE BEING AROUND THOSE TWO...

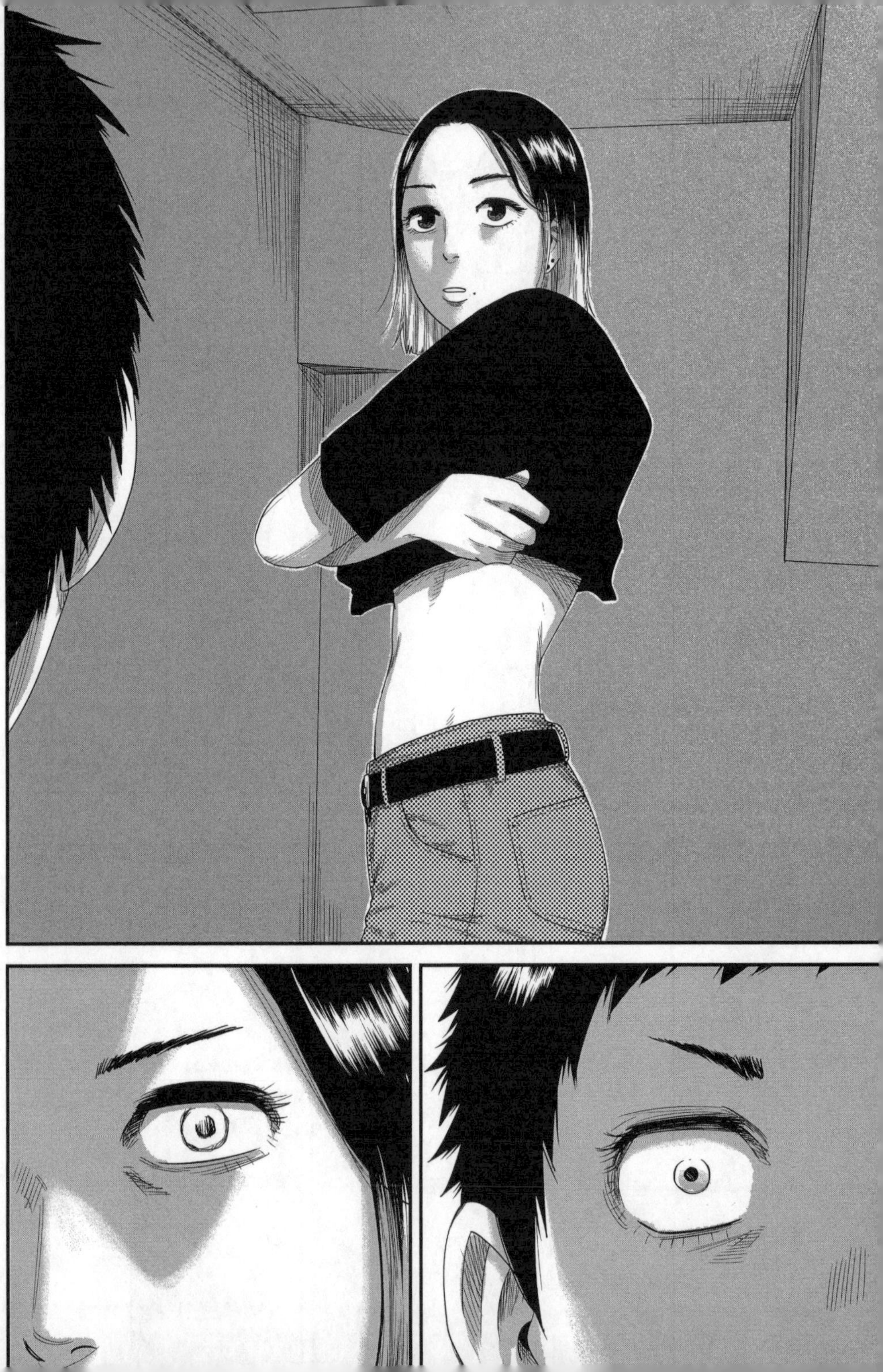

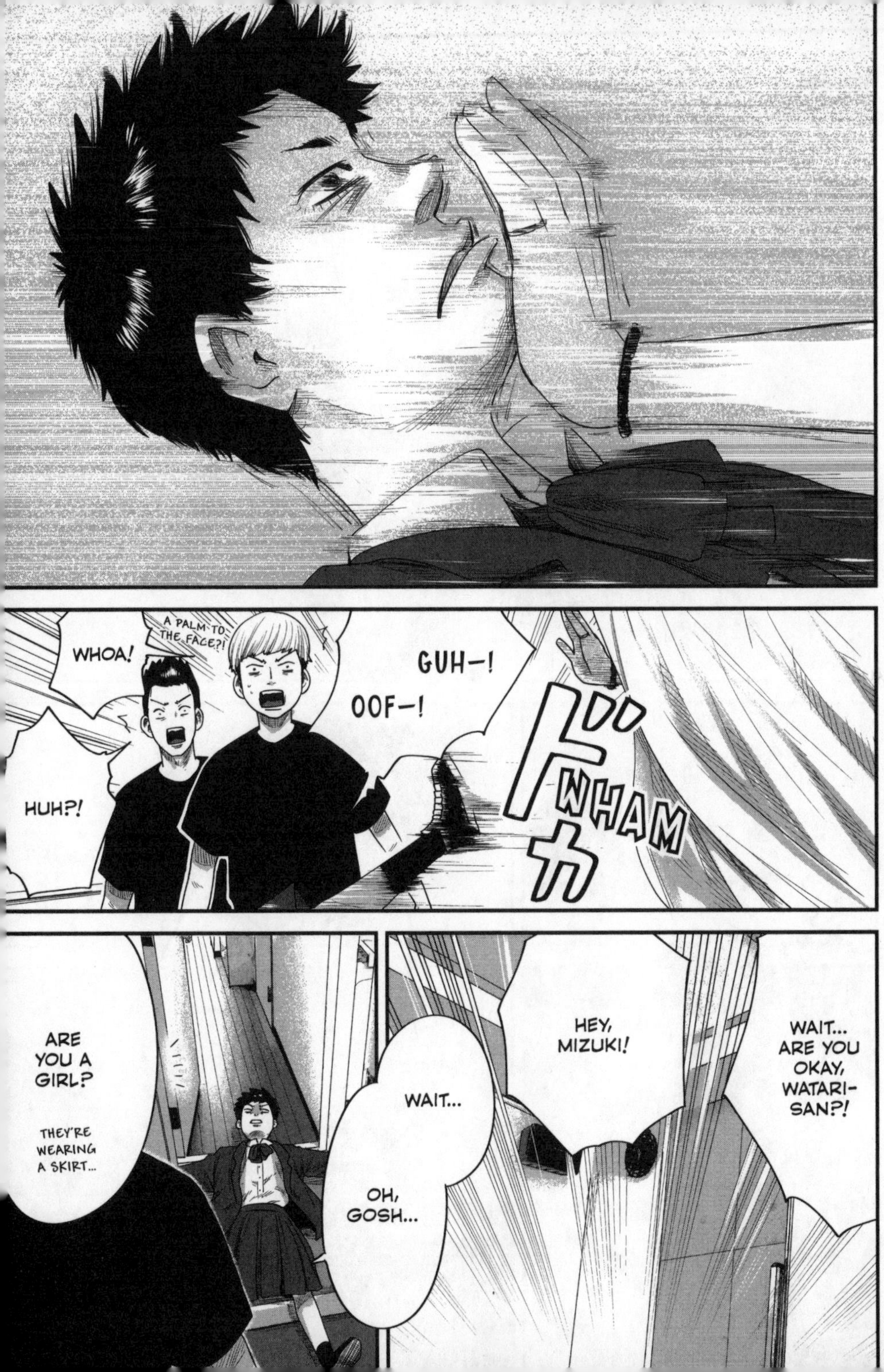
GUH-!
OOF-!
WHAM
A PALM TO THE FACE?!
WHOA!
HUH?!
WAIT... ARE YOU OKAY, WATARI-SAN?!
HEY, MIZUKI!
WAIT...
OH, GOSH...
ARE YOU A GIRL?
THEY'RE WEARING A SKIRT...

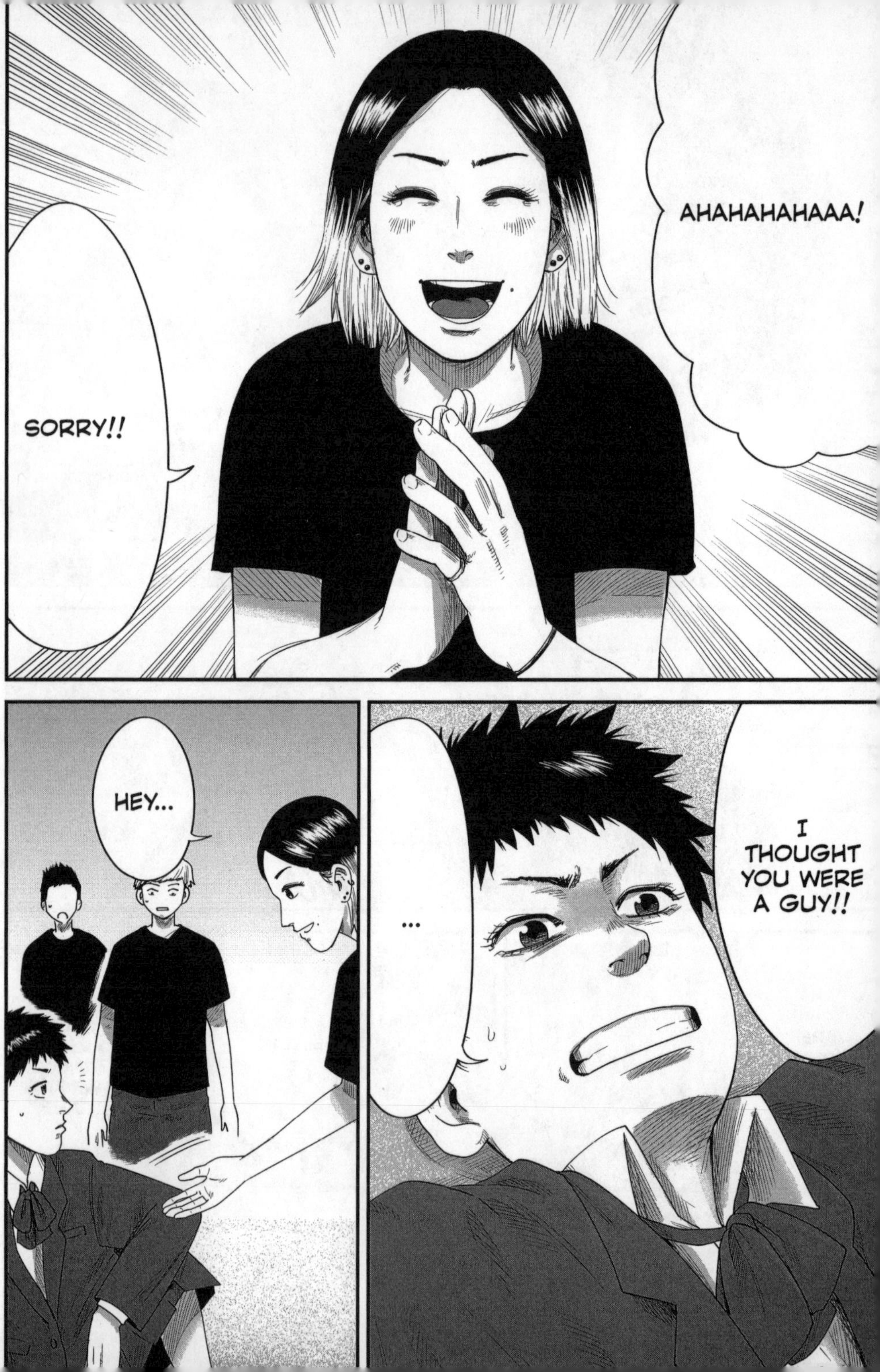
AHAHAHAHAAA!
SORRY!!
I THOUGHT YOU WERE A GUY!!
...
HEY...

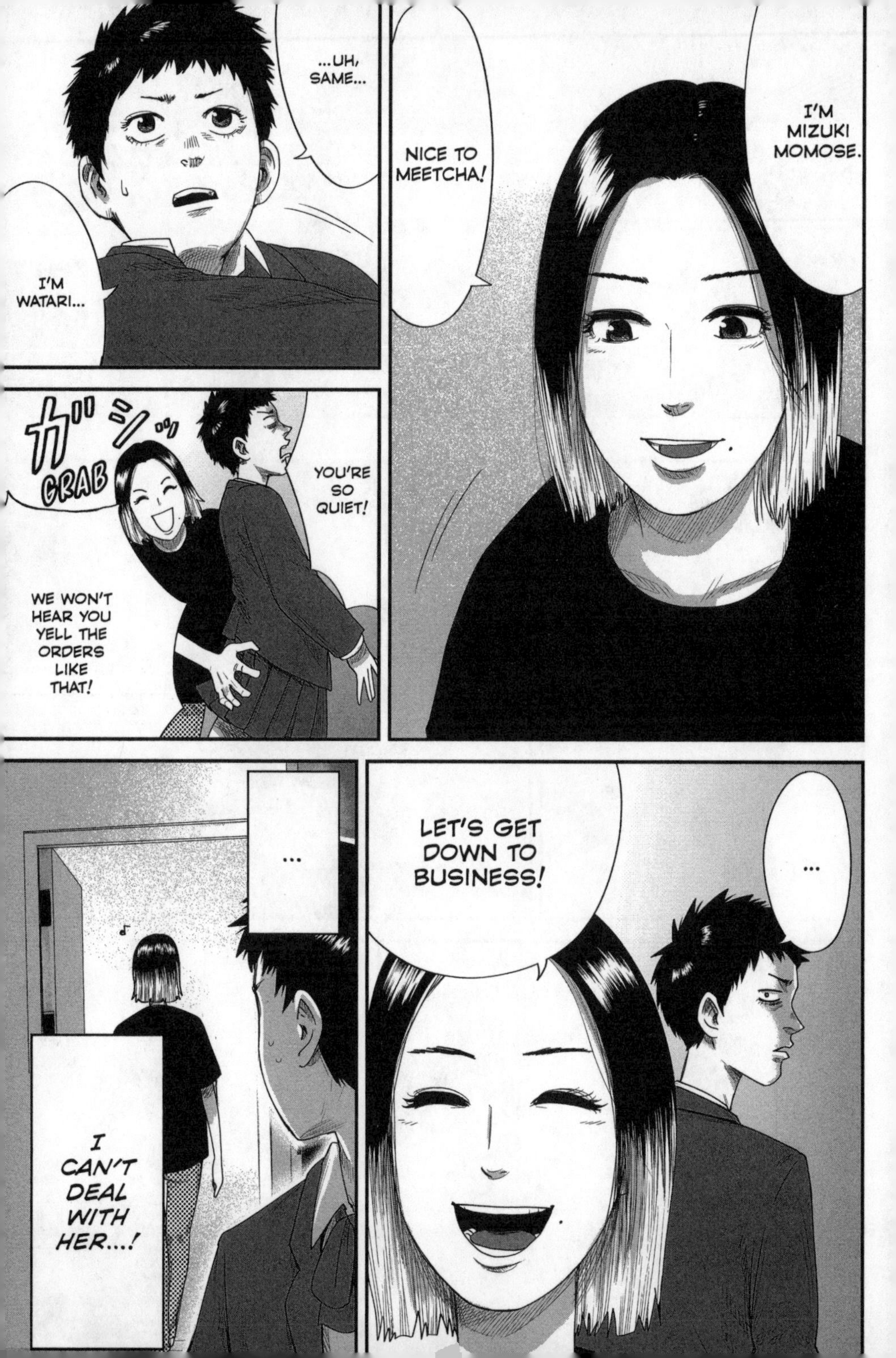
I'M MIZUKI MOMOSE.
NICE TO MEETCHA!
...UH, SAME...
I'M WATARI...
YOU'RE SO QUIET!
ガシッ
GRAB
WE WON'T HEAR YOU YELL THE ORDERS LIKE THAT!
...
LET'S GET DOWN TO BUSINESS!
...
I CAN'T DEAL WITH HER...!

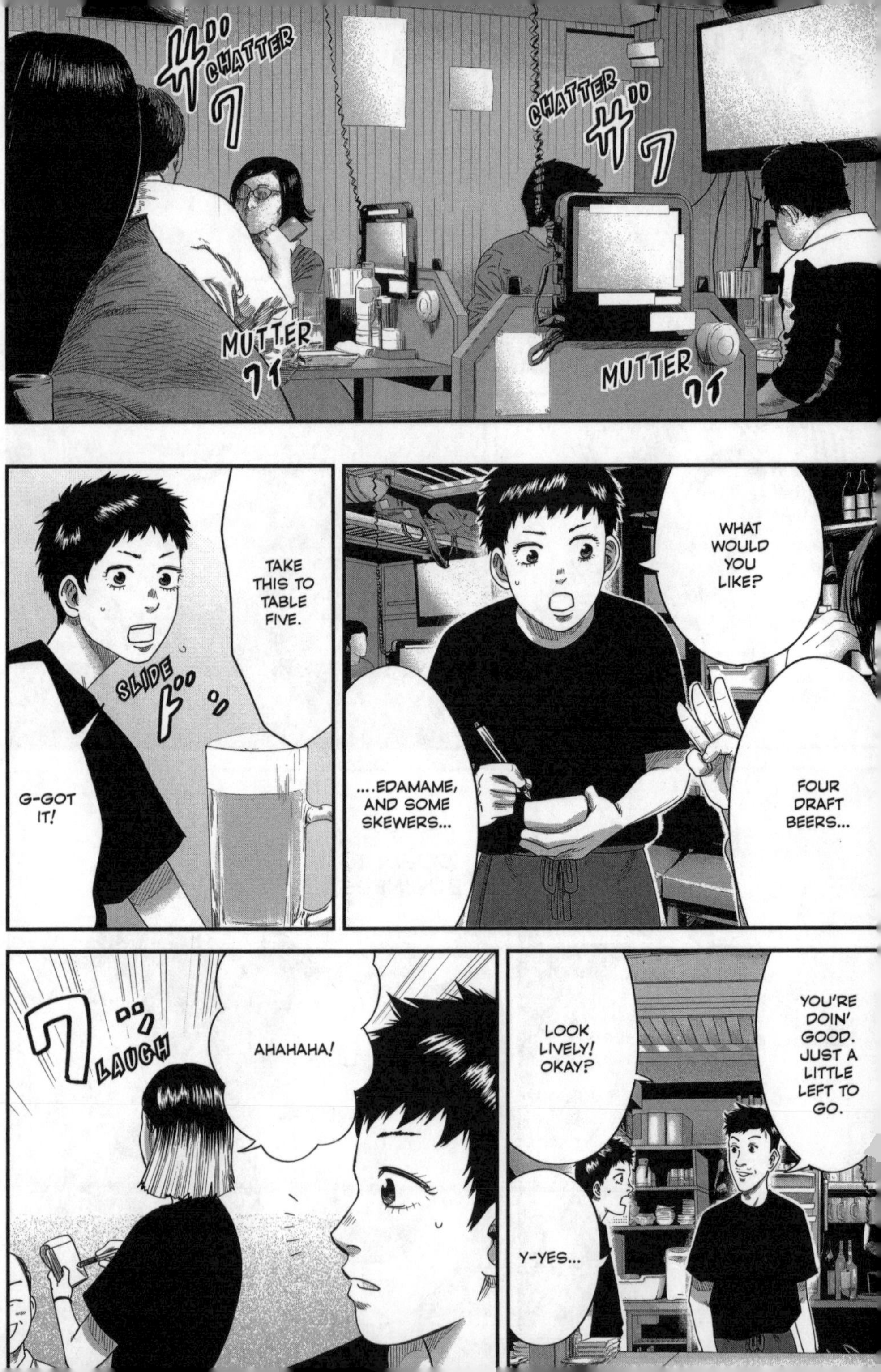
CHATTER
CHATTER
MUTTER
MUTTER
WHAT WOULD YOU LIKE?
FOUR DRAFT BEERS...
....EDAMAME, AND SOME SKEWERS...
TAKE THIS TO TABLE FIVE.
SLIDE
G-GOT IT!
YOU'RE DOIN' GOOD. JUST A LITTLE LEFT TO GO.
LOOK LIVELY! OKAY?
Y-YES...
AHAHAHA!
LAUGH

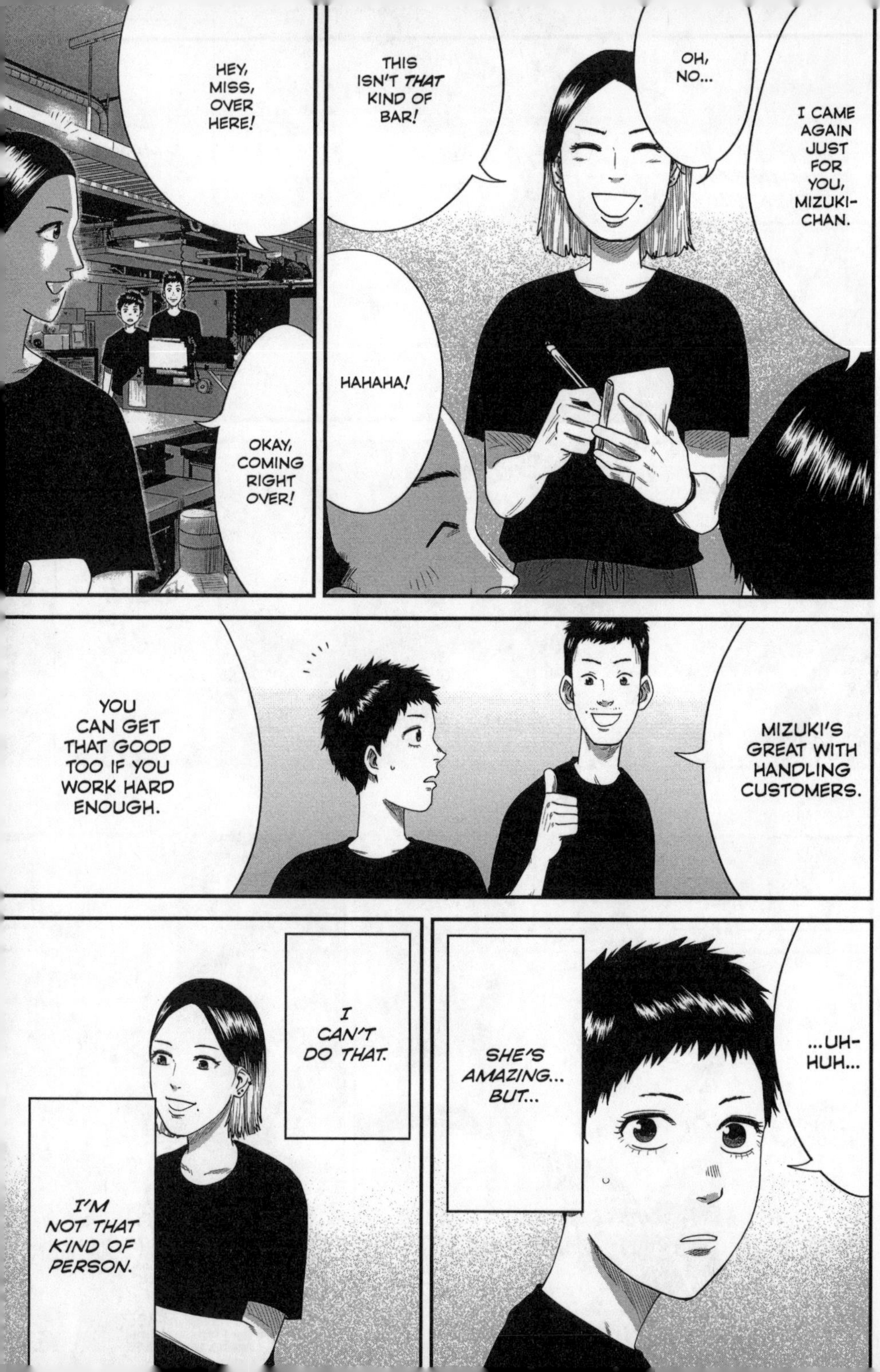
I CAME AGAIN JUST FOR YOU, MIZUKI-CHAN.
OH, NO...
THIS ISN'T *THAT* KIND OF BAR!
HAHAHA!
HEY, MISS, OVER HERE!
OKAY, COMING RIGHT OVER!
MIZUKI'S GREAT WITH HANDLING CUSTOMERS.
YOU CAN GET THAT GOOD TOO IF YOU WORK HARD ENOUGH.
...UH-HUH...
SHE'S AMAZING... BUT...
I CAN'T DO THAT.
I'M NOT THAT KIND OF PERSON.

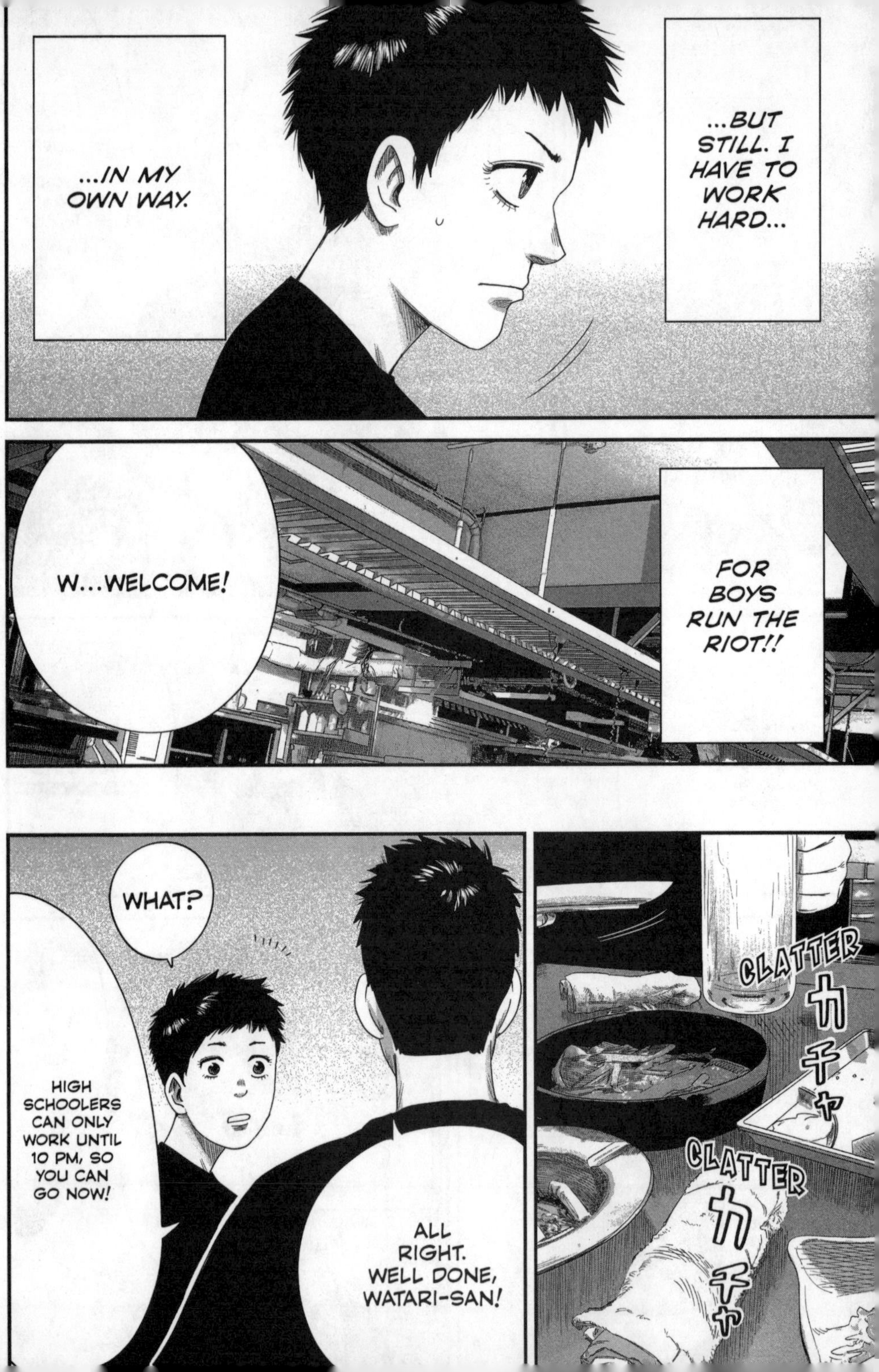

...BUT STILL. I HAVE TO WORK HARD...
...IN MY OWN WAY.
FOR BOYS RUN THE RIOT!!
W...WELCOME!
CLATTER
カチャ
CLATTER
カチャ
ALL RIGHT. WELL DONE, WATARI-SAN!
HIGH SCHOOLERS CAN ONLY WORK UNTIL 10 PM, SO YOU CAN GO NOW!
WHAT?

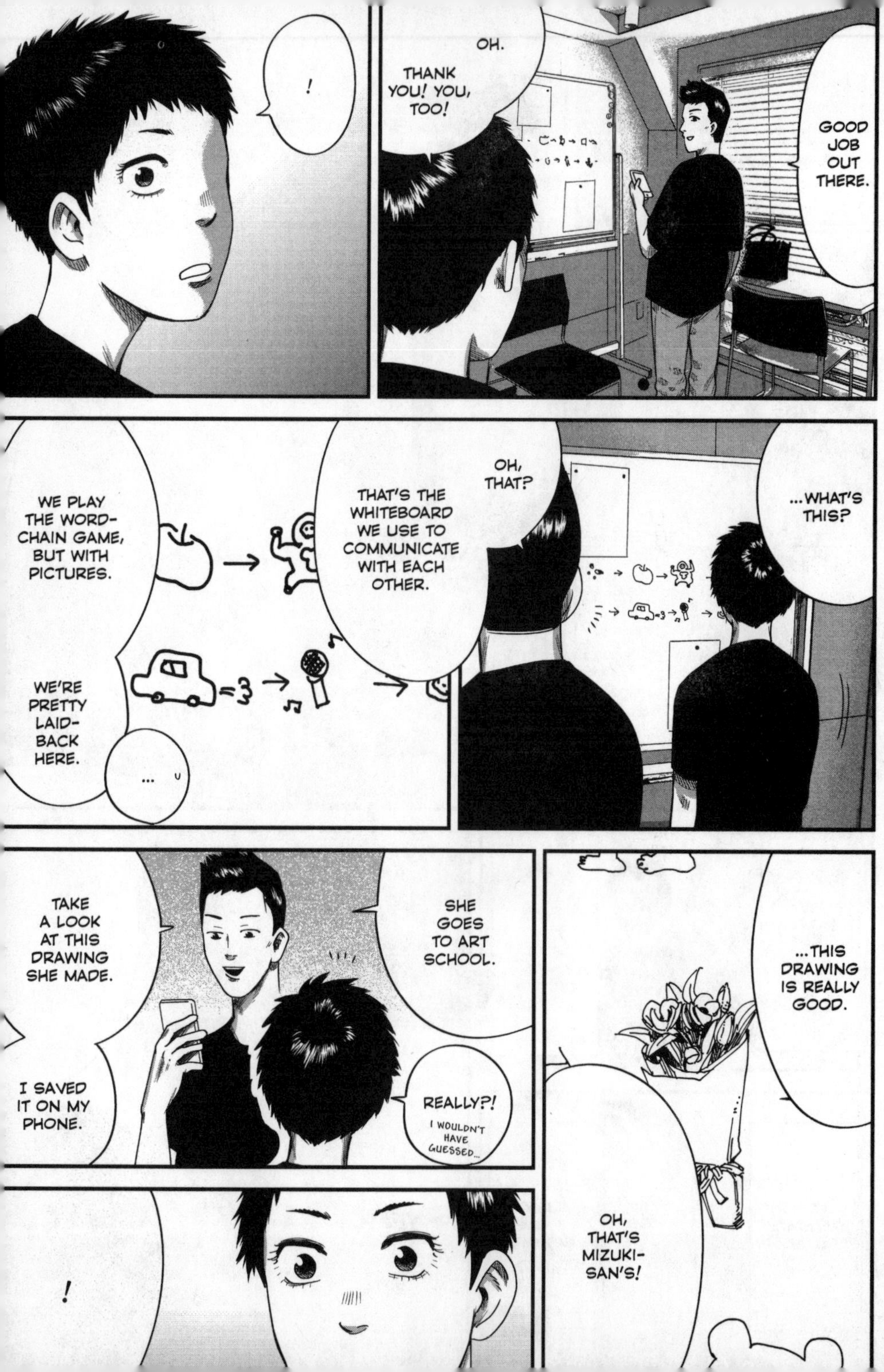
GOOD JOB OUT THERE.
OH.
THANK YOU! YOU, TOO!
!
...WHAT'S THIS?
OH, THAT?
THAT'S THE WHITEBOARD WE USE TO COMMUNICATE WITH EACH OTHER.
WE PLAY THE WORD-CHAIN GAME, BUT WITH PICTURES.
WE'RE PRETTY LAID-BACK HERE.
...
...THIS DRAWING IS REALLY GOOD.
OH, THAT'S MIZUKI-SAN'S!
SHE GOES TO ART SCHOOL.
TAKE A LOOK AT THIS DRAWING SHE MADE.
I SAVED IT ON MY PHONE.
REALLY?!
I WOULDN'T HAVE GUESSED...
!

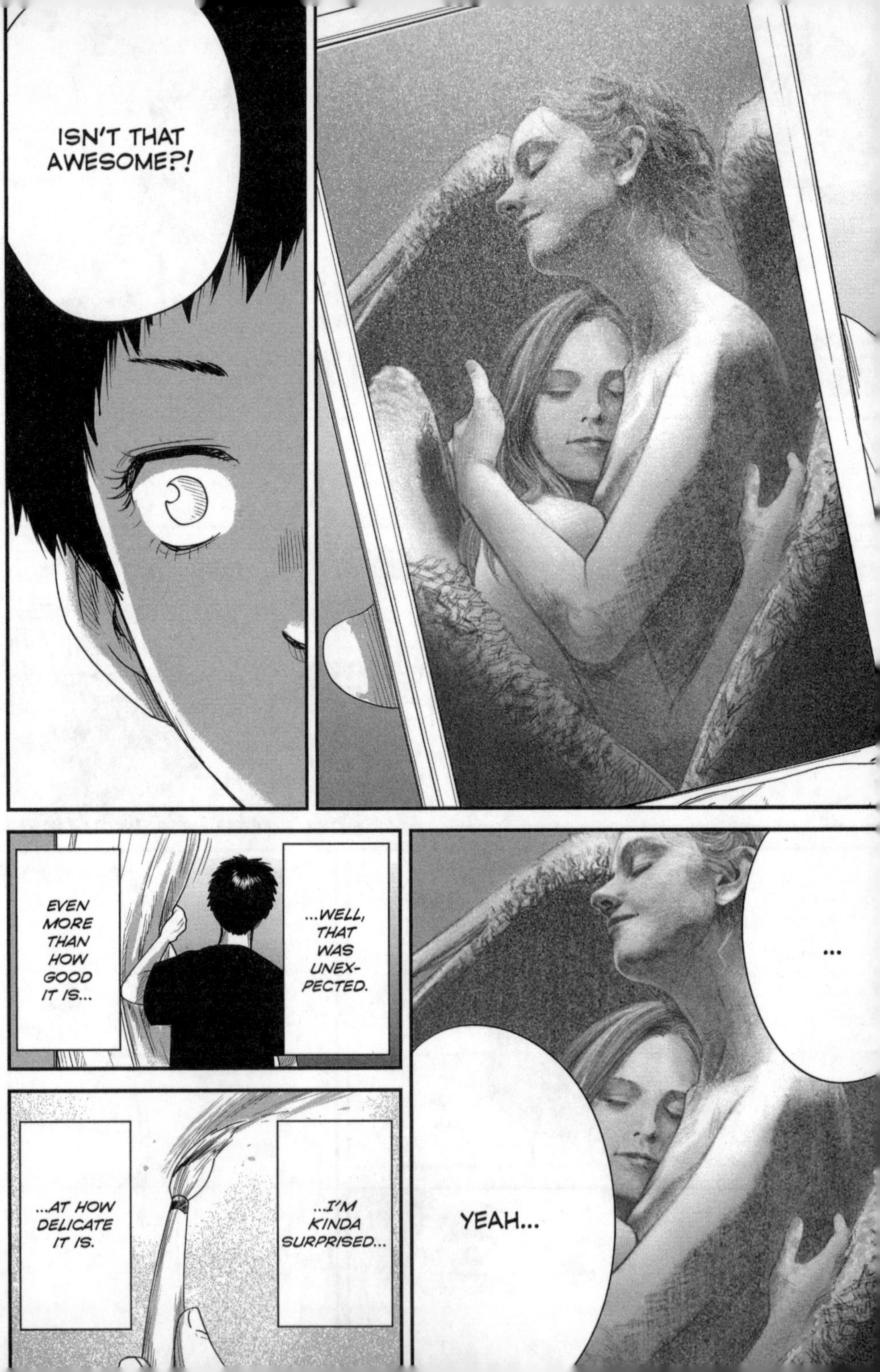
ISN'T THAT AWESOME?!
...
YEAH...
...WELL, THAT WAS UNEXPECTED.
EVEN MORE THAN HOW GOOD IT IS...
...I'M KINDA SURPRISED...
...AT HOW DELICATE IT IS.

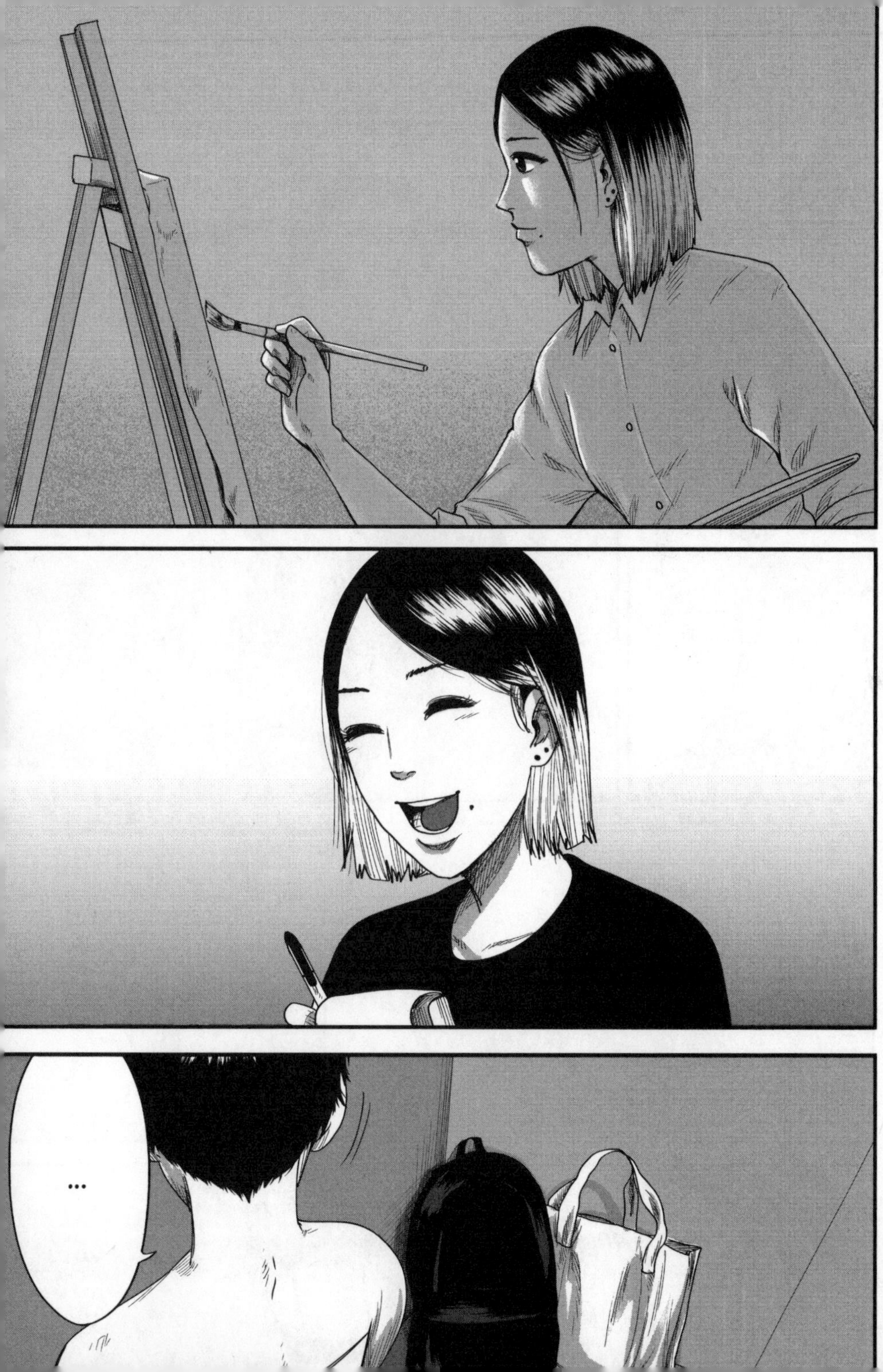
...

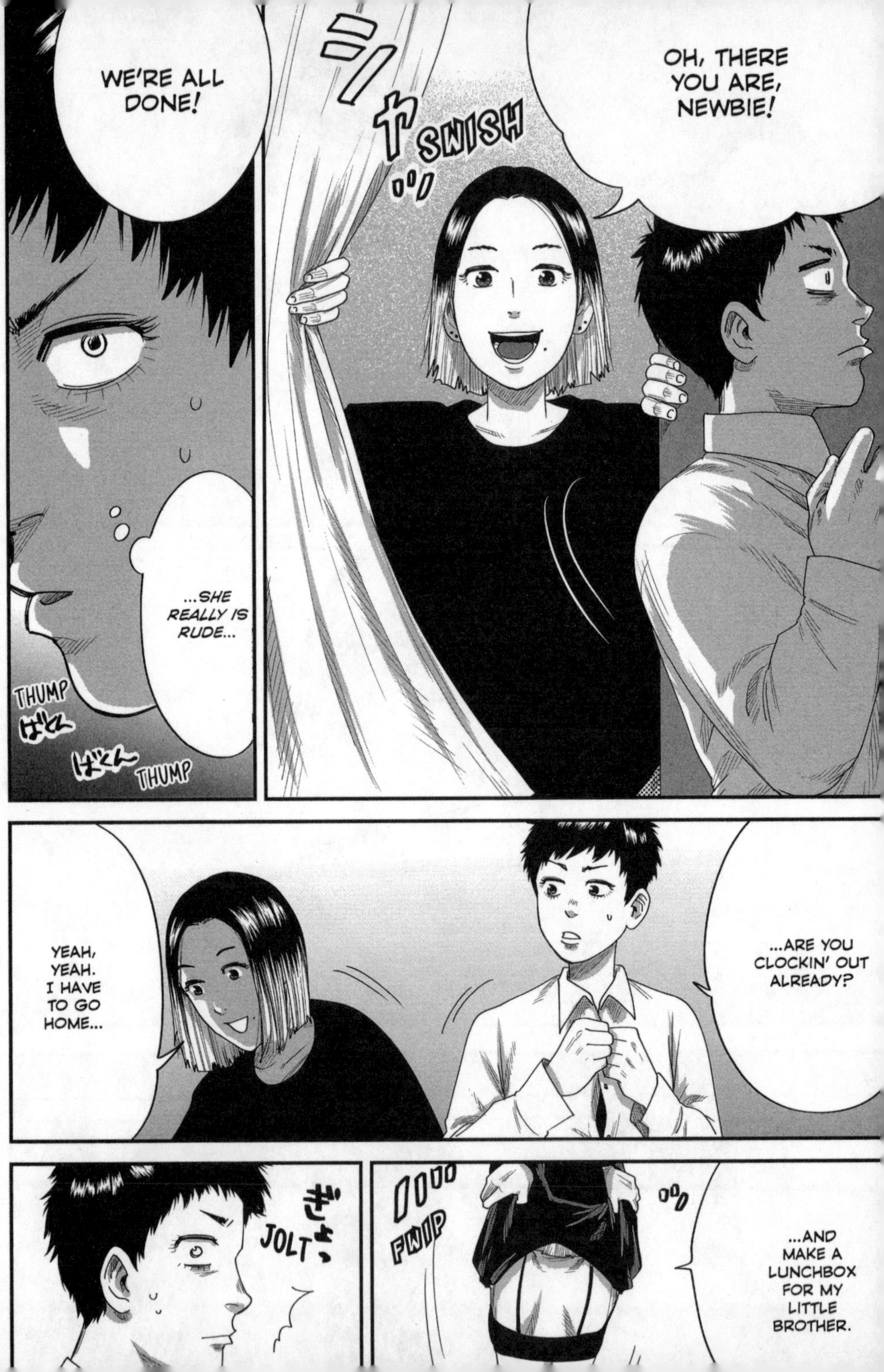
OH, THERE YOU ARE, NEWBIE!
SWISH
WE'RE ALL DONE!
...SHE REALLY IS RUDE...
THUMP
THUMP
...ARE YOU CLOCKIN' OUT ALREADY?
YEAH, YEAH. I HAVE TO GO HOME...
...AND MAKE A LUNCHBOX FOR MY LITTLE BROTHER.
FWIP
JOLT

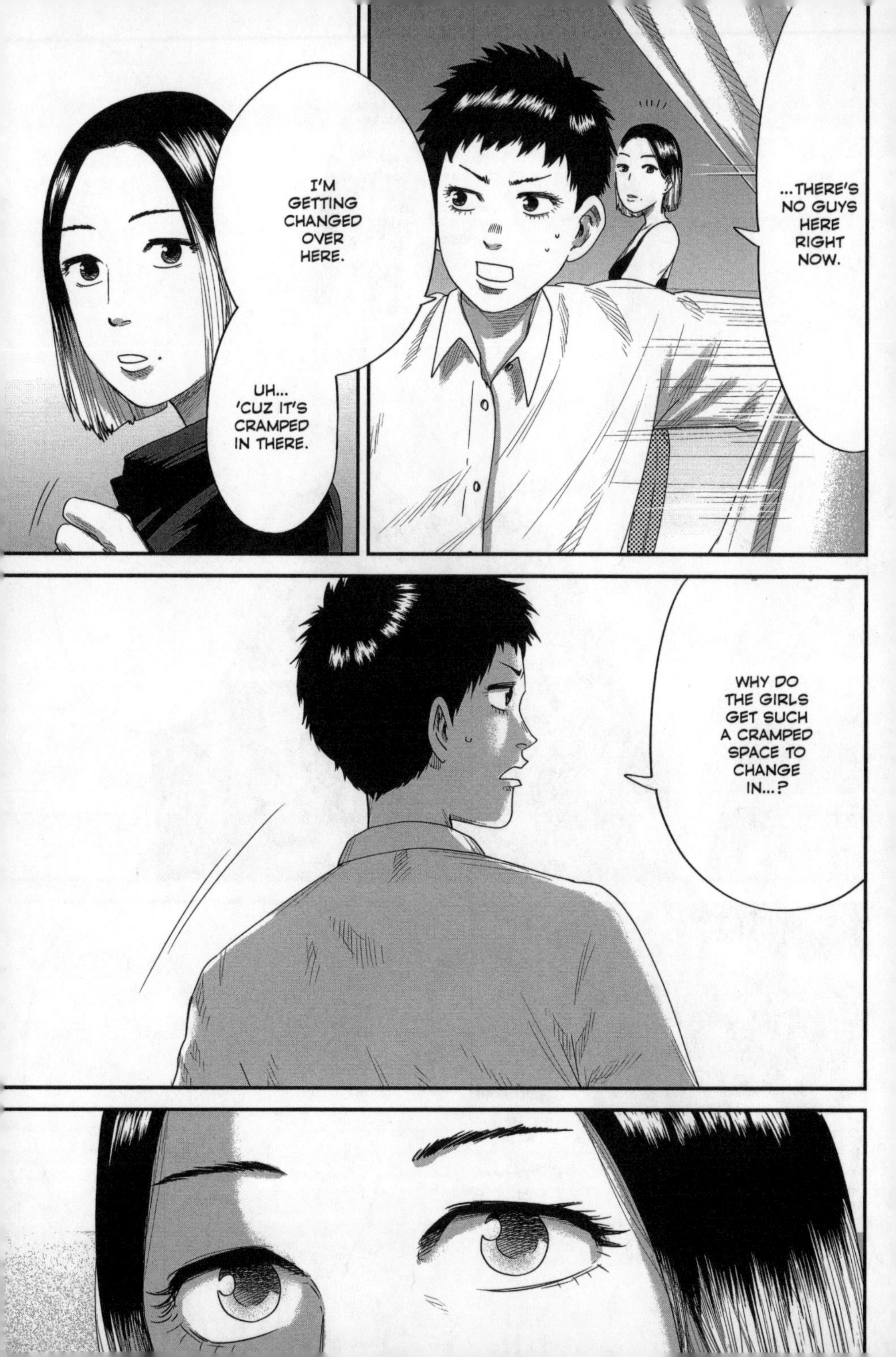
...THERE'S NO GUYS HERE RIGHT NOW.
I'M GETTING CHANGED OVER HERE.
UH... 'CUZ IT'S CRAMPED IN THERE.
WHY DO THE GIRLS GET SUCH A CRAMPED SPACE TO CHANGE IN...?

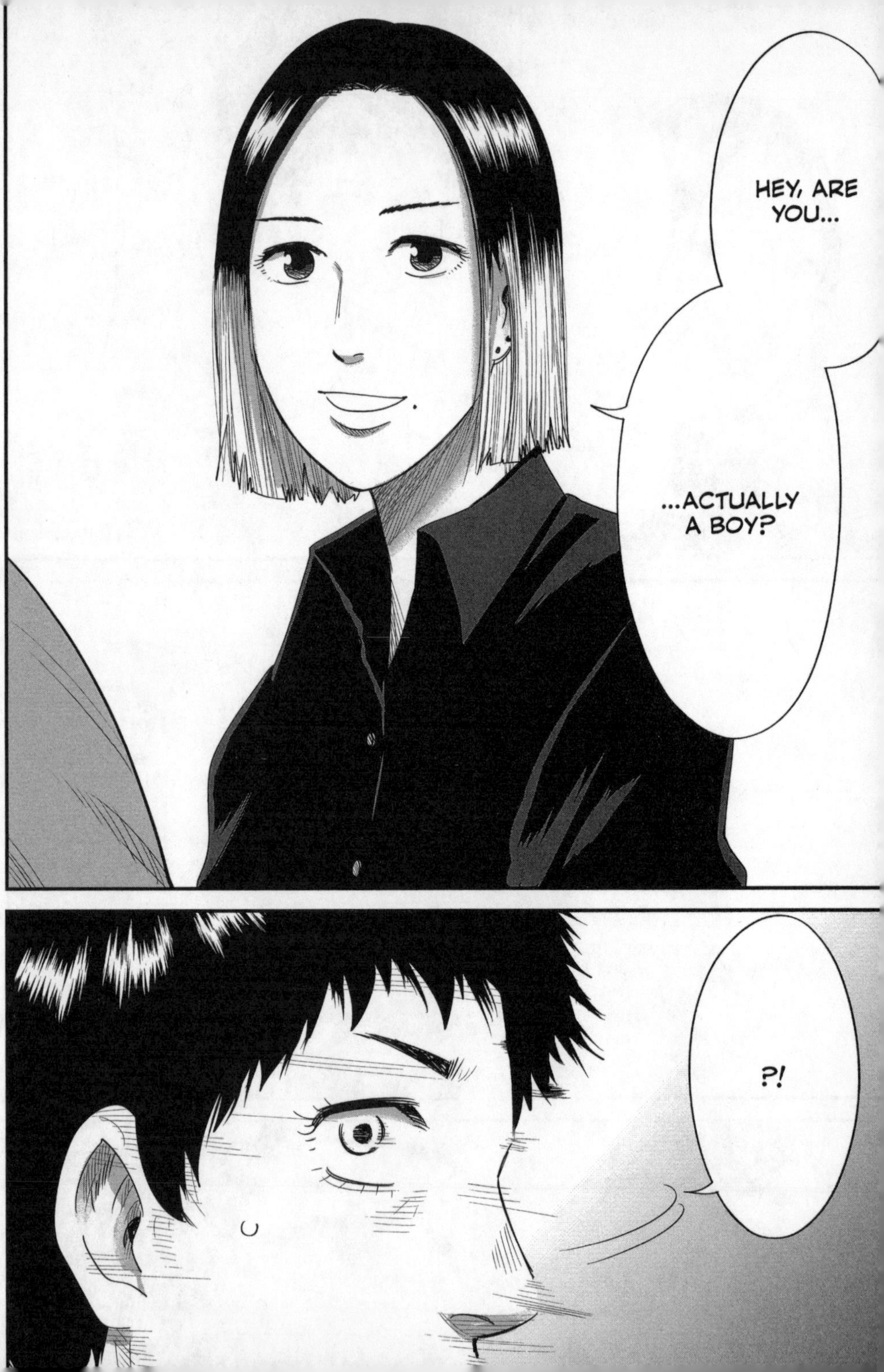
HEY, ARE YOU...
...ACTUALLY A BOY?
?!

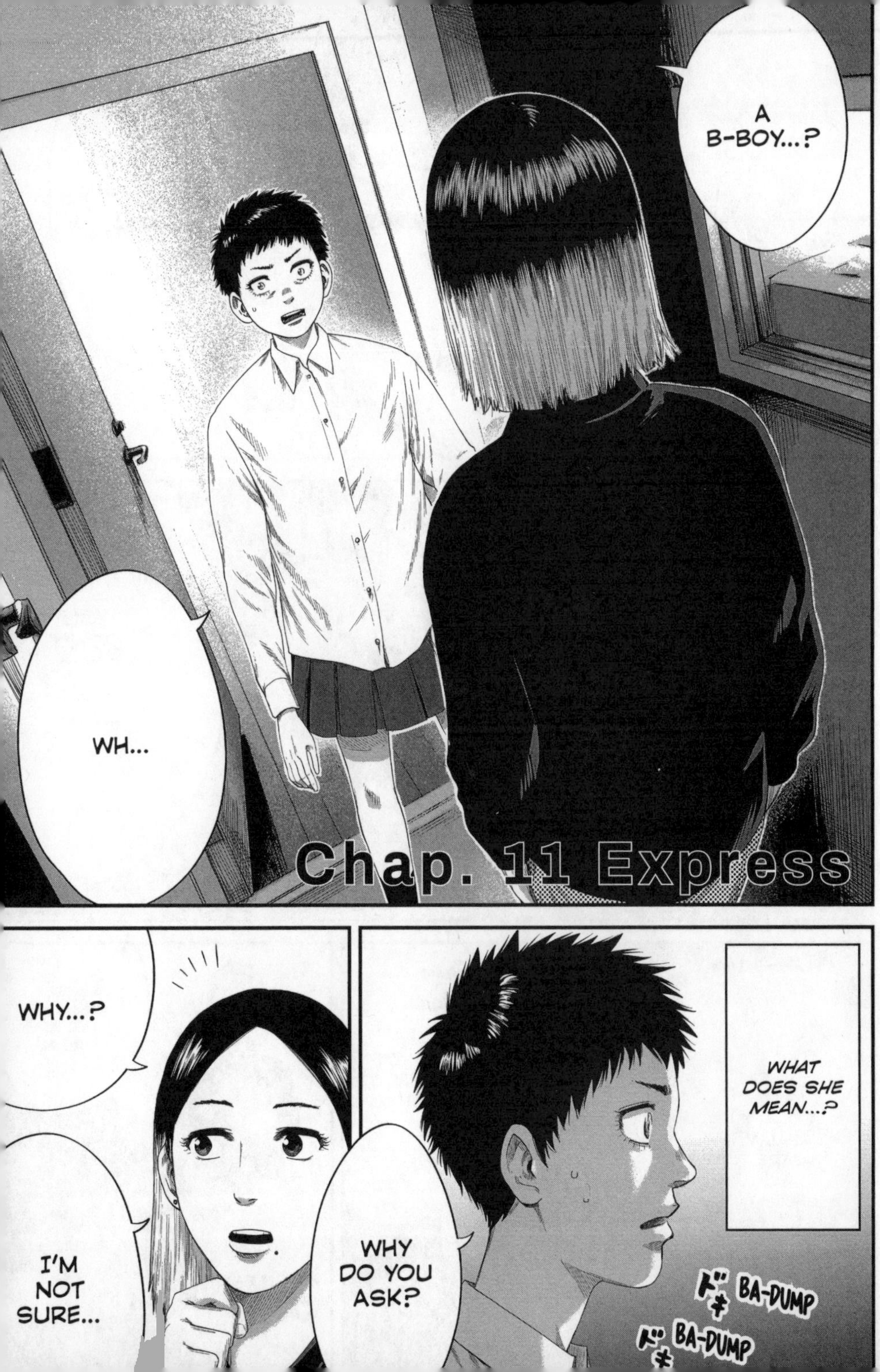
A B-BOY...?
WH...
Chap. 11 Express
WHAT DOES SHE MEAN...?
ドキ BA-DUMP
ドキ BA-DUMP
WHY...?
WHY DO YOU ASK?
I'M NOT SURE...

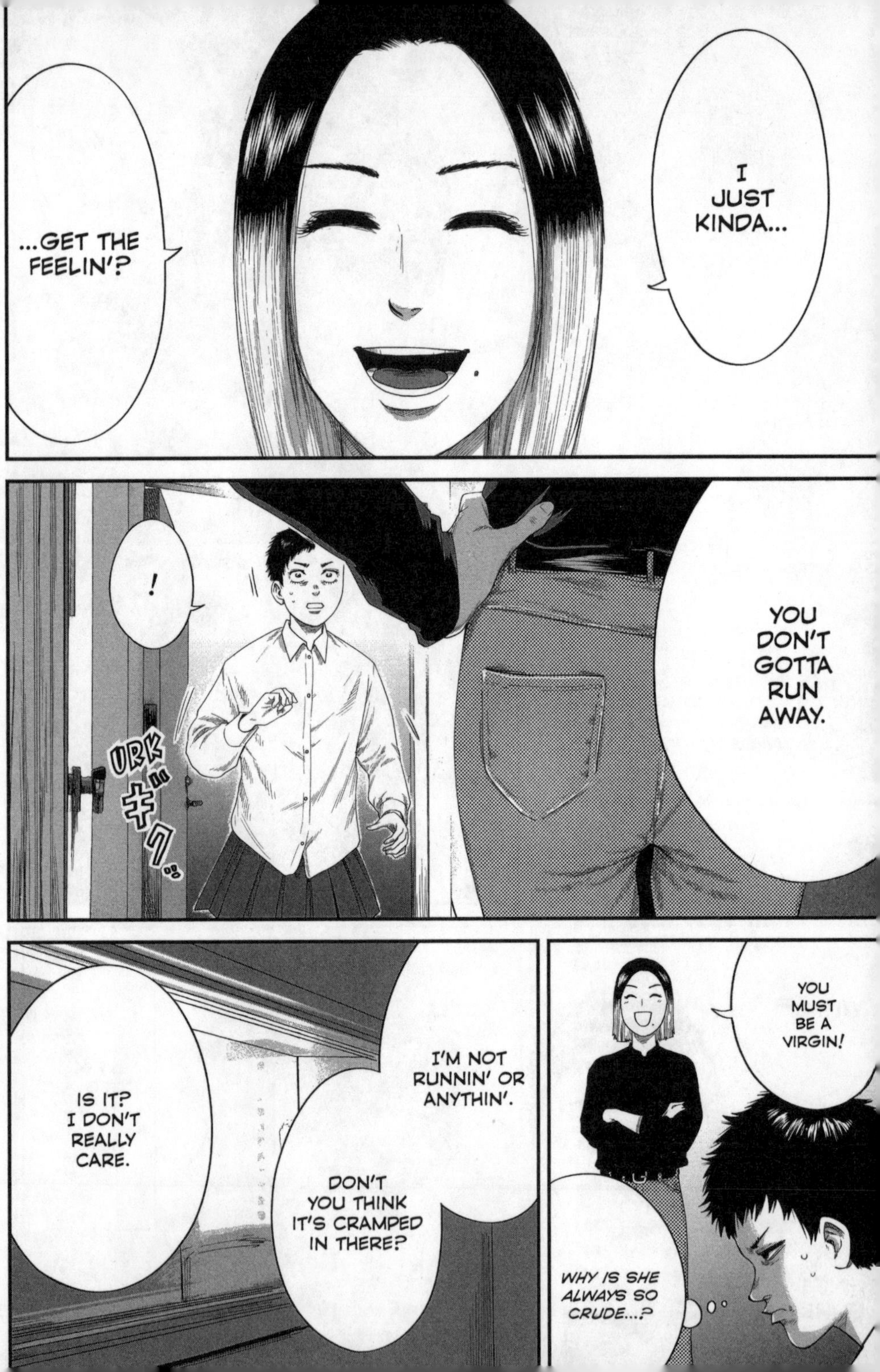
I JUST KINDA...
...GET THE FEELIN'?
YOU DON'T GOTTA RUN AWAY.
!
URK
ギク
YOU MUST BE A VIRGIN!
WHY IS SHE ALWAYS SO CRUDE...?
I'M NOT RUNNIN' OR ANYTHIN'.
DON'T YOU THINK IT'S CRAMPED IN THERE?
IS IT? I DON'T REALLY CARE.

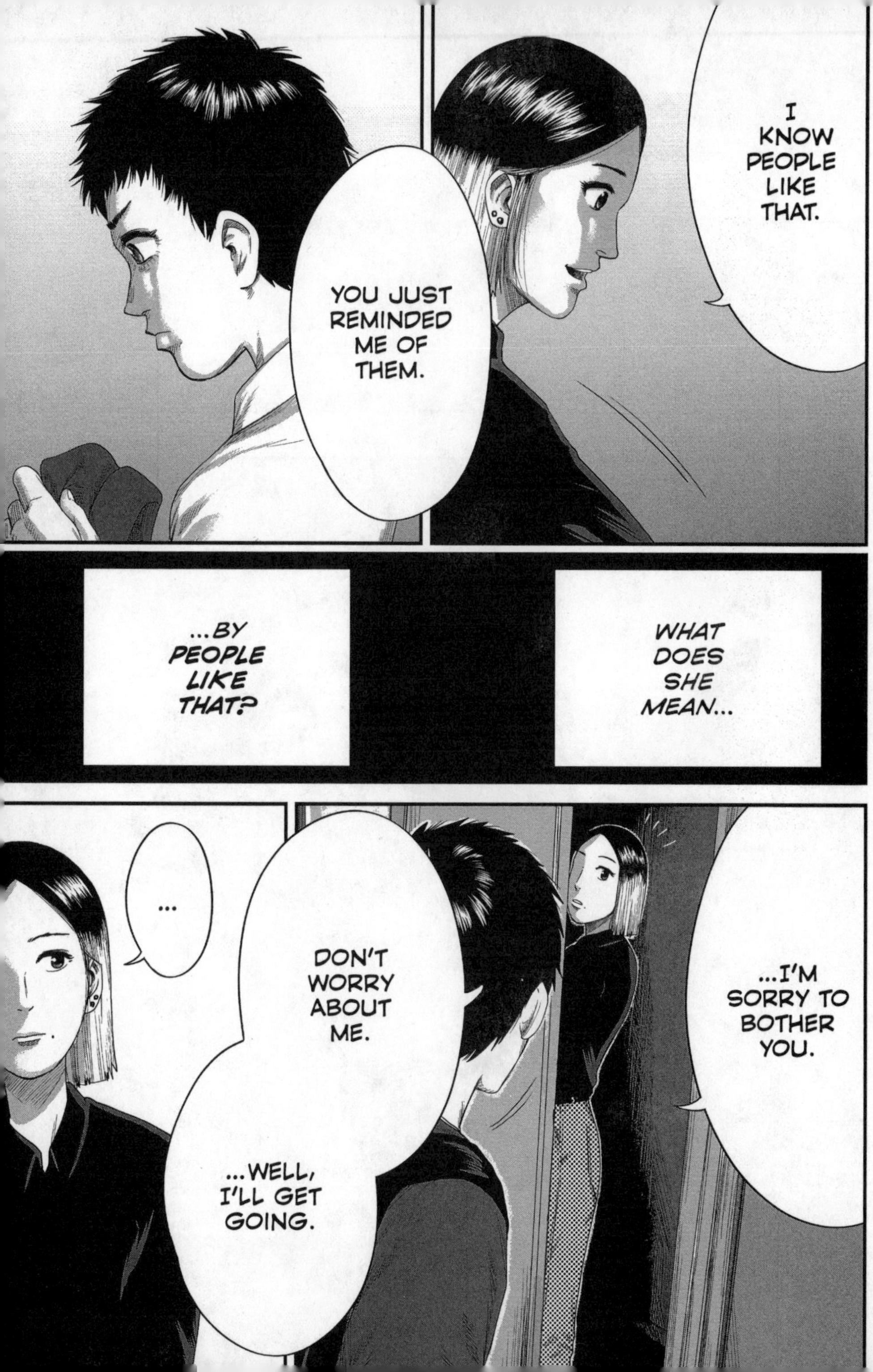
I KNOW PEOPLE LIKE THAT.
YOU JUST REMINDED ME OF THEM.
WHAT DOES SHE MEAN...
...BY PEOPLE LIKE THAT?
...I'M SORRY TO BOTHER YOU.
DON'T WORRY ABOUT ME.
...WELL, I'LL GET GOING.
...

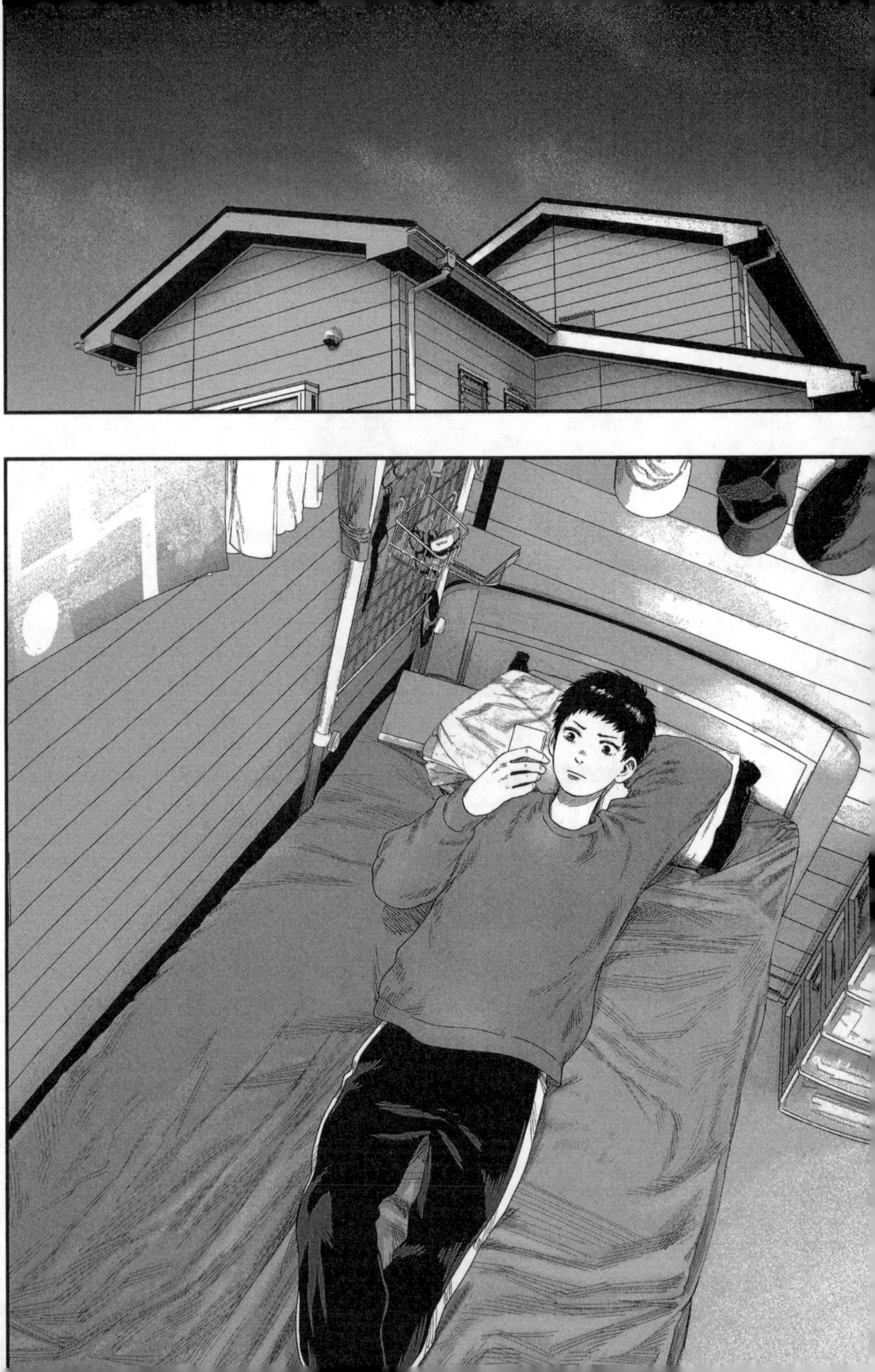

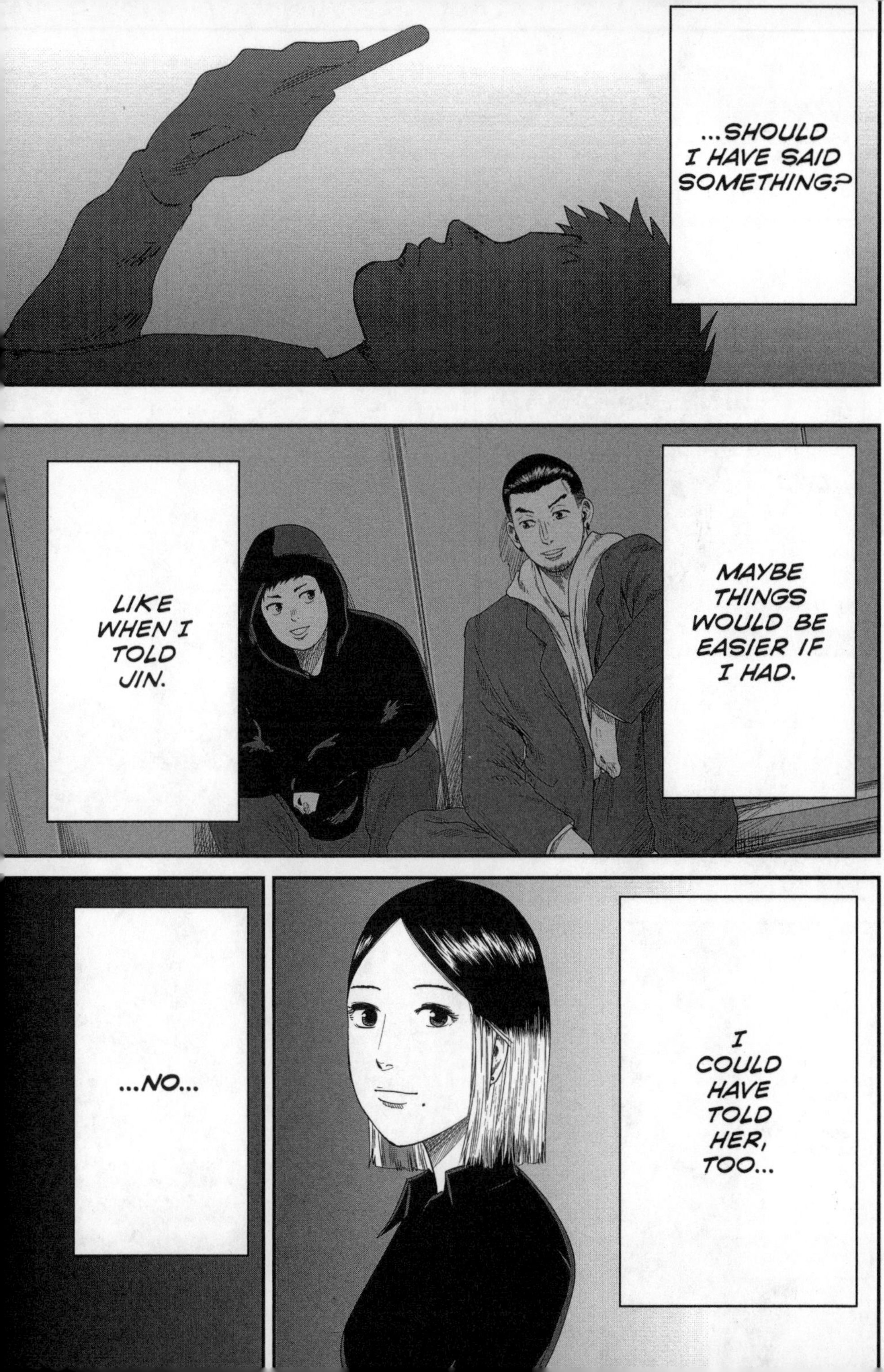
...SHOULD I HAVE SAID SOMETHING?
MAYBE THINGS WOULD BE EASIER IF I HAD.
LIKE WHEN I TOLD JIN.
I COULD HAVE TOLD HER, TOO...
...NO...

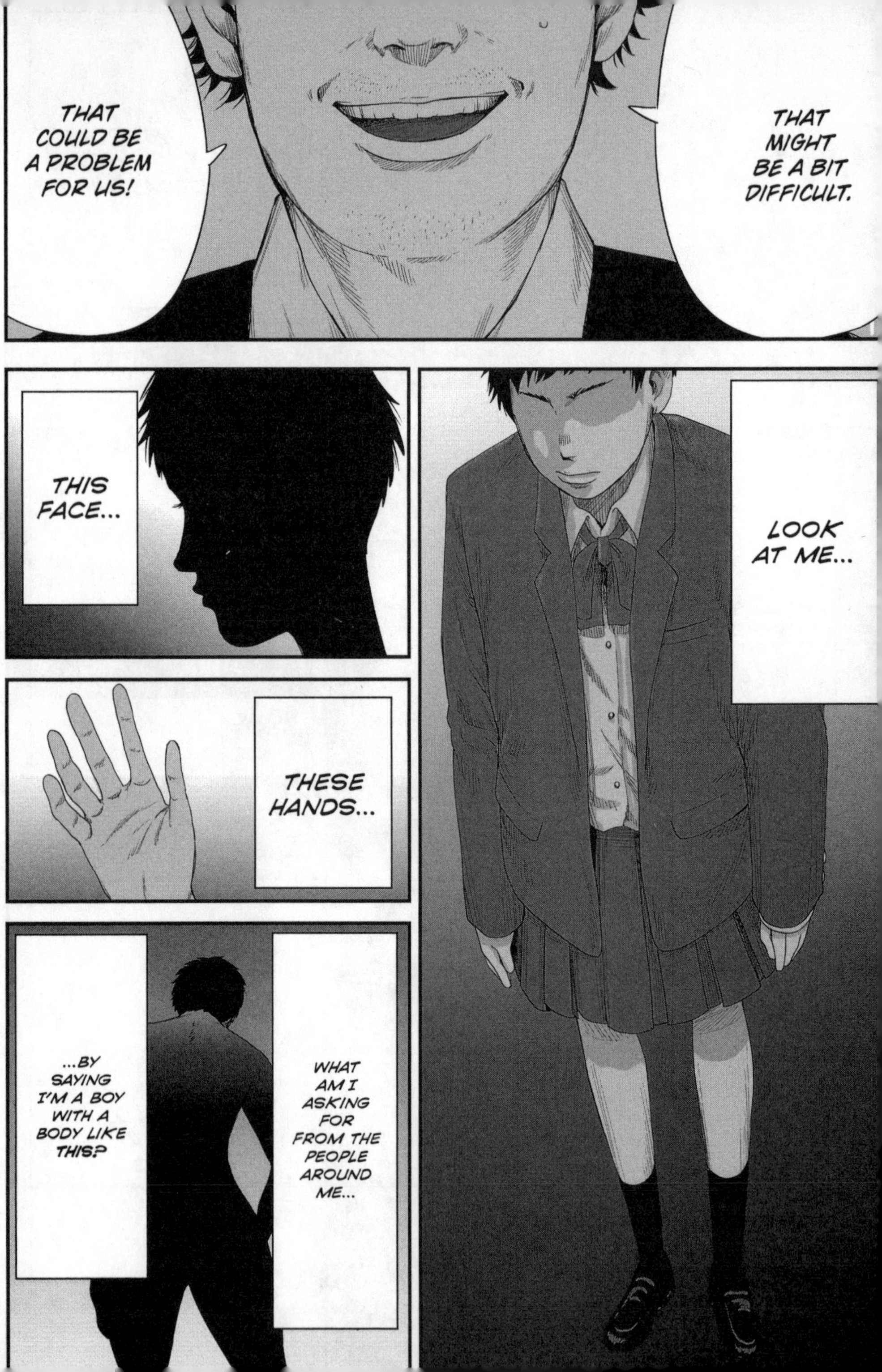
THAT MIGHT BE A BIT DIFFICULT.
THAT COULD BE A PROBLEM FOR US!
LOOK AT ME...
THIS FACE...
THESE HANDS...
WHAT AM I ASKING FOR FROM THE PEOPLE AROUND ME...
...BY SAYING I'M A BOY WITH A BODY LIKE THIS?

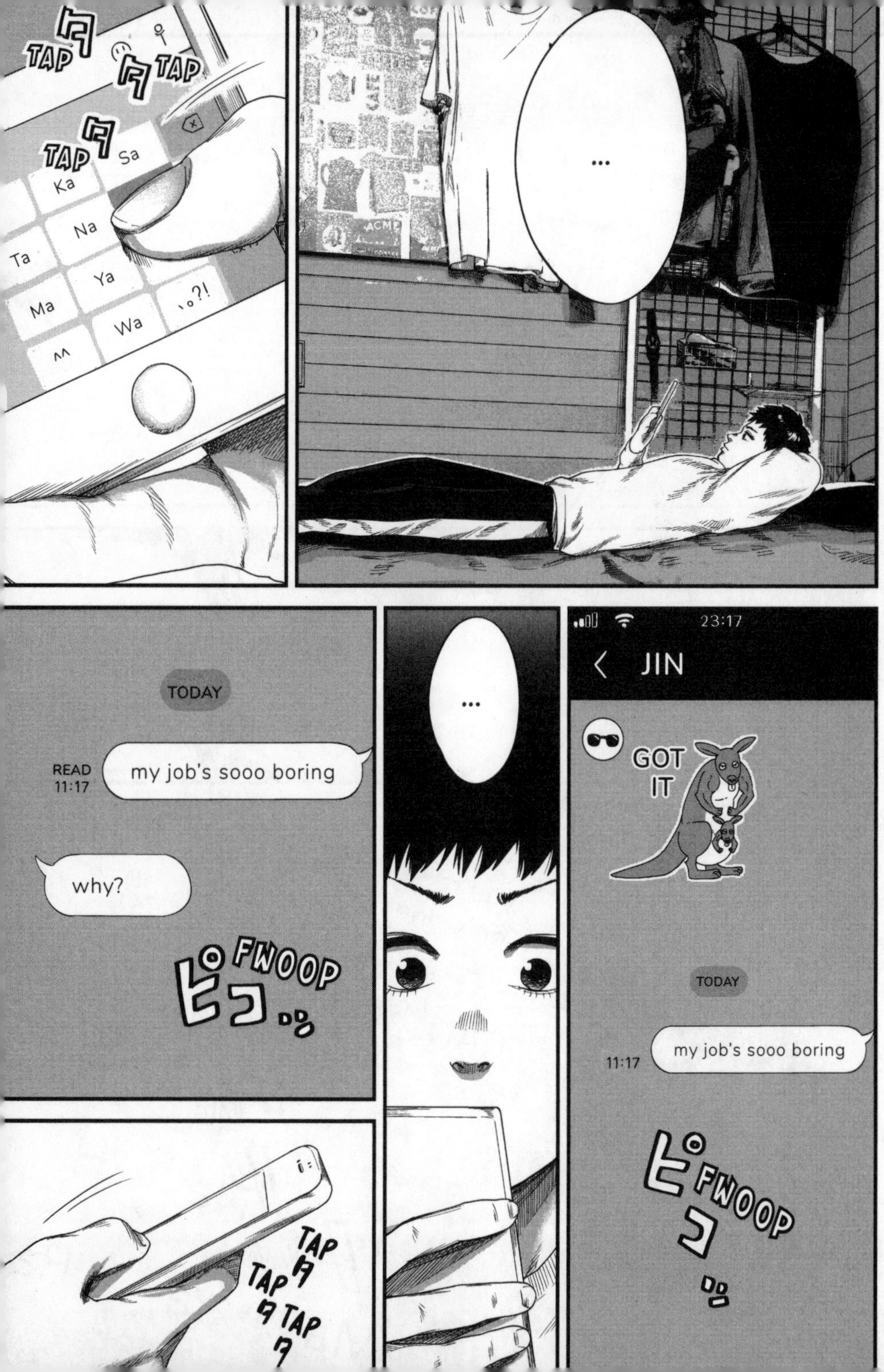

...
TAP TAP TAP
Sa
Ka
Na
Ta
Ya
Ma
Wa
、。?!
^^
23:17
JIN
GOT IT
TODAY
11:17
my job's sooo boring
FWOOP
...
TODAY
READ 11:17
my job's sooo boring
why?
FWOOP
TAP TAP TAP

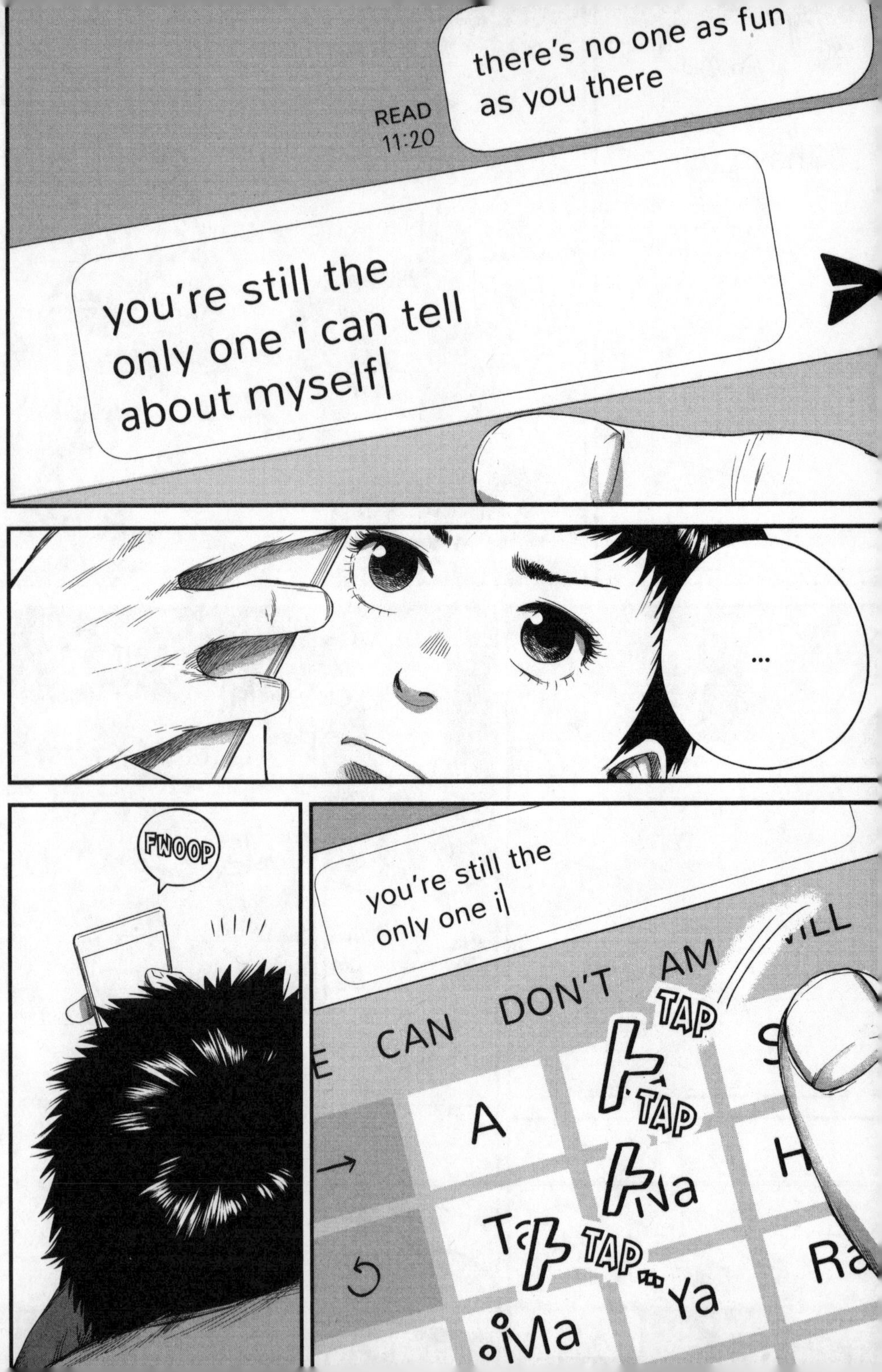

there's no one as fun as you there
READ 11:20
you're still the only one i can tell about myself
...
FWOOP
you're still the only one i
CAN DON'T AM
TAP
TAP
TAP
A
Ta
Ya
Ma
H
Ra

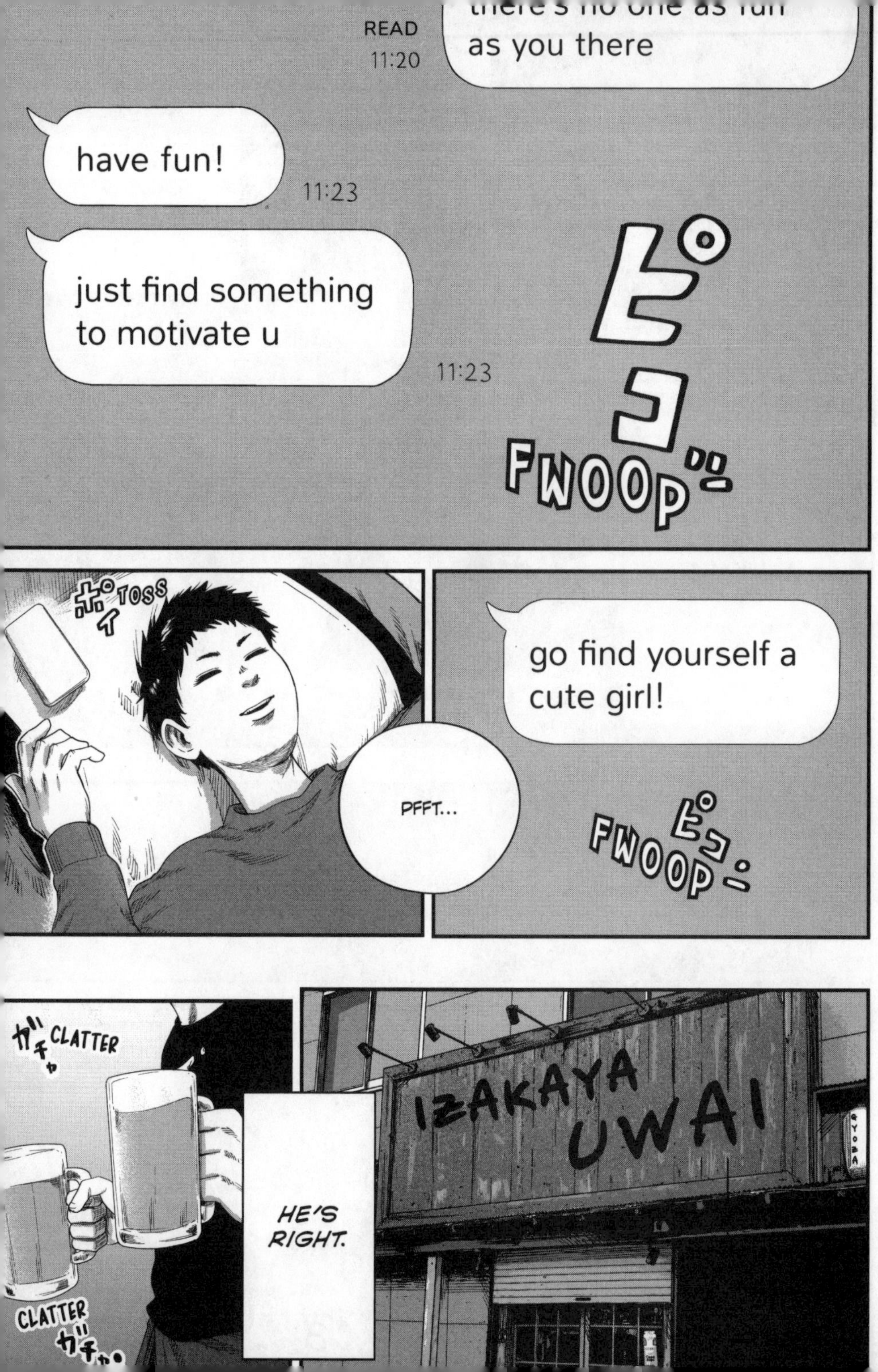

there's no one as fun as you there
READ 11:20
have fun!
11:23
just find something to motivate u
11:23
ピコ
FWOOP
go find yourself a cute girl!
ピコ
FWOOP
ポイ TOSS
PFFT...
IZAKAYA UWAI
HE'S RIGHT.
ガチャ CLATTER
CLATTER ガチャ

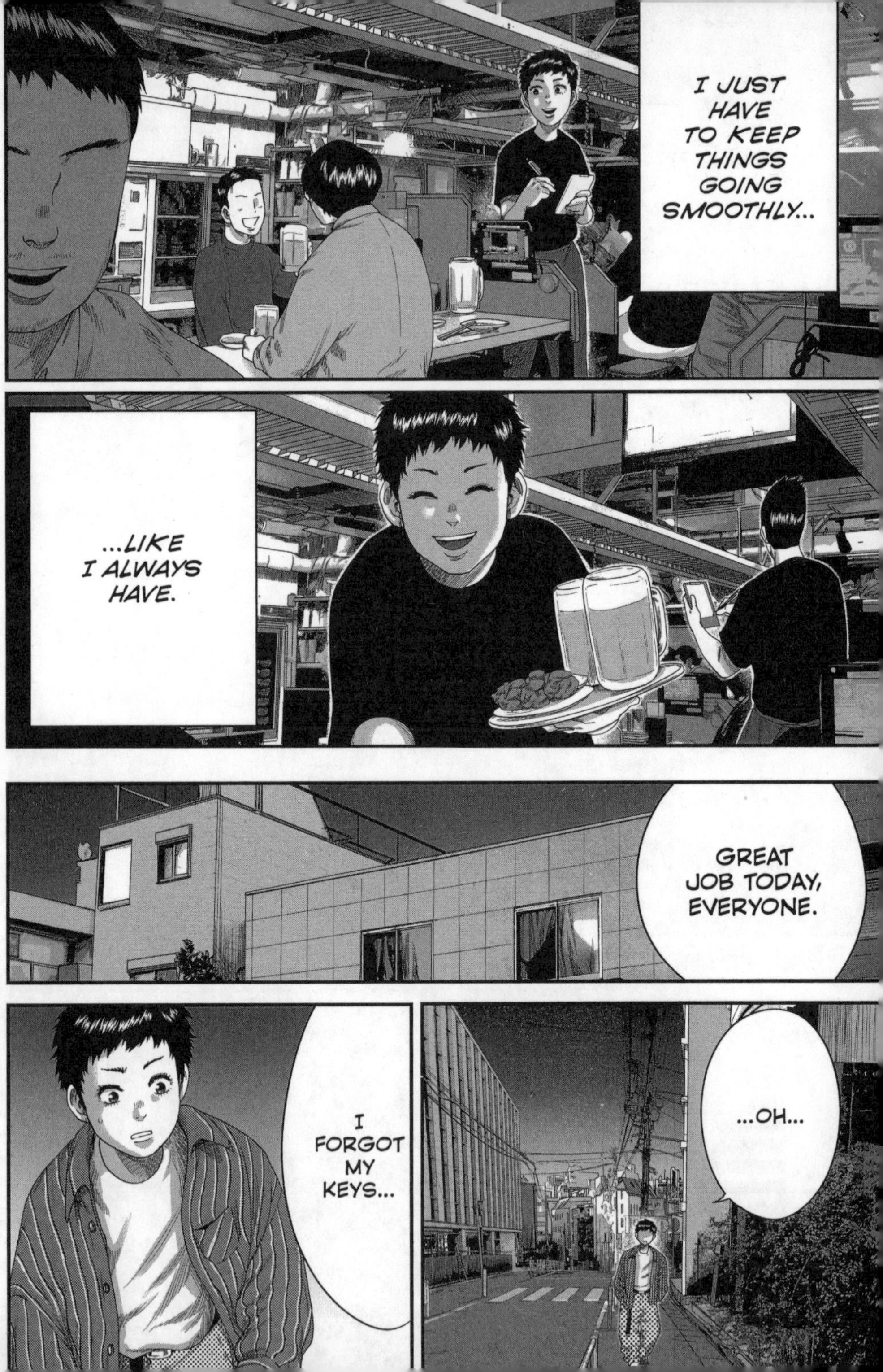
I JUST HAVE TO KEEP THINGS GOING SMOOTHLY...
...LIKE I ALWAYS HAVE.
GREAT JOB TODAY, EVERYONE.
...OH...
I FORGOT MY KEYS...

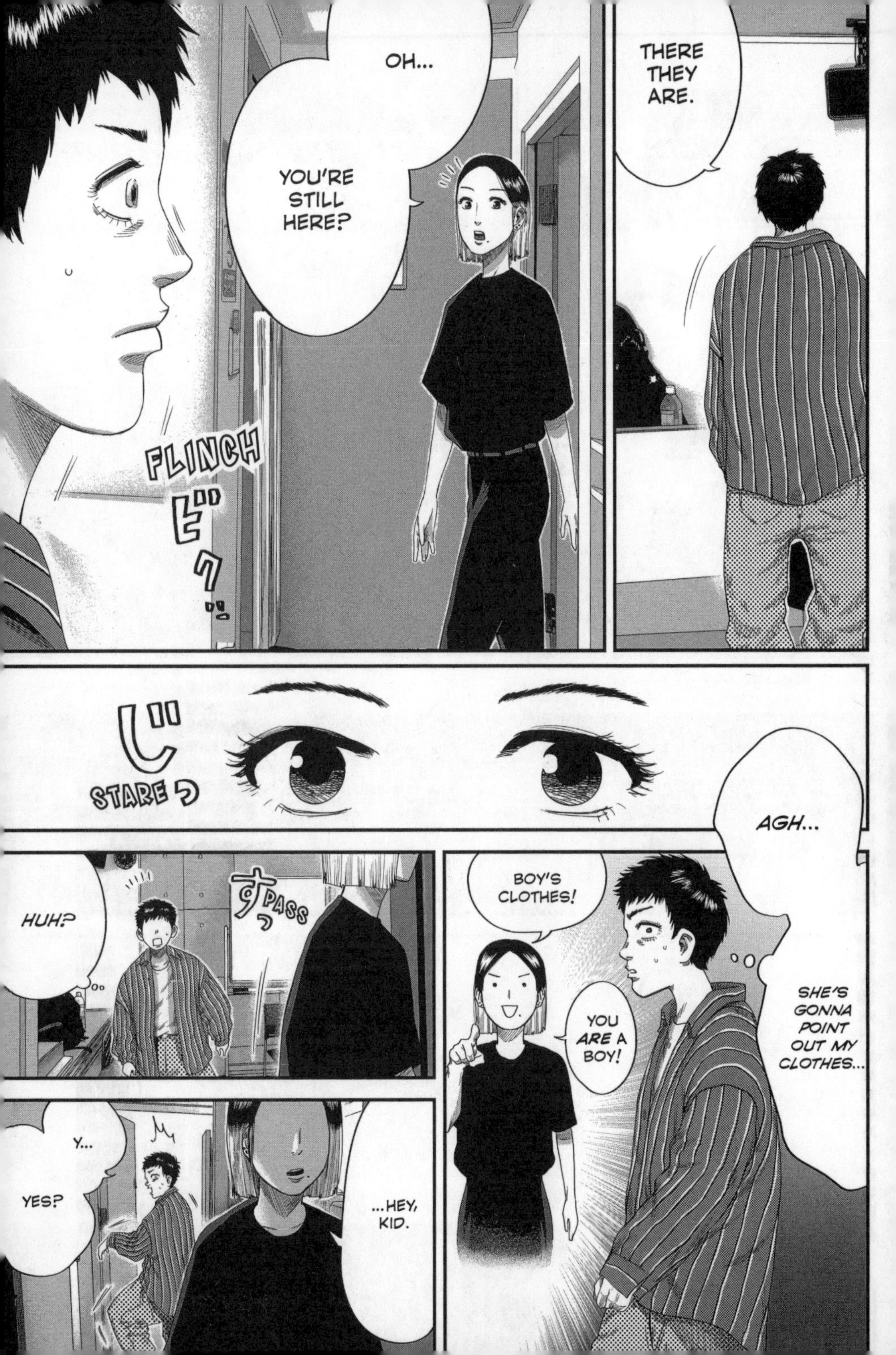
THERE THEY ARE.
OH...
YOU'RE STILL HERE?
FLINCH
ビクッ
じーっ
STARE
AGH...
SHE'S GONNA POINT OUT MY CLOTHES...
BOY'S CLOTHES!
YOU ARE A BOY!
すっ
PASS
HUH?
...HEY, KID.
Y...
YES?

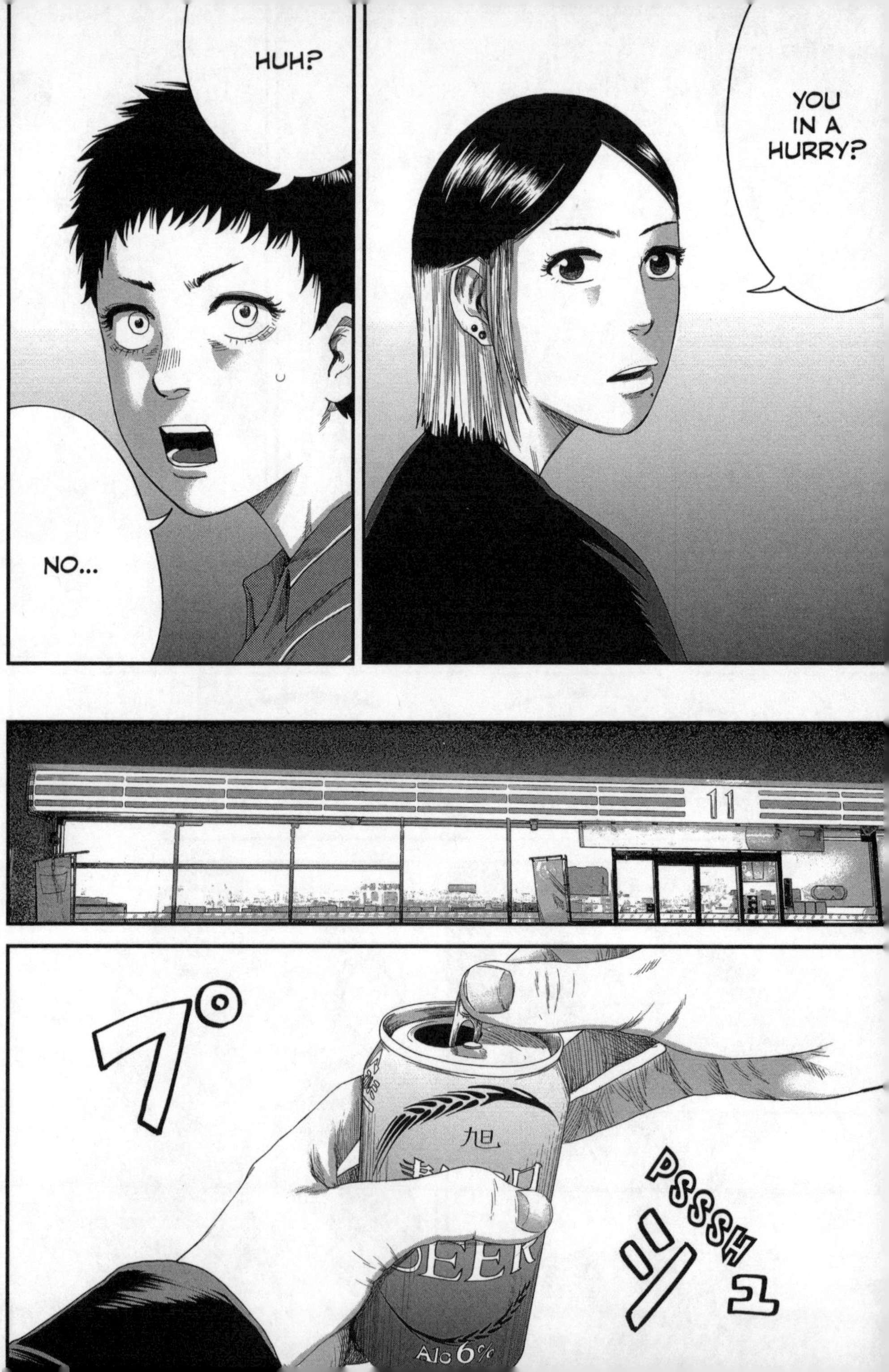
YOU IN A HURRY?
HUH?
NO...
11
旭
Alc 6%
PSSSH

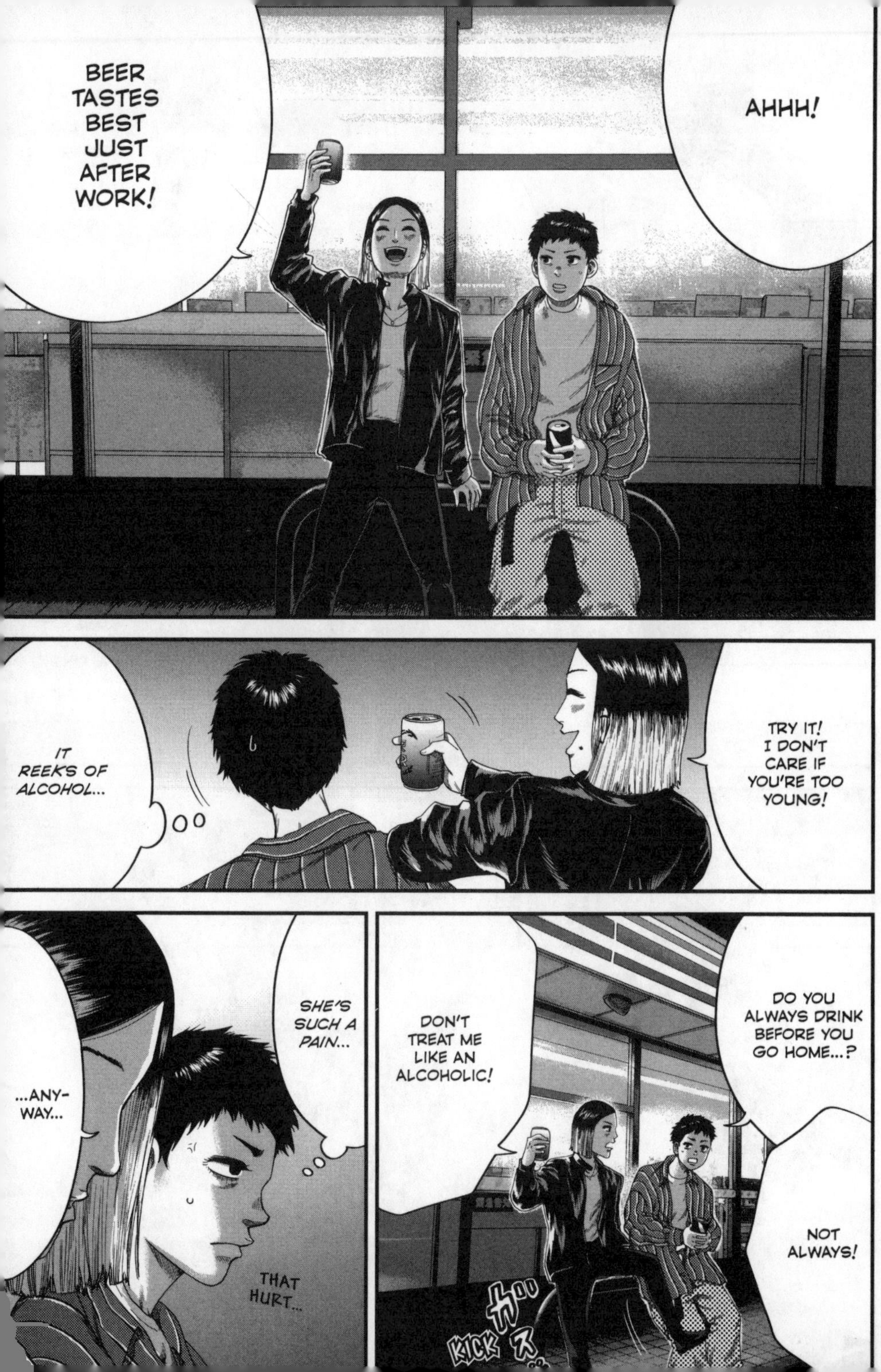
AHHH!
BEER TASTES BEST JUST AFTER WORK!
TRY IT! I DON'T CARE IF YOU'RE TOO YOUNG!
IT REEKS OF ALCOHOL...
DO YOU ALWAYS DRINK BEFORE YOU GO HOME...?
NOT ALWAYS!
DON'T TREAT ME LIKE AN ALCOHOLIC!
KICK
SHE'S SUCH A PAIN...
...ANY-WAY...
THAT HURT...

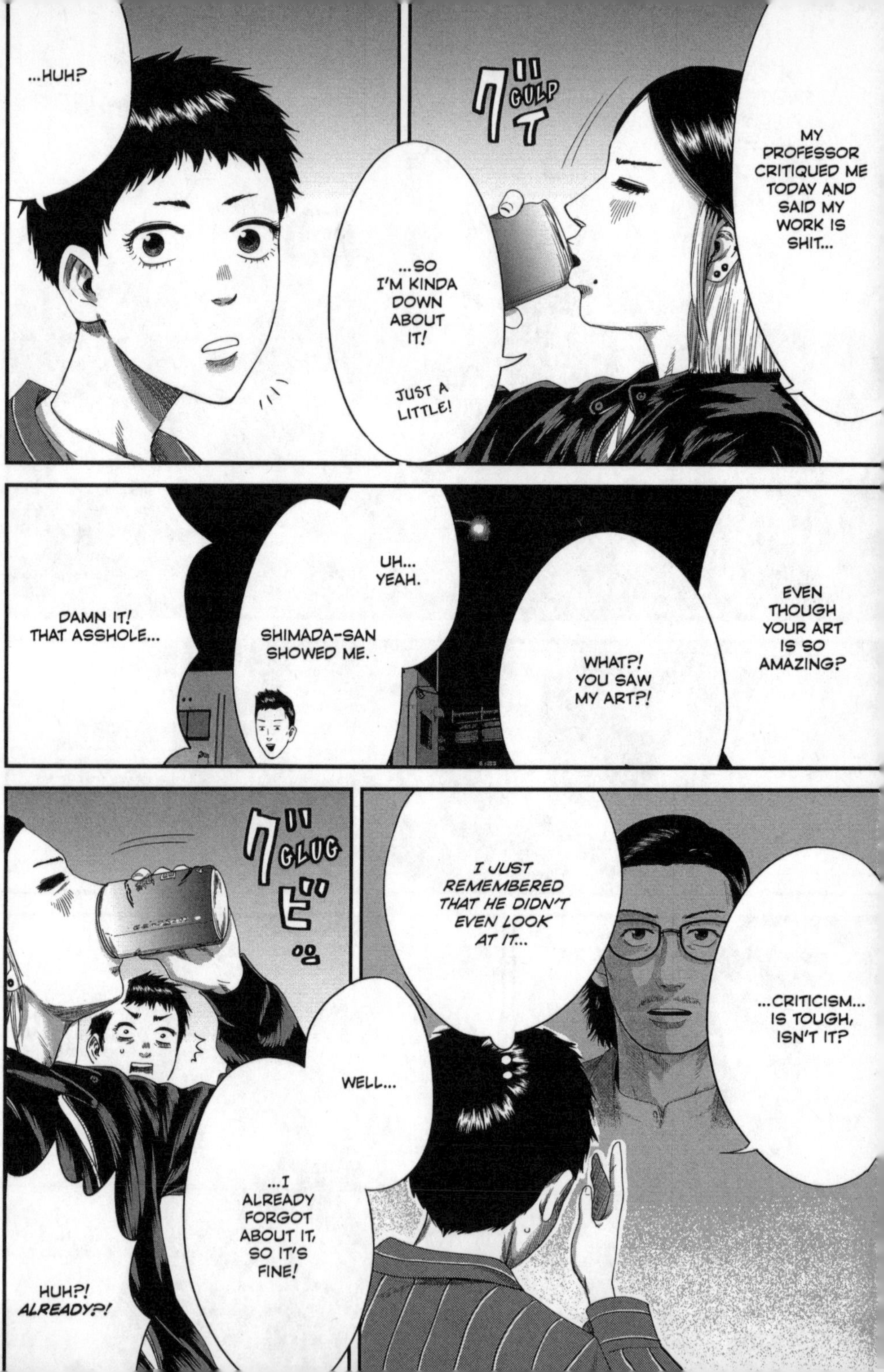
MY PROFESSOR CRITIQUED ME TODAY AND SAID MY WORK IS SHIT...
GULP
...SO I'M KINDA DOWN ABOUT IT!
JUST A LITTLE!
...HUH?
EVEN THOUGH YOUR ART IS SO AMAZING?
WHAT?! YOU SAW MY ART?!
UH... YEAH.
SHIMADA-SAN SHOWED ME.
DAMN IT! THAT ASSHOLE...
...CRITICISM... IS TOUGH, ISN'T IT?
I JUST REMEMBERED THAT HE DIDN'T EVEN LOOK AT IT...
WELL...
...I ALREADY FORGOT ABOUT IT, SO IT'S FINE!
GLUG
HUH?! ALREADY?!

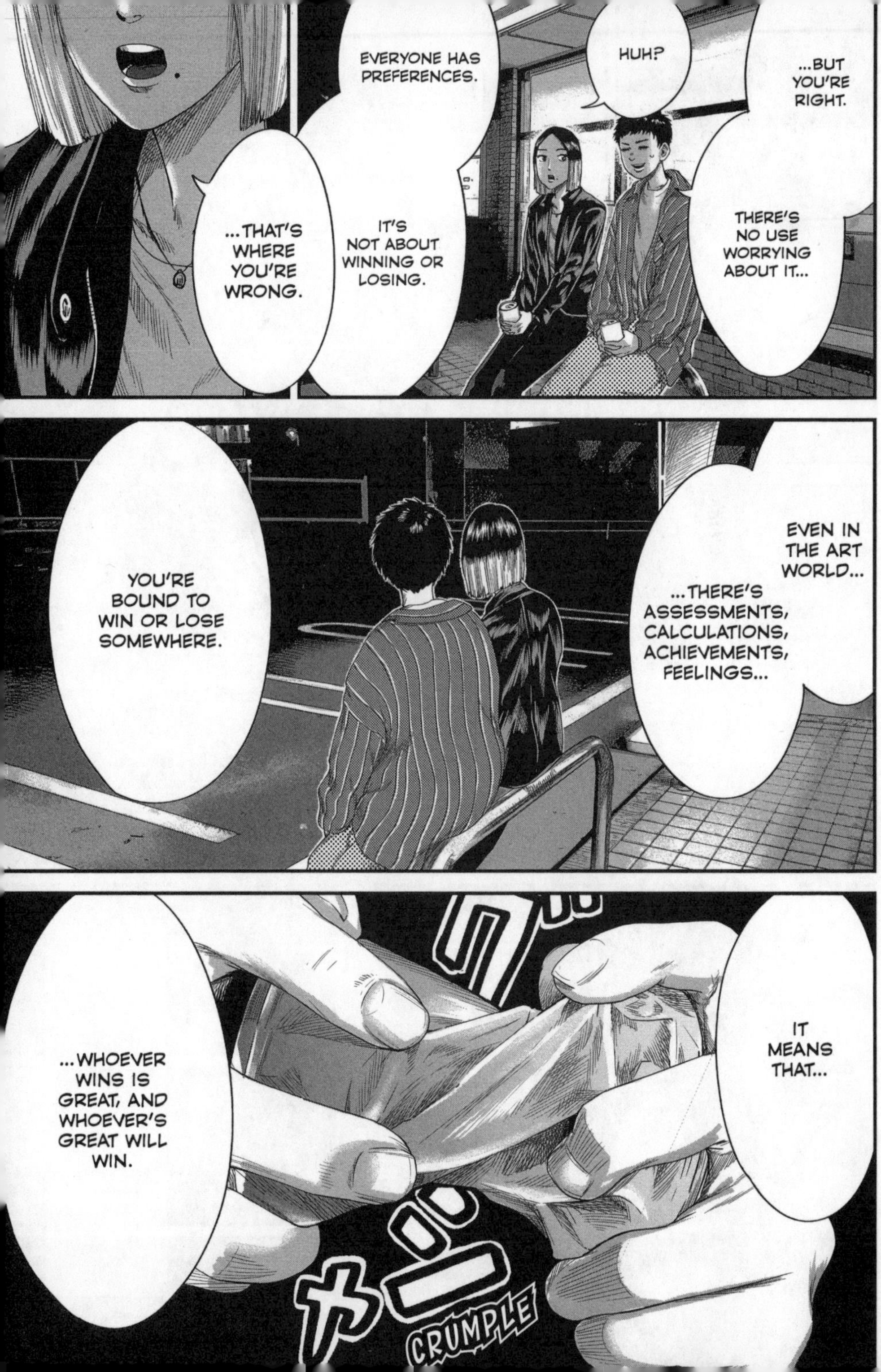
...BUT YOU'RE RIGHT.
THERE'S NO USE WORRYING ABOUT IT...
HUH?
EVERYONE HAS PREFERENCES.
IT'S NOT ABOUT WINNING OR LOSING.
...THAT'S WHERE YOU'RE WRONG.
EVEN IN THE ART WORLD...
...THERE'S ASSESSMENTS, CALCULATIONS, ACHIEVEMENTS, FEELINGS...
YOU'RE BOUND TO WIN OR LOSE SOMEWHERE.
IT MEANS THAT...
...WHOEVER WINS IS GREAT, AND WHOEVER'S GREAT WILL WIN.
CRUMPLE

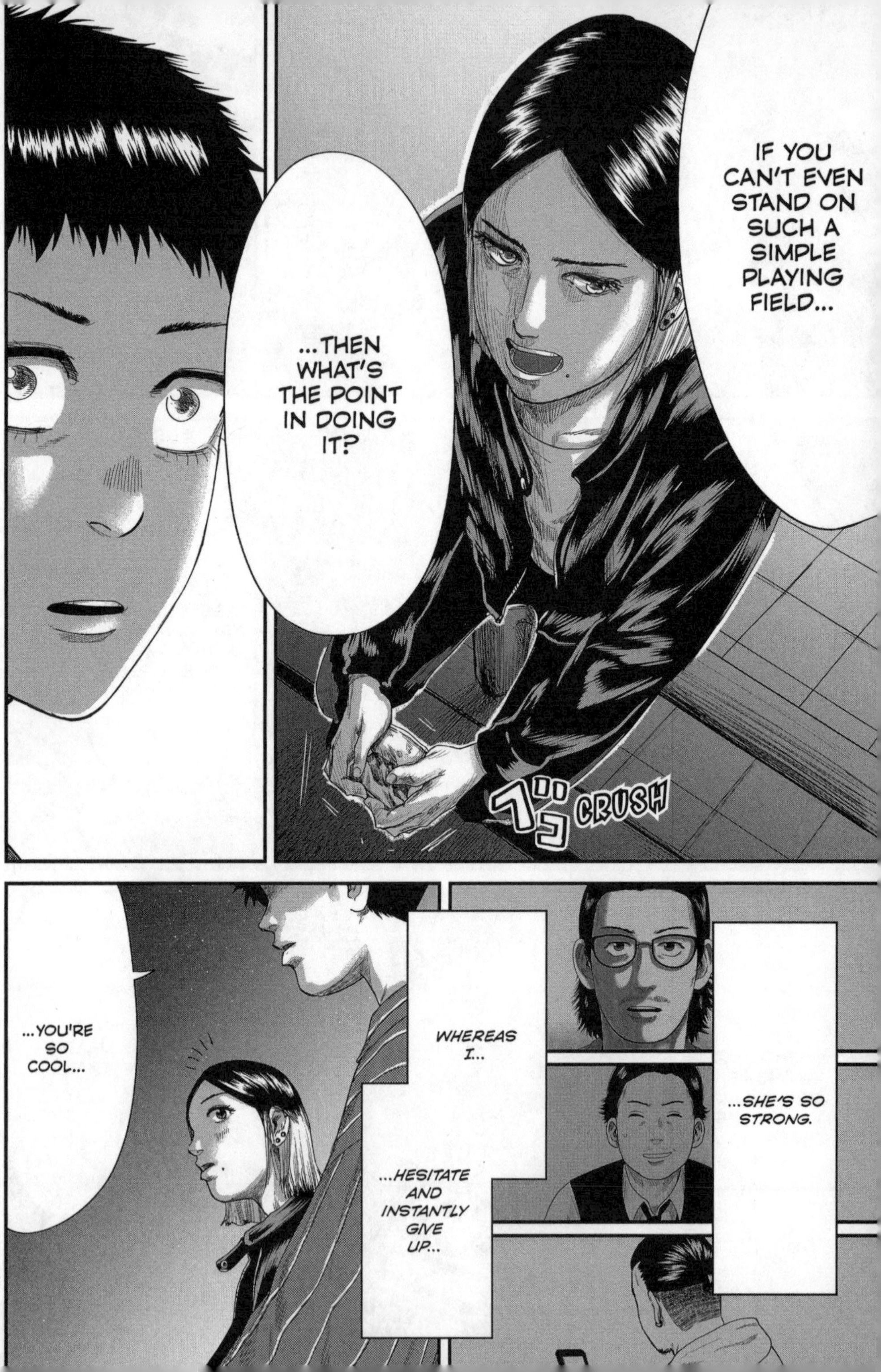
IF YOU CAN'T EVEN STAND ON SUCH A SIMPLE PLAYING FIELD...
...THEN WHAT'S THE POINT IN DOING IT?
CRUSH
...SHE'S SO STRONG.
WHEREAS I...
...HESITATE AND INSTANTLY GIVE UP...
...YOU'RE SO COOL...

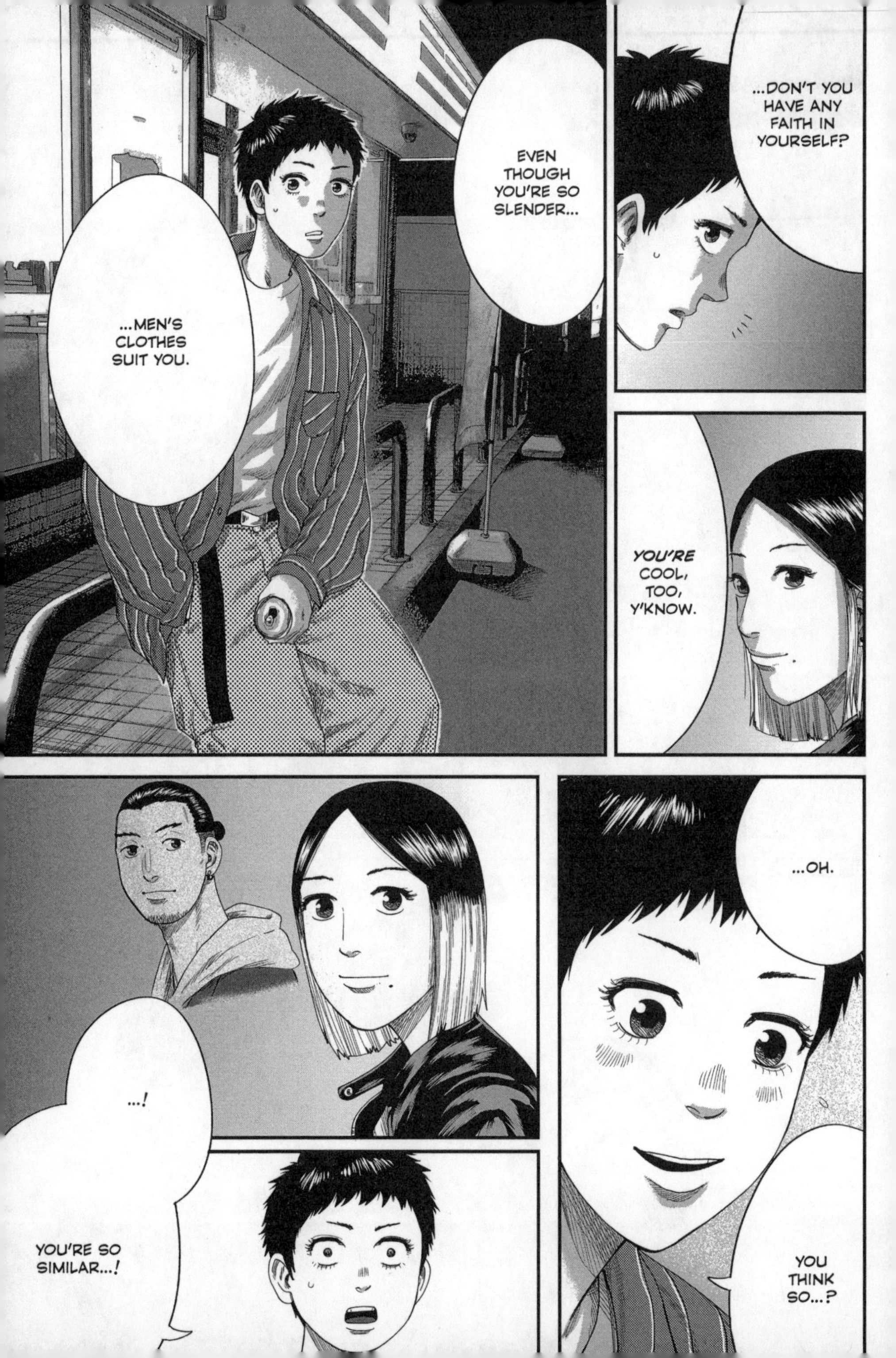
...DON'T YOU HAVE ANY FAITH IN YOURSELF?
YOU'RE COOL, TOO, Y'KNOW.
EVEN THOUGH YOU'RE SO SLENDER...
...MEN'S CLOTHES SUIT YOU.
...OH.
YOU THINK SO...?
...!
YOU'RE SO SIMILAR...!

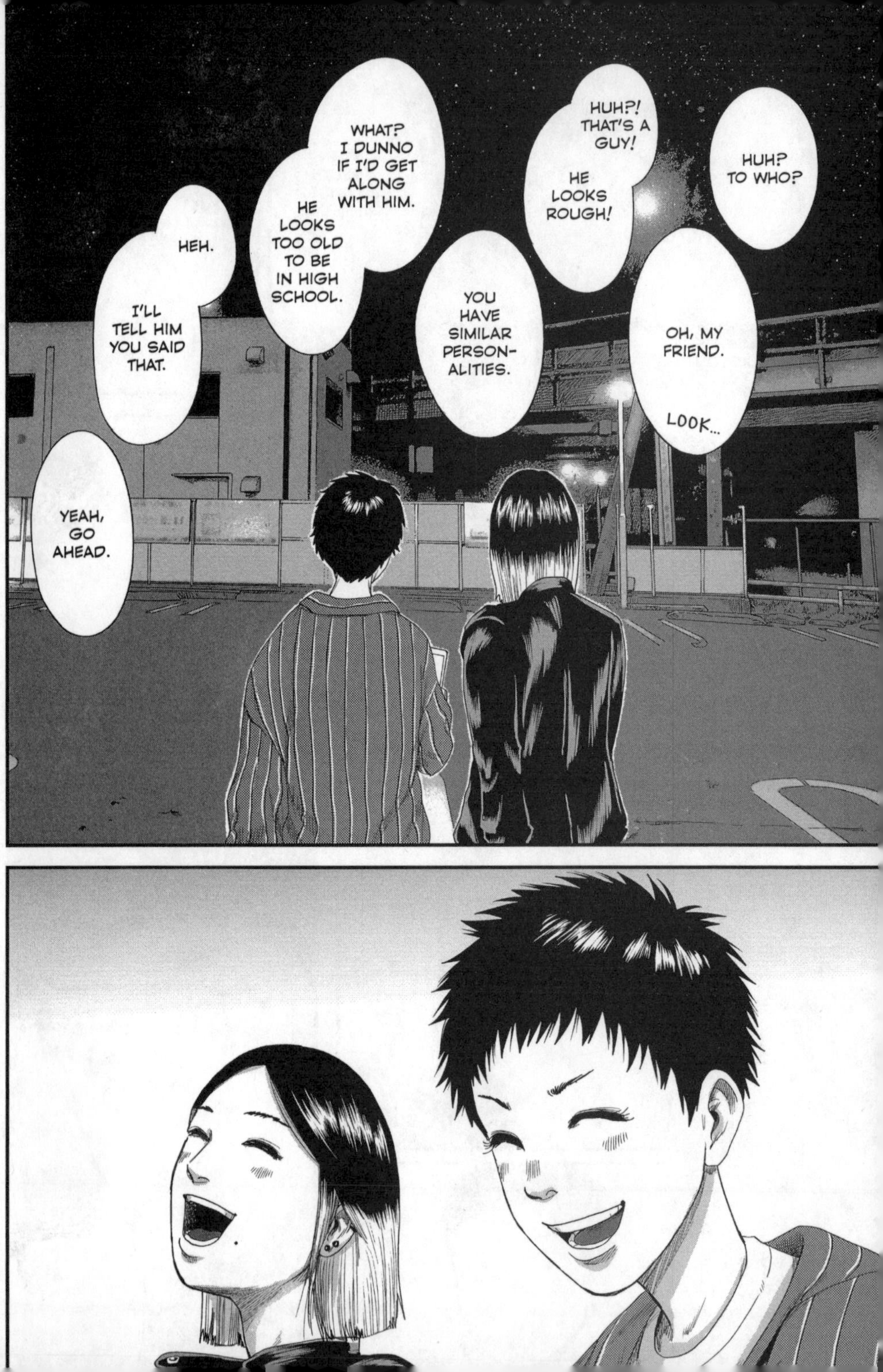
HUH? TO WHO?
OH, MY FRIEND.
LOOK...
HUH?! THAT'S A GUY!
HE LOOKS ROUGH!
YOU HAVE SIMILAR PERSON-ALITIES.
WHAT? I DUNNO IF I'D GET ALONG WITH HIM.
HE LOOKS TOO OLD TO BE IN HIGH SCHOOL.
HEH.
I'LL TELL HIM YOU SAID THAT.
YEAH, GO AHEAD.

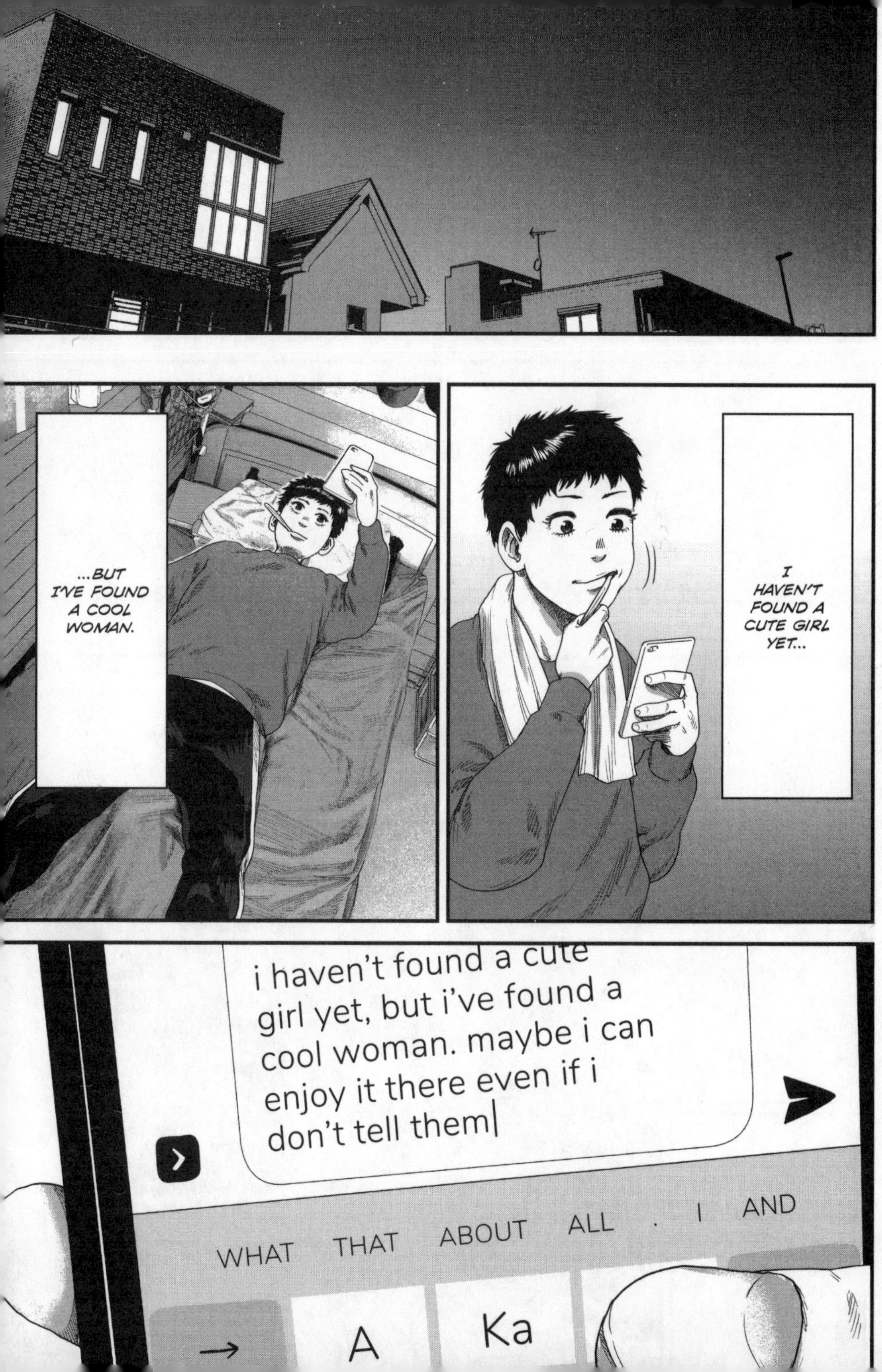
I HAVEN'T FOUND A CUTE GIRL YET...
...BUT I'VE FOUND A COOL WOMAN.
i haven't found a cute girl yet, but i've found a cool woman. maybe i can enjoy it there even if i don't tell them
WHAT THAT ABOUT ALL . I AND
→ A Ka

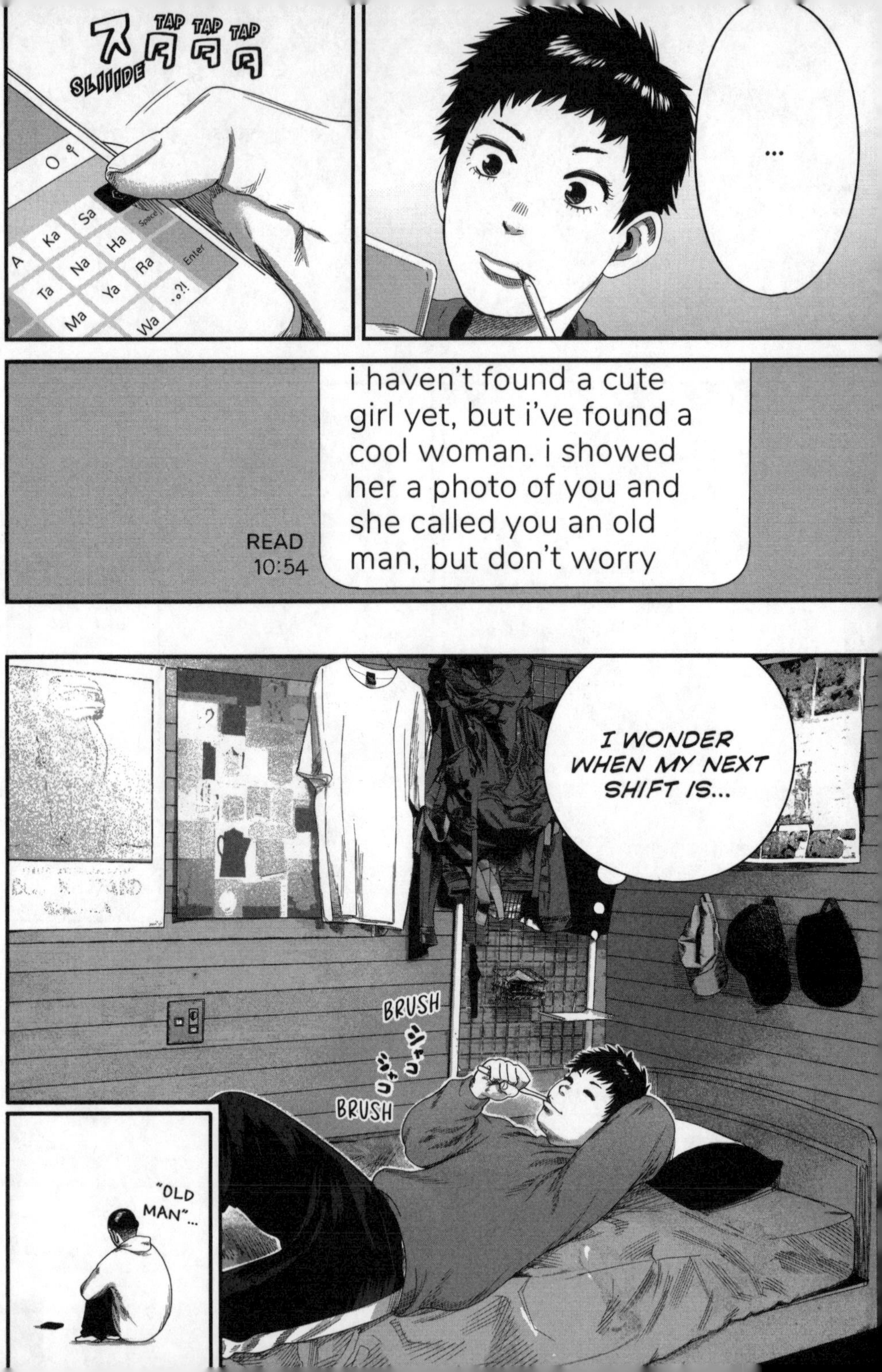
...
TAP TAP TAP
SLIIIDE
A Ka Sa
Ta Na Ha
Ma Ya Ra
Wa
Space
Enter
i haven't found a cute girl yet, but i've found a cool woman. i showed her a photo of you and she called you an old man, but don't worry
READ 10:54
I WONDER WHEN MY NEXT SHIFT IS...
BRUSH
BRUSH
"OLD MAN"...

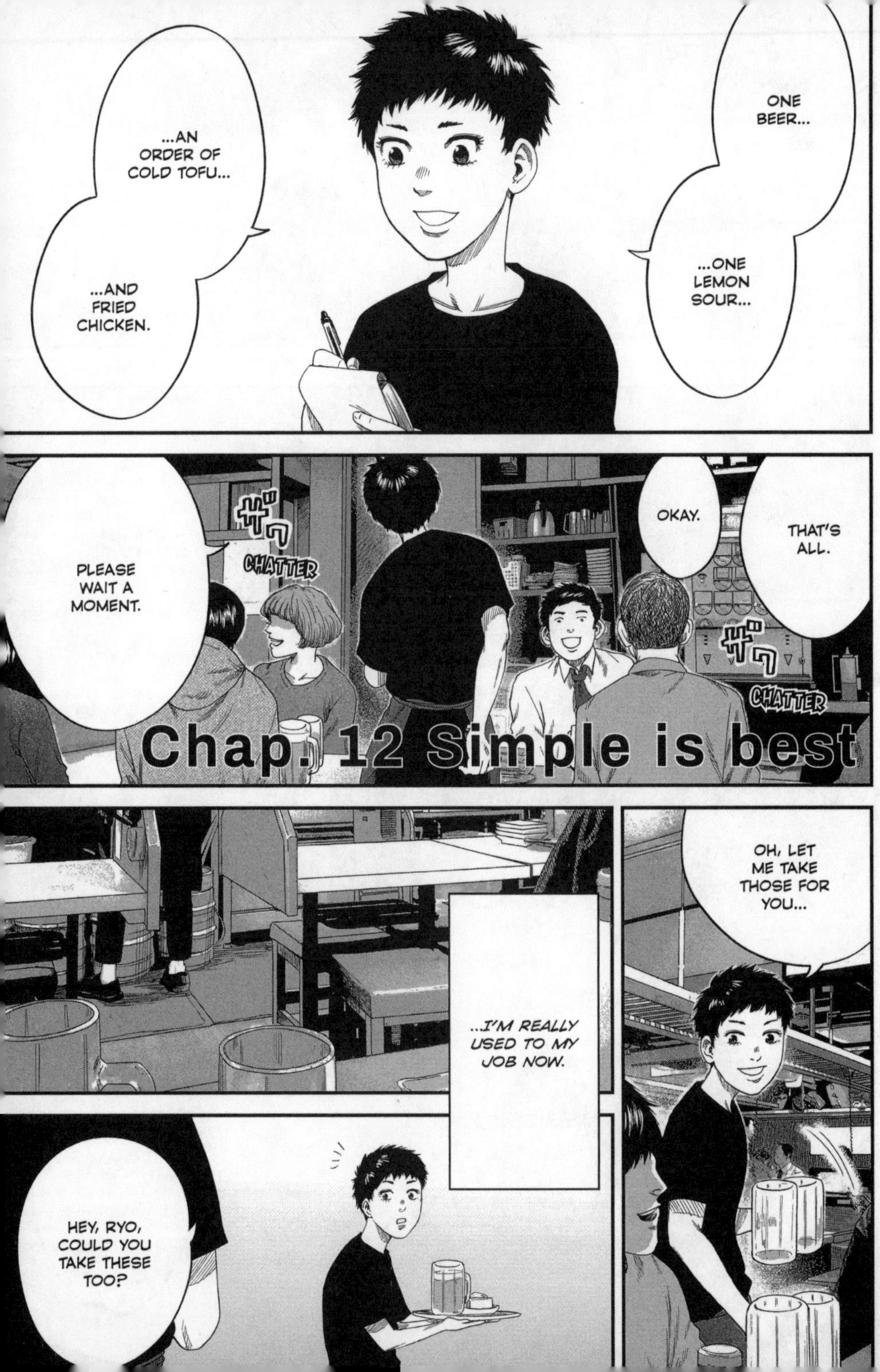
ONE BEER...
...ONE LEMON SOUR...
...AN ORDER OF COLD TOFU...
...AND FRIED CHICKEN.
THAT'S ALL.
OKAY.
ザワ
CHATTER
ザワ
CHATTER
PLEASE WAIT A MOMENT.
Chap. 12 Simple is best
OH, LET ME TAKE THOSE FOR YOU...
...I'M REALLY USED TO MY JOB NOW.
HEY, RYO, COULD YOU TAKE THESE TOO?

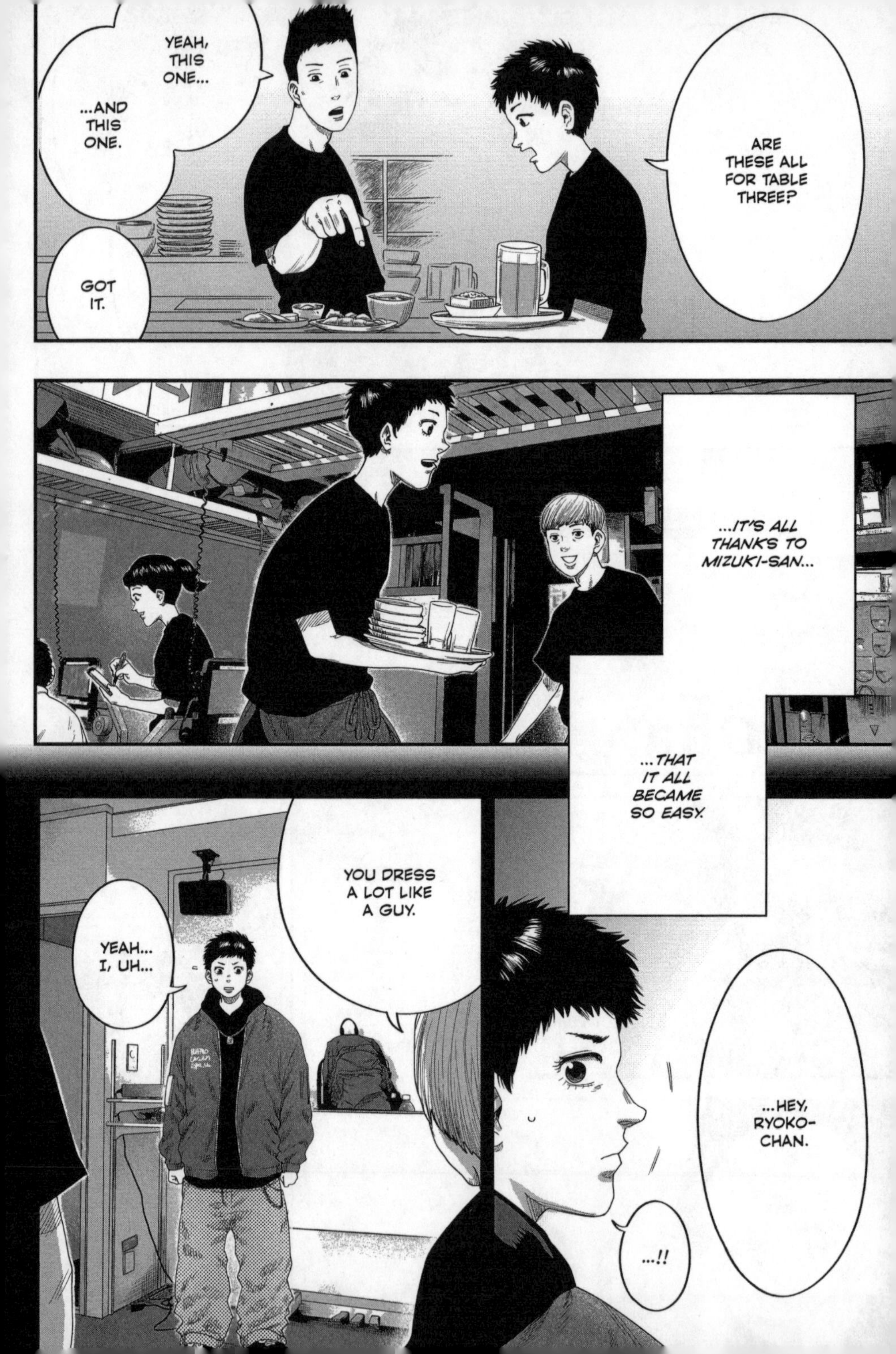
ARE THESE ALL FOR TABLE THREE?
YEAH, THIS ONE...
...AND THIS ONE.
GOT IT.
...IT'S ALL THANKS TO MIZUKI-SAN...
...THAT IT ALL BECAME SO EASY.
...HEY, RYOKO-CHAN.
...!!
YOU DRESS A LOT LIKE A GUY.
YEAH... I, UH...

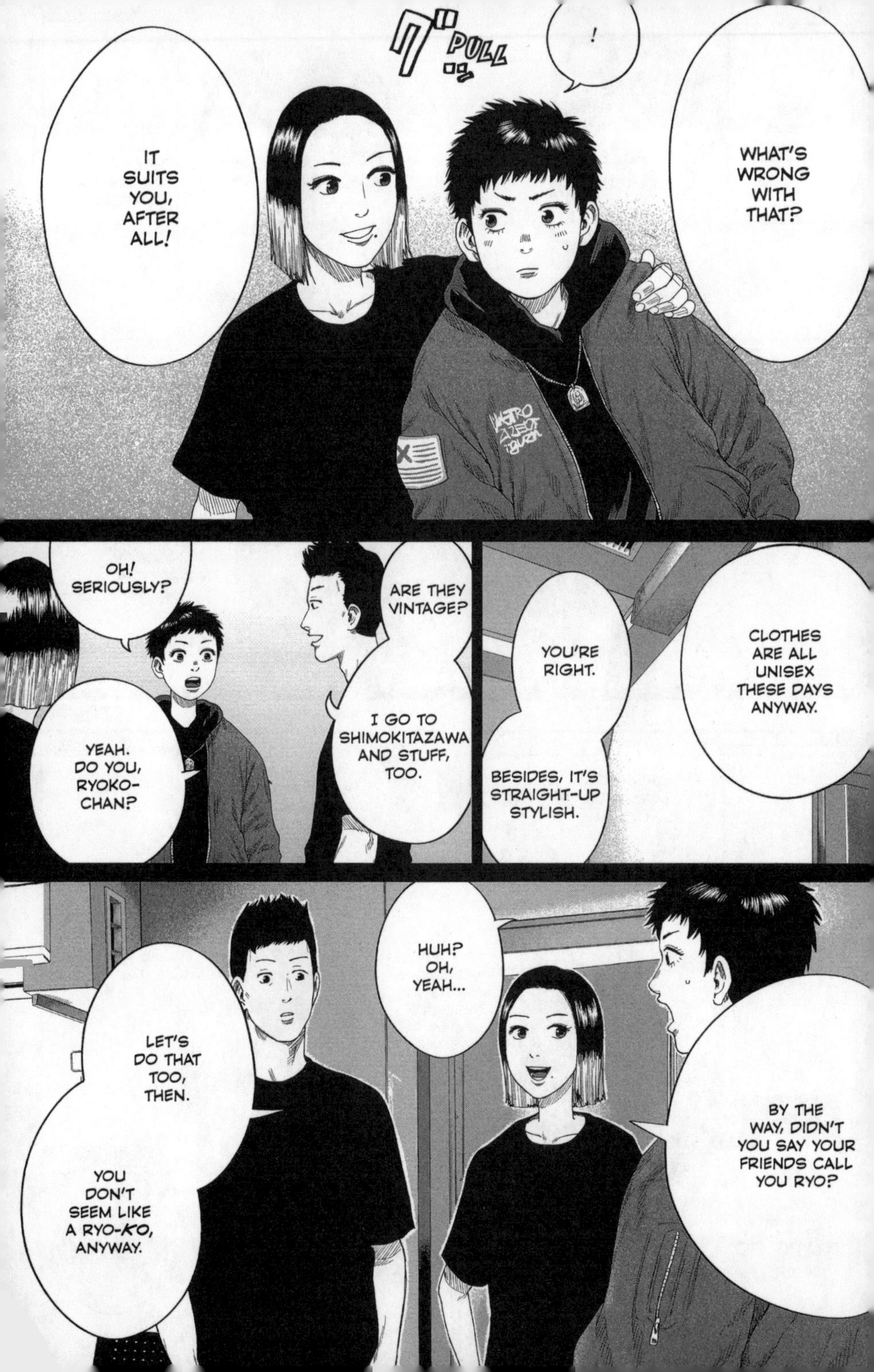
PULL
!
WHAT'S WRONG WITH THAT?
IT SUITS YOU, AFTER ALL!
CLOTHES ARE ALL UNISEX THESE DAYS ANYWAY.
YOU'RE RIGHT.
BESIDES, IT'S STRAIGHT-UP STYLISH.
ARE THEY VINTAGE?
I GO TO SHIMOKITAZAWA AND STUFF, TOO.
OH! SERIOUSLY?
YEAH. DO YOU, RYOKO-CHAN?
BY THE WAY, DIDN'T YOU SAY YOUR FRIENDS CALL YOU RYO?
HUH? OH, YEAH...
LET'S DO THAT TOO, THEN.
YOU DON'T SEEM LIKE A RYO-*KO*, ANYWAY.

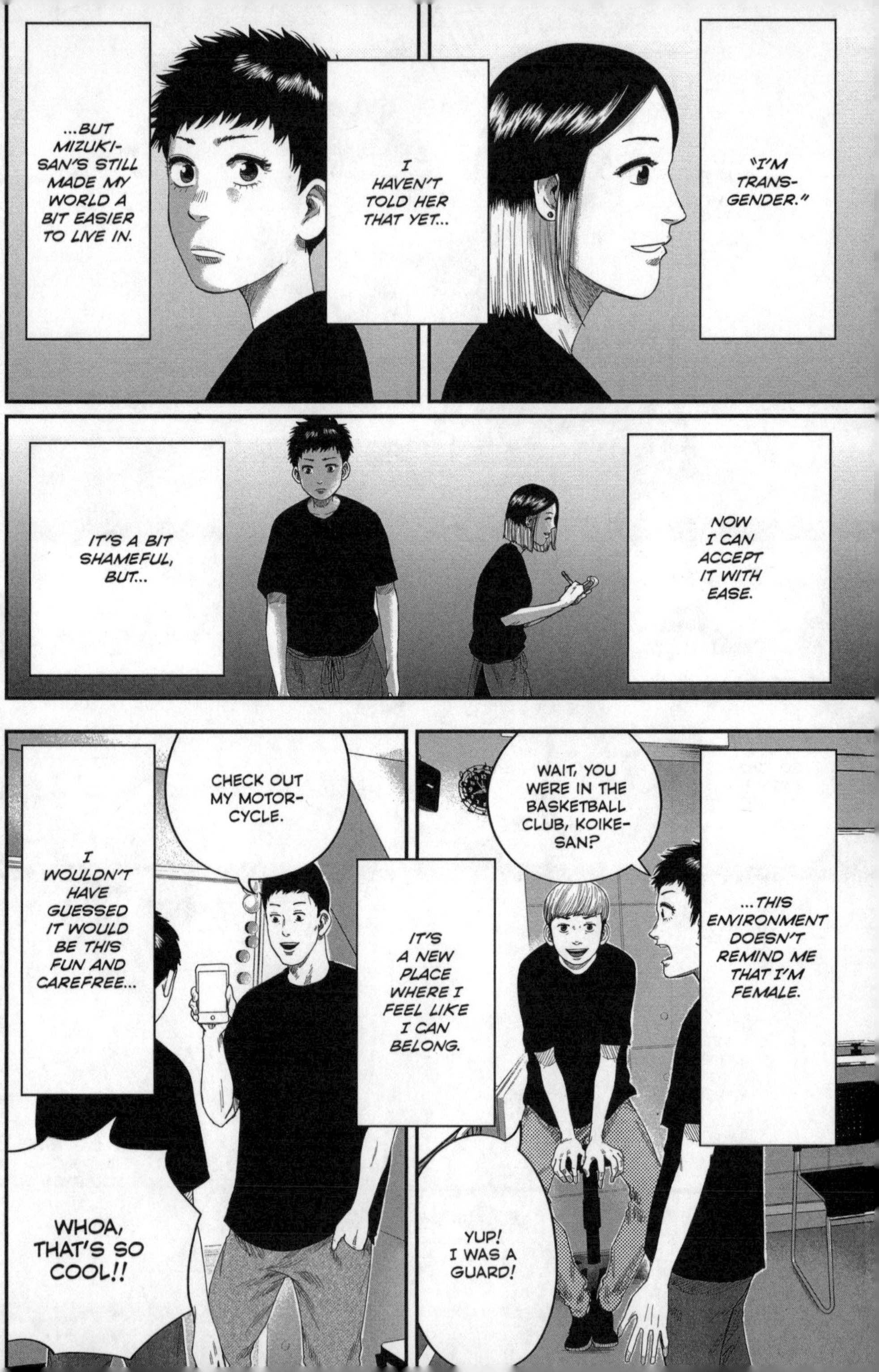
"I'M TRANS-GENDER."
I HAVEN'T TOLD HER THAT YET...
...BUT MIZUKI-SAN'S STILL MADE MY WORLD A BIT EASIER TO LIVE IN.
NOW I CAN ACCEPT IT WITH EASE.
IT'S A BIT SHAMEFUL, BUT...
...THIS ENVIRONMENT DOESN'T REMIND ME THAT I'M FEMALE.
WAIT, YOU WERE IN THE BASKETBALL CLUB, KOIKE-SAN?
YUP! I WAS A GUARD!
IT'S A NEW PLACE WHERE I FEEL LIKE I CAN BELONG.
I WOULDN'T HAVE GUESSED IT WOULD BE THIS FUN AND CAREFREE...
CHECK OUT MY MOTOR-CYCLE.
WHOA, THAT'S SO COOL!!

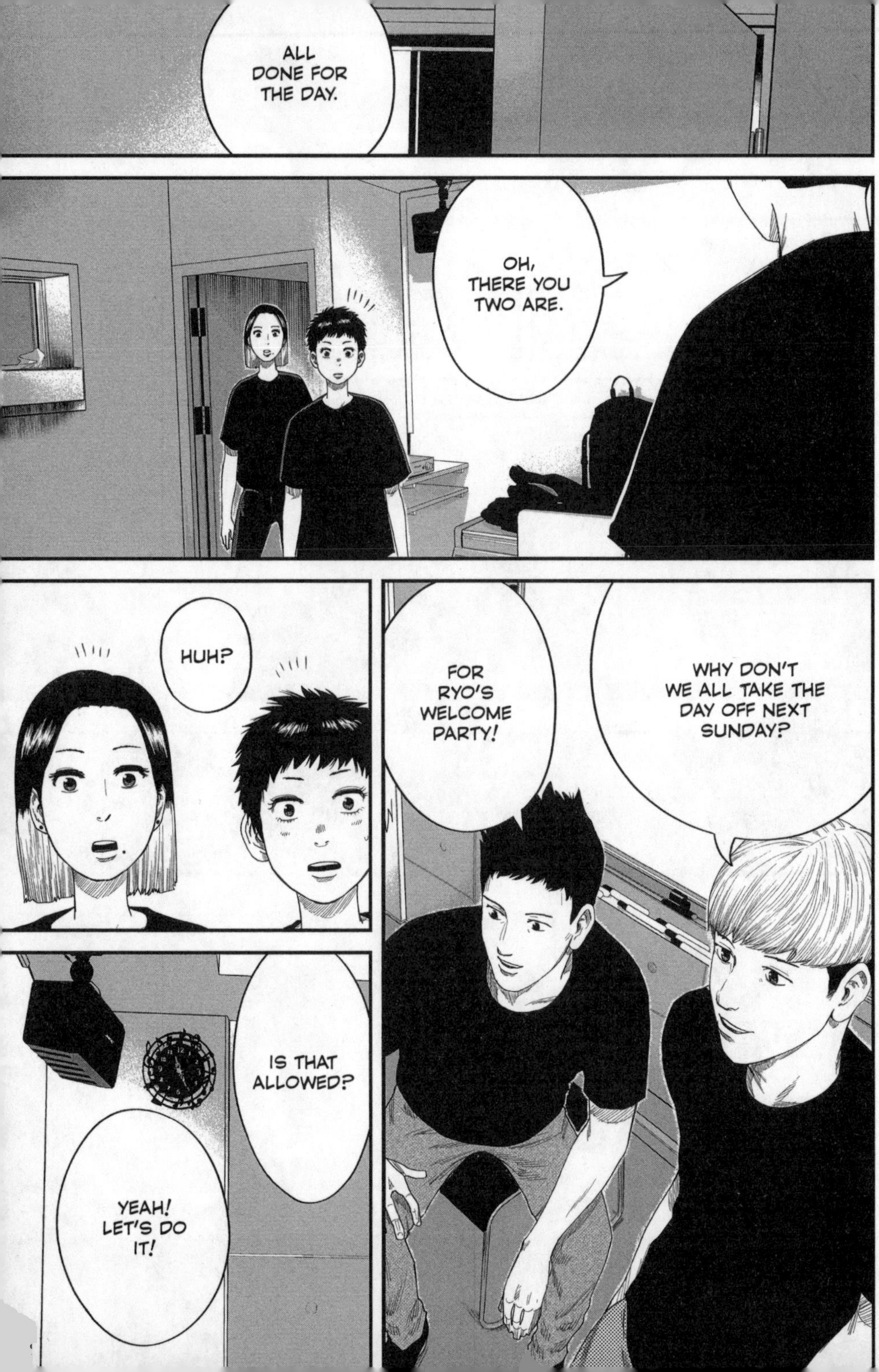
ALL DONE FOR THE DAY.
OH, THERE YOU TWO ARE.
WHY DON'T WE ALL TAKE THE DAY OFF NEXT SUNDAY?
FOR RYO'S WELCOME PARTY!
HUH?
IS THAT ALLOWED?
YEAH! LET'S DO IT!

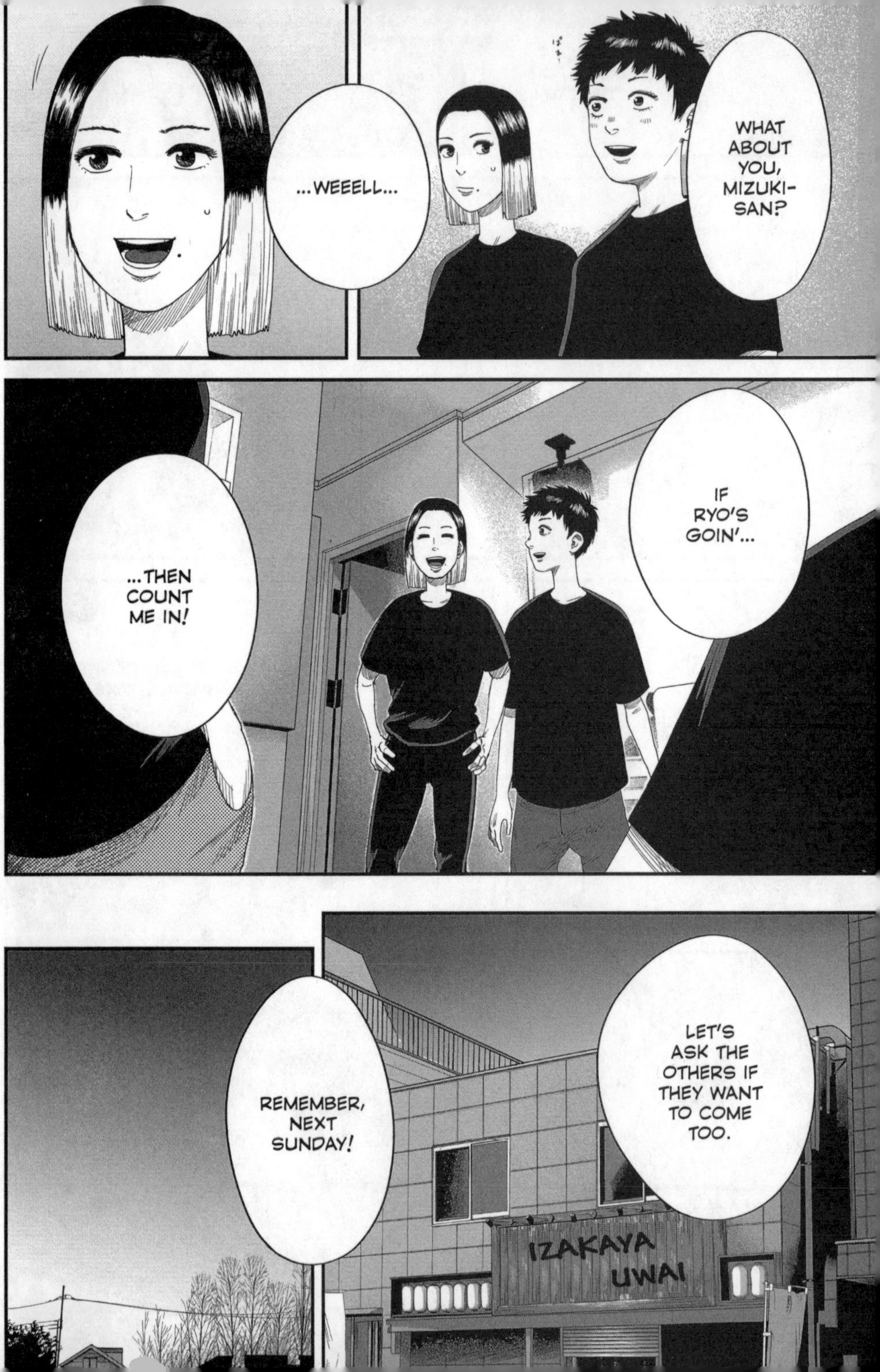
WHAT ABOUT YOU, MIZUKI-SAN?
...WEEELL...
IF RYO'S GOIN'...
...THEN COUNT ME IN!
LET'S ASK THE OTHERS IF THEY WANT TO COME TOO.
REMEMBER, NEXT SUNDAY!
IZAKAYA UWAI

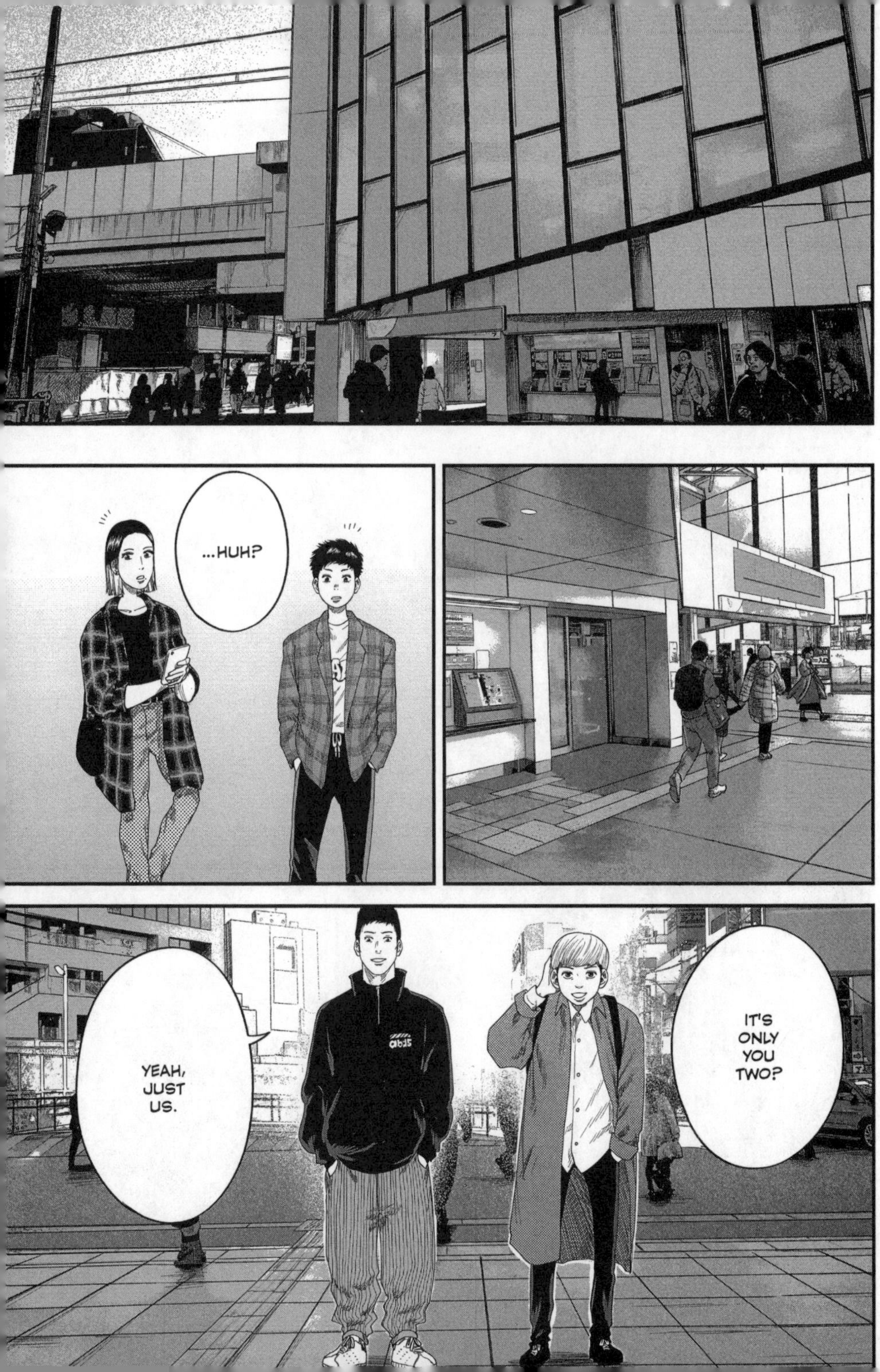
...HUH?
IT'S ONLY YOU TWO?
YEAH, JUST US.

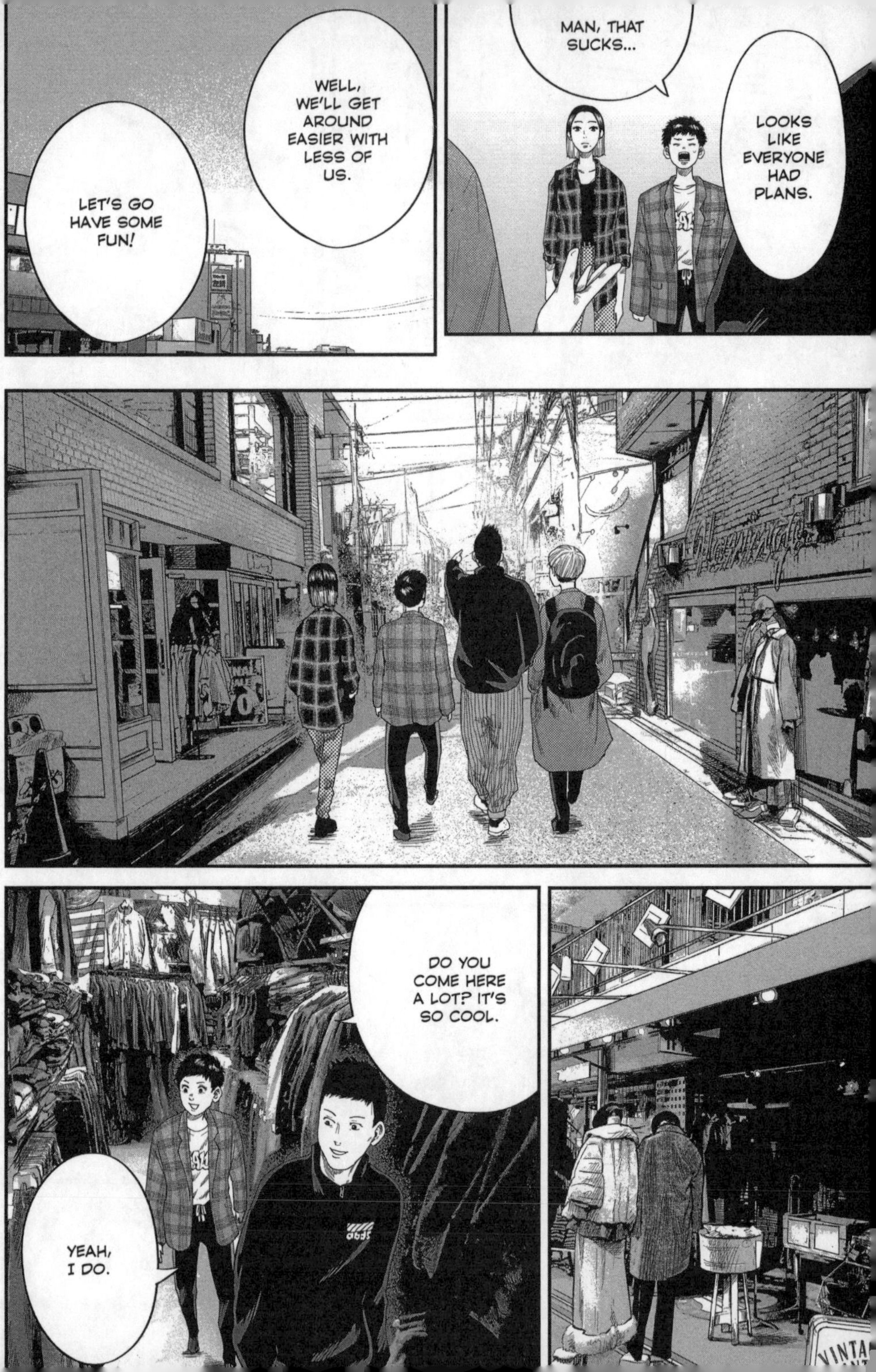
MAN, THAT SUCKS...
LOOKS LIKE EVERYONE HAD PLANS.
WELL, WE'LL GET AROUND EASIER WITH LESS OF US.
LET'S GO HAVE SOME FUN!
DO YOU COME HERE A LOT? IT'S SO COOL.
YEAH, I DO.

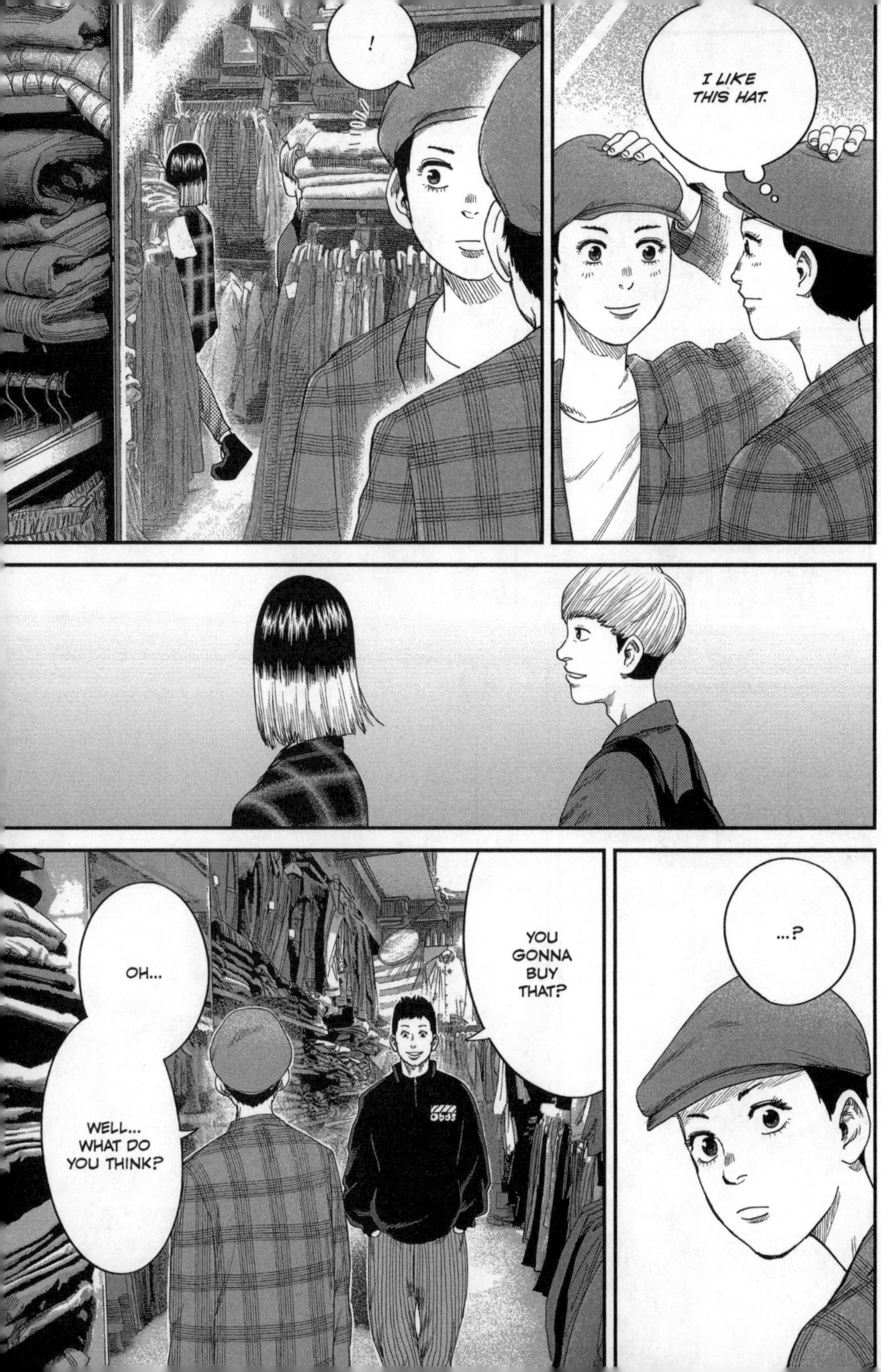
I LIKE THIS HAT.
!
...?
YOU GONNA BUY THAT?
OH...
WELL... WHAT DO YOU THINK?

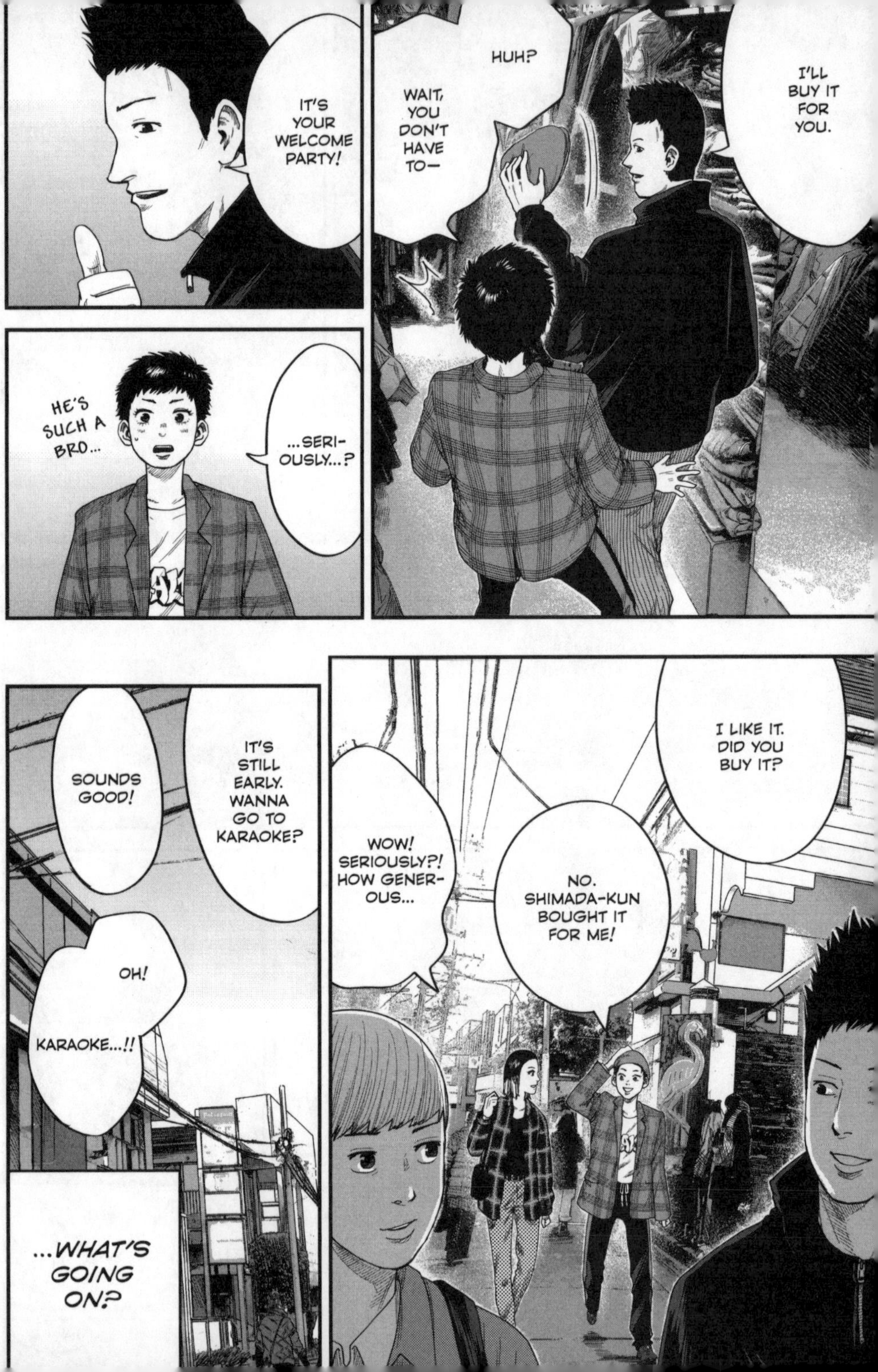
I'LL BUY IT FOR YOU.
HUH?
WAIT, YOU DON'T HAVE TO—
IT'S YOUR WELCOME PARTY!
...SERI-OUSLY...?
HE'S SUCH A BRO...
I LIKE IT. DID YOU BUY IT?
NO. SHIMADA-KUN BOUGHT IT FOR ME!
WOW! SERIOUSLY?! HOW GENER-OUS...
IT'S STILL EARLY. WANNA GO TO KARAOKE?
SOUNDS GOOD!
OH!
KARAOKE...!!
...WHAT'S GOING ON?

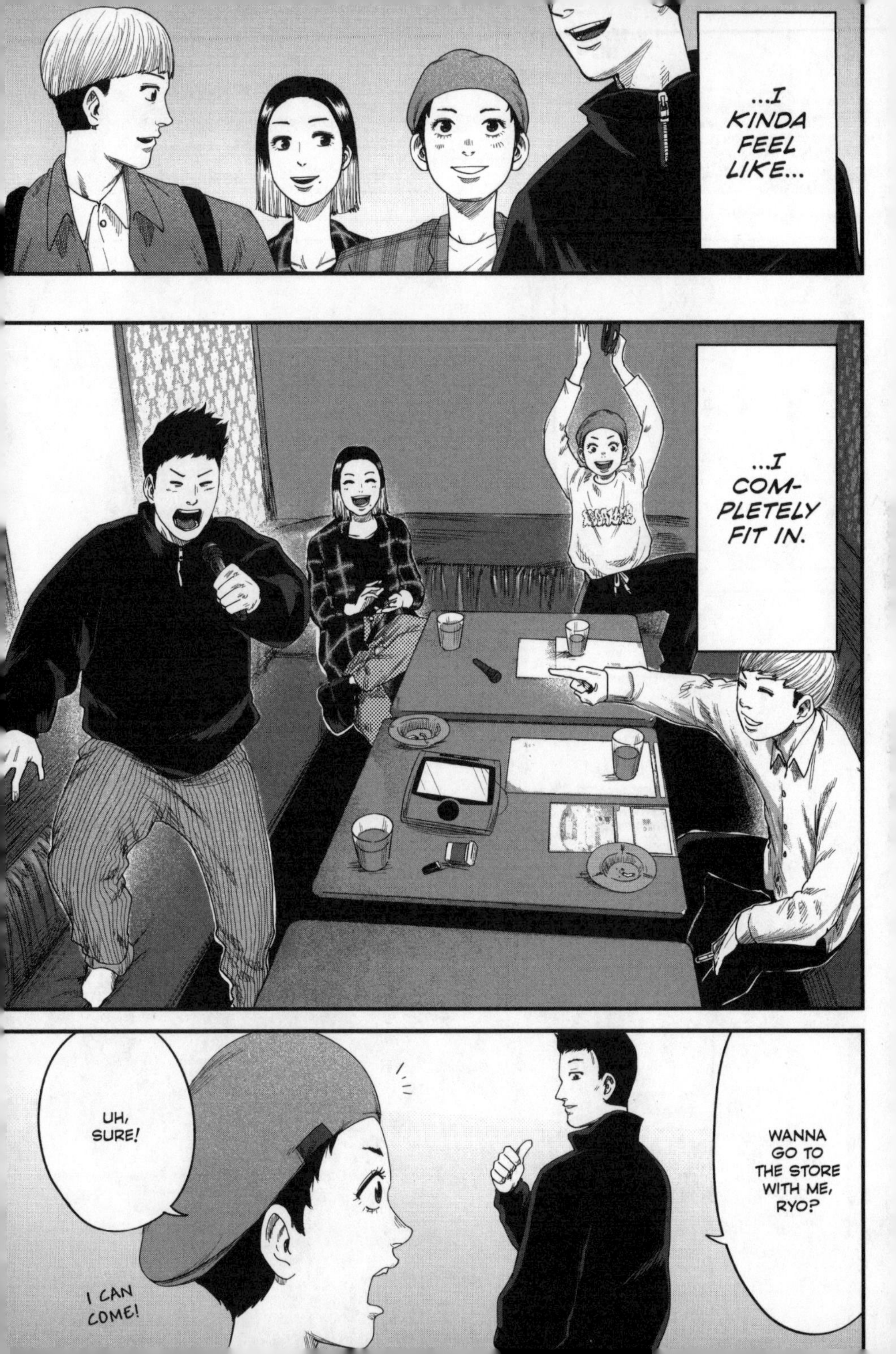
...I KINDA FEEL LIKE...
...I COMPLETELY FIT IN.
WANNA GO TO THE STORE WITH ME, RYO?
UH, SURE!
I CAN COME!

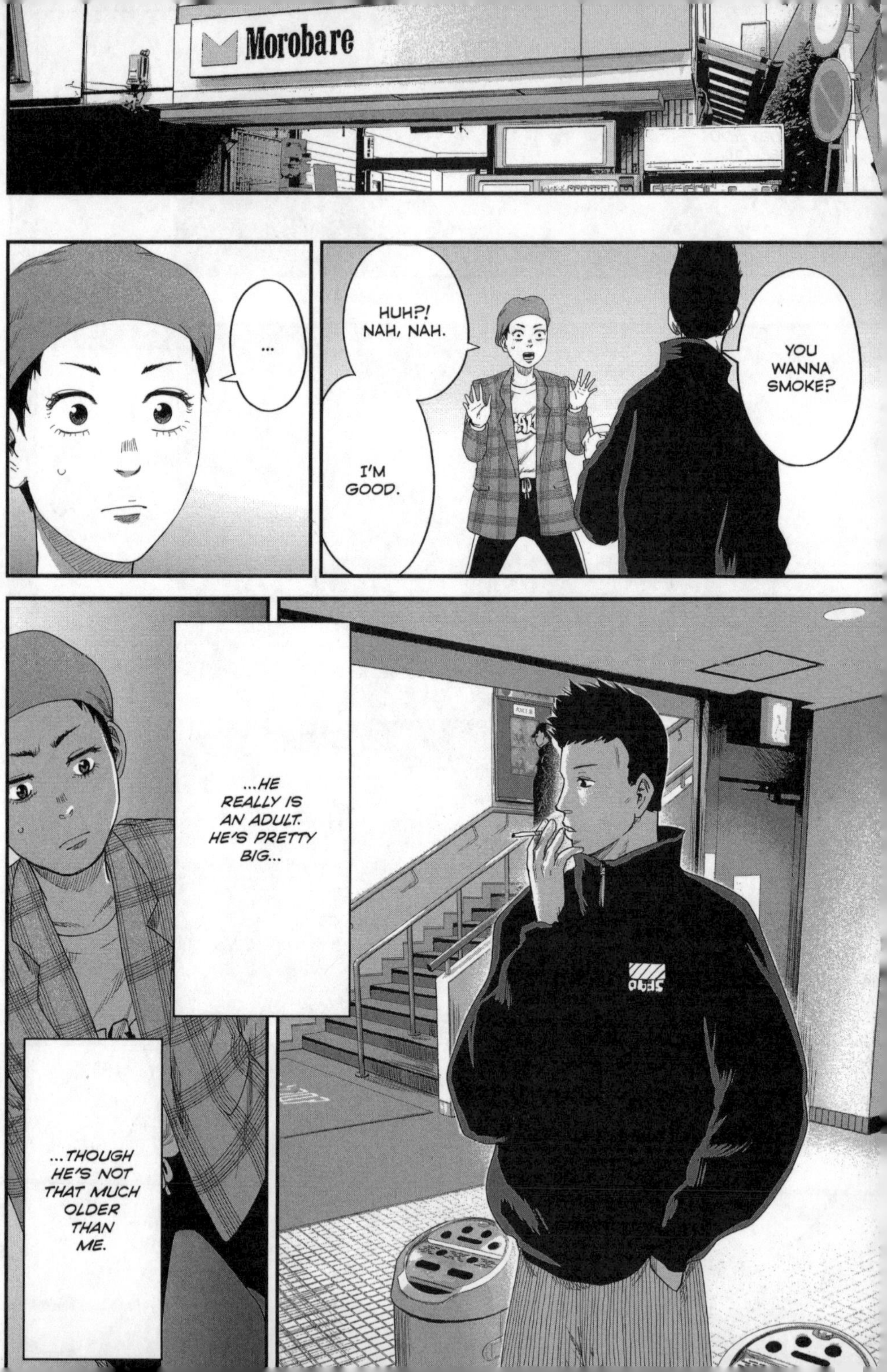
Morobare
YOU WANNA SMOKE?
HUH?! NAH, NAH.
I'M GOOD.
...
...HE REALLY IS AN ADULT. HE'S PRETTY BIG...
...THOUGH HE'S NOT THAT MUCH OLDER THAN ME.

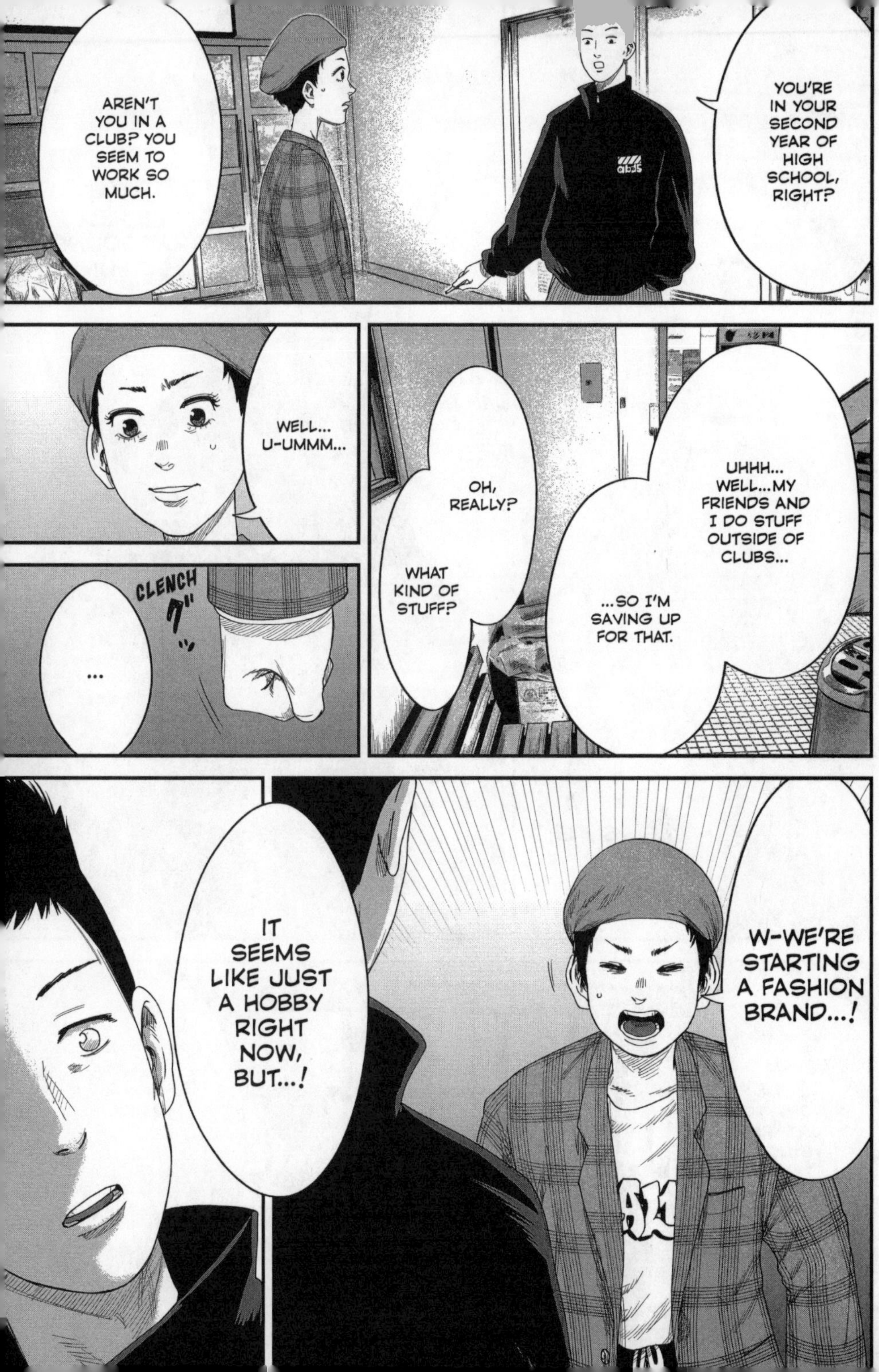
YOU'RE IN YOUR SECOND YEAR OF HIGH SCHOOL, RIGHT?
AREN'T YOU IN A CLUB? YOU SEEM TO WORK SO MUCH.
UHHH... WELL...MY FRIENDS AND I DO STUFF OUTSIDE OF CLUBS...
...SO I'M SAVING UP FOR THAT.
OH, REALLY?
WHAT KIND OF STUFF?
WELL... U-UMMM...
CLENCH
...
W-WE'RE STARTING A FASHION BRAND...!
IT SEEMS LIKE JUST A HOBBY RIGHT NOW, BUT...!

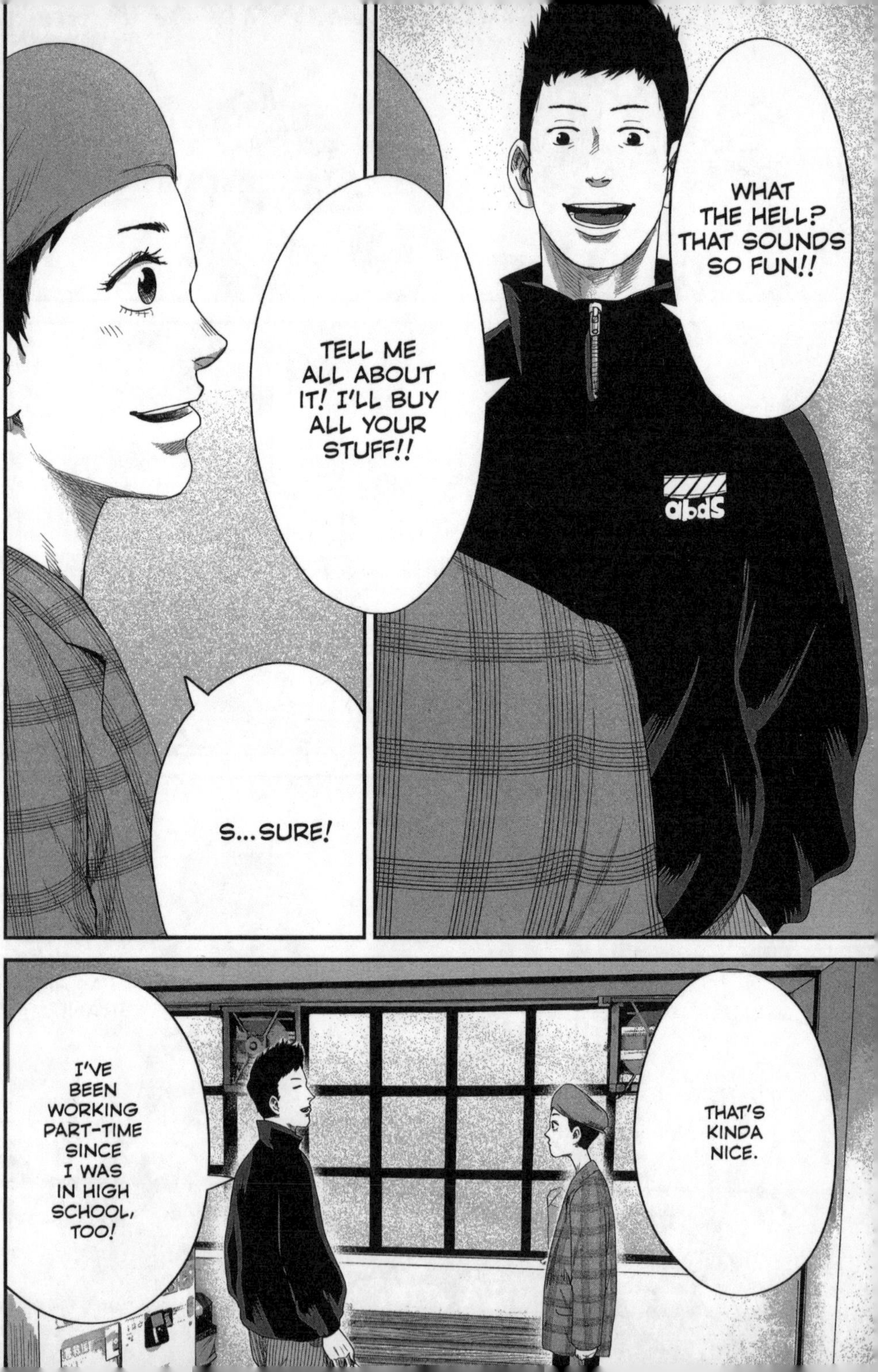
WHAT THE HELL? THAT SOUNDS SO FUN!!
TELL ME ALL ABOUT IT! I'LL BUY ALL YOUR STUFF!!
S...SURE!
THAT'S KINDA NICE.
I'VE BEEN WORKING PART-TIME SINCE I WAS IN HIGH SCHOOL, TOO!

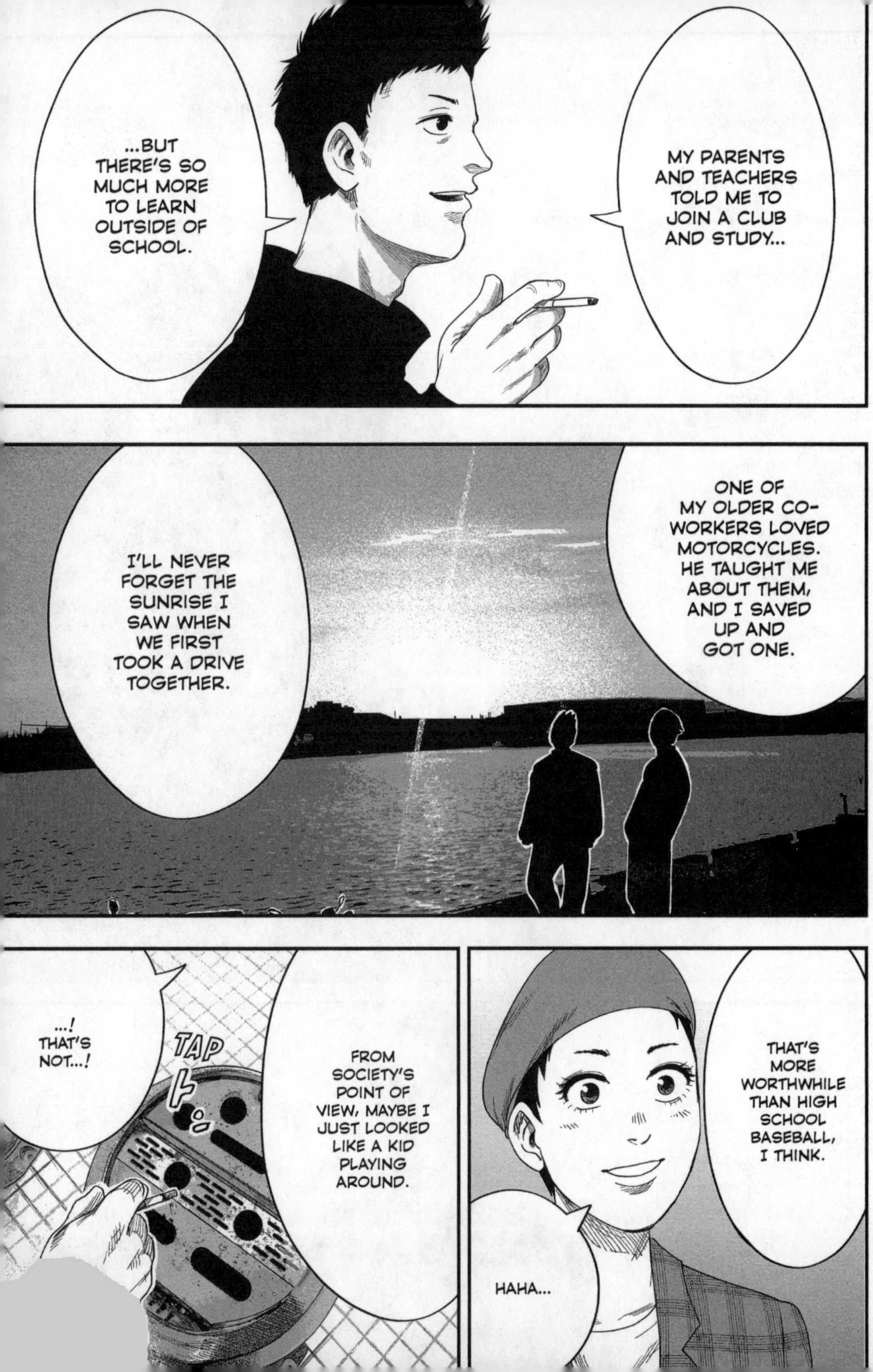
MY PARENTS AND TEACHERS TOLD ME TO JOIN A CLUB AND STUDY...
...BUT THERE'S SO MUCH MORE TO LEARN OUTSIDE OF SCHOOL.
ONE OF MY OLDER CO-WORKERS LOVED MOTORCYCLES. HE TAUGHT ME ABOUT THEM, AND I SAVED UP AND GOT ONE.
I'LL NEVER FORGET THE SUNRISE I SAW WHEN WE FIRST TOOK A DRIVE TOGETHER.
THAT'S MORE WORTHWHILE THAN HIGH SCHOOL BASEBALL, I THINK.
HAHA...
FROM SOCIETY'S POINT OF VIEW, MAYBE I JUST LOOKED LIKE A KID PLAYING AROUND.
TAP
...! THAT'S NOT...!

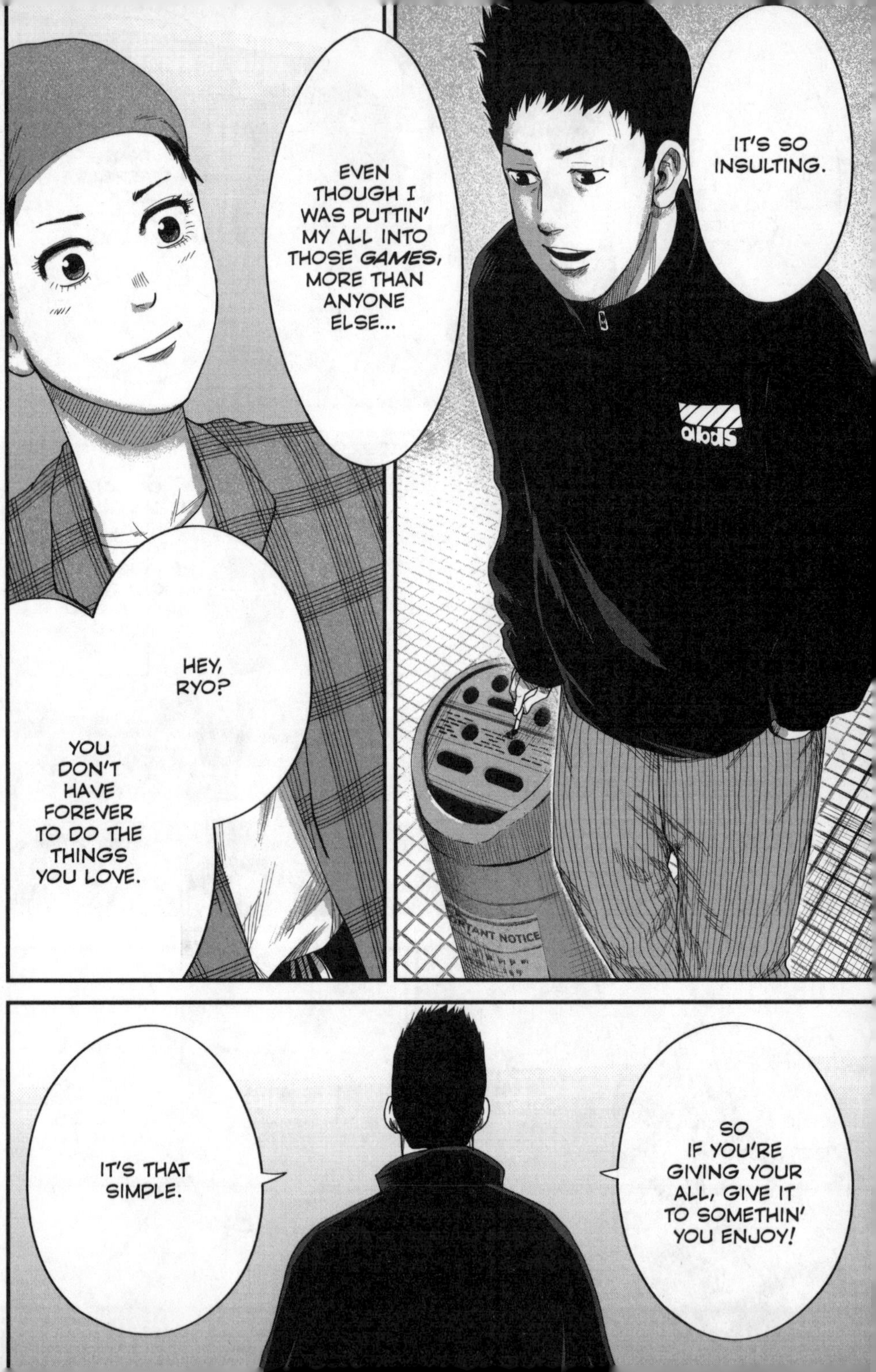
IT'S SO INSULTING.
EVEN THOUGH I WAS PUTTIN' MY ALL INTO THOSE *GAMES*, MORE THAN ANYONE ELSE...
HEY, RYO?
YOU DON'T HAVE FOREVER TO DO THE THINGS YOU LOVE.
SO IF YOU'RE GIVING YOUR ALL, GIVE IT TO SOMETHIN' YOU ENJOY!
IT'S THAT SIMPLE.

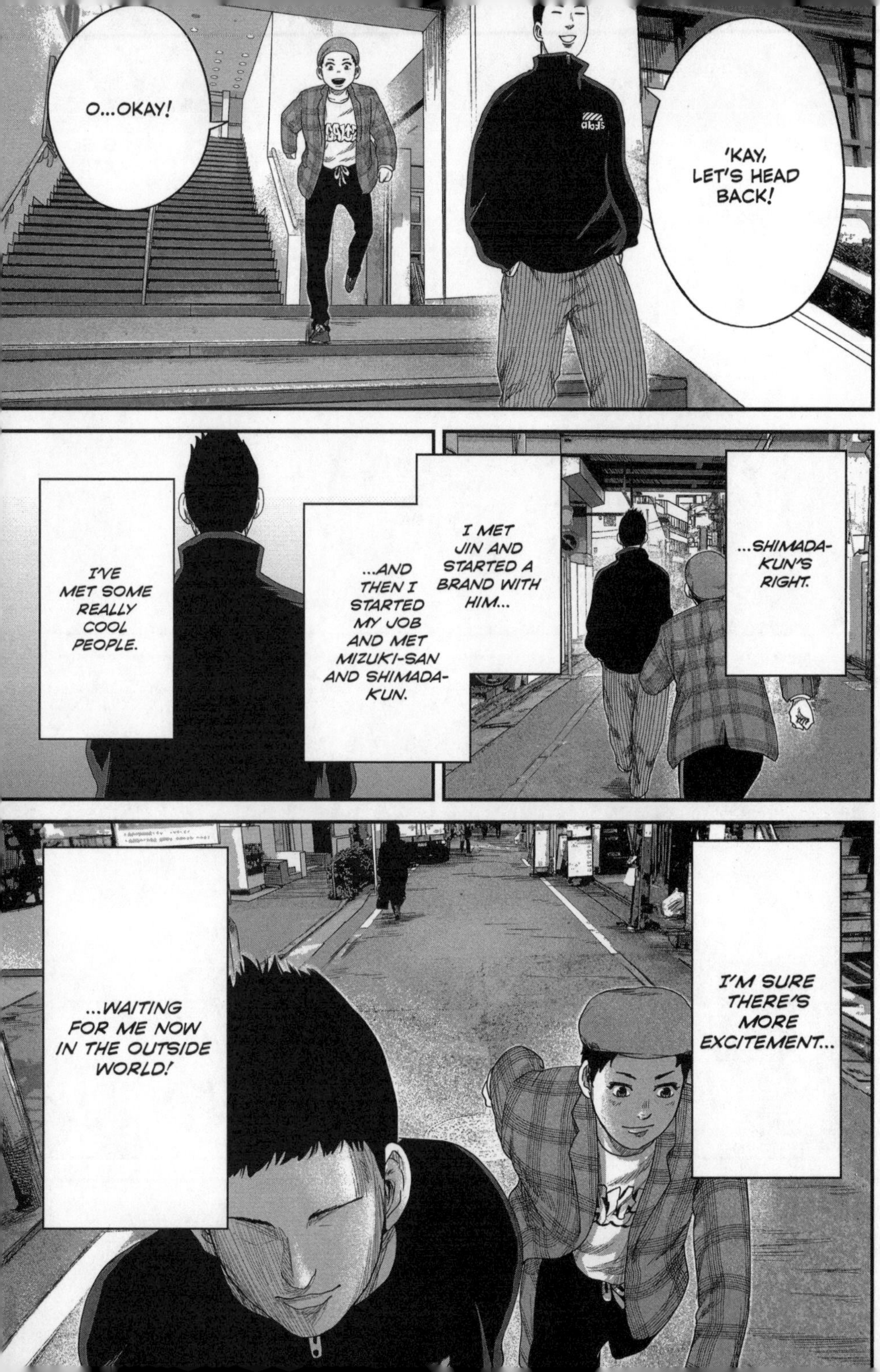
'KAY, LET'S HEAD BACK!
O...OKAY!
...SHIMADA-KUN'S RIGHT.
I MET JIN AND STARTED A BRAND WITH HIM...
...AND THEN I STARTED MY JOB AND MET MIZUKI-SAN AND SHIMADA-KUN.
I'VE MET SOME REALLY COOL PEOPLE.
I'M SURE THERE'S MORE EXCITEMENT...
...WAITING FOR ME NOW IN THE OUTSIDE WORLD!

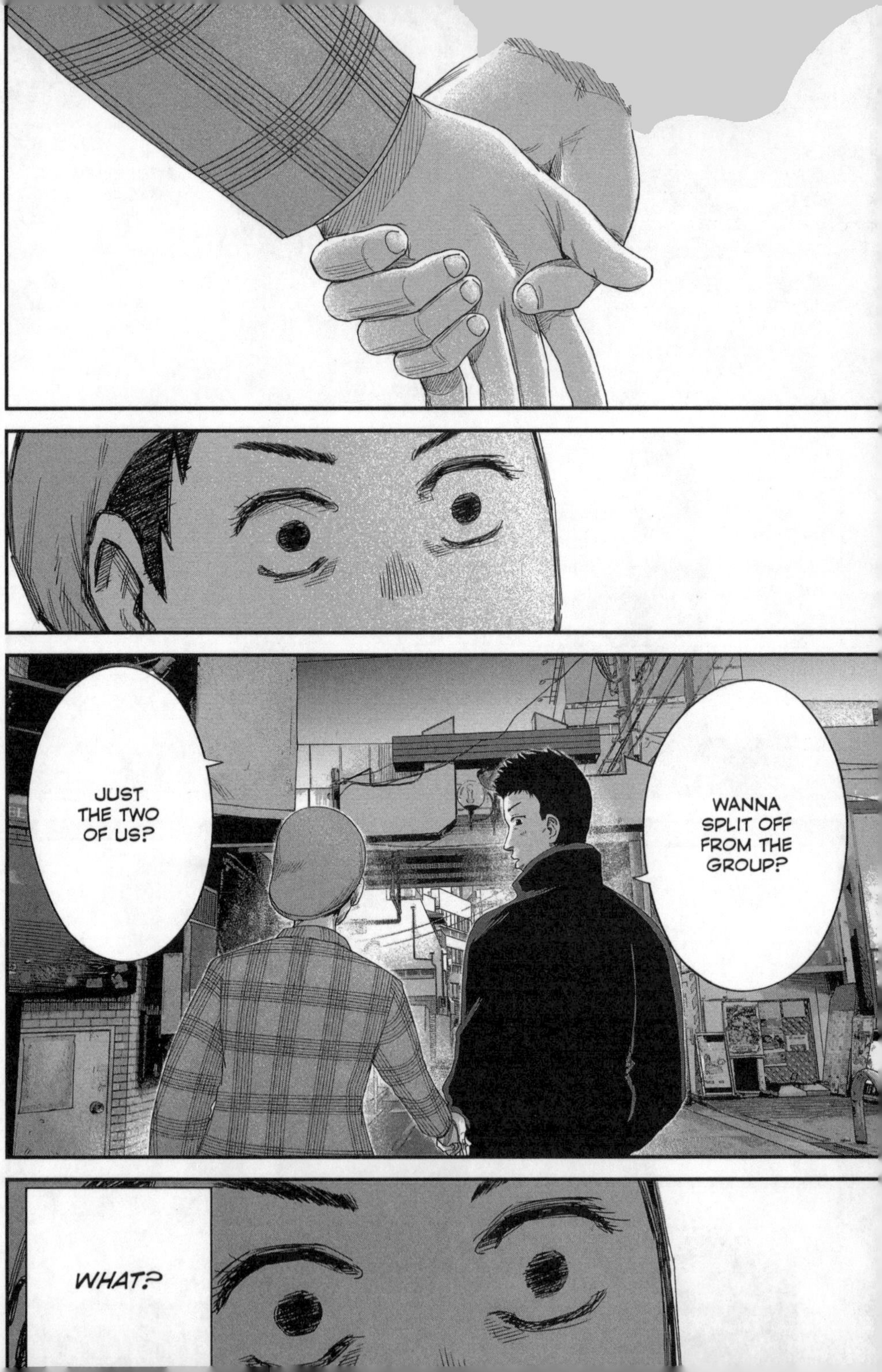
WANNA SPLIT OFF FROM THE GROUP?
JUST THE TWO OF US?
WHAT?

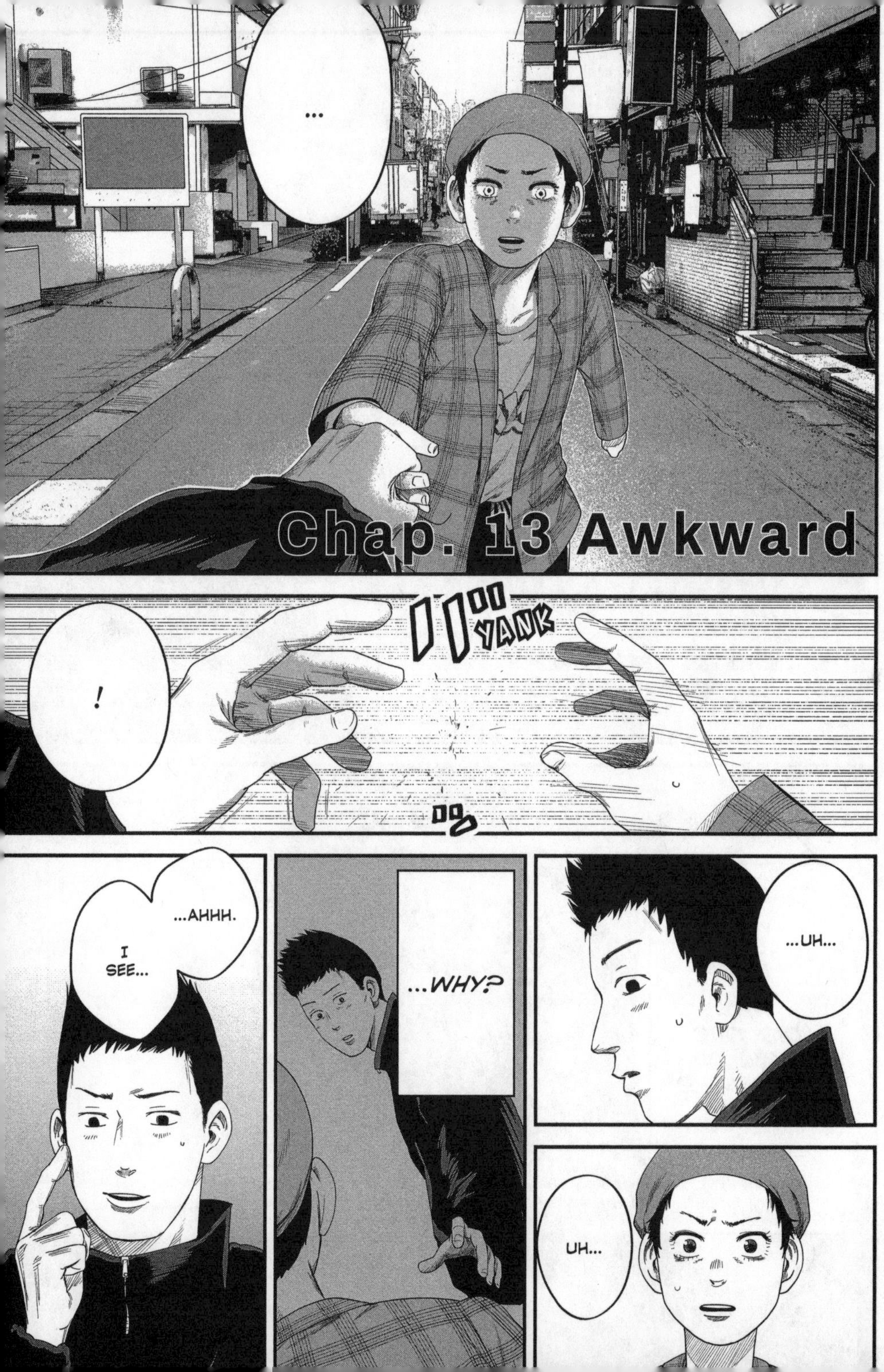
...
Chap. 13 Awkward
!
YANK
...UH...
UH...
...WHY?
...AHHH. I SEE...

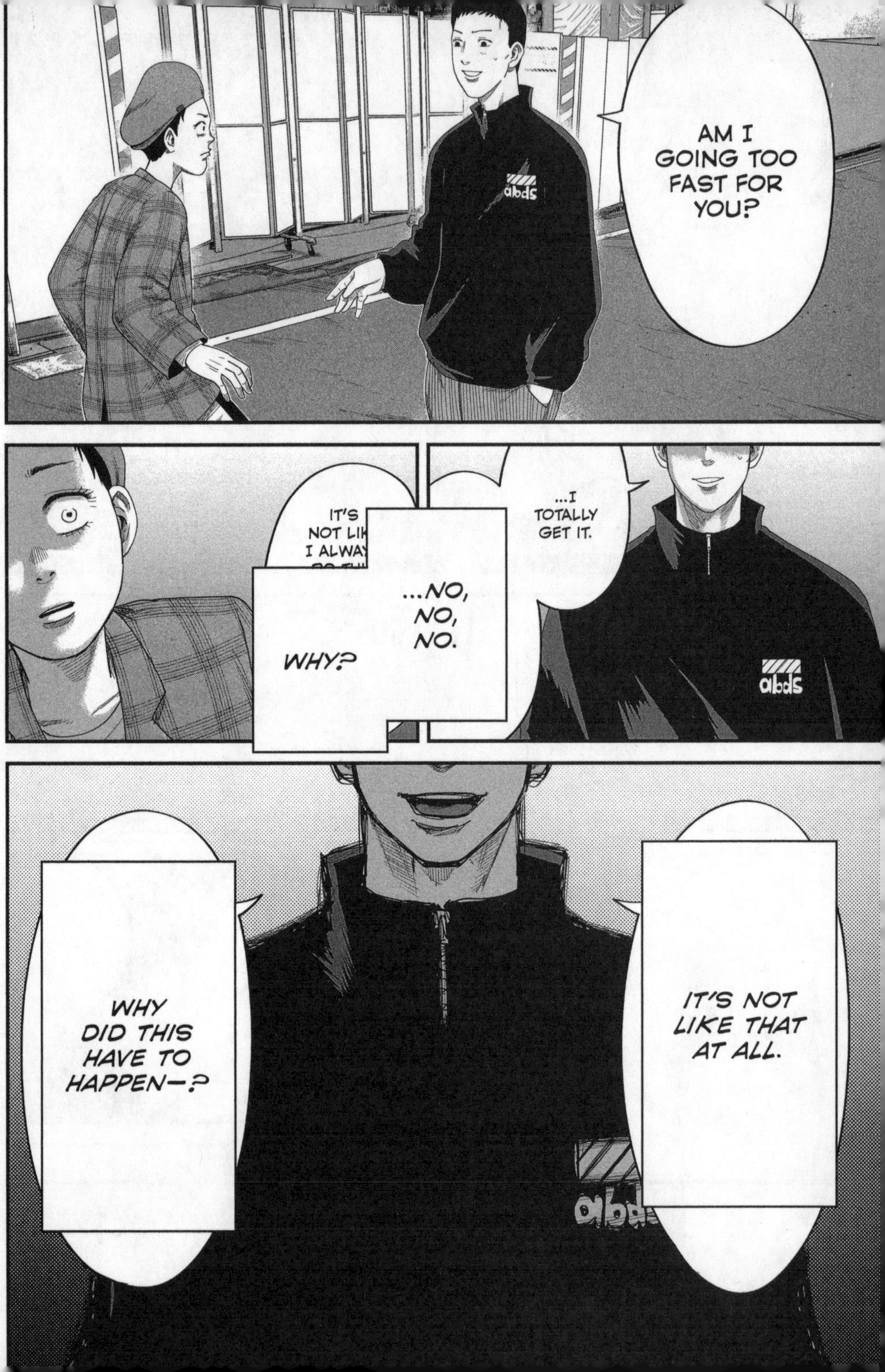
AM I GOING TOO FAST FOR YOU?
...I TOTALLY GET IT.
...NO, NO, NO.
WHY?
IT'S NOT LIKE THAT AT ALL.
WHY DID THIS HAVE TO HAPPEN—?

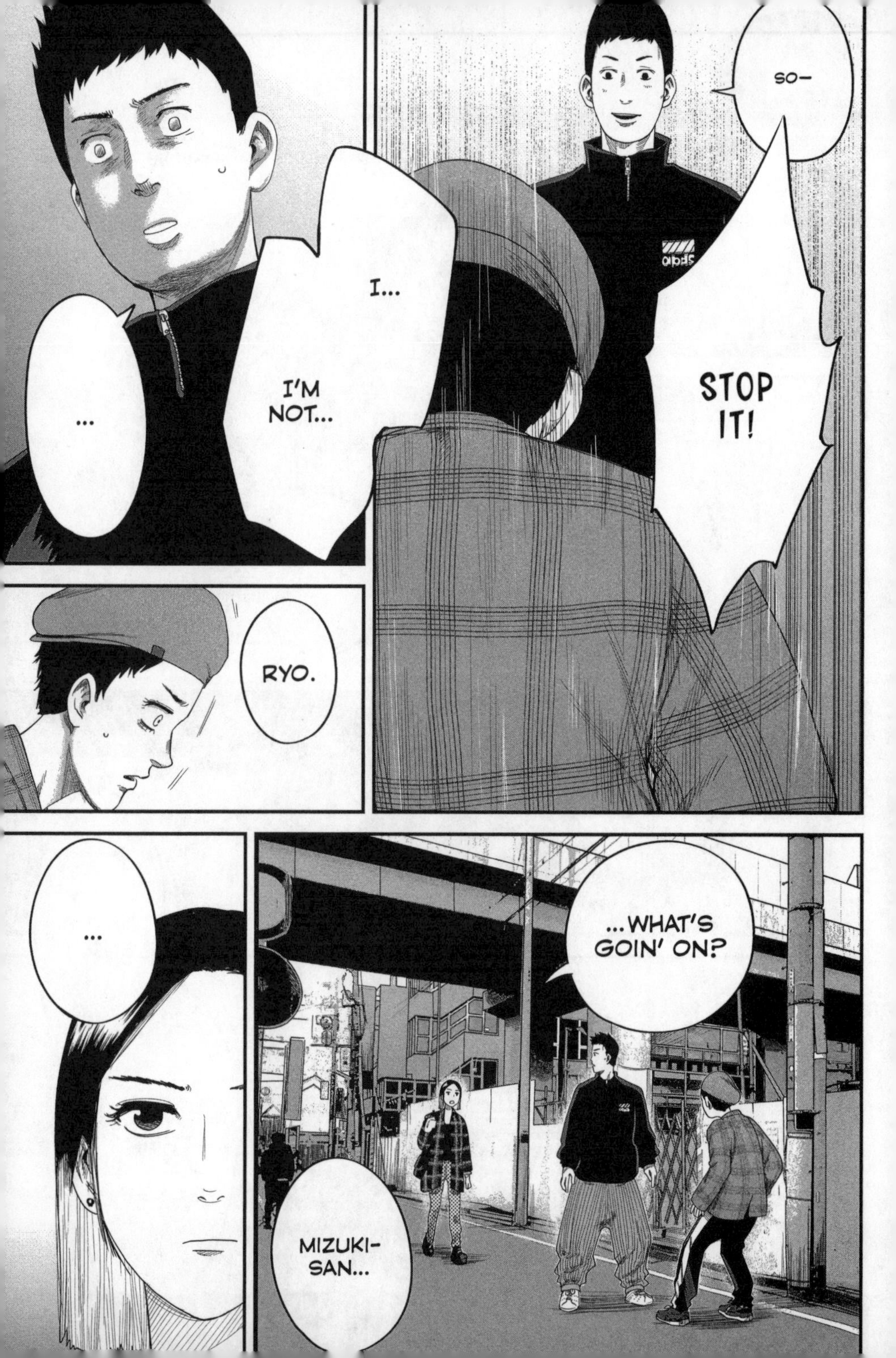
SO—
STOP IT!
I... I'M NOT...
...
RYO.
...WHAT'S GOIN' ON?
MIZUKI-SAN...
...

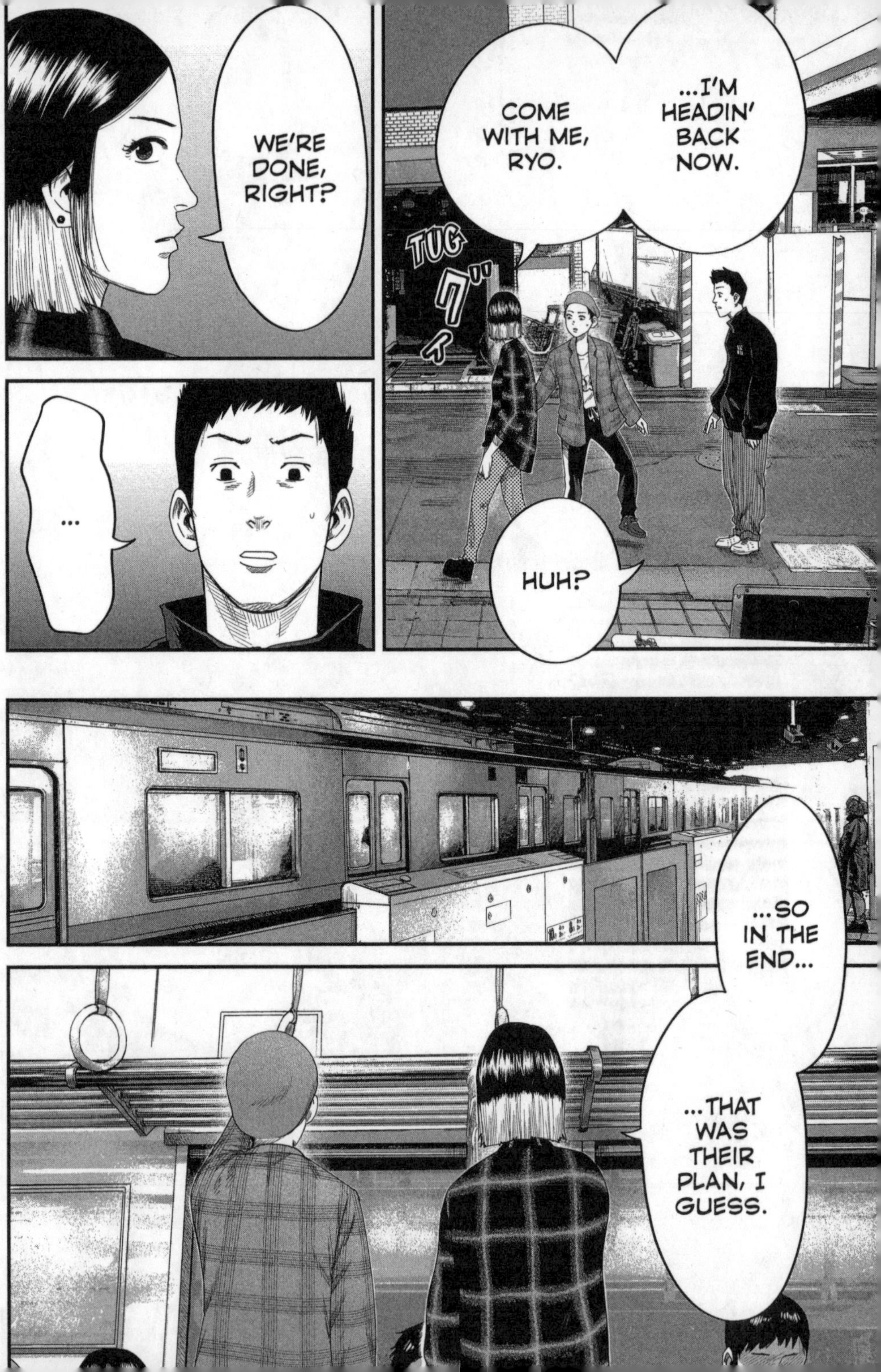
...I'M HEADIN' BACK NOW.
COME WITH ME, RYO.
TUG
HUH?
WE'RE DONE, RIGHT?
...
...SO IN THE END...
...THAT WAS THEIR PLAN, I GUESS.

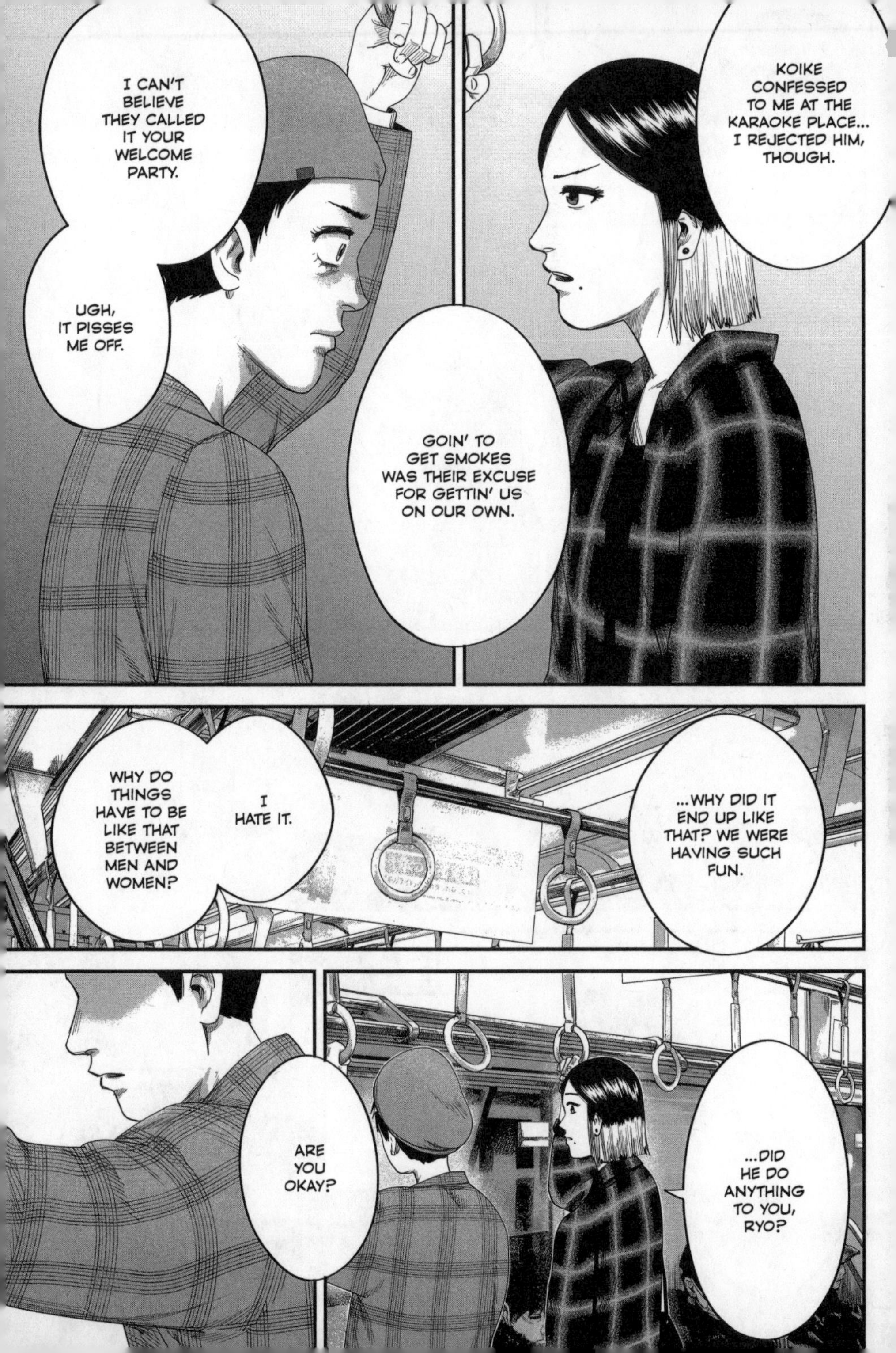
KOIKE CONFESSED TO ME AT THE KARAOKE PLACE... I REJECTED HIM, THOUGH.
GOIN' TO GET SMOKES WAS THEIR EXCUSE FOR GETTIN' US ON OUR OWN.
I CAN'T BELIEVE THEY CALLED IT YOUR WELCOME PARTY.
UGH, IT PISSES ME OFF.
...WHY DID IT END UP LIKE THAT? WE WERE HAVING SUCH FUN.
I HATE IT.
WHY DO THINGS HAVE TO BE LIKE THAT BETWEEN MEN AND WOMEN?
...DID HE DO ANYTHING TO YOU, RYO?
ARE YOU OKAY?

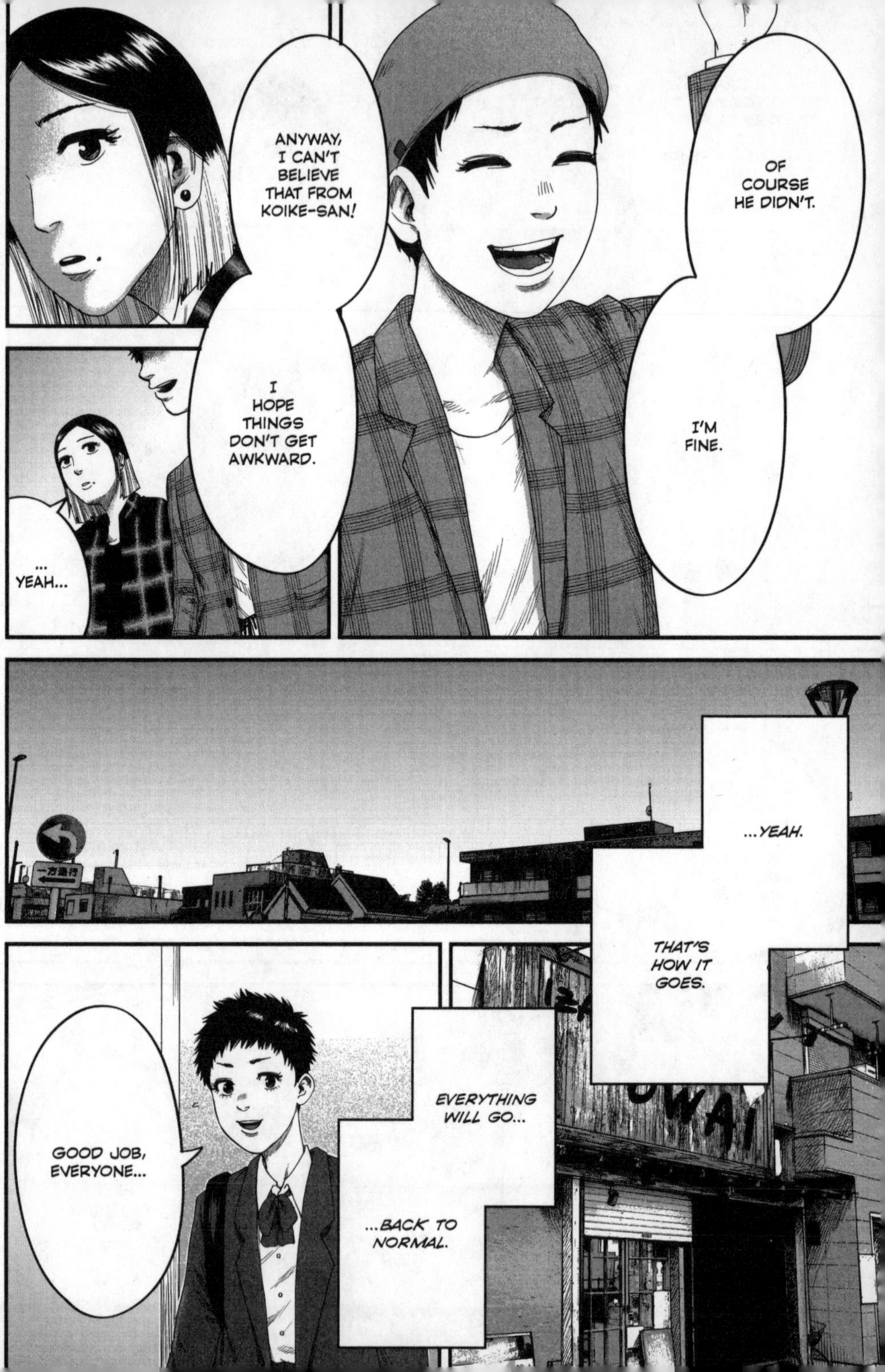
OF COURSE HE DIDN'T.
I'M FINE.
ANYWAY, I CAN'T BELIEVE THAT FROM KOIKE-SAN!
I HOPE THINGS DON'T GET AWKWARD.
... YEAH...
...YEAH.
THAT'S HOW IT GOES.
EVERYTHING WILL GO...
...BACK TO NORMAL.
GOOD JOB, EVERYONE...

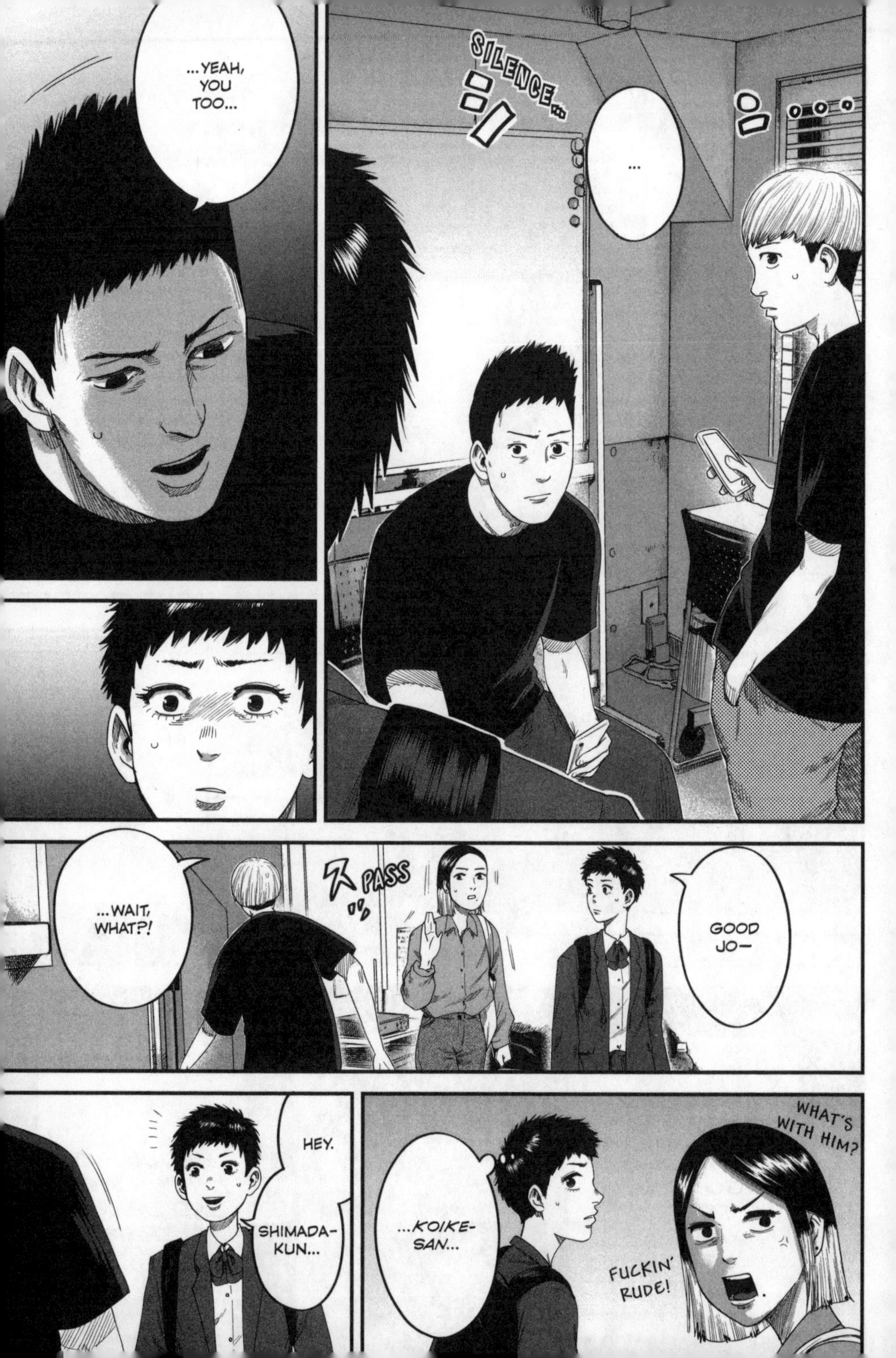
SILENCE...
...
...YEAH, YOU TOO...
GOOD JO—
PASS
...WAIT, WHAT?!
WHAT'S WITH HIM?
...KOIKE-SAN...
FUCKIN' RUDE!
HEY.
SHIMADA-KUN...

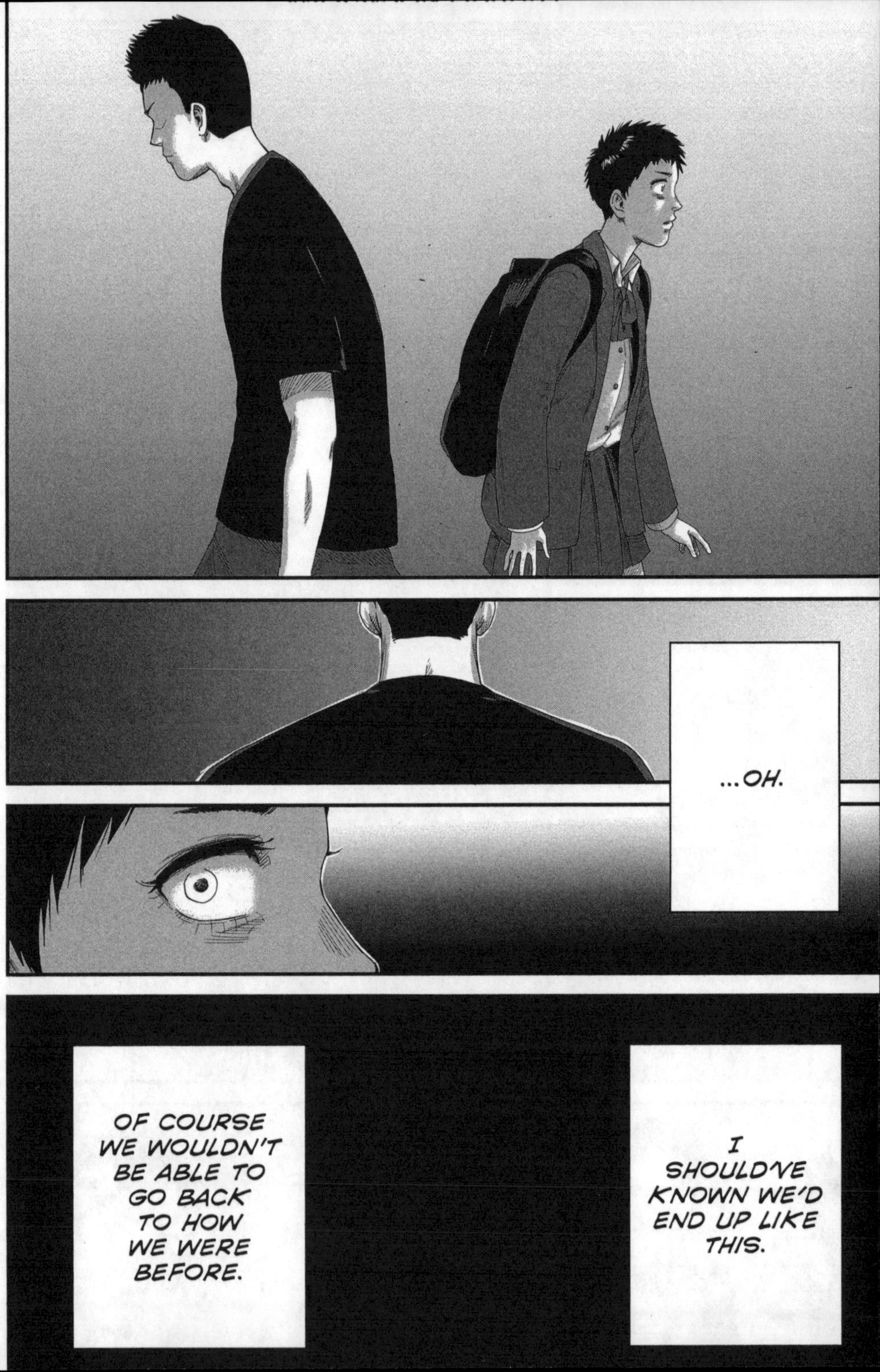
...OH.
I SHOULD'VE KNOWN WE'D END UP LIKE THIS.
OF COURSE WE WOULDN'T BE ABLE TO GO BACK TO HOW WE WERE BEFORE.

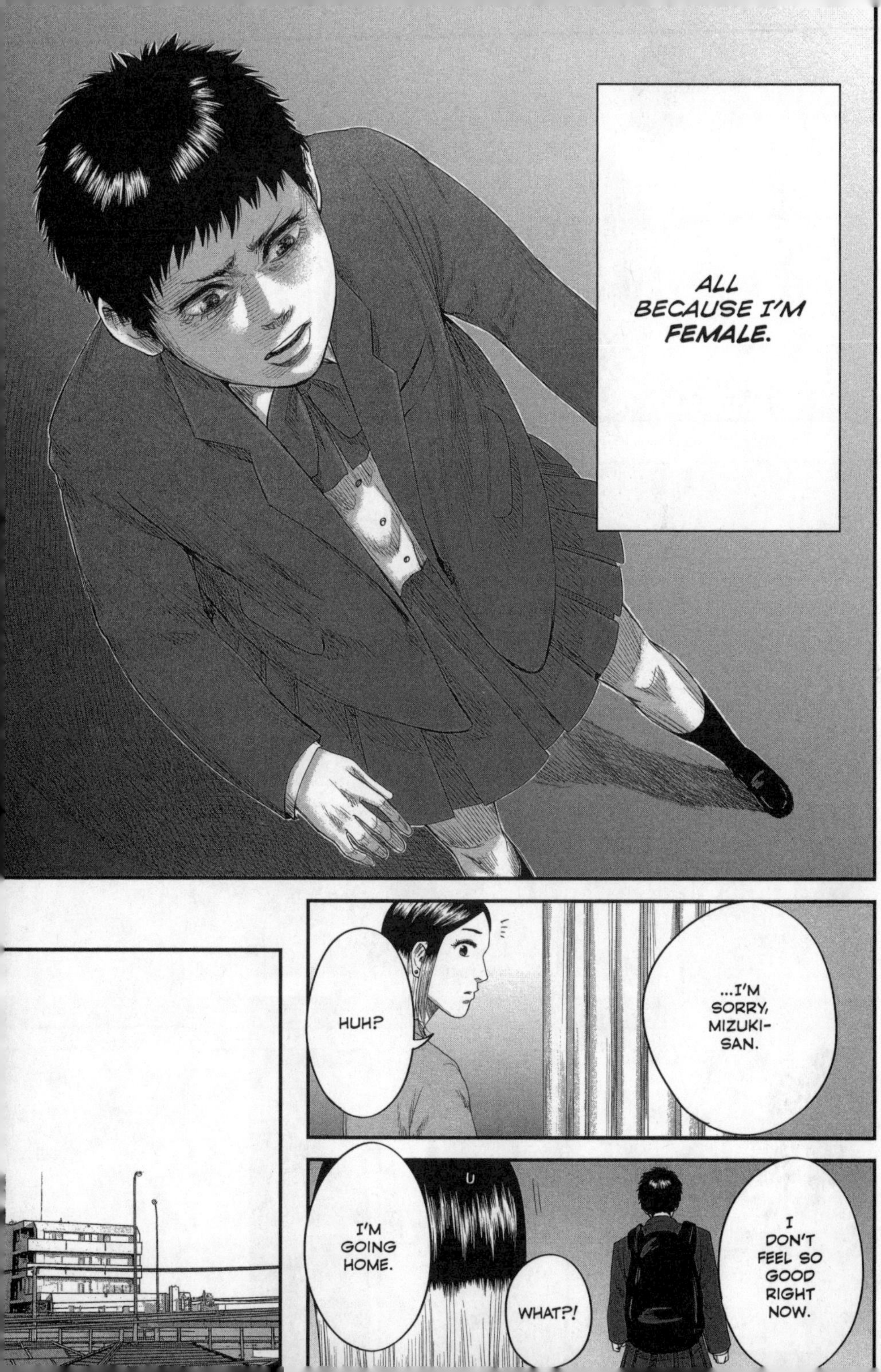

ALL BECAUSE I'M FEMALE.
...I'M SORRY, MIZUKI-SAN.
HUH?
I DON'T FEEL SO GOOD RIGHT NOW.
I'M GOING HOME.
WHAT?!

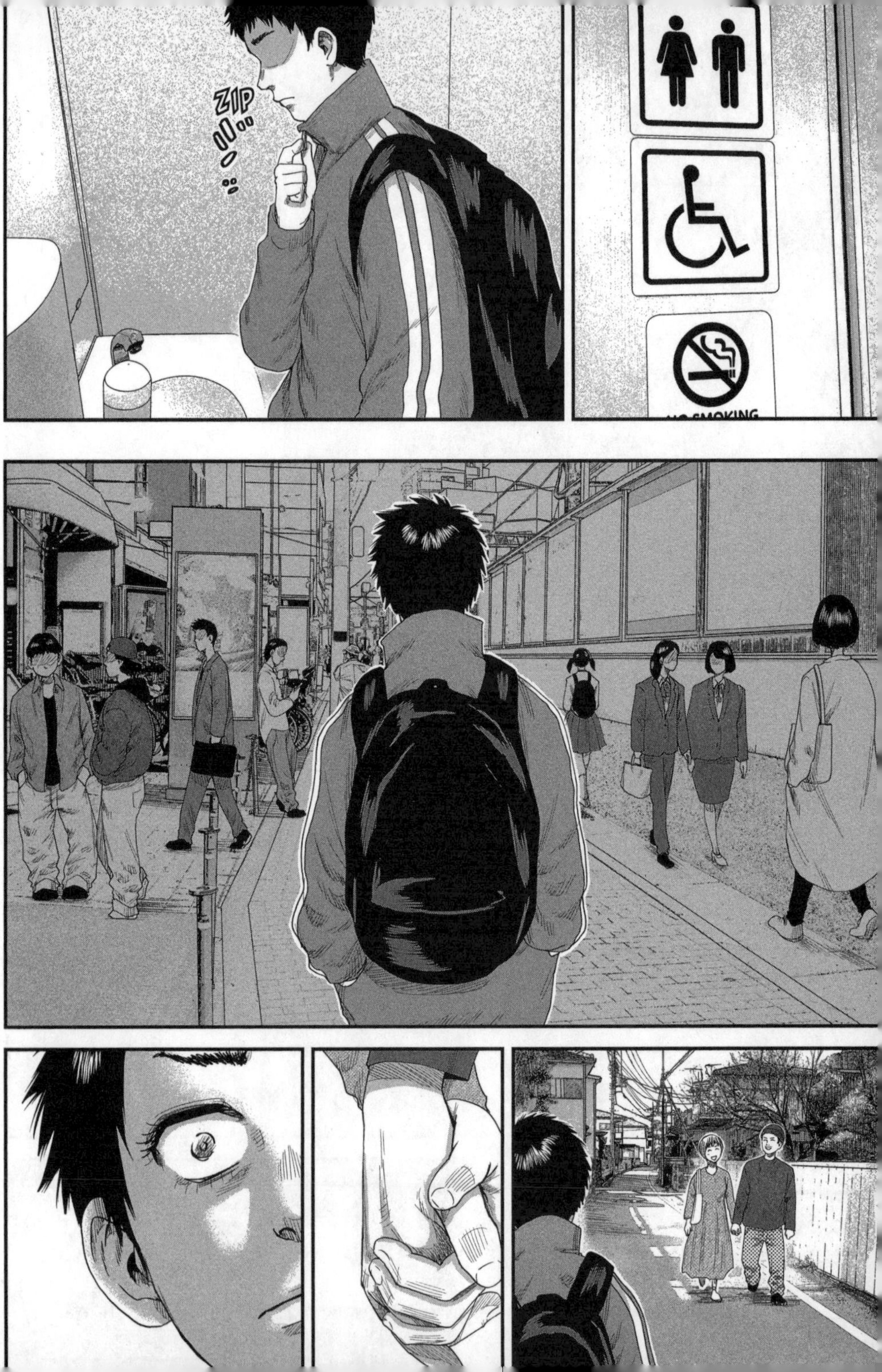
ZIP

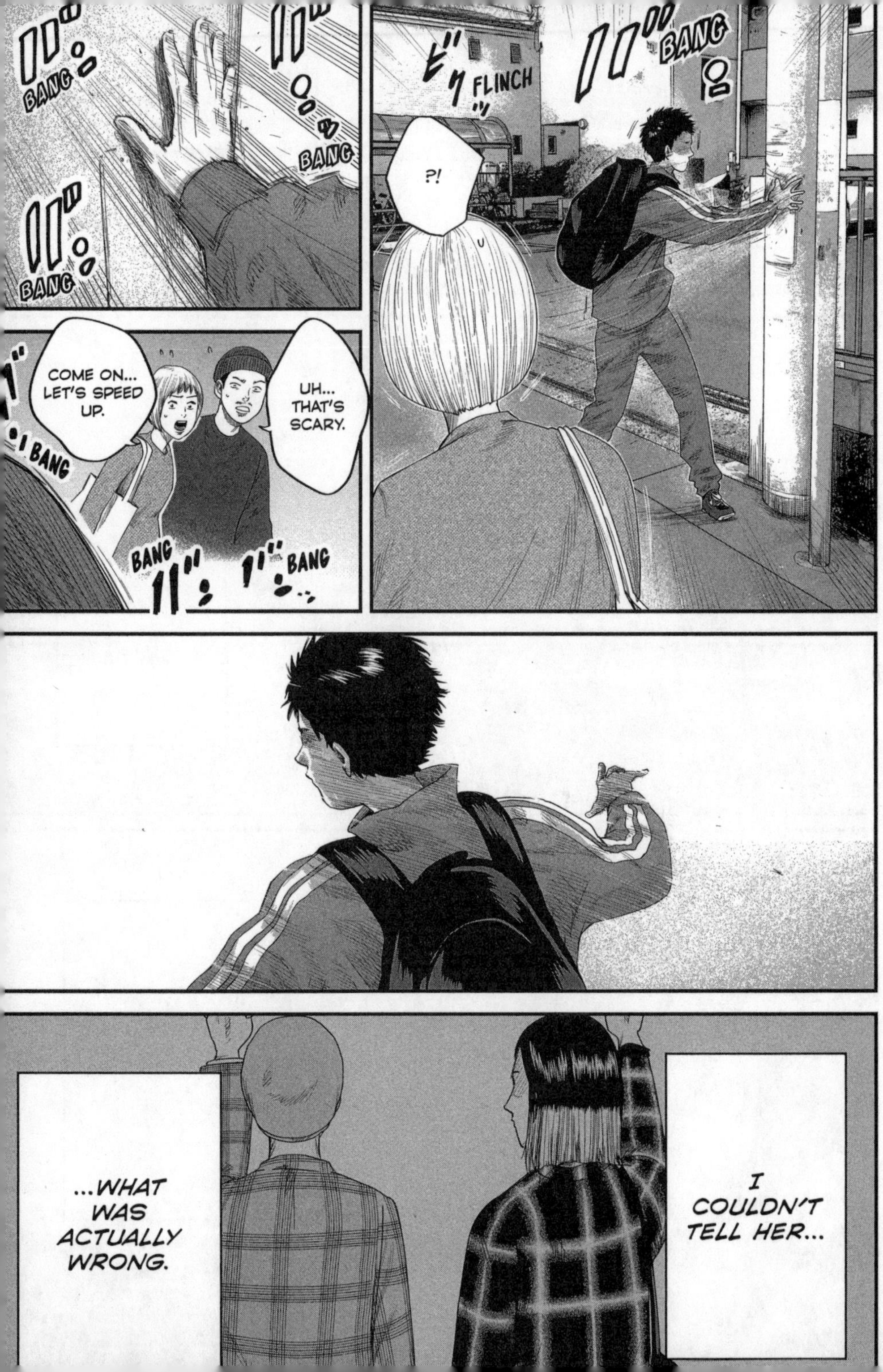
BANG
FLINCH
?!
BANG
BANG
BANG
UH... THAT'S SCARY.
COME ON... LET'S SPEED UP.
BANG
BANG
BANG
I COULDN'T TELL HER...
...WHAT WAS ACTUALLY WRONG.

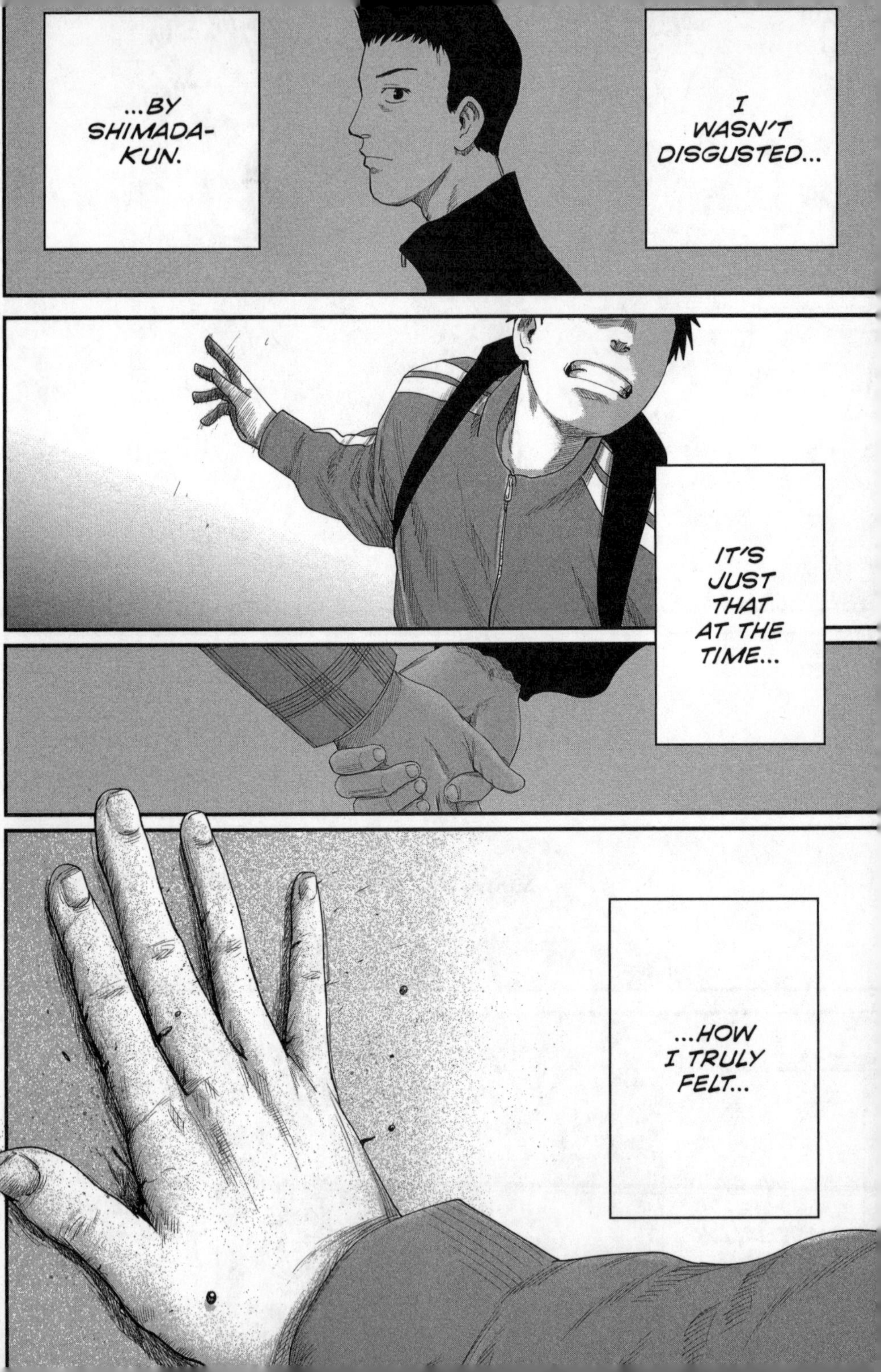
I WASN'T DISGUSTED...
...BY SHIMADA-KUN.
IT'S JUST THAT AT THE TIME...
...HOW I TRULY FELT...

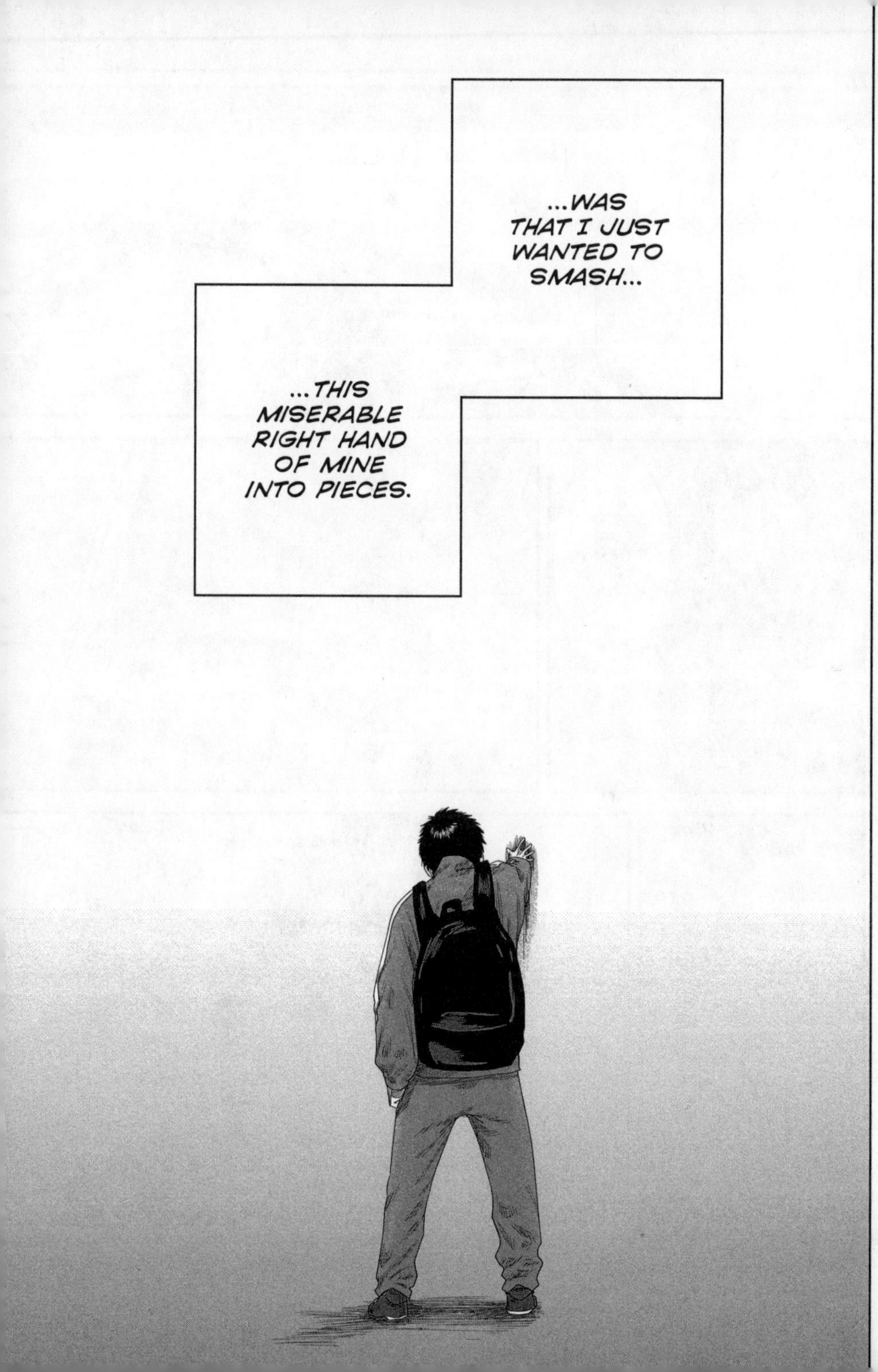
...WAS THAT I JUST WANTED TO SMASH...
...THIS MISERABLE RIGHT HAND OF MINE INTO PIECES.

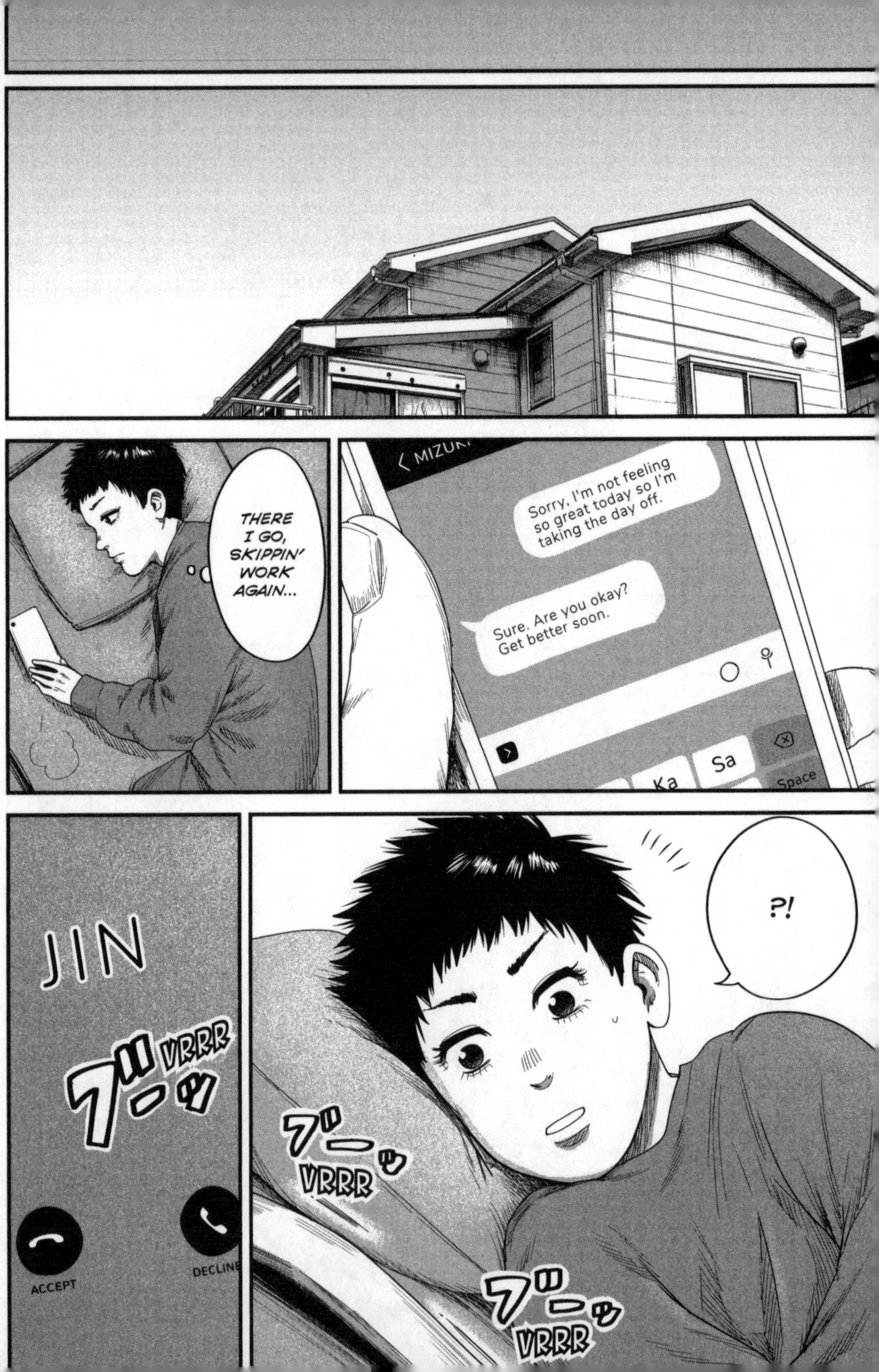
Sorry, I'm not feeling so great today so I'm taking the day off.
Sure. Are you okay? Get better soon.
Ka
Sa
Space
THERE I GO, SKIPPIN' WORK AGAIN...
?!
ブーッ VRRR
ブーッ VRRR
JIN
ブーッ VRRR
ACCEPT
DECLINE

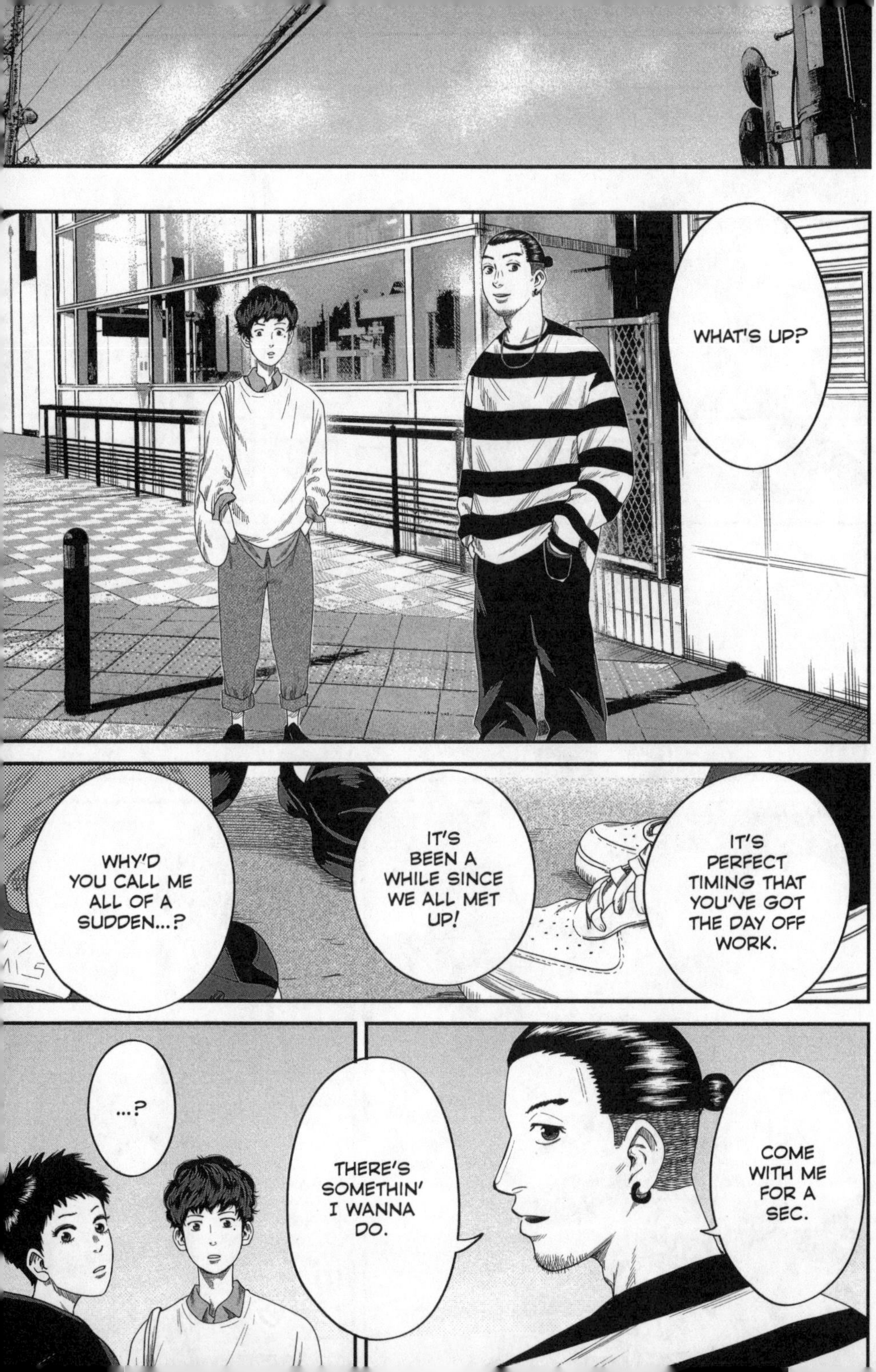
WHAT'S UP?
IT'S PERFECT TIMING THAT YOU'VE GOT THE DAY OFF WORK.
IT'S BEEN A WHILE SINCE WE ALL MET UP!
WHY'D YOU CALL ME ALL OF A SUDDEN...?
COME WITH ME FOR A SEC.
THERE'S SOMETHIN' I WANNA DO.
...?

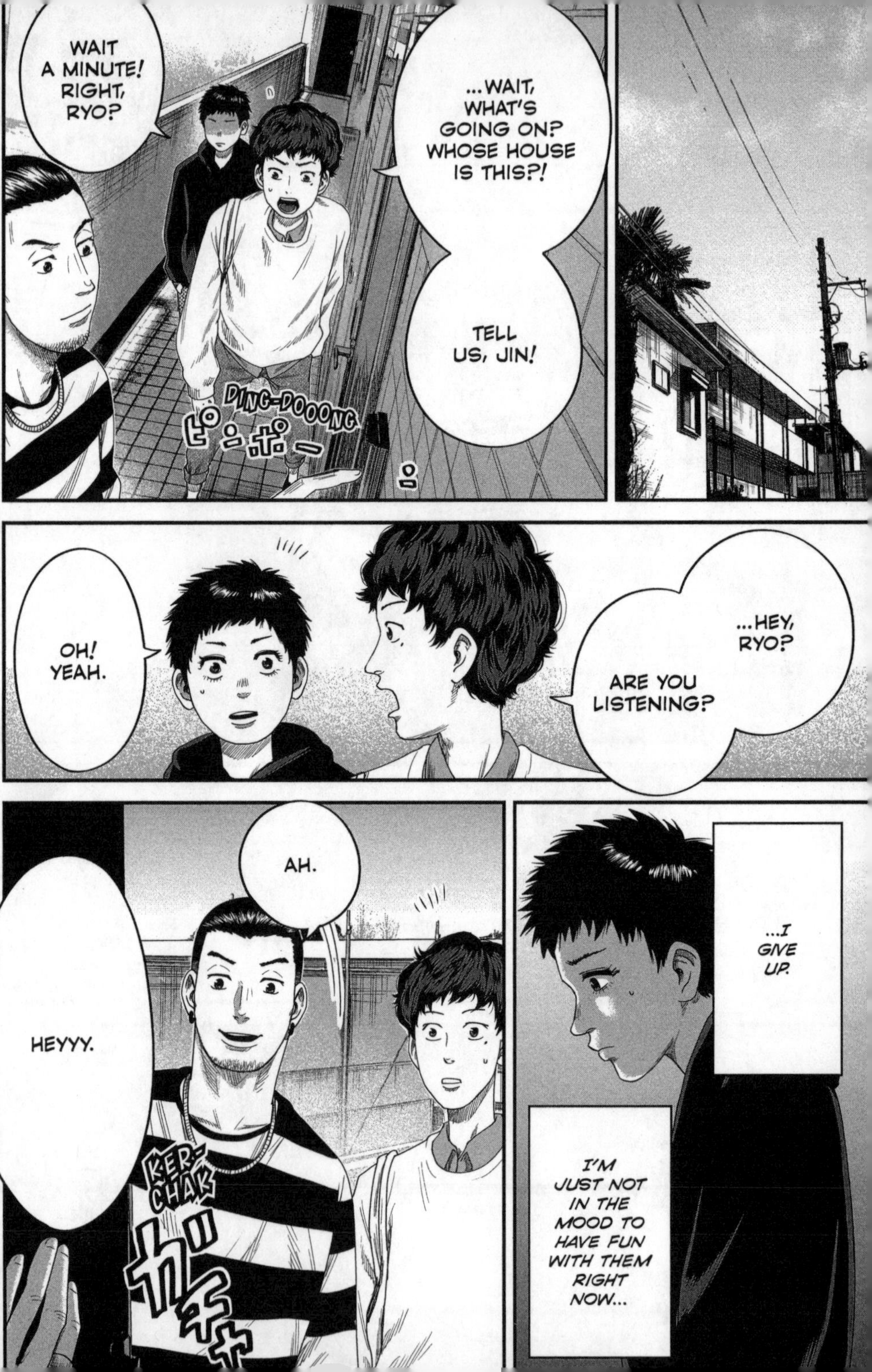
...WAIT, WHAT'S GOING ON? WHOSE HOUSE IS THIS?!
TELL US, JIN!
WAIT A MINUTE! RIGHT, RYO?
DING-DOOONG
...HEY, RYO?
ARE YOU LISTENING?
OH! YEAH.
...I GIVE UP.
I'M JUST NOT IN THE MOOD TO HAVE FUN WITH THEM RIGHT NOW...
AH.
HEYYY.
KER-CHAK

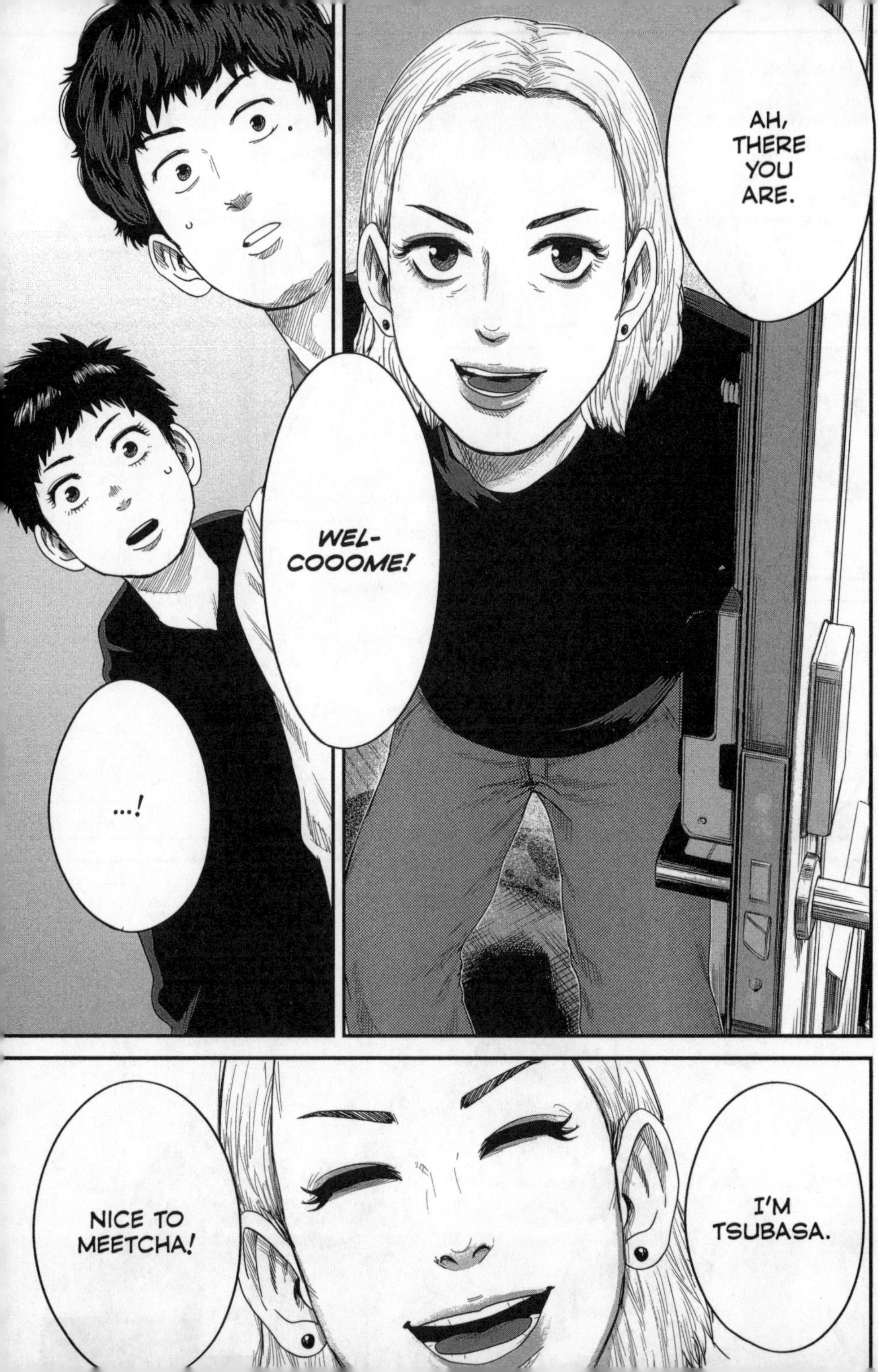
AH, THERE YOU ARE.
WEL-COOOME!
...!
I'M TSUBASA.
NICE TO MEETCHA!

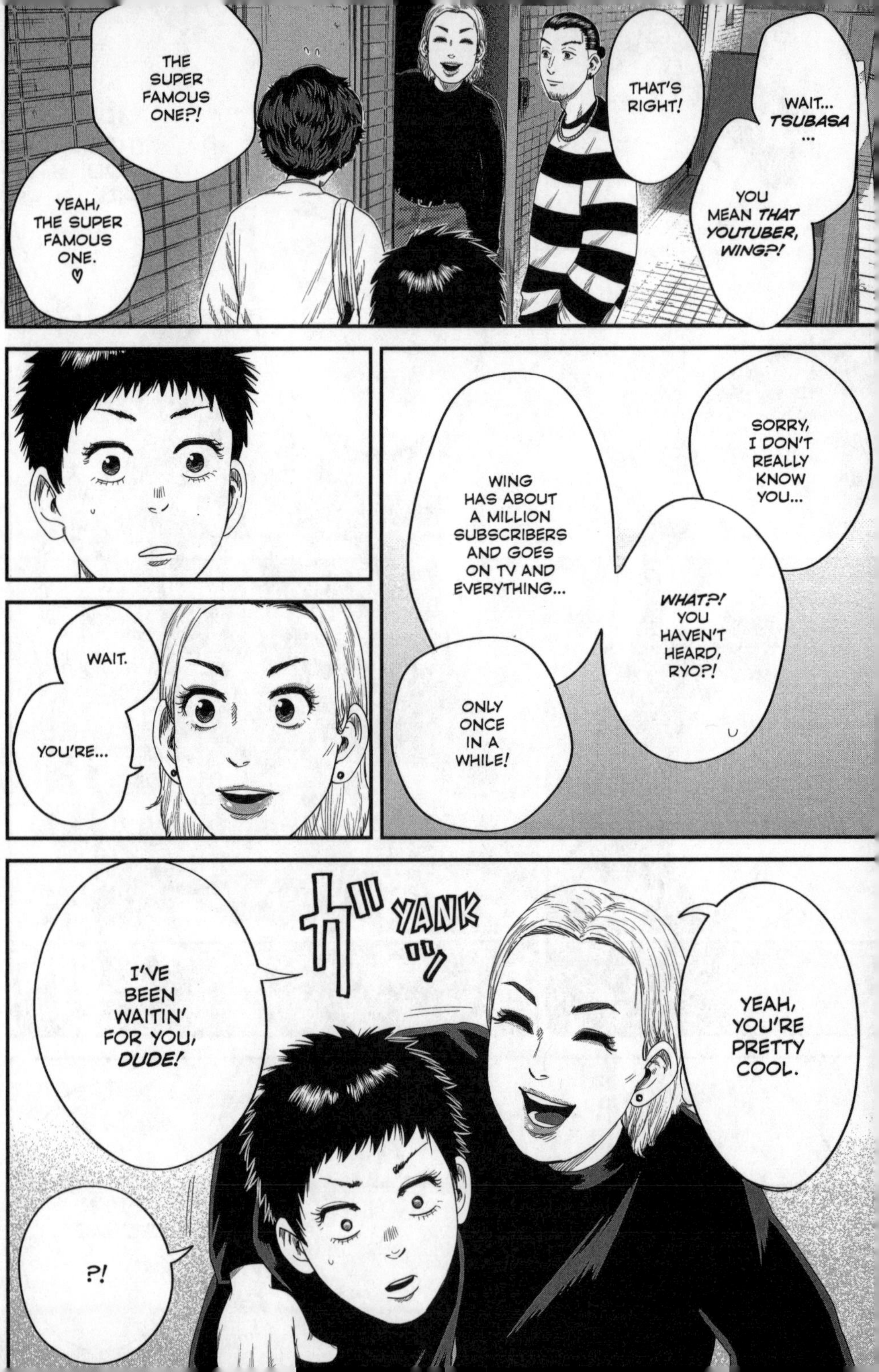
WAIT... TSUBASA ...
YOU MEAN THAT YOUTUBER, WING?!
THAT'S RIGHT!
THE SUPER FAMOUS ONE?!
YEAH, THE SUPER FAMOUS ONE. ♡
SORRY, I DON'T REALLY KNOW YOU...
WING HAS ABOUT A MILLION SUBSCRIBERS AND GOES ON TV AND EVERYTHING...
WHAT?! YOU HAVEN'T HEARD, RYO?!
ONLY ONCE IN A WHILE!
WAIT.
YOU'RE...
YEAH, YOU'RE PRETTY COOL.
YANK
I'VE BEEN WAITIN' FOR YOU, DUDE!
?!

Chap. 14 Tough

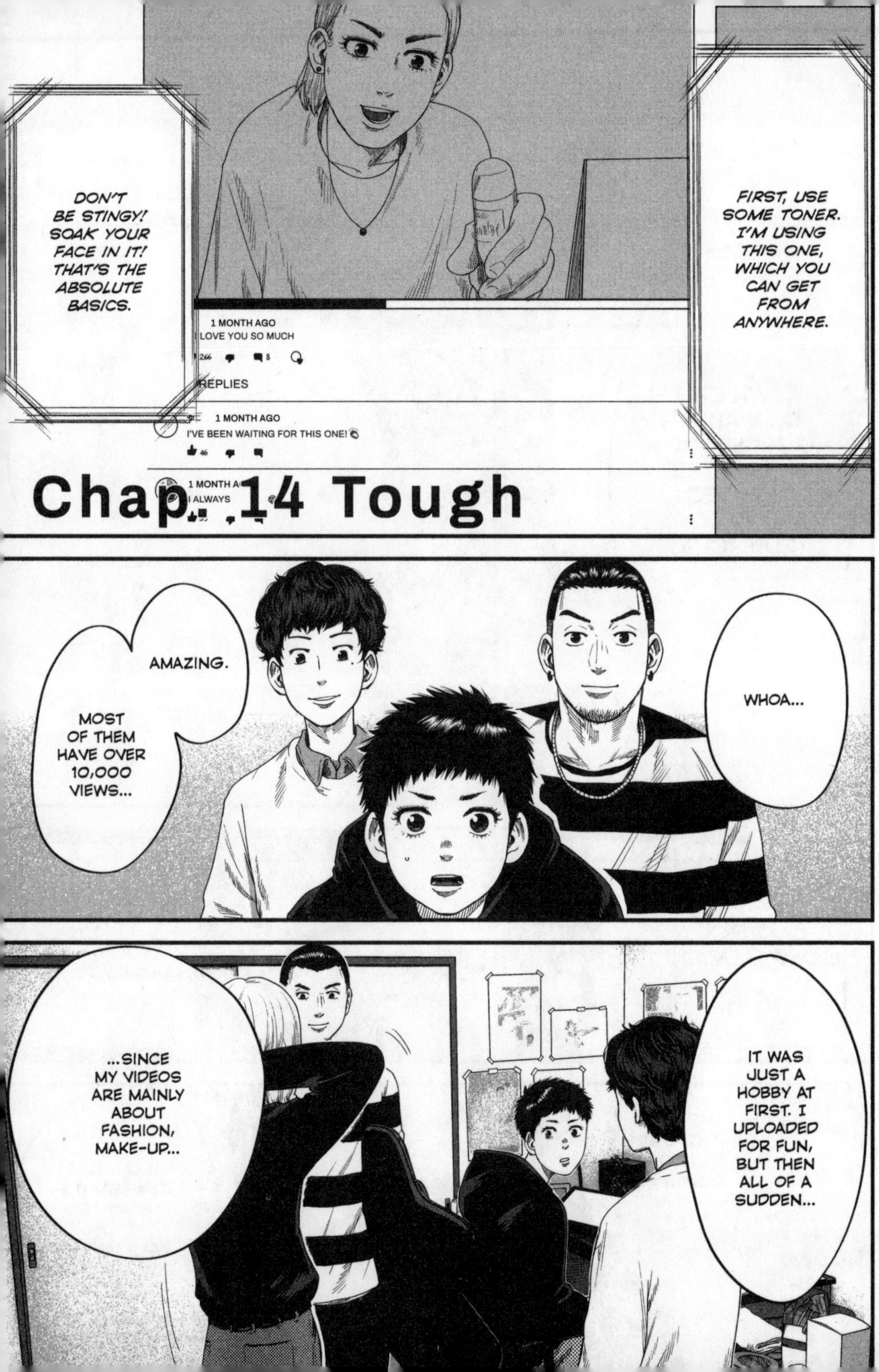
FIRST, USE SOME TONER. I'M USING THIS ONE, WHICH YOU CAN GET FROM ANYWHERE.
DON'T BE STINGY! SOAK YOUR FACE IN IT! THAT'S THE ABSOLUTE BASICS.
1 MONTH AGO
LOVE YOU SO MUCH
266 8
REPLIES
1 MONTH AGO
I'VE BEEN WAITING FOR THIS ONE!
46
1 MONTH A
I ALWAYS
WHOA...
AMAZING.
MOST OF THEM HAVE OVER 10,000 VIEWS...
IT WAS JUST A HOBBY AT FIRST. I UPLOADED FOR FUN, BUT THEN ALL OF A SUDDEN...
...SINCE MY VIDEOS ARE MAINLY ABOUT FASHION, MAKE-UP...

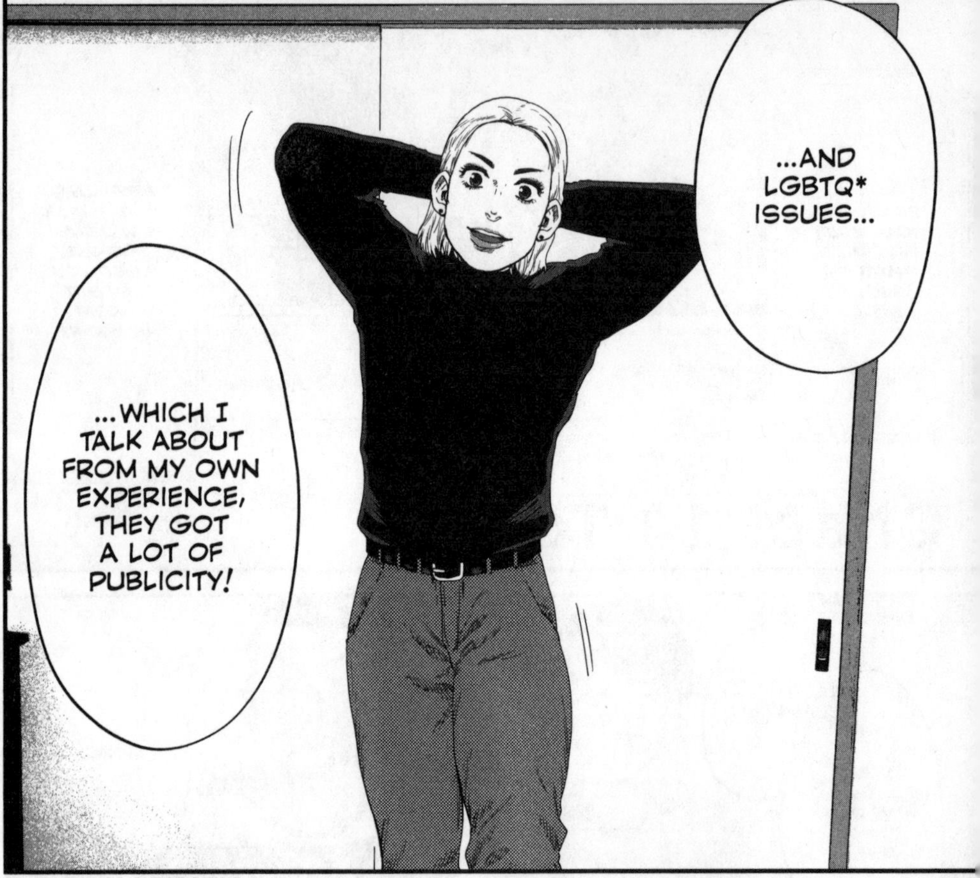
...AND LGBTQ* ISSUES...
...WHICH I TALK ABOUT FROM MY OWN EXPERIENCE, THEY GOT A LOT OF PUBLICITY!

*Q = QUEER OR QUESTIONING

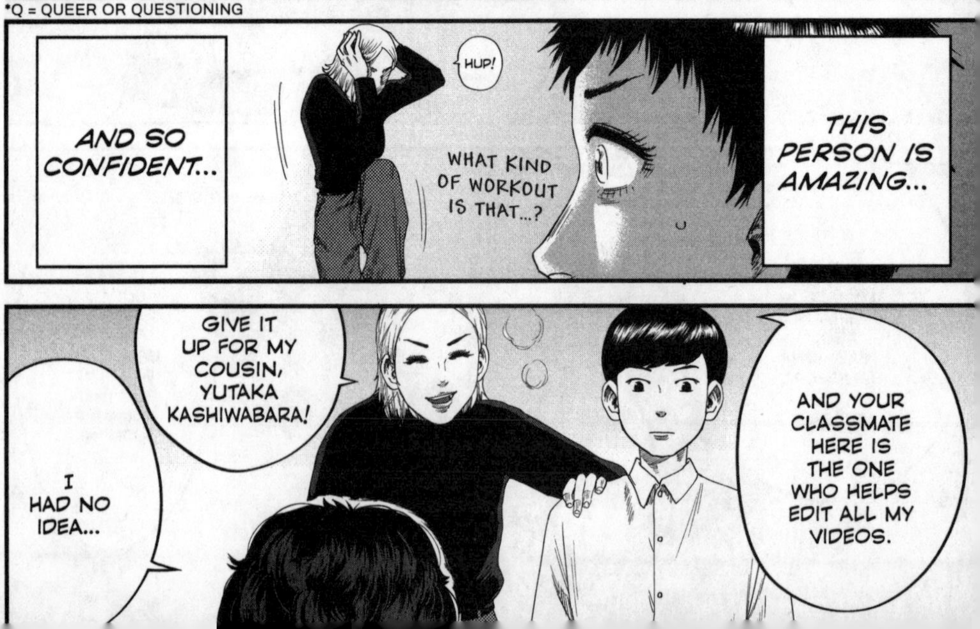
THIS PERSON IS AMAZING...
HUP!
WHAT KIND OF WORKOUT IS THAT...?
AND SO CONFIDENT...
GIVE IT UP FOR MY COUSIN, YUTAKA KASHIWABARA!
AND YOUR CLASSMATE HERE IS THE ONE WHO HELPS EDIT ALL MY VIDEOS.
I HAD NO IDEA...

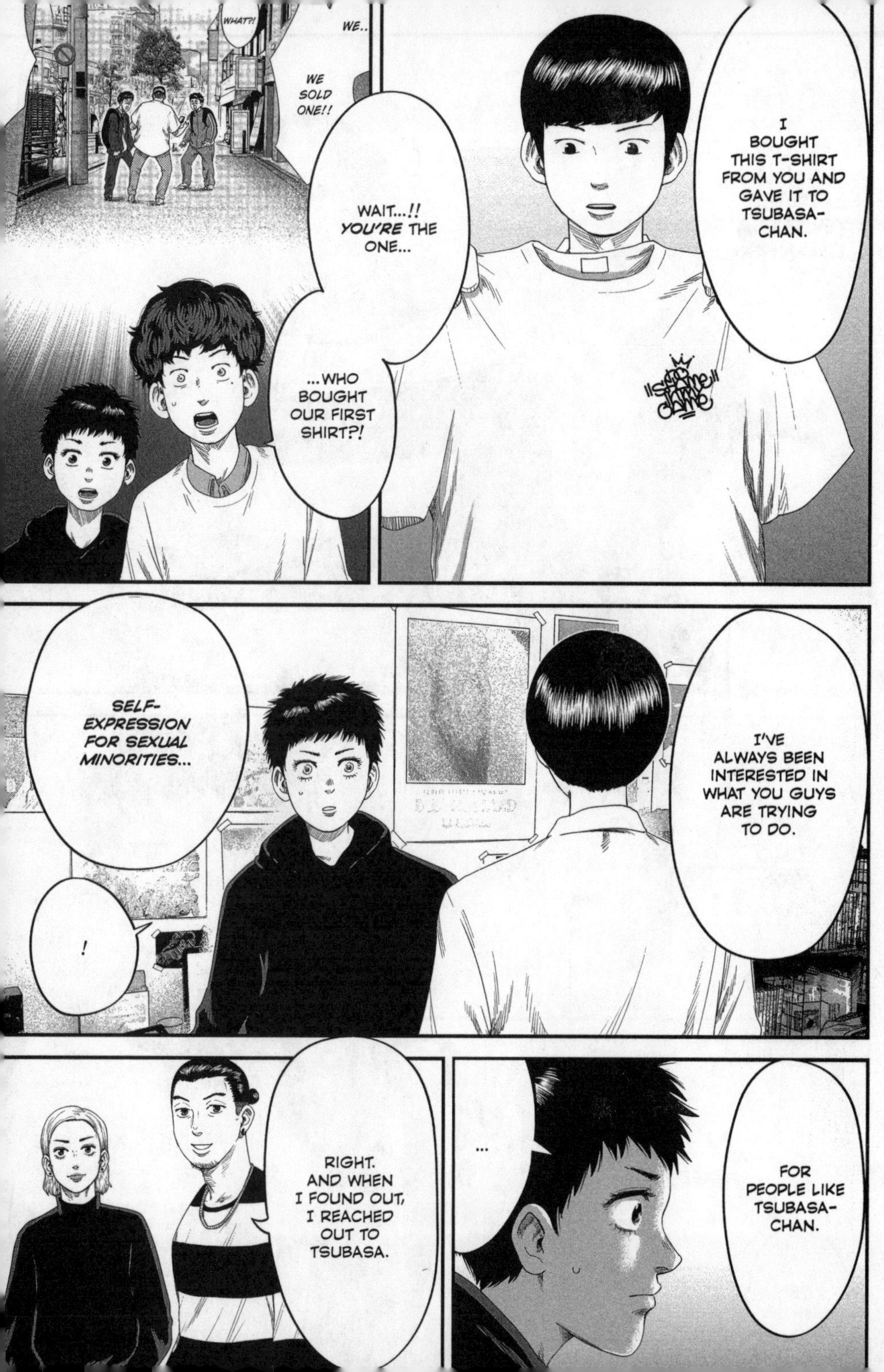
I BOUGHT THIS T-SHIRT FROM YOU AND GAVE IT TO TSUBASA-CHAN.
WE..
WHAT?!
WE SOLD ONE!!
WAIT...!! *YOU'RE* THE ONE...
...WHO BOUGHT OUR FIRST SHIRT?!
I'VE ALWAYS BEEN INTERESTED IN WHAT YOU GUYS ARE TRYING TO DO.
SELF-EXPRESSION FOR SEXUAL MINORITIES...
!
FOR PEOPLE LIKE TSUBASA-CHAN.
...
RIGHT. AND WHEN I FOUND OUT, I REACHED OUT TO TSUBASA.

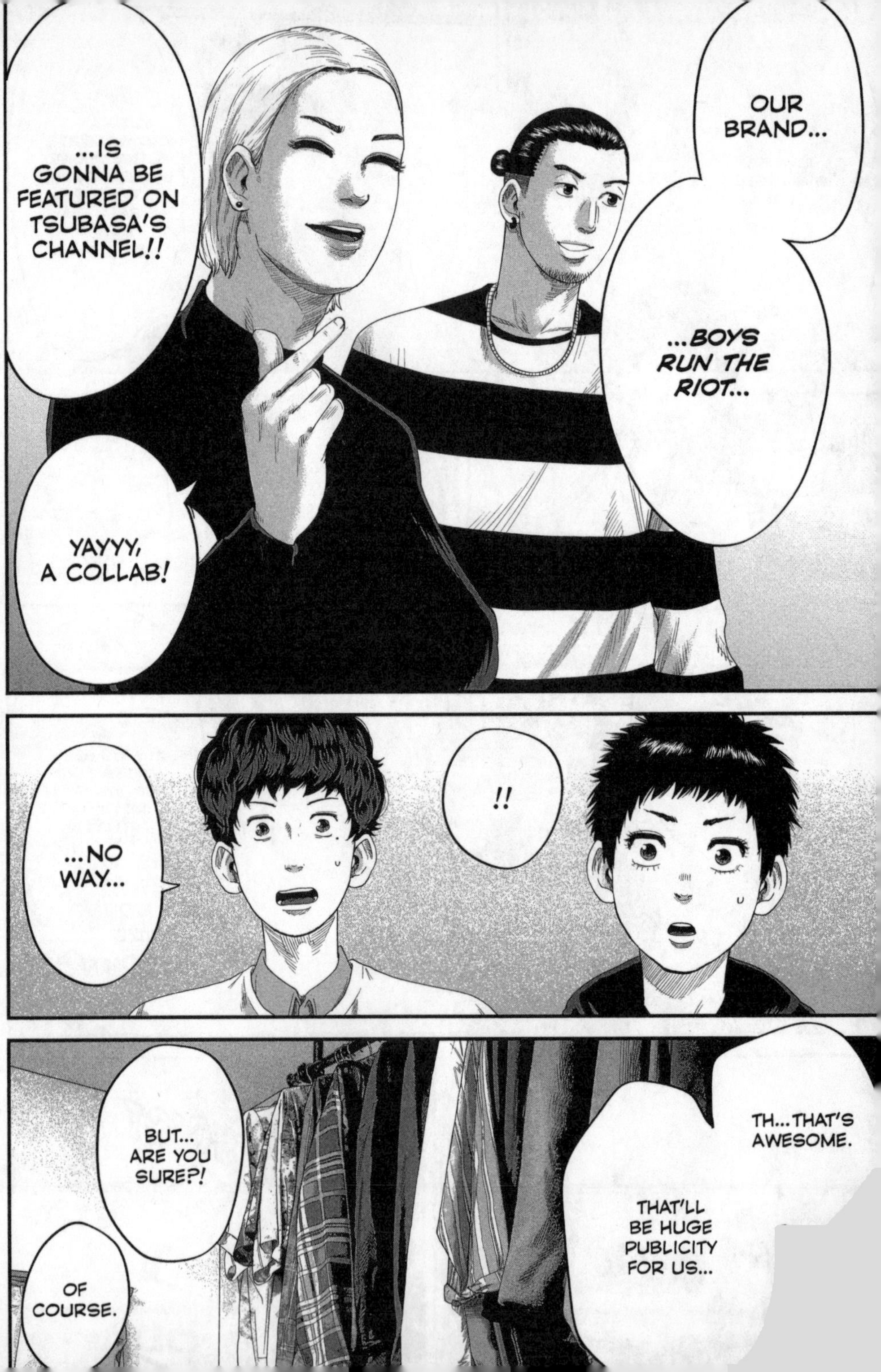
OUR BRAND...
...BOYS RUN THE RIOT...
...IS GONNA BE FEATURED ON TSUBASA'S CHANNEL!!
YAYYY, A COLLAB!
!!
...NO WAY...
TH...THAT'S AWESOME.
THAT'LL BE HUGE PUBLICITY FOR US...
BUT... ARE YOU SURE?!
OF COURSE.

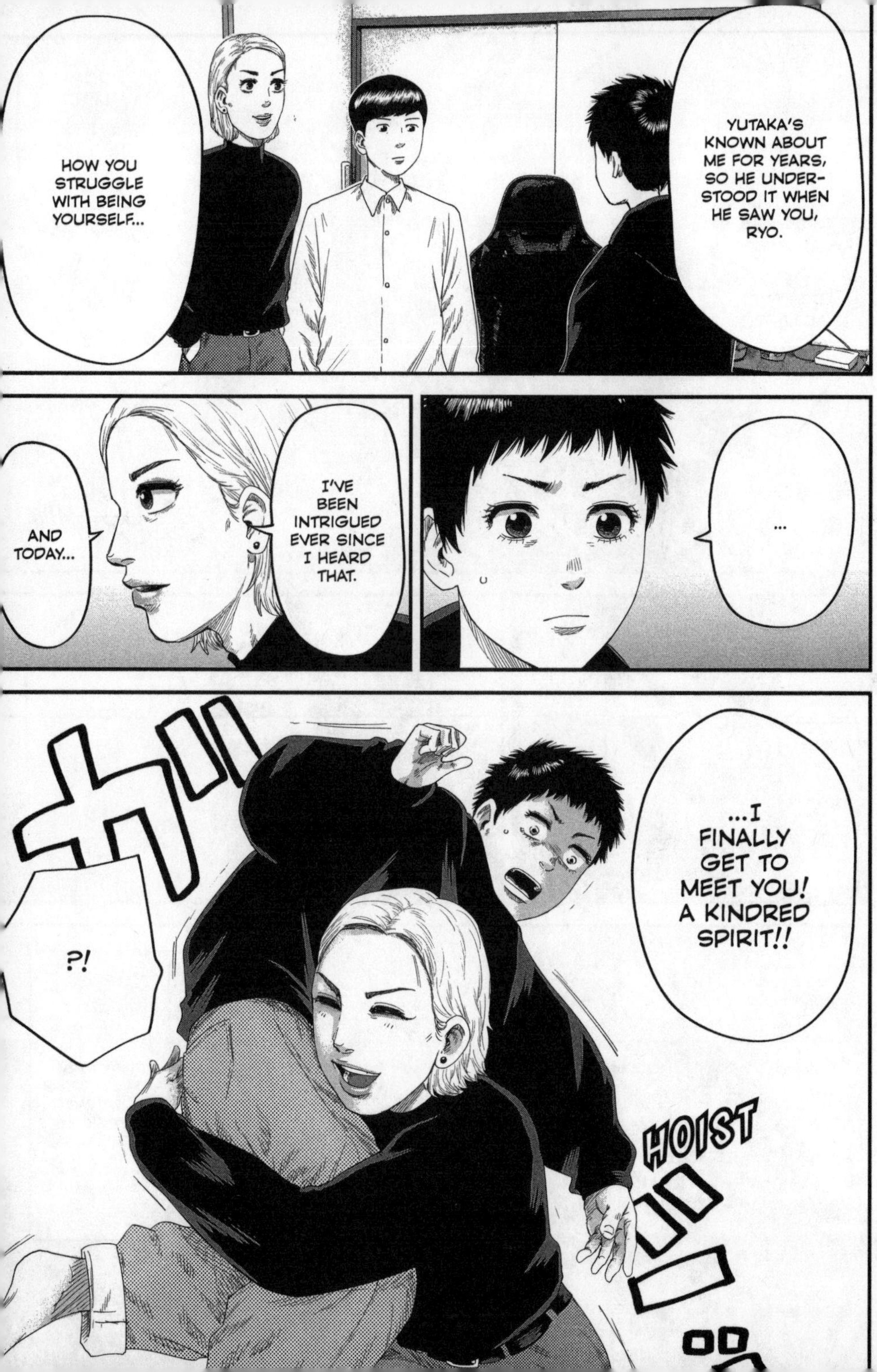
YUTAKA'S KNOWN ABOUT ME FOR YEARS, SO HE UNDER-STOOD IT WHEN HE SAW YOU, RYO.
HOW YOU STRUGGLE WITH BEING YOURSELF...
...
I'VE BEEN INTRIGUED EVER SINCE I HEARD THAT.
AND TODAY...
...I FINALLY GET TO MEET YOU! A KINDRED SPIRIT!!
?!
HOIST

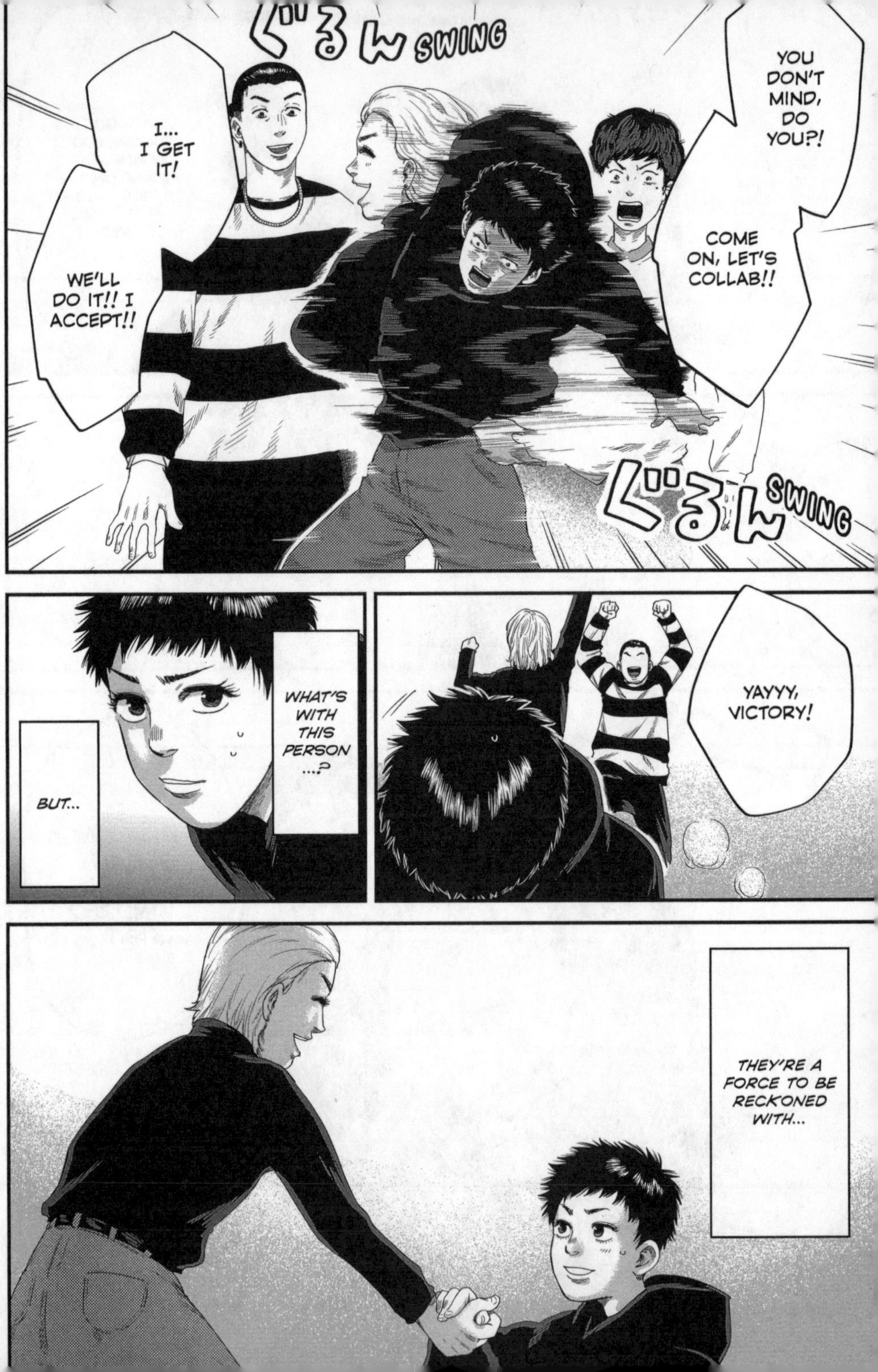
YOU DON'T MIND, DO YOU?!
COME ON, LET'S COLLAB!!
ぐるん SWING
I... I GET IT!
WE'LL DO IT!! I ACCEPT!!
ぐるん SWING
YAYYY, VICTORY!
WHAT'S WITH THIS PERSON ...?
BUT...
THEY'RE A FORCE TO BE RECKONED WITH...

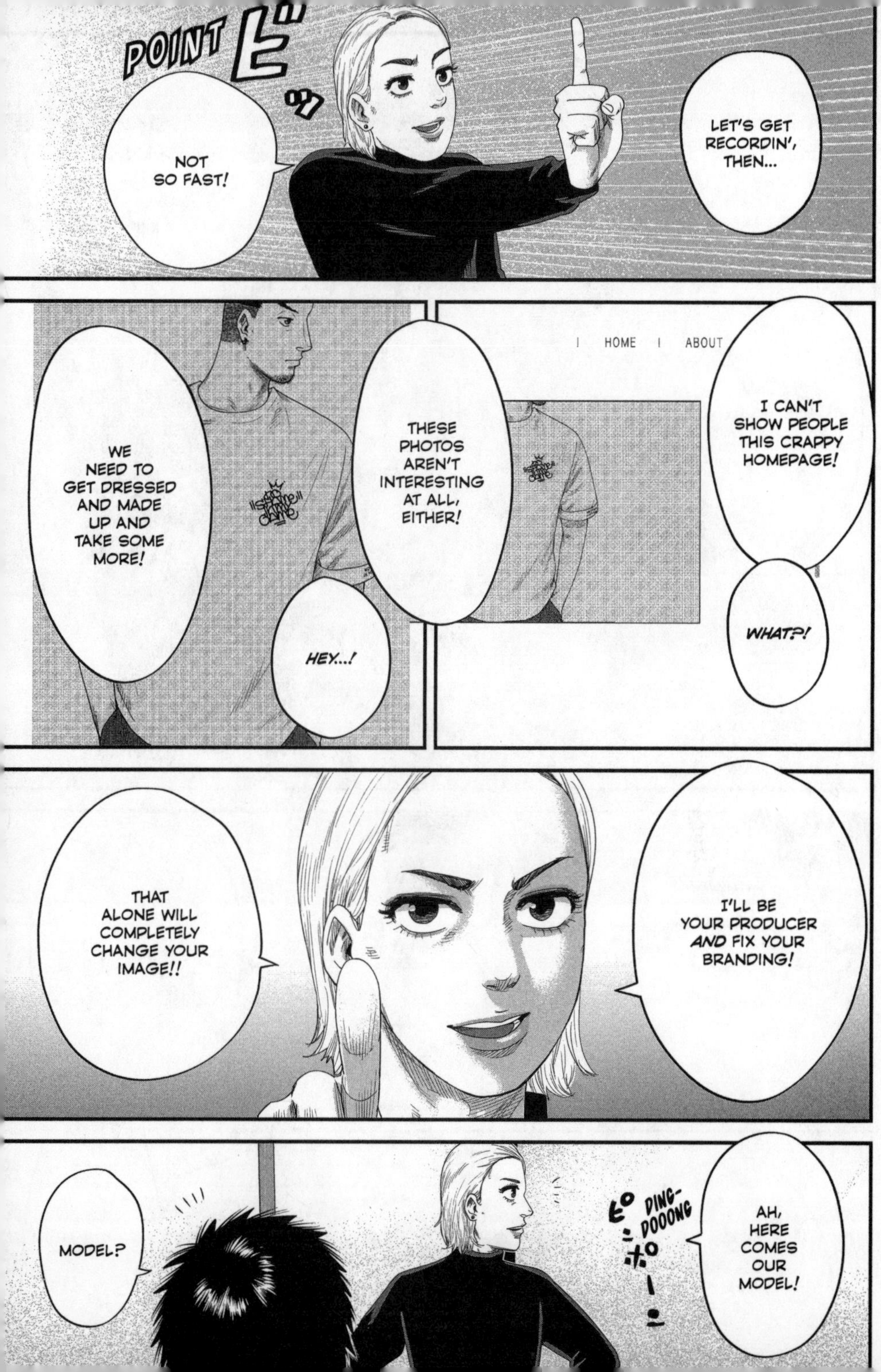
LET'S GET RECORDIN', THEN...
POINT
NOT SO FAST!
I HOME I ABOUT
I CAN'T SHOW PEOPLE THIS CRAPPY HOMEPAGE!
WHAT?!
THESE PHOTOS AREN'T INTERESTING AT ALL, EITHER!
WE NEED TO GET DRESSED AND MADE UP AND TAKE SOME MORE!
HEY...!
I'LL BE YOUR PRODUCER *AND* FIX YOUR BRANDING!
THAT ALONE WILL COMPLETELY CHANGE YOUR IMAGE!!
DING-DOOONG
AH, HERE COMES OUR MODEL!
MODEL?

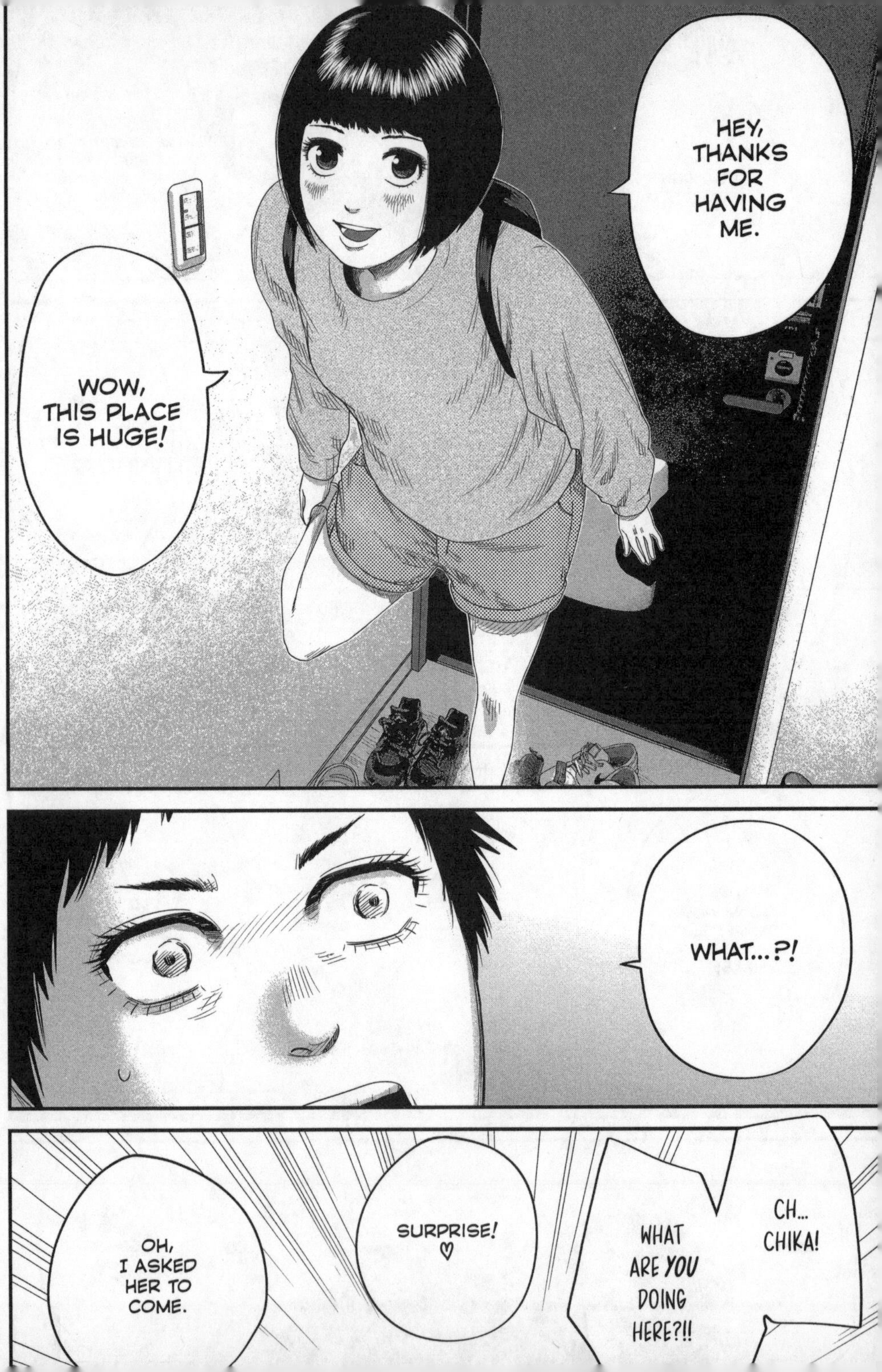
HEY, THANKS FOR HAVING ME.
WOW, THIS PLACE IS HUGE!
WHAT...?!
CH... CHIKA!
WHAT ARE *YOU* DOING HERE?!!
SURPRISE! ♡
OH, I ASKED HER TO COME.

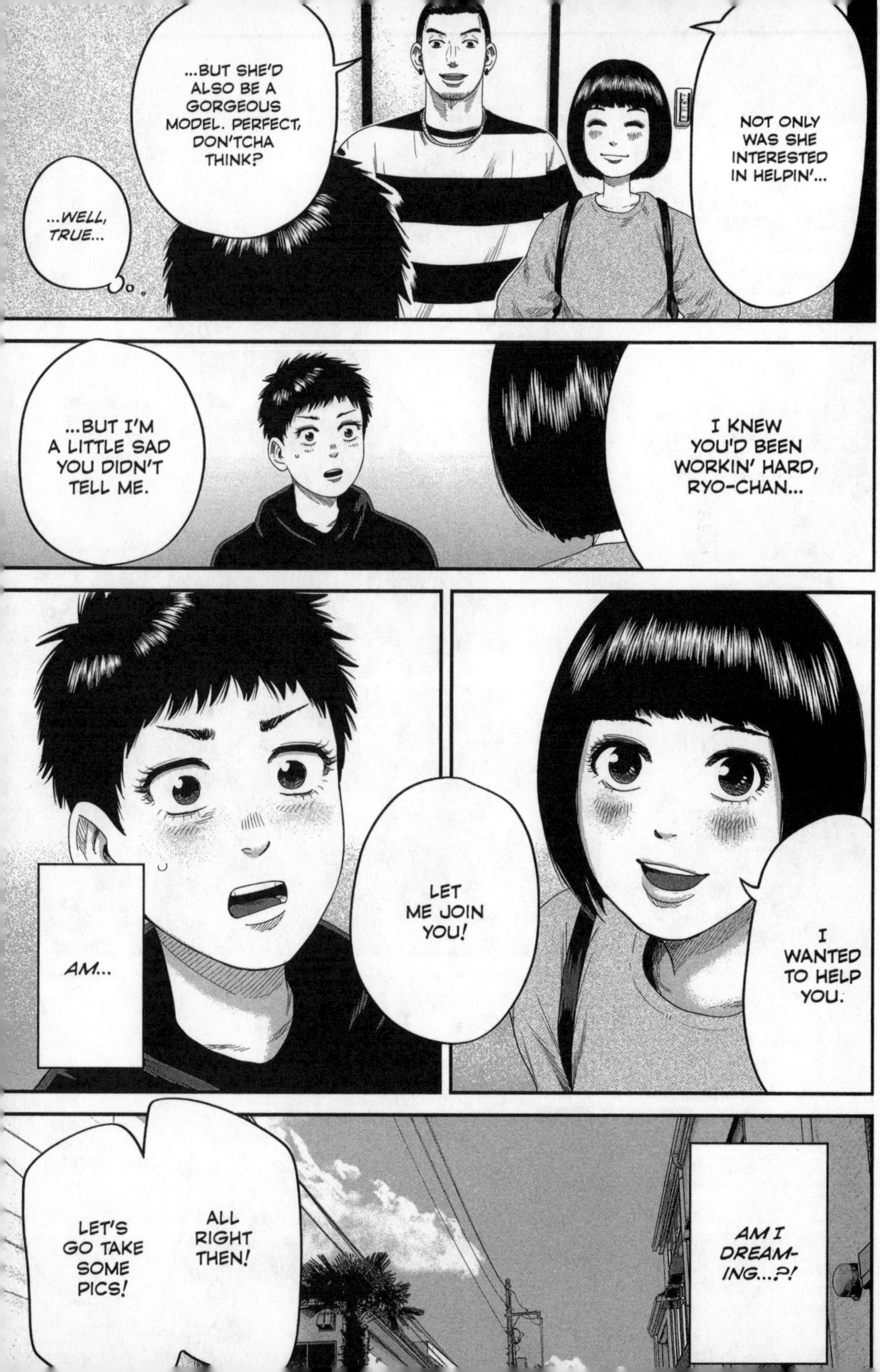
NOT ONLY WAS SHE INTERESTED IN HELPIN'...
...BUT SHE'D ALSO BE A GORGEOUS MODEL. PERFECT, DON'TCHA THINK?
...WELL, TRUE...
I KNEW YOU'D BEEN WORKIN' HARD, RYO-CHAN...
...BUT I'M A LITTLE SAD YOU DIDN'T TELL ME.
I WANTED TO HELP YOU.
LET ME JOIN YOU!
AM...
AM I DREAM-ING...?!
ALL RIGHT THEN!
LET'S GO TAKE SOME PICS!

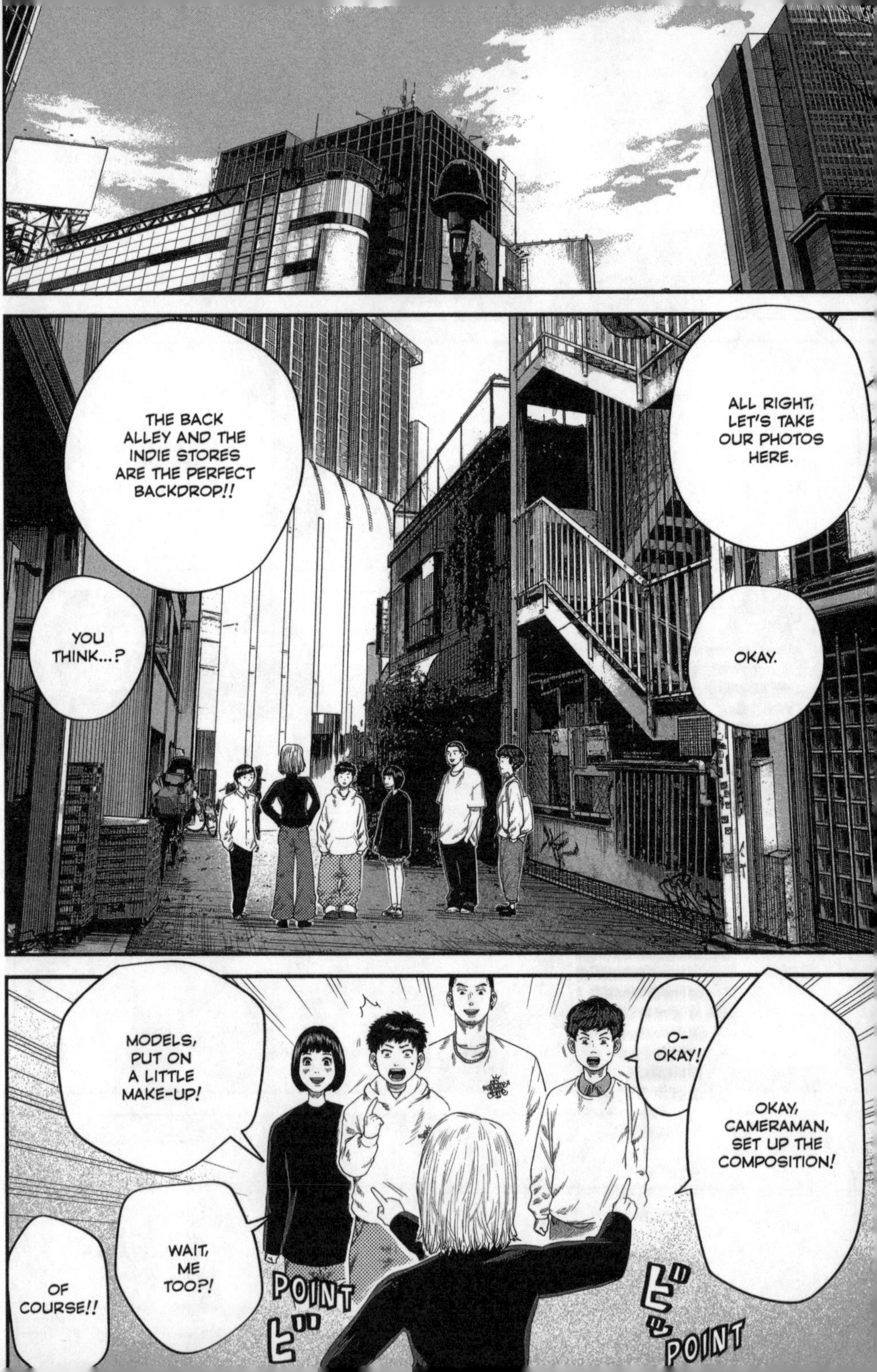
ALL RIGHT, LET'S TAKE OUR PHOTOS HERE.
THE BACK ALLEY AND THE INDIE STORES ARE THE PERFECT BACKDROP!!
OKAY.
YOU THINK...?
OKAY, CAMERAMAN, SET UP THE COMPOSITION!
O-OKAY!
MODELS, PUT ON A LITTLE MAKE-UP!
POINT
POINT
WAIT, ME TOO?!
OF COURSE!!

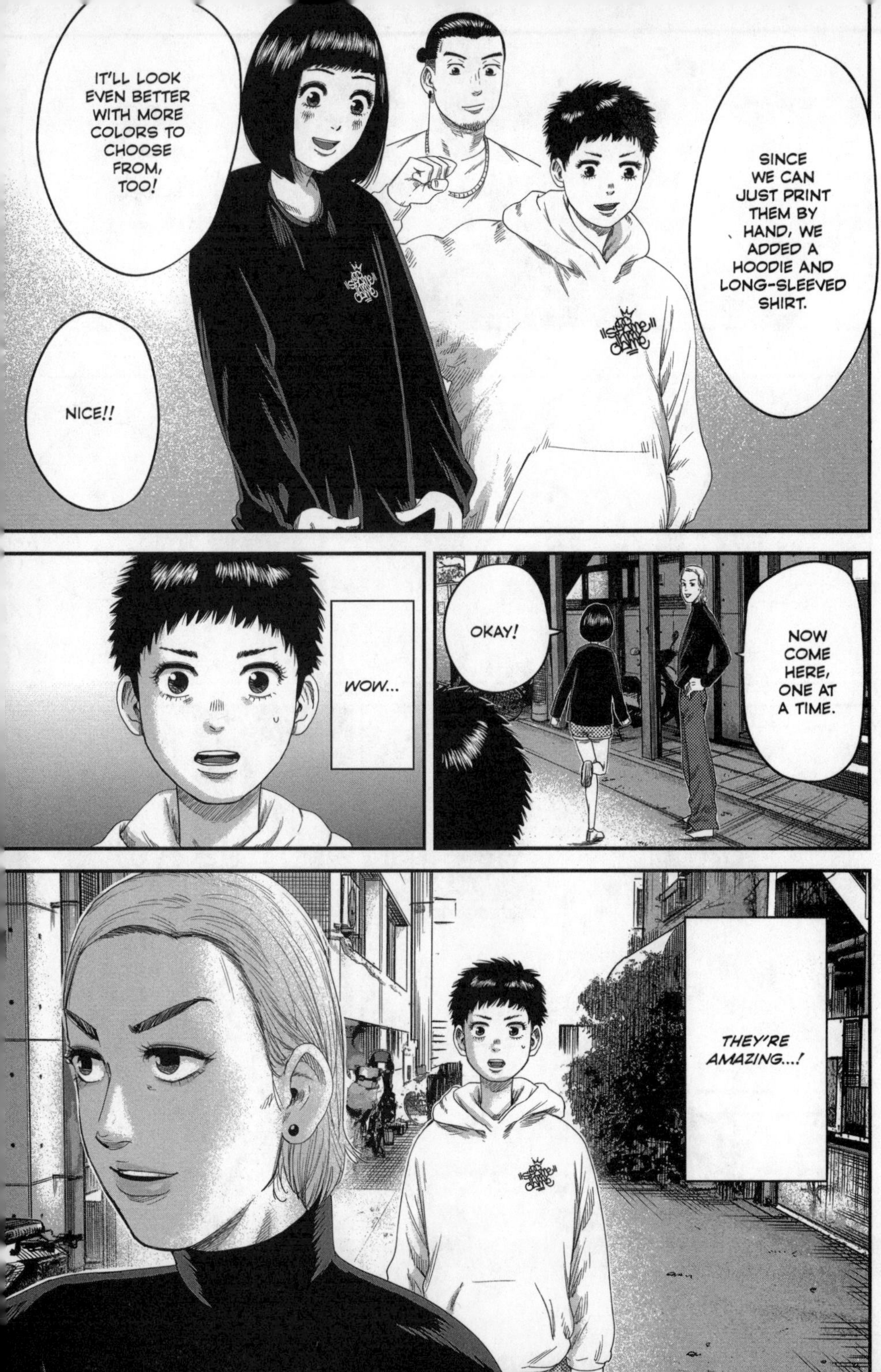
SINCE WE CAN JUST PRINT THEM BY HAND, WE ADDED A HOODIE AND LONG-SLEEVED SHIRT.
IT'LL LOOK EVEN BETTER WITH MORE COLORS TO CHOOSE FROM, TOO!
NICE!!
NOW COME HERE, ONE AT A TIME.
OKAY!
WOW...
THEY'RE AMAZING...!

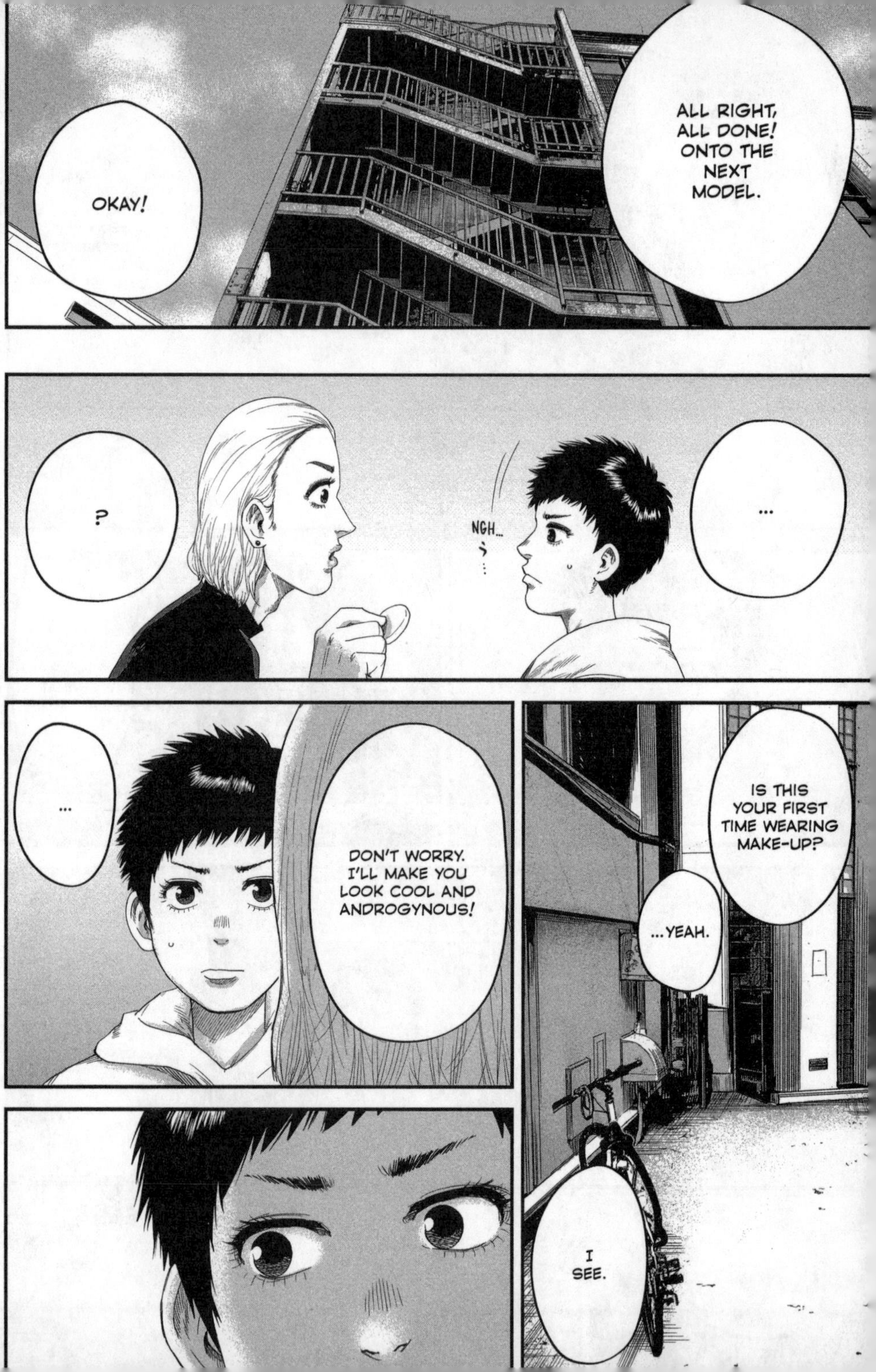
ALL RIGHT, ALL DONE! ONTO THE NEXT MODEL.
OKAY!
...
NGH...
?
IS THIS YOUR FIRST TIME WEARING MAKE-UP?
...YEAH.
I SEE.
DON'T WORRY. I'LL MAKE YOU LOOK COOL AND ANDROGYNOUS!
...

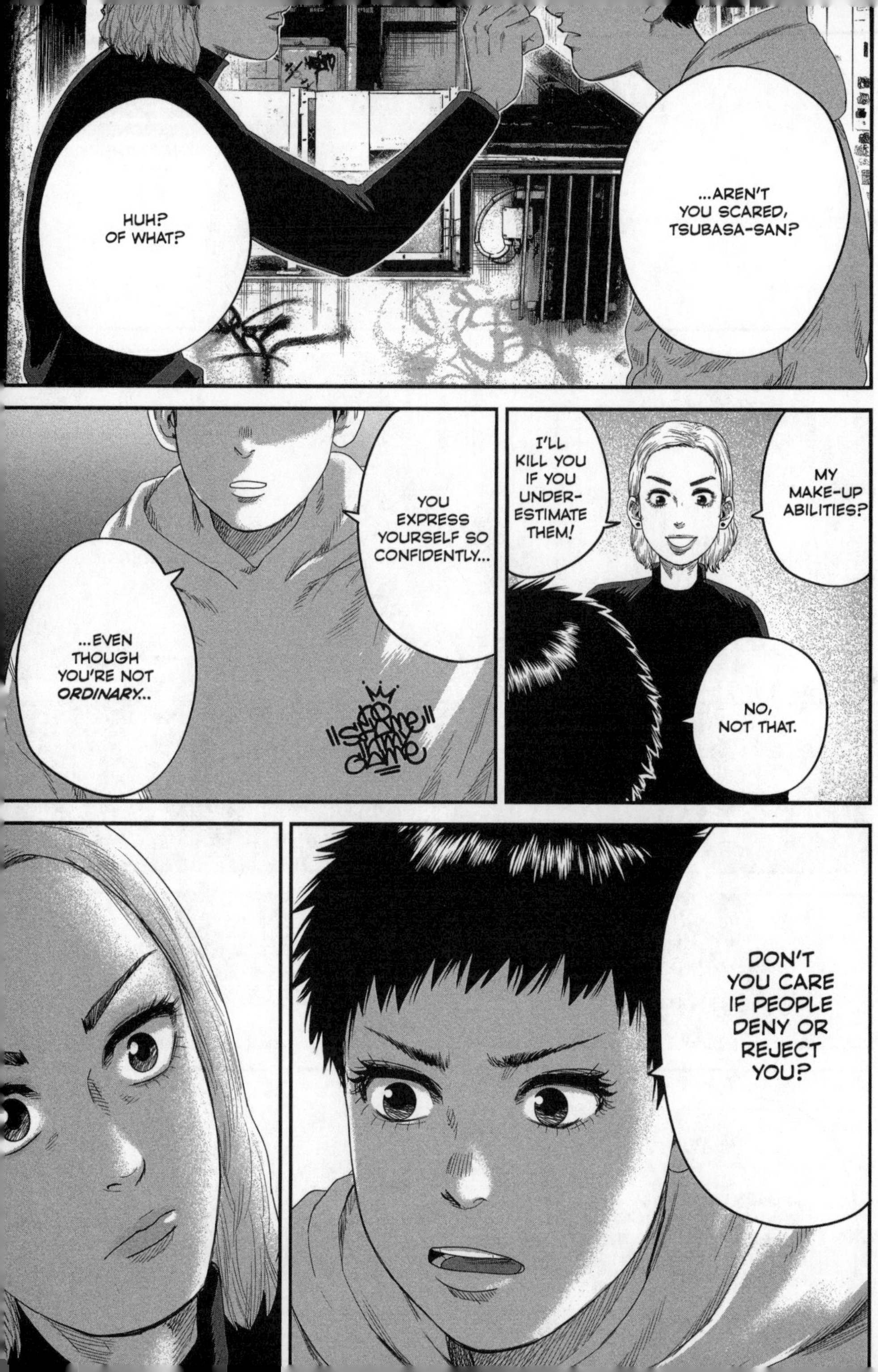
...AREN'T YOU SCARED, TSUBASA-SAN?
HUH? OF WHAT?
MY MAKE-UP ABILITIES?
I'LL KILL YOU IF YOU UNDER-ESTIMATE THEM!
NO, NOT THAT.
YOU EXPRESS YOURSELF SO CONFIDENTLY...
...EVEN THOUGH YOU'RE NOT *ORDINARY*...
DON'T YOU CARE IF PEOPLE DENY OR REJECT YOU?

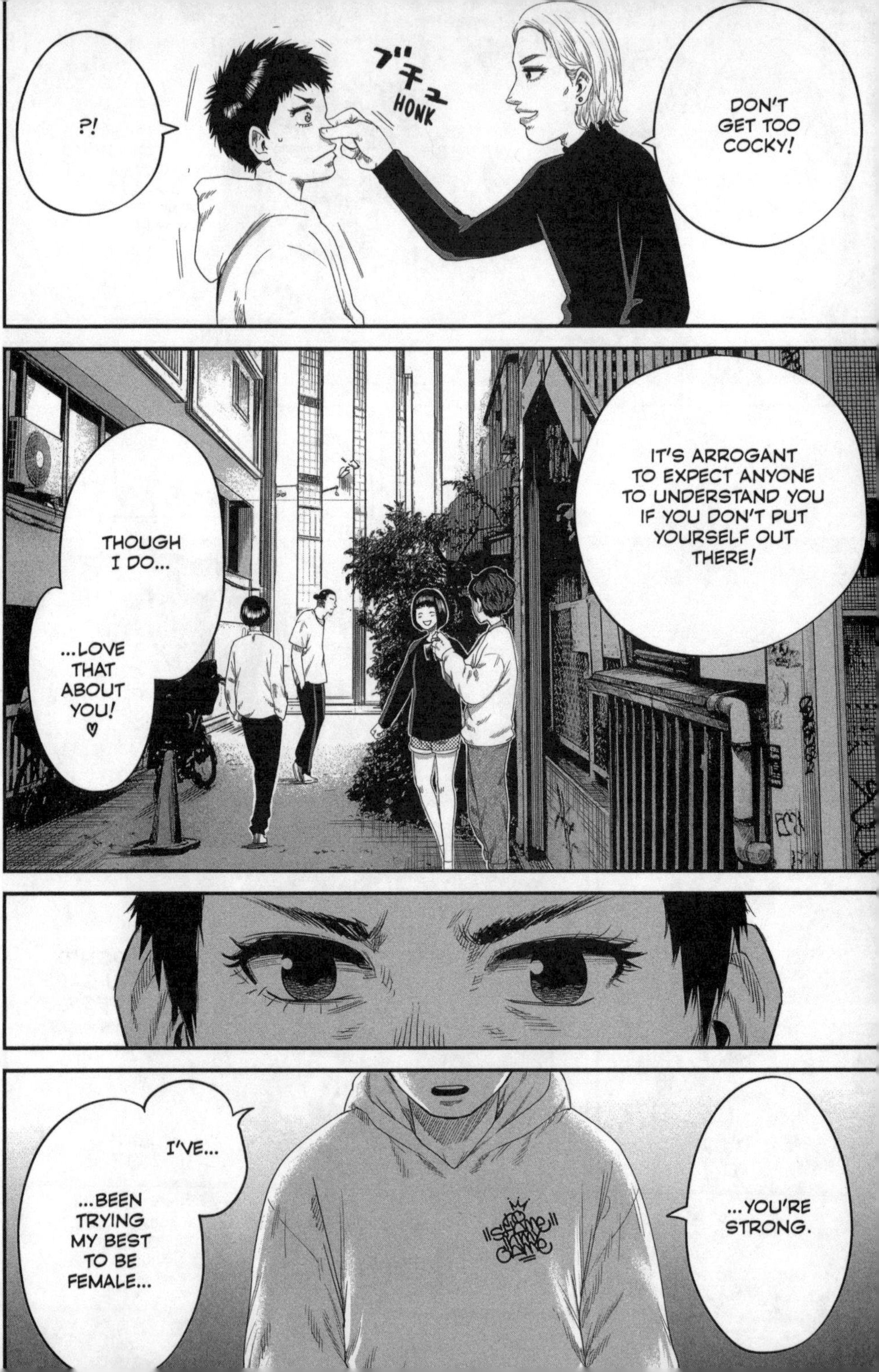
DON'T GET TOO COCKY!
ブチュ
HONK
?!
IT'S ARROGANT TO EXPECT ANYONE TO UNDERSTAND YOU IF YOU DON'T PUT YOURSELF OUT THERE!
THOUGH I DO...
...LOVE THAT ABOUT YOU! ♡
...YOU'RE STRONG.
I'VE...
...BEEN TRYING MY BEST TO BE FEMALE...

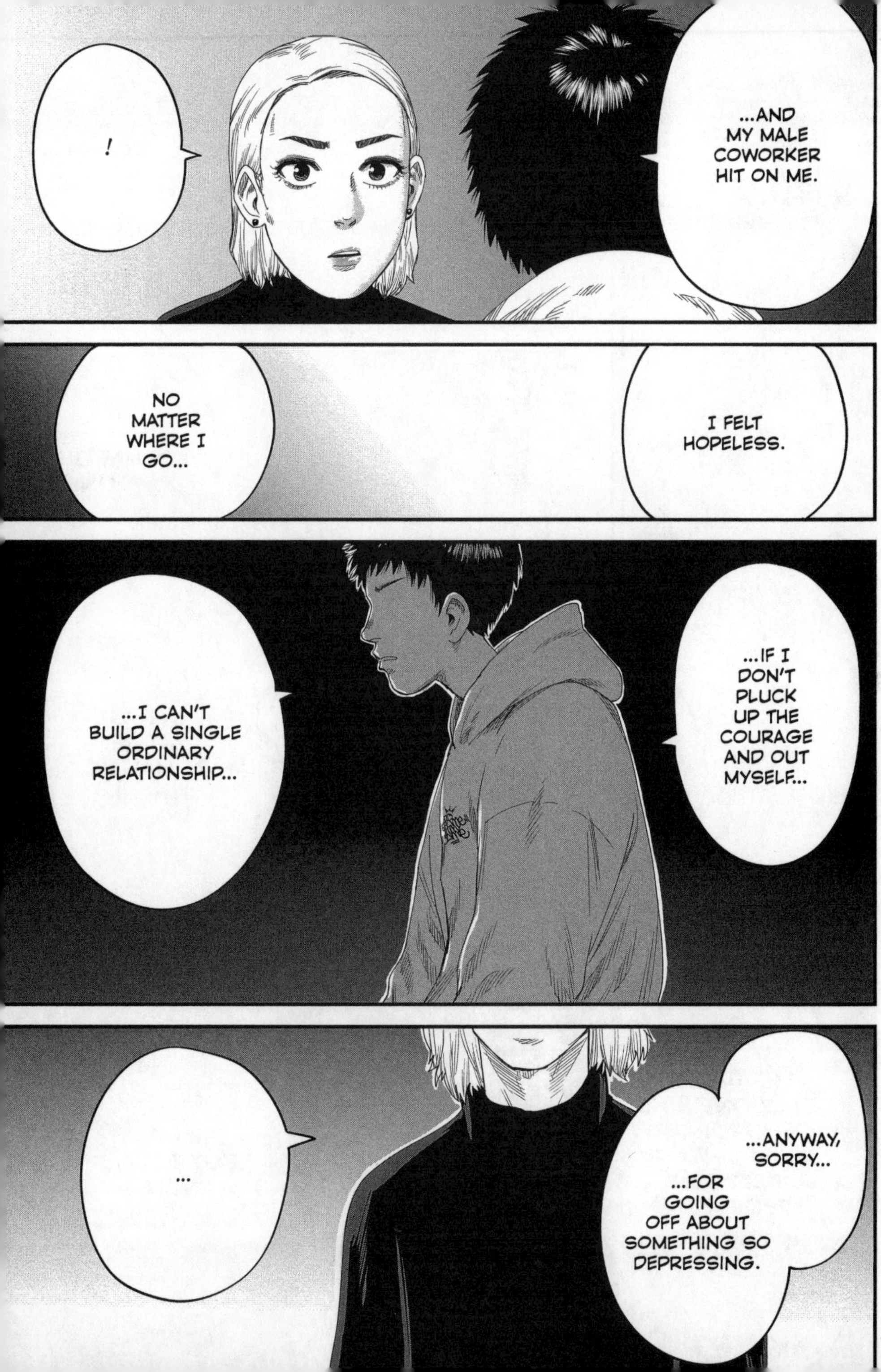
...AND MY MALE COWORKER HIT ON ME.
!
I FELT HOPELESS.
NO MATTER WHERE I GO...
...IF I DON'T PLUCK UP THE COURAGE AND OUT MYSELF...
...I CAN'T BUILD A SINGLE ORDINARY RELATIONSHIP...
...ANYWAY, SORRY...
...FOR GOING OFF ABOUT SOMETHING SO DEPRESSING.
...

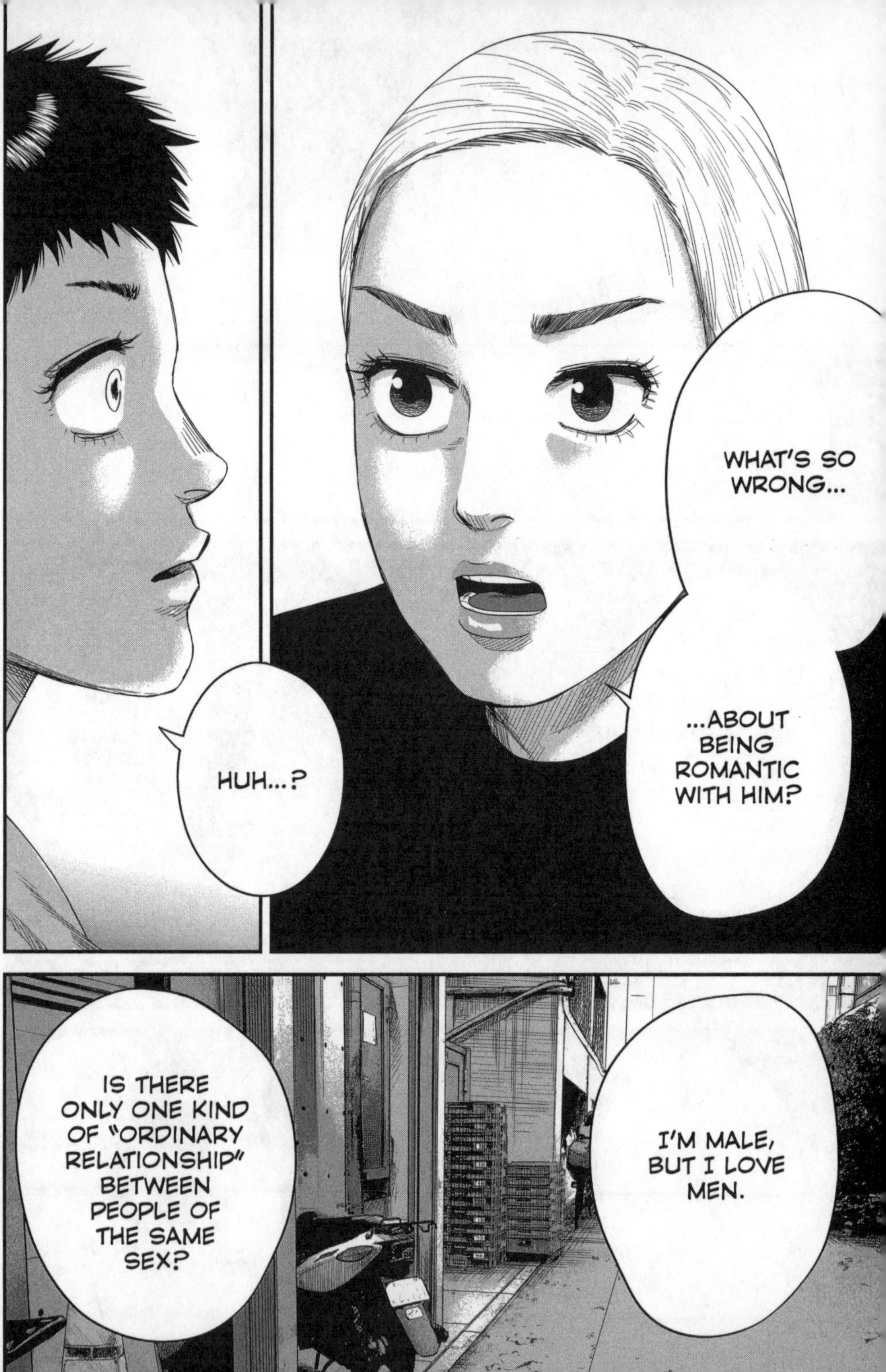
WHAT'S SO WRONG...
...ABOUT BEING ROMANTIC WITH HIM?
HUH...?
I'M MALE, BUT I LOVE MEN.
IS THERE ONLY ONE KIND OF "ORDINARY RELATIONSHIP" BETWEEN PEOPLE OF THE SAME SEX?

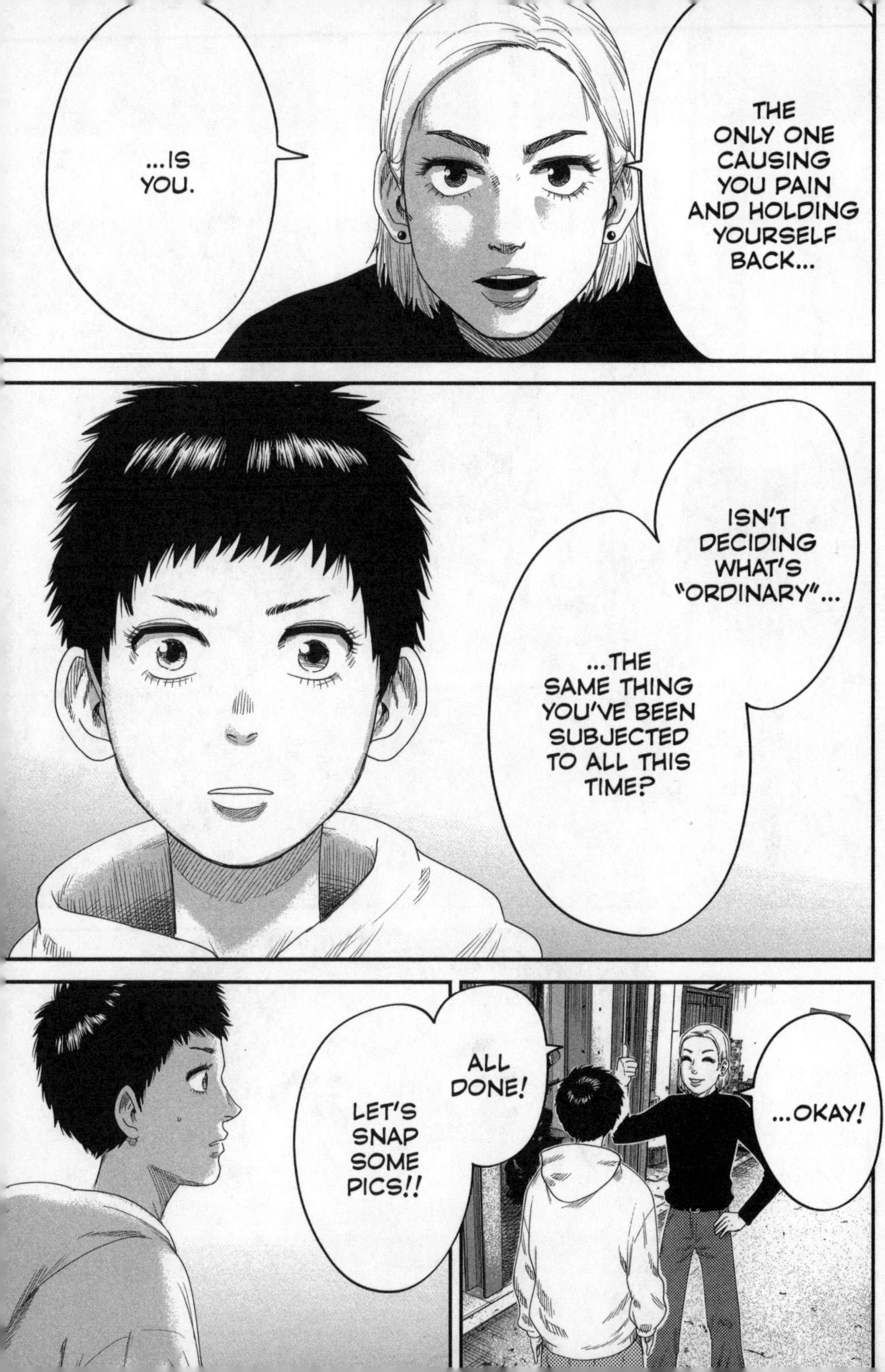
THE ONLY ONE CAUSING YOU PAIN AND HOLDING YOURSELF BACK...
...IS YOU.
ISN'T DECIDING WHAT'S "ORDINARY"...
...THE SAME THING YOU'VE BEEN SUBJECTED TO ALL THIS TIME?
...OKAY!
ALL DONE! LET'S SNAP SOME PICS!!

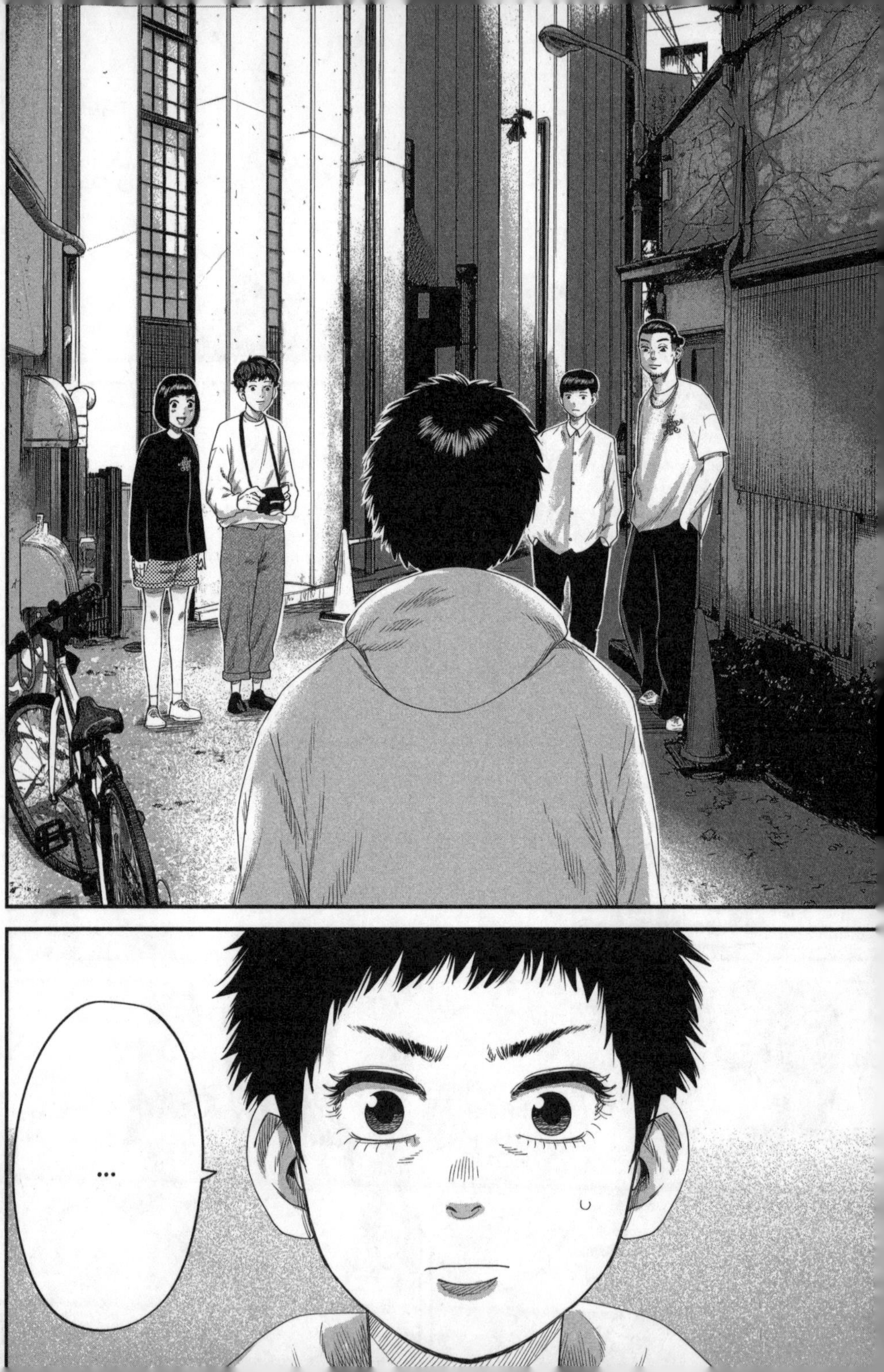
...

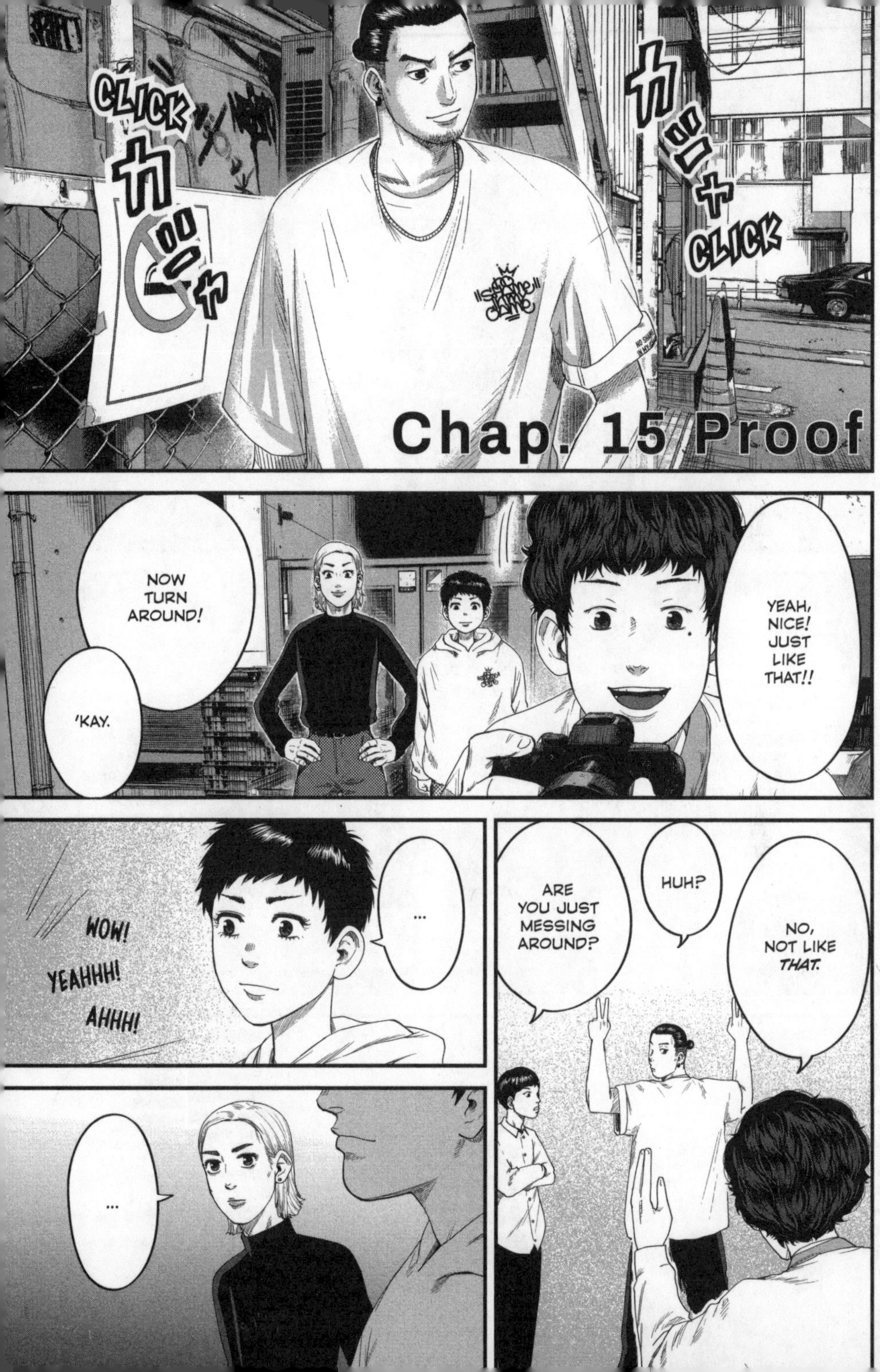

カシャ
CLICK
CLICK
カシャ
Chap. 15 Proof
YEAH, NICE! JUST LIKE THAT!!
NOW TURN AROUND!
'KAY.
NO, NOT LIKE THAT.
HUH?
ARE YOU JUST MESSING AROUND?
...
WOW!
YEAHHH!
AHHH!
...

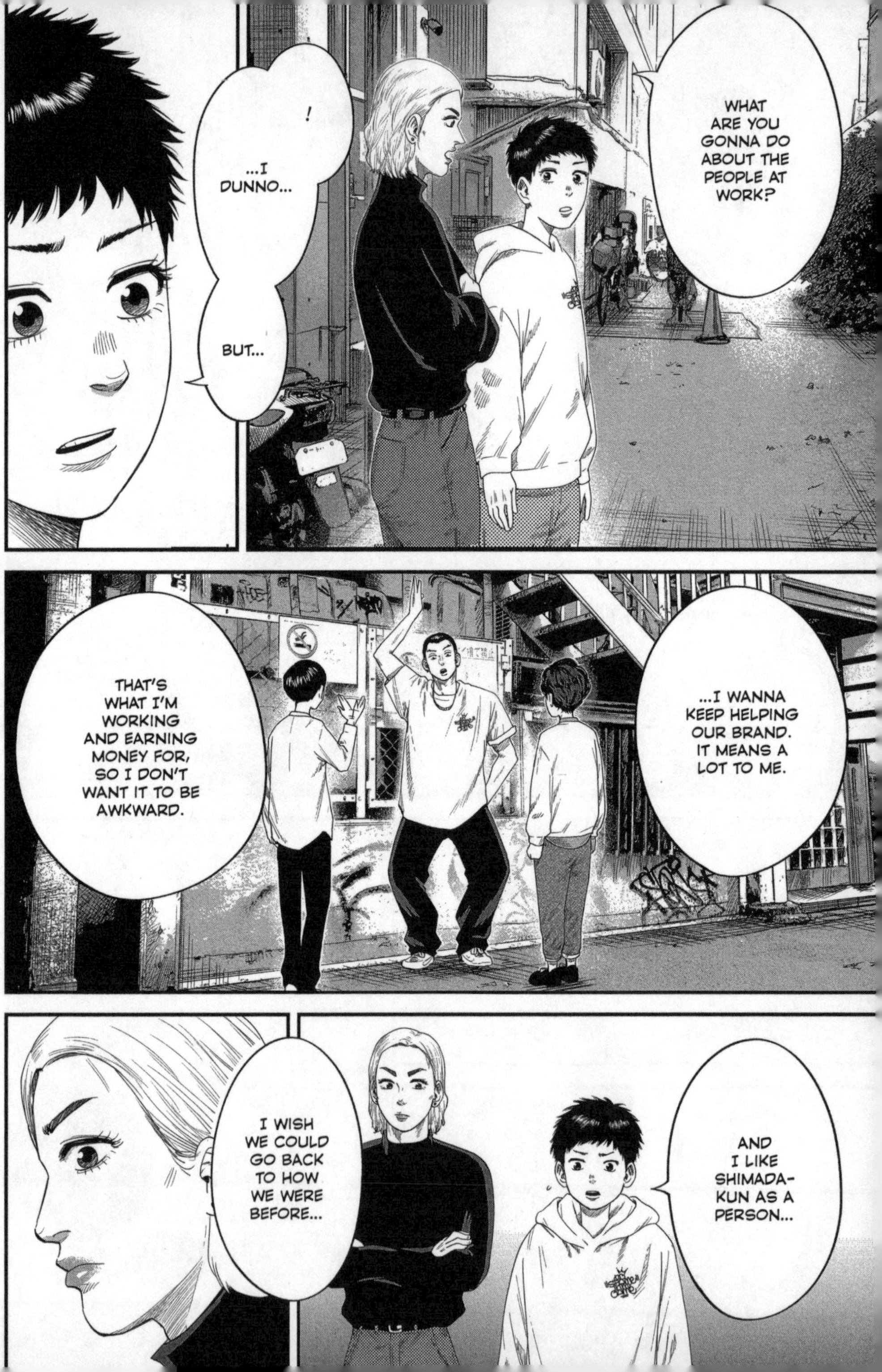

WHAT ARE YOU GONNA DO ABOUT THE PEOPLE AT WORK?
!
...I DUNNO...
BUT...
...I WANNA KEEP HELPING OUR BRAND. IT MEANS A LOT TO ME.
THAT'S WHAT I'M WORKING AND EARNING MONEY FOR, SO I DON'T WANT IT TO BE AWKWARD.
AND I LIKE SHIMADA-KUN AS A PERSON...
I WISH WE COULD GO BACK TO HOW WE WERE BEFORE...

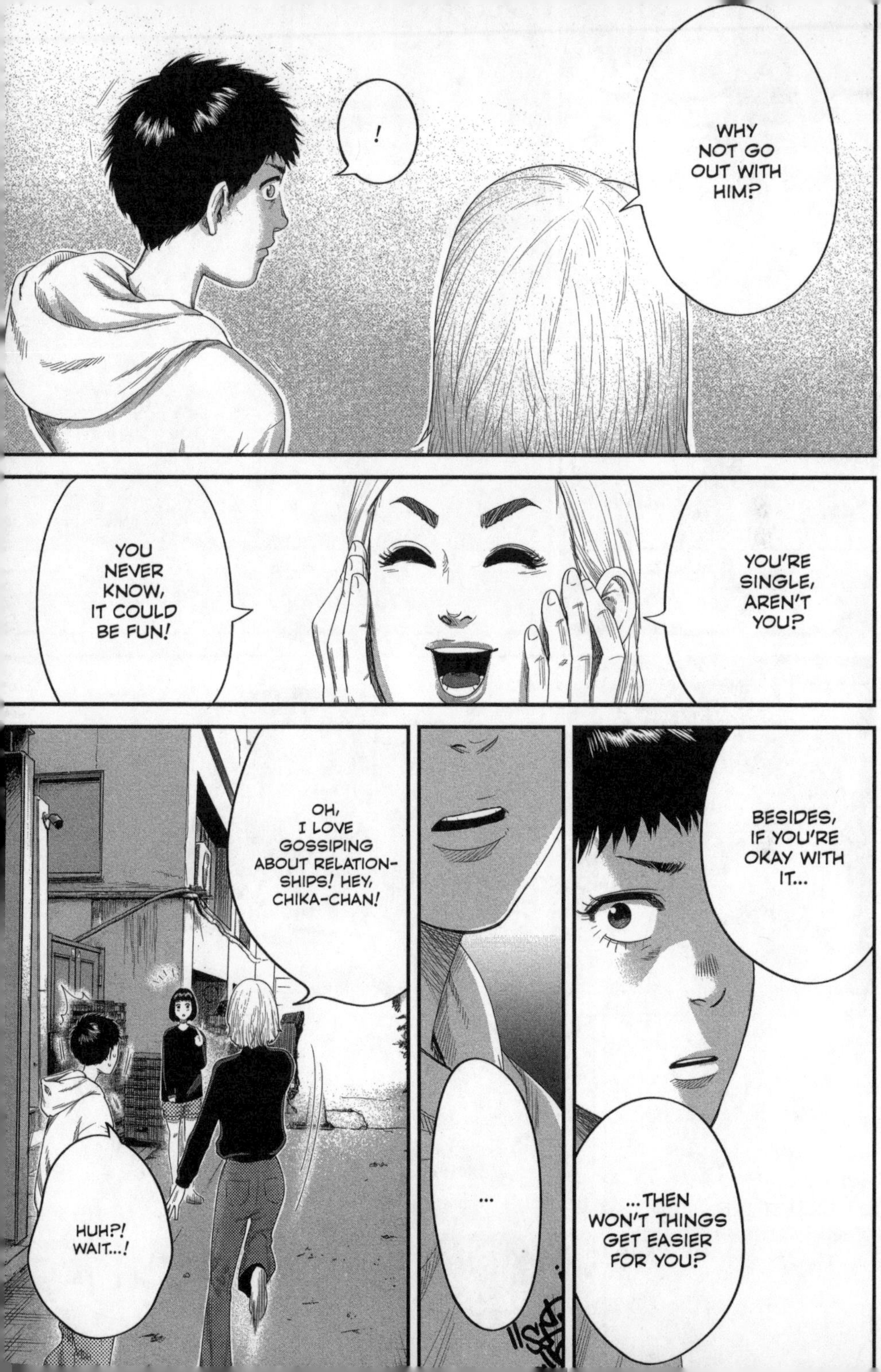
WHY NOT GO OUT WITH HIM?
!
YOU'RE SINGLE, AREN'T YOU?
YOU NEVER KNOW, IT COULD BE FUN!
BESIDES, IF YOU'RE OKAY WITH IT...
...THEN WON'T THINGS GET EASIER FOR YOU?
...
OH, I LOVE GOSSIPING ABOUT RELATION-SHIPS! HEY, CHIKA-CHAN!
HUH?! WAIT...!

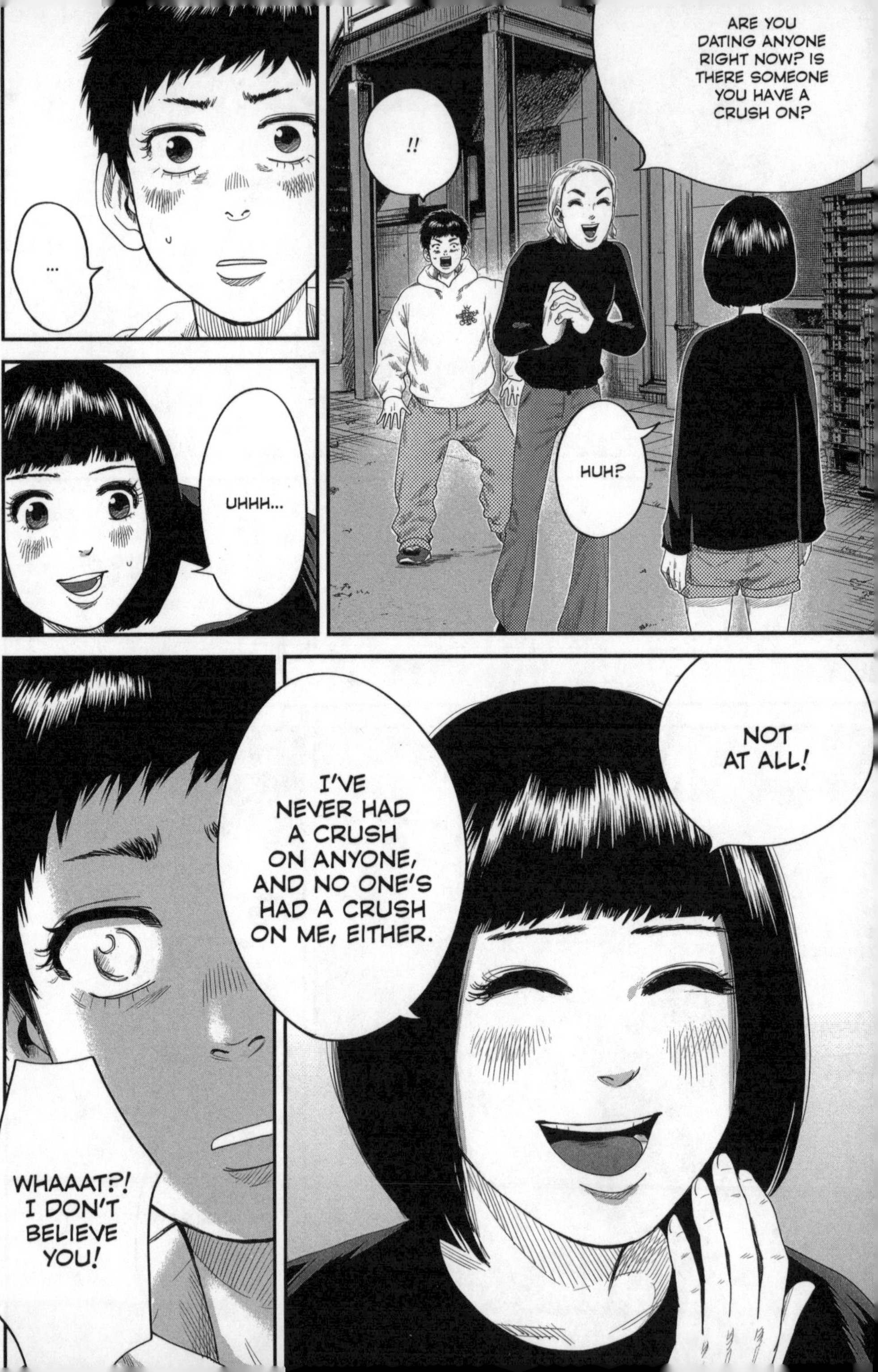
ARE YOU DATING ANYONE RIGHT NOW? IS THERE SOMEONE YOU HAVE A CRUSH ON?
!!
HUH?
...
UHHH...
NOT AT ALL!
I'VE NEVER HAD A CRUSH ON ANYONE, AND NO ONE'S HAD A CRUSH ON ME, EITHER.
WHAAAT?! I DON'T BELIEVE YOU!

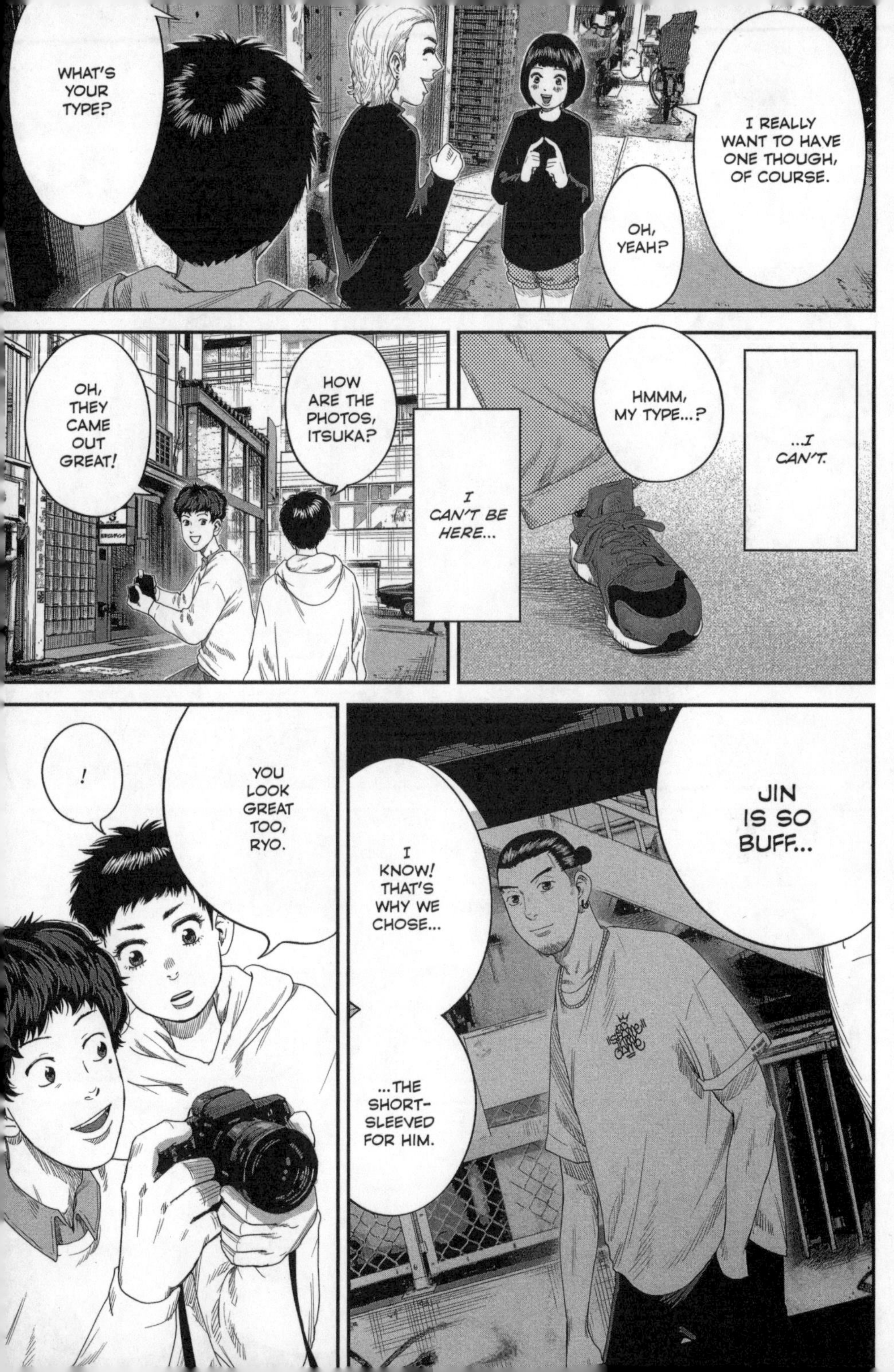
I REALLY WANT TO HAVE ONE THOUGH, OF COURSE.
OH, YEAH?
WHAT'S YOUR TYPE?
HMMM, MY TYPE...?
...I CAN'T.
I CAN'T BE HERE...
HOW ARE THE PHOTOS, ITSUKA?
OH, THEY CAME OUT GREAT!
JIN IS SO BUFF...
I KNOW! THAT'S WHY WE CHOSE...
...THE SHORT-SLEEVED FOR HIM.
YOU LOOK GREAT TOO, RYO.
!

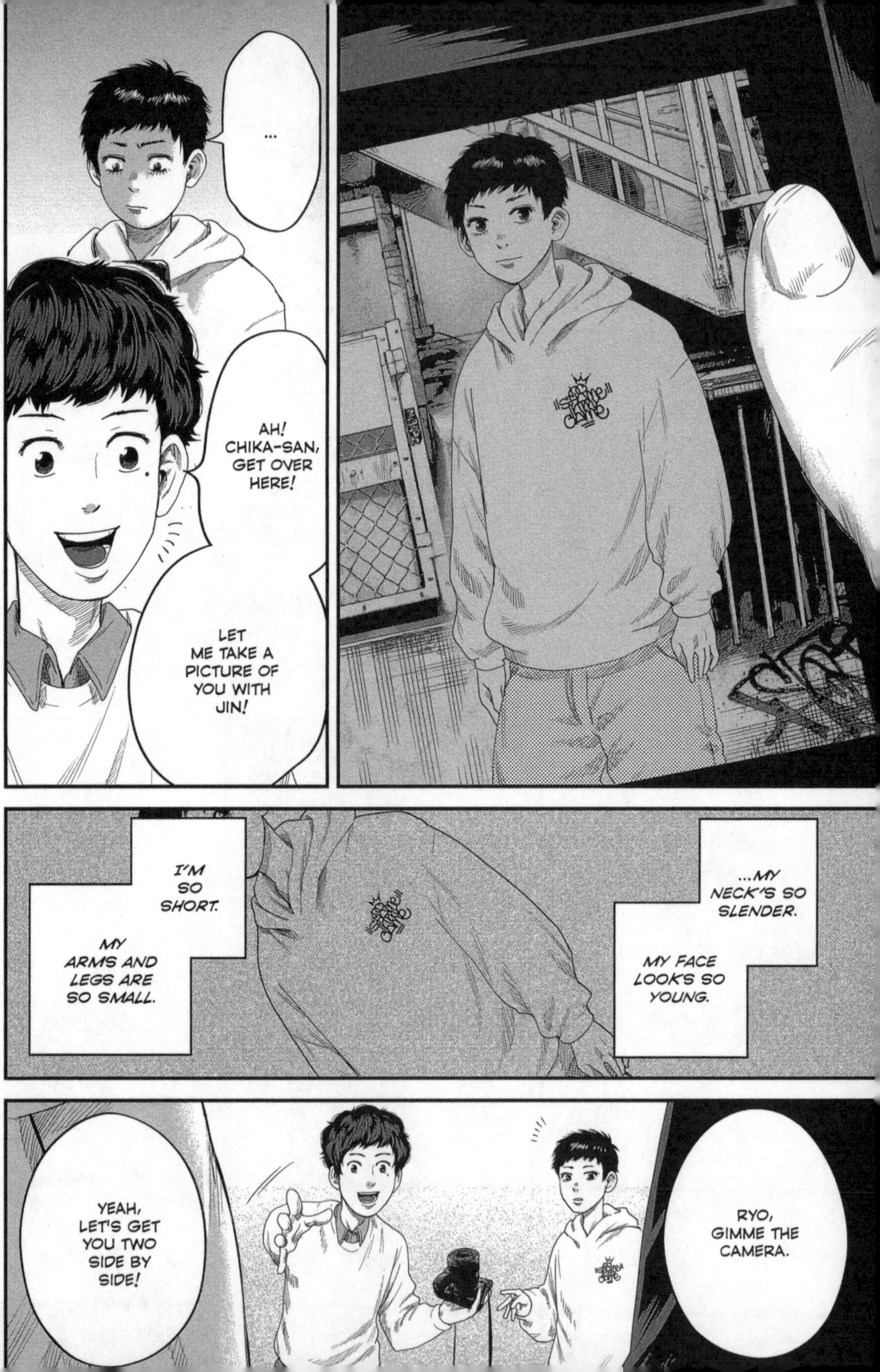
...
AH! CHIKA-SAN, GET OVER HERE!
LET ME TAKE A PICTURE OF YOU WITH JIN!
...MY NECK'S SO SLENDER.
MY FACE LOOKS SO YOUNG.
I'M SO SHORT.
MY ARMS AND LEGS ARE SO SMALL.
RYO, GIMME THE CAMERA.
YEAH, LET'S GET YOU TWO SIDE BY SIDE!

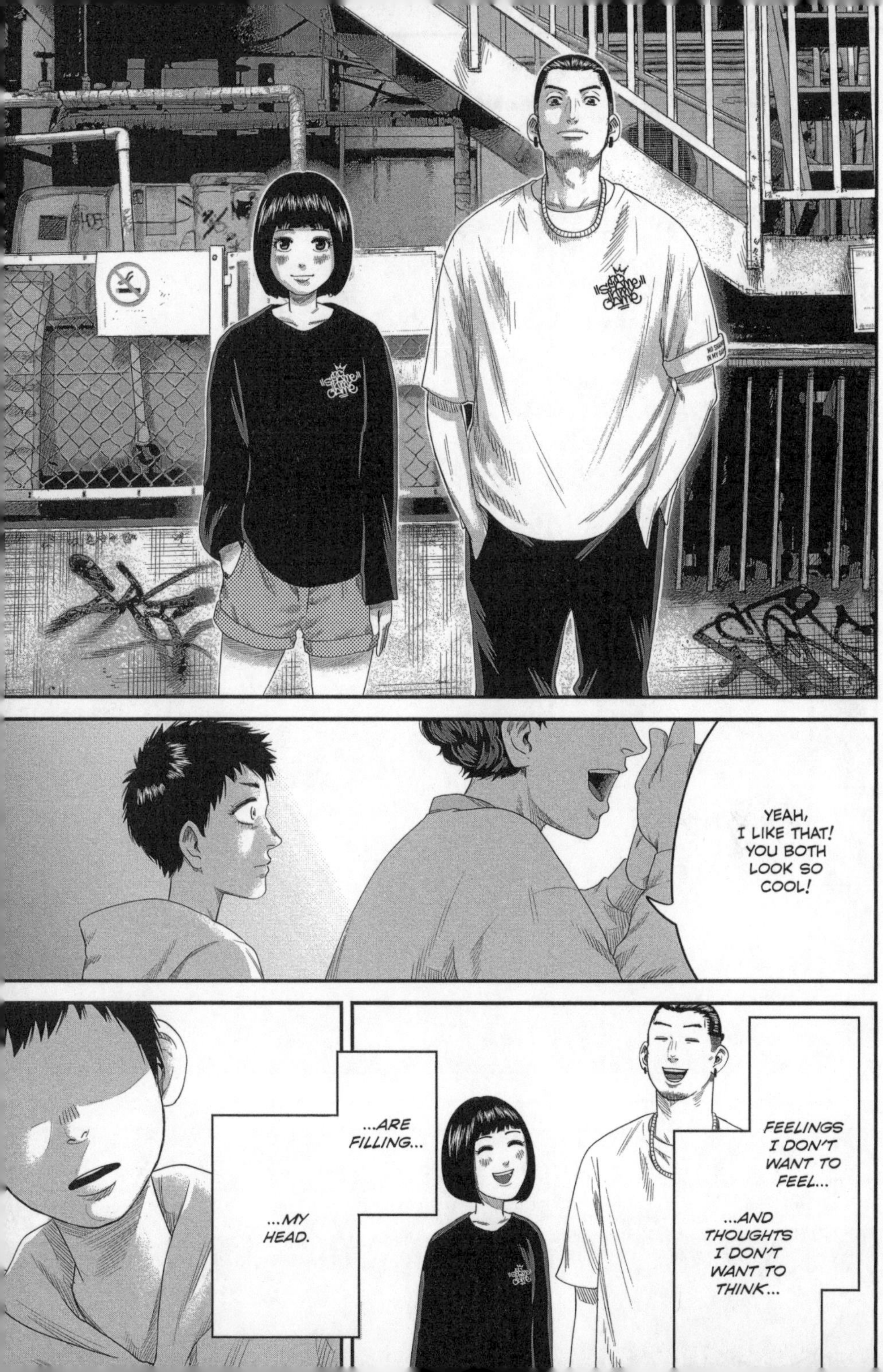
YEAH, I LIKE THAT! YOU BOTH LOOK SO COOL!
FEELINGS I DON'T WANT TO FEEL...
...AND THOUGHTS I DON'T WANT TO THINK...
...ARE FILLING...
...MY HEAD.

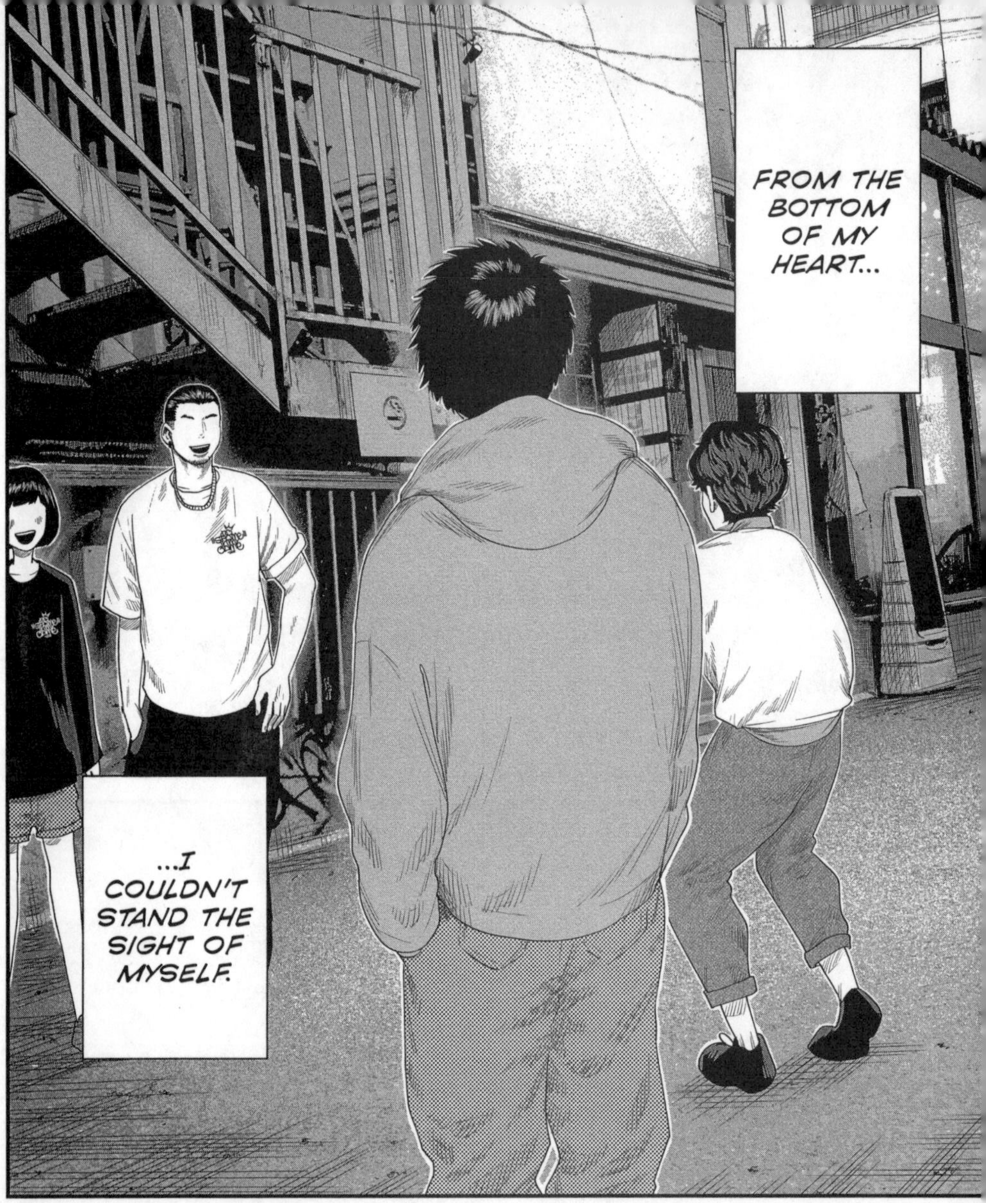
FROM THE BOTTOM OF MY HEART...
...I COULDN'T STAND THE SIGHT OF MYSELF.
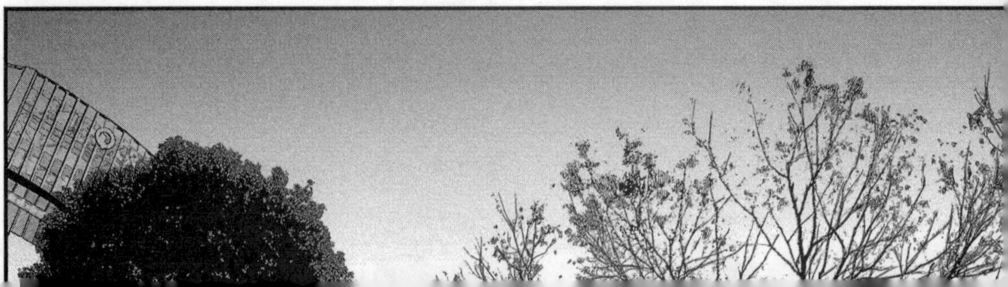

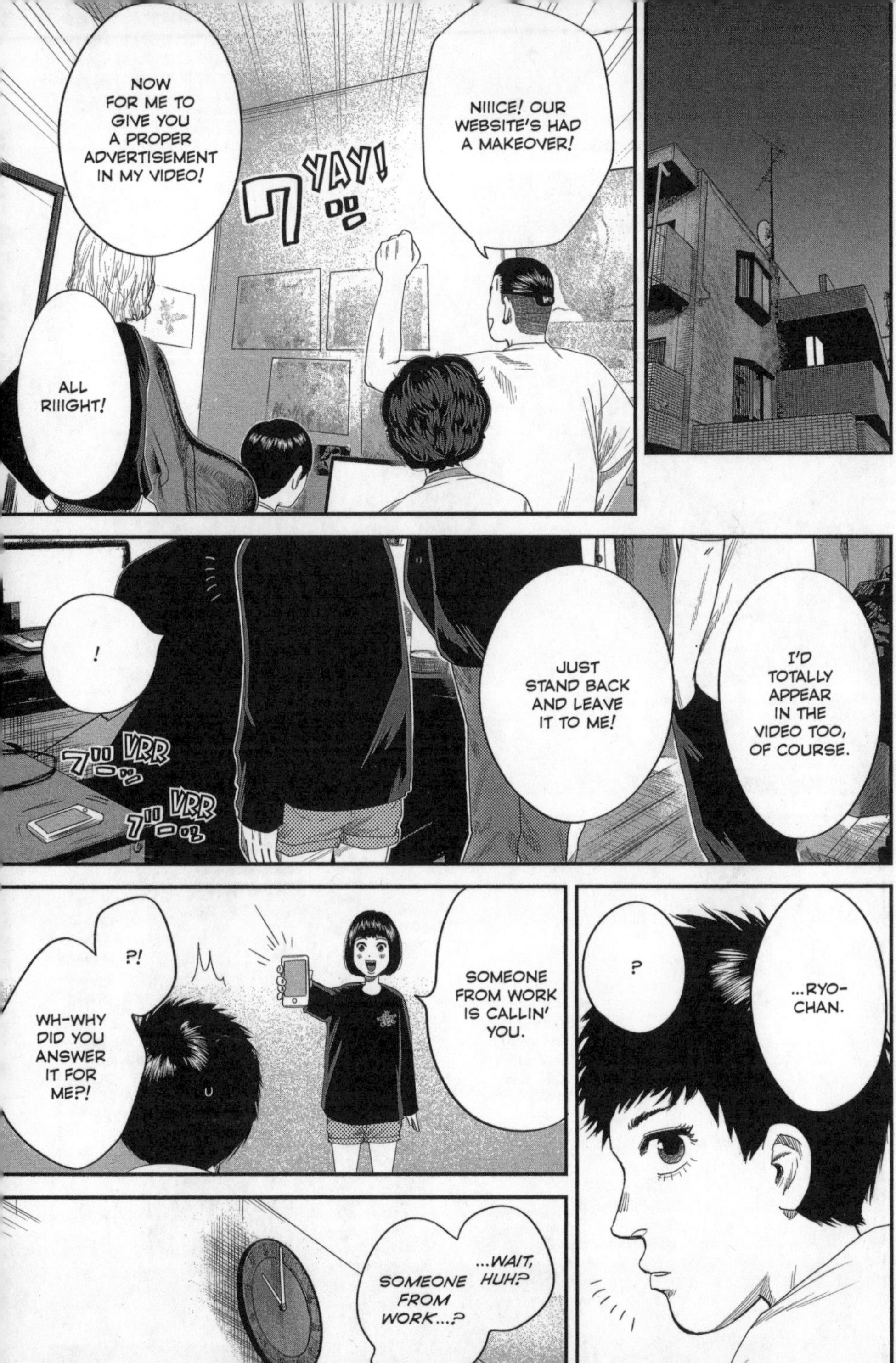
NIIICE! OUR WEBSITE'S HAD A MAKEOVER!
YAY!
NOW FOR ME TO GIVE YOU A PROPER ADVERTISEMENT IN MY VIDEO!
ALL RIIIGHT!
I'D TOTALLY APPEAR IN THE VIDEO TOO, OF COURSE.
JUST STAND BACK AND LEAVE IT TO ME!
!
VRR
VRR
...RYO-CHAN.
?
SOMEONE FROM WORK IS CALLIN' YOU.
?!
WH-WHY DID YOU ANSWER IT FOR ME?!
...WAIT, HUH?
SOMEONE FROM WORK...?

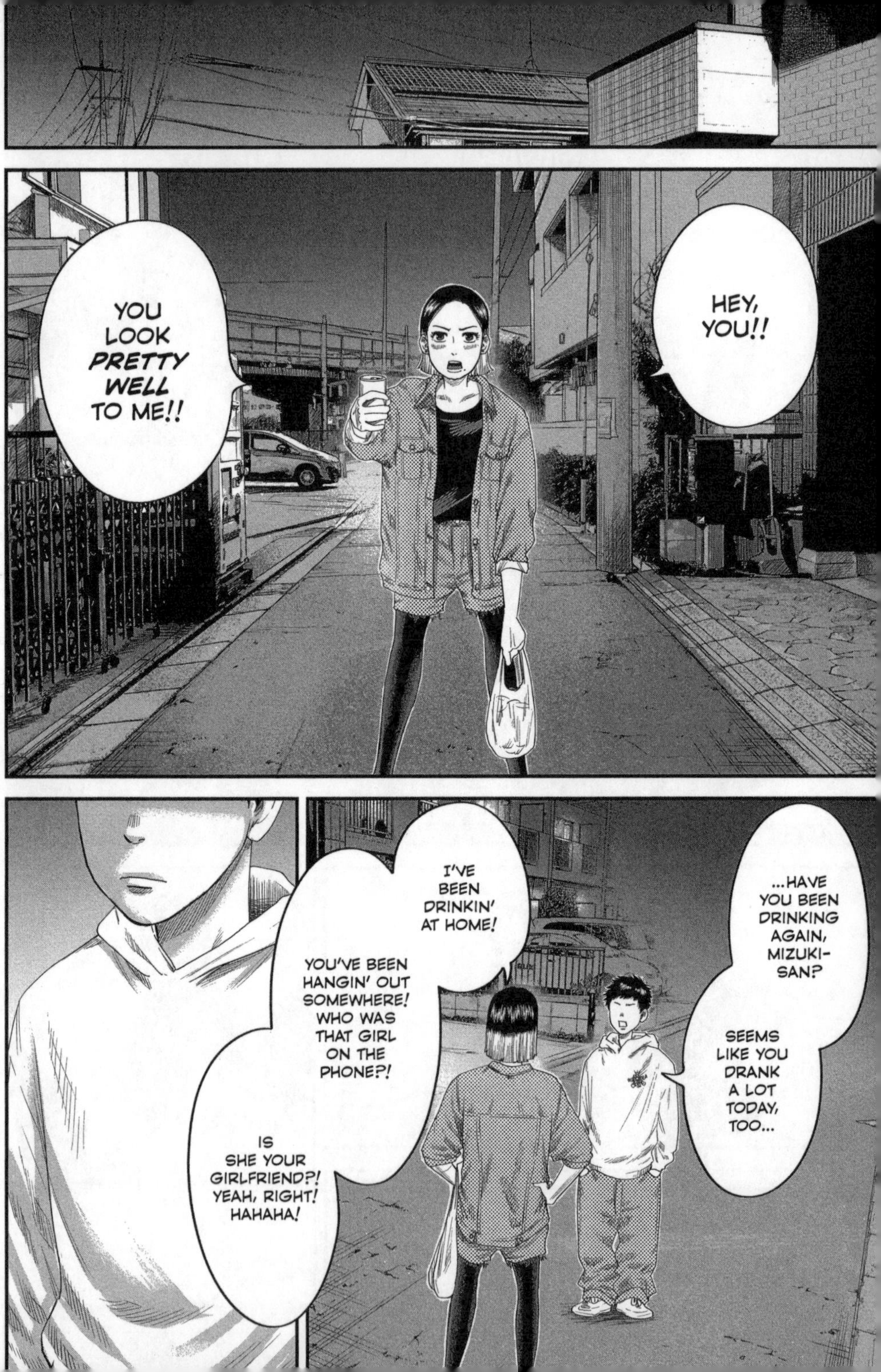
HEY, YOU!!
YOU LOOK PRETTY WELL TO ME!!
...HAVE YOU BEEN DRINKING AGAIN, MIZUKI-SAN?
SEEMS LIKE YOU DRANK A LOT TODAY, TOO...
I'VE BEEN DRINKIN' AT HOME!
YOU'VE BEEN HANGIN' OUT SOMEWHERE! WHO WAS THAT GIRL ON THE PHONE?!
IS SHE YOUR GIRLFRIEND?! YEAH, RIGHT! HAHAHA!

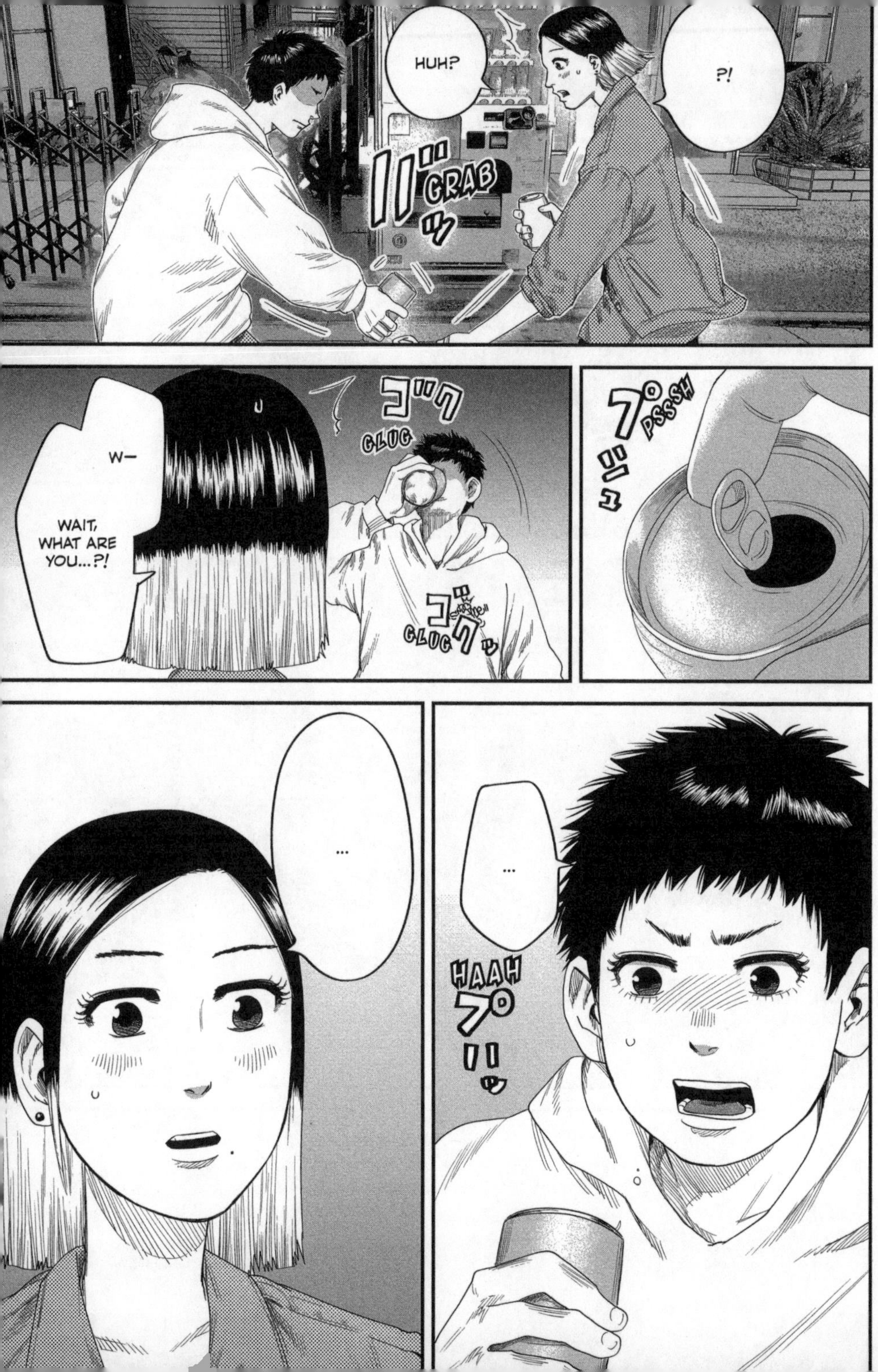
?!
HUH?
GRAB
PSSSH
GLUG
W—
WAIT, WHAT ARE YOU...?!
GLUG
...
HAAH
...

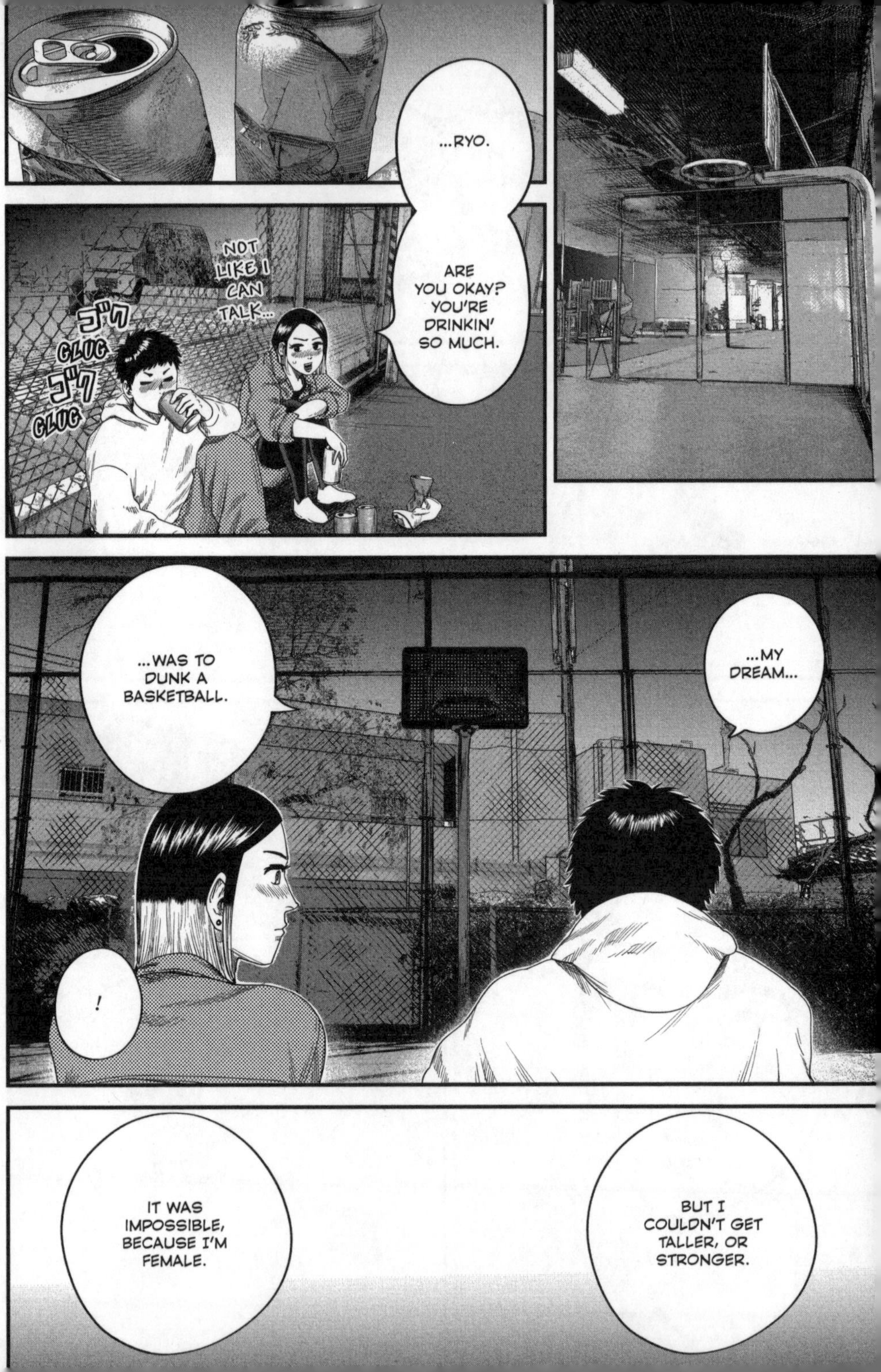
...RYO.
ARE YOU OKAY? YOU'RE DRINKIN' SO MUCH.
NOT LIKE I CAN TALK...
ゴク
GLUG
ゴク
GLUG
...MY DREAM...
...WAS TO DUNK A BASKETBALL.
!
BUT I COULDN'T GET TALLER, OR STRONGER.
IT WAS IMPOSSIBLE, BECAUSE I'M FEMALE.

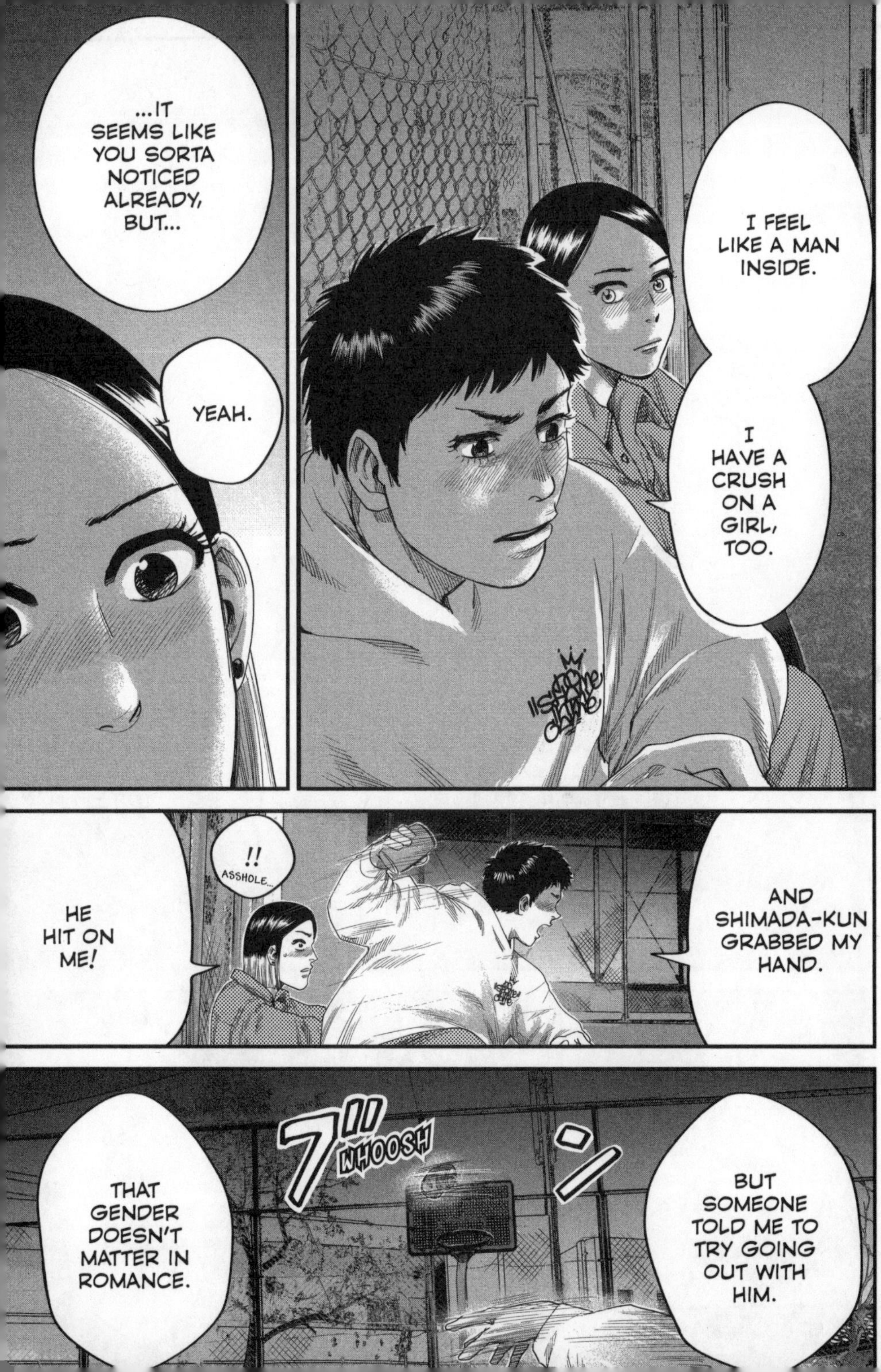
I FEEL LIKE A MAN INSIDE.
I HAVE A CRUSH ON A GIRL, TOO.
...IT SEEMS LIKE YOU SORTA NOTICED ALREADY, BUT...
YEAH.
AND SHIMADA-KUN GRABBED MY HAND.
!!
ASSHOLE...
HE HIT ON ME!
BUT SOMEONE TOLD ME TO TRY GOING OUT WITH HIM.
WHOOSH
THAT GENDER DOESN'T MATTER IN ROMANCE.

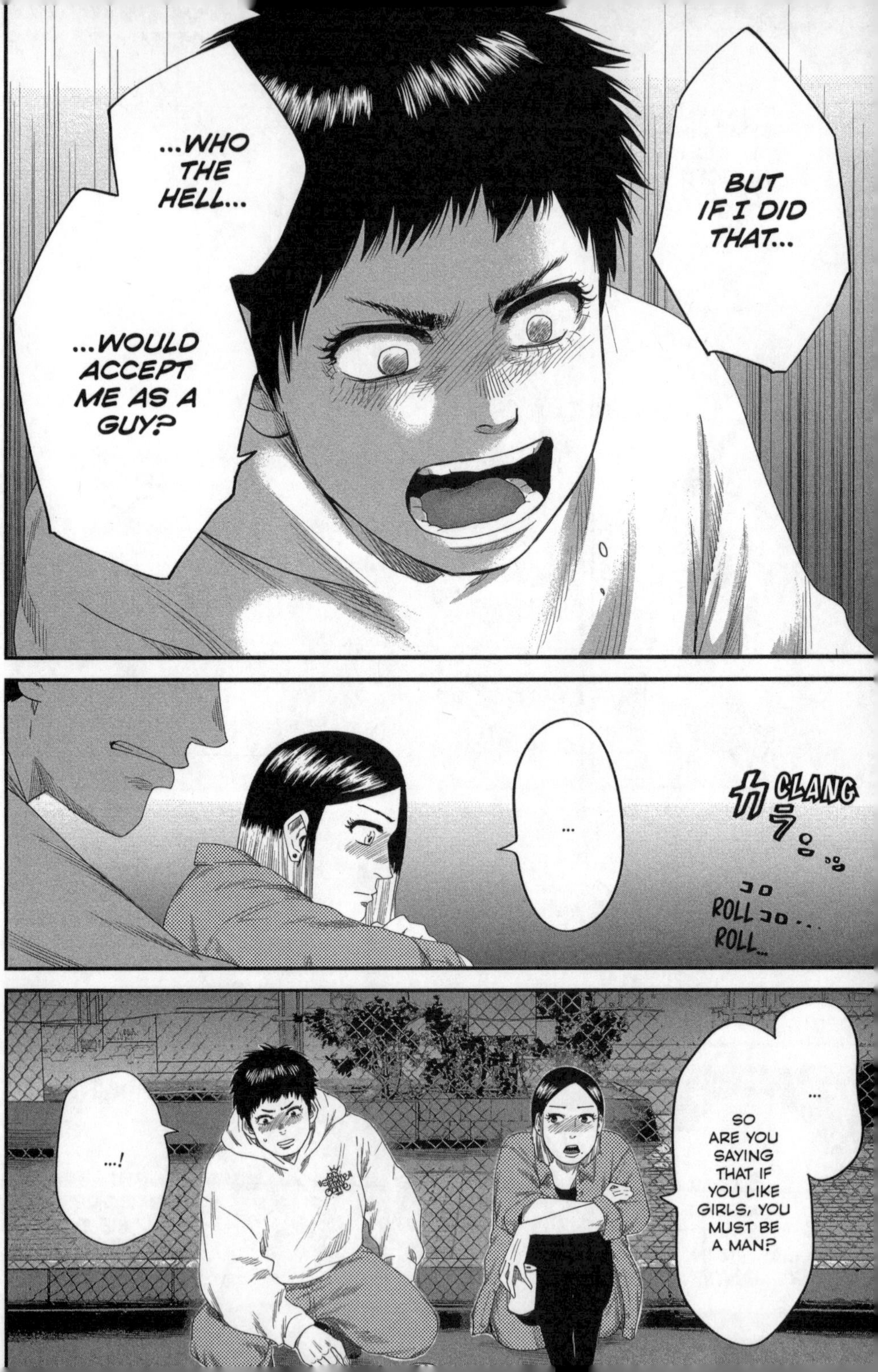
BUT IF I DID THAT...
...WHO THE HELL...
...WOULD ACCEPT ME AS A GUY?
CLANG
ROLL ROLL...
...
...
SO ARE YOU SAYING THAT IF YOU LIKE GIRLS, YOU MUST BE A MAN?
...!

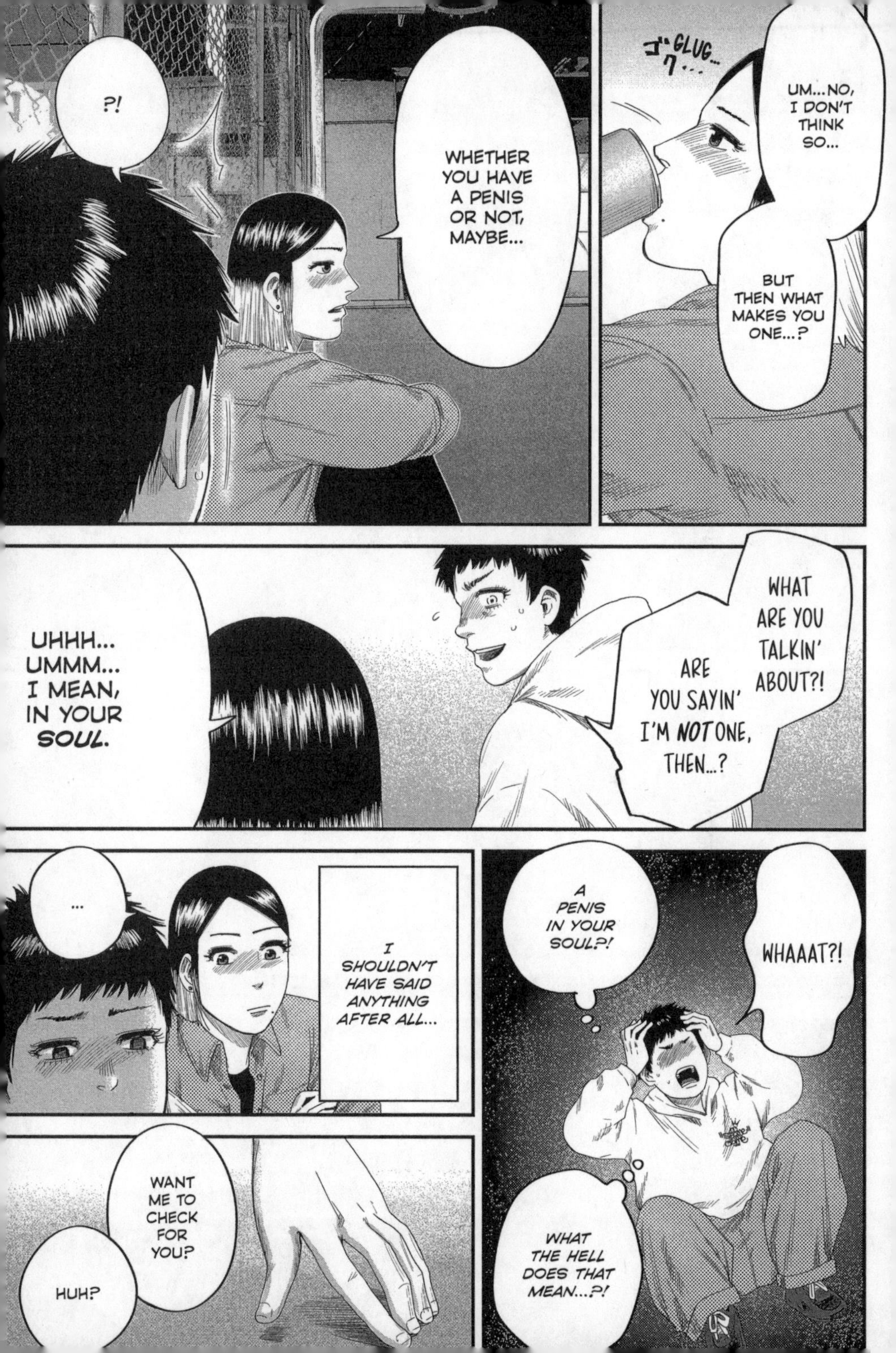
ゴクッ GLUG...
UM...NO, I DON'T THINK SO...
BUT THEN WHAT MAKES YOU ONE...?
WHETHER YOU HAVE A PENIS OR NOT, MAYBE...
?!
WHAT ARE YOU TALKIN' ABOUT?!
ARE YOU SAYIN' I'M **NOT** ONE, THEN...?
UHHH... UMMM... I MEAN, IN YOUR **SOUL**.
WHAAAT?!
A PENIS IN YOUR SOUL?!
WHAT THE HELL DOES THAT MEAN...?!
I SHOULDN'T HAVE SAID ANYTHING AFTER ALL...
...
WANT ME TO CHECK FOR YOU?
HUH?

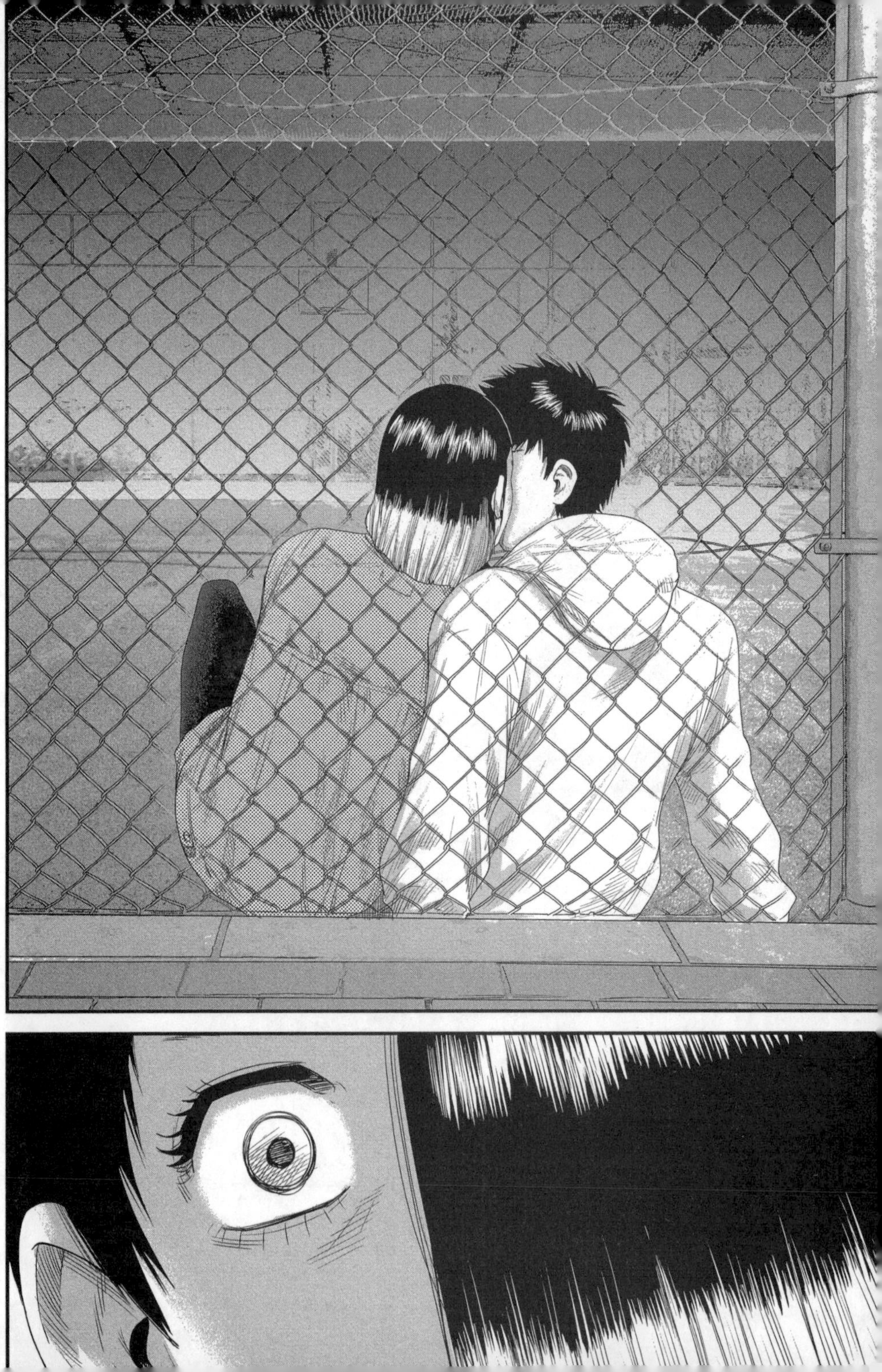

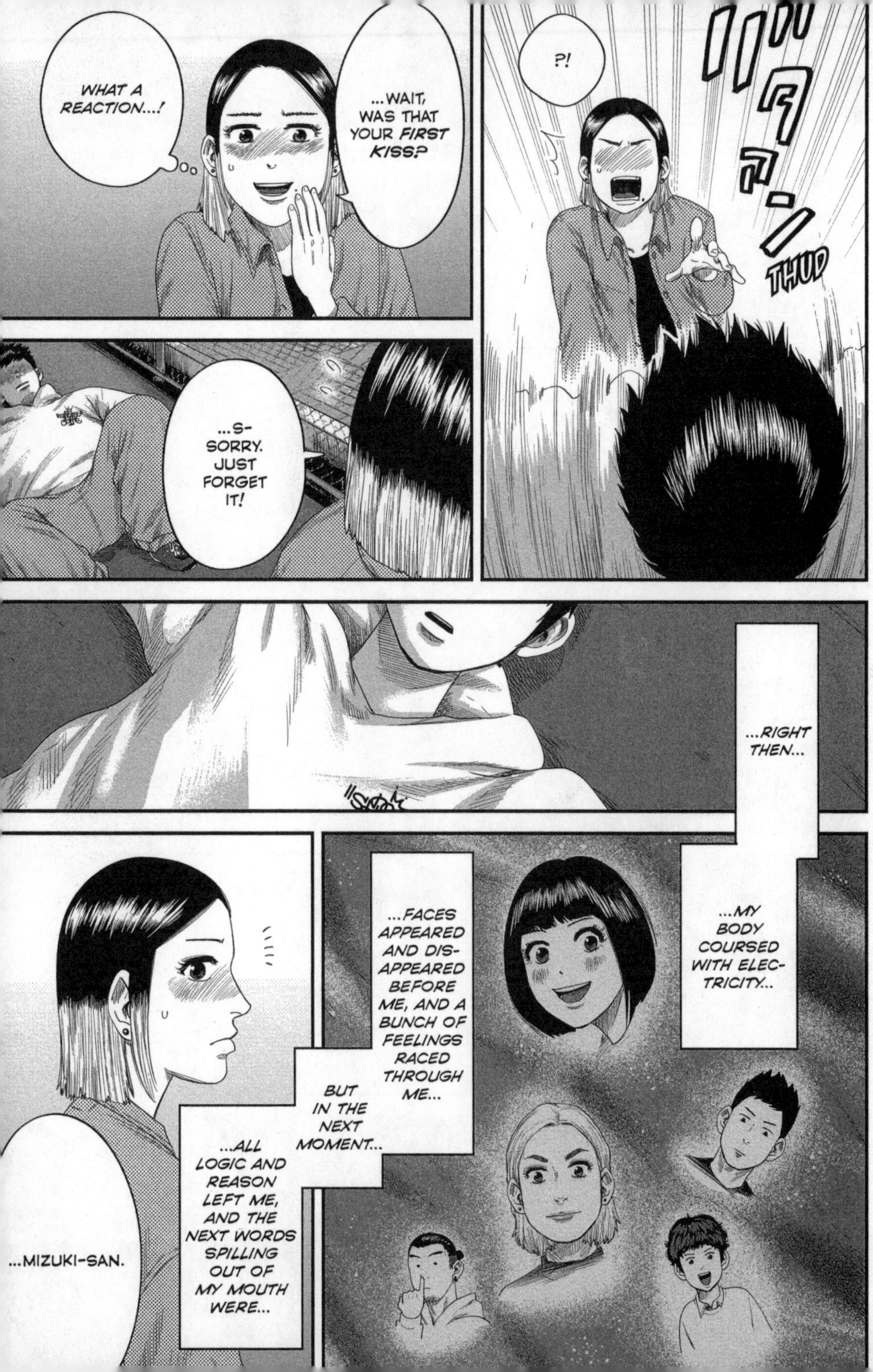
?!
THUD
...WAIT, WAS THAT YOUR *FIRST KISS?*
WHAT A REACTION...!
...S-SORRY. JUST FORGET IT!
...RIGHT THEN...
...MY BODY COURSED WITH ELECTRICITY...
...FACES APPEARED AND DISAPPEARED BEFORE ME, AND A BUNCH OF FEELINGS RACED THROUGH ME...
BUT IN THE NEXT MOMENT...
...ALL LOGIC AND REASON LEFT ME, AND THE NEXT WORDS SPILLING OUT OF MY MOUTH WERE...
...MIZUKI-SAN.

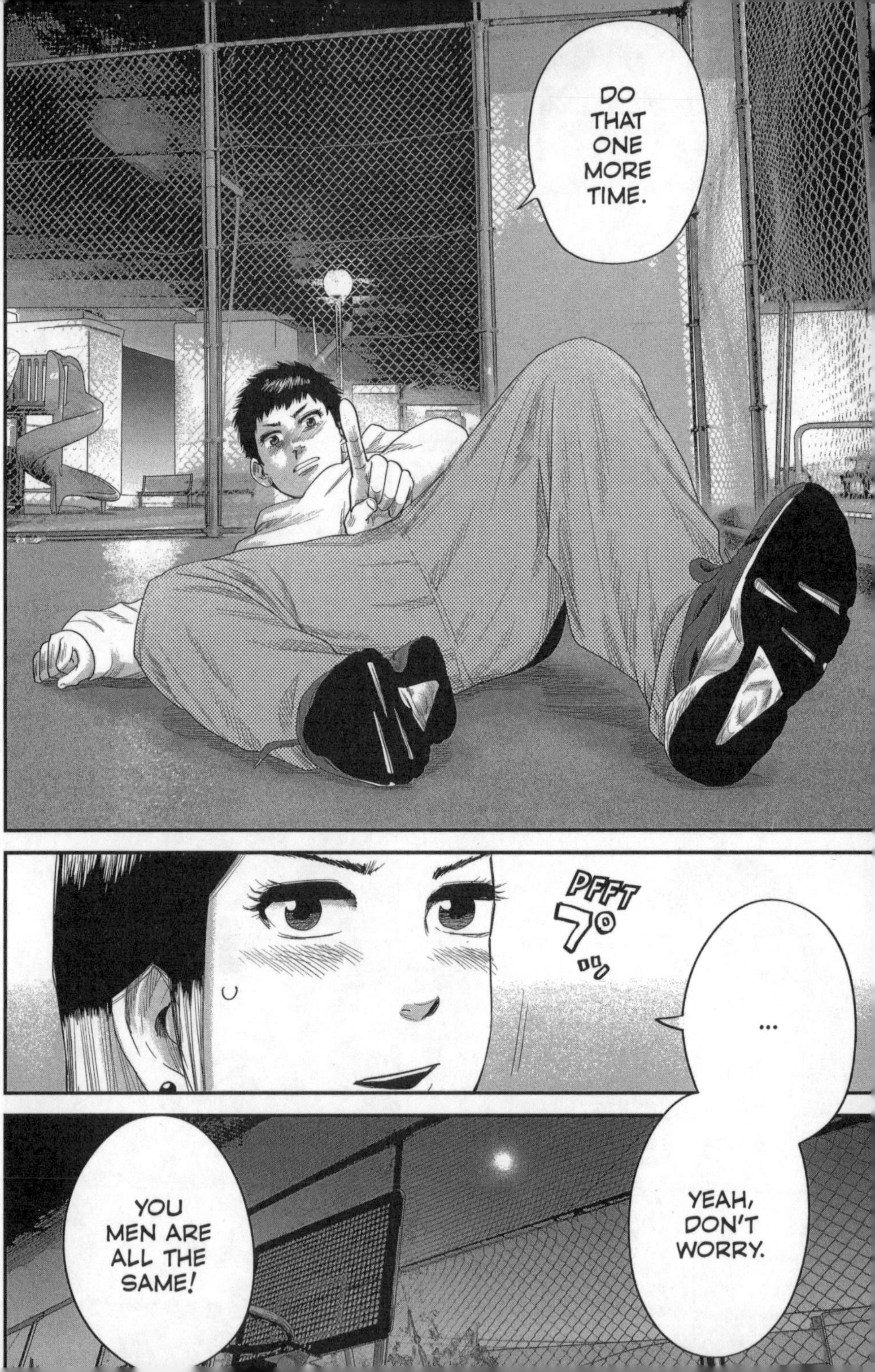
DO THAT ONE MORE TIME.
PFFT
...
YEAH, DON'T WORRY.
YOU MEN ARE ALL THE SAME!

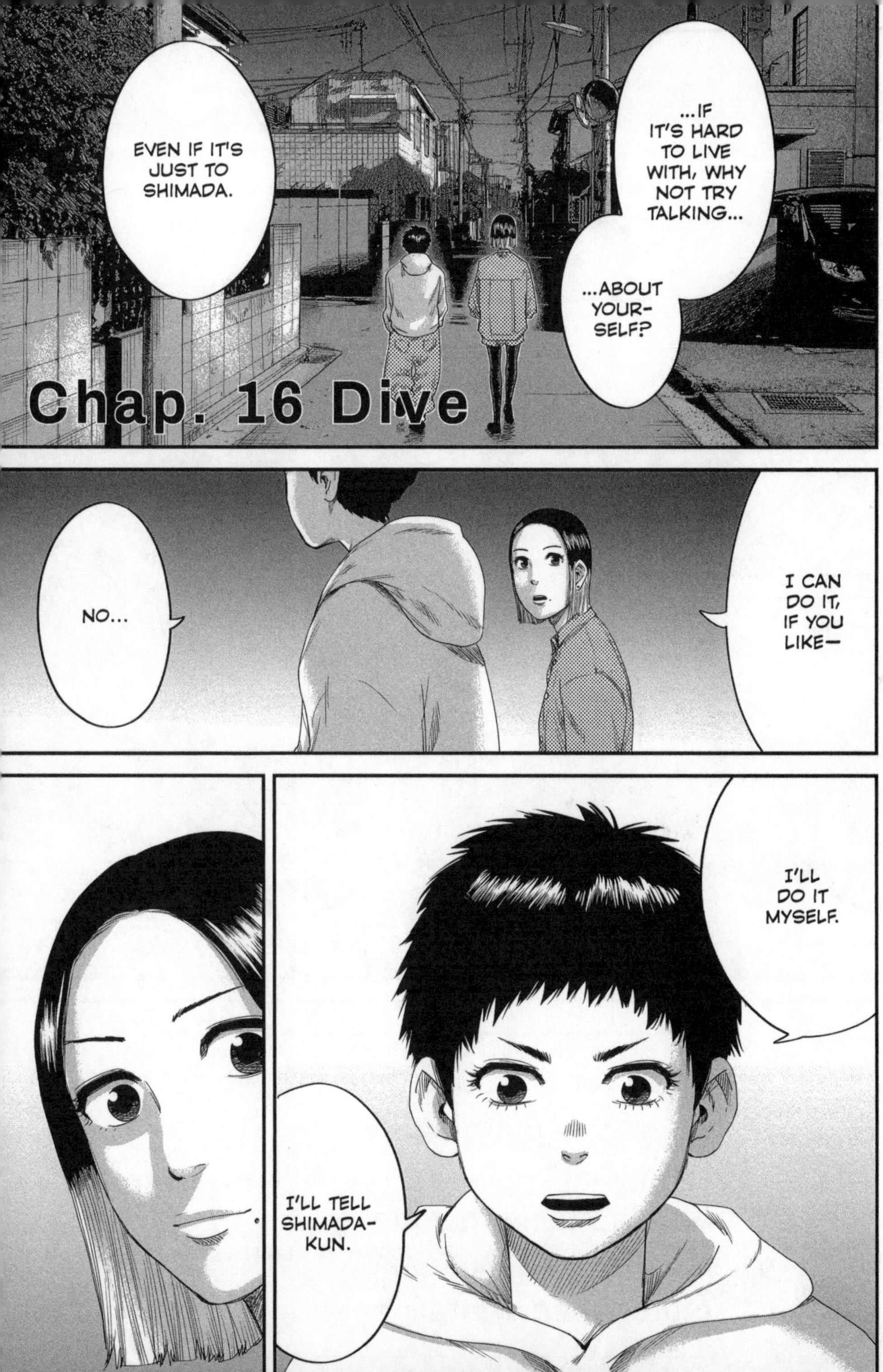
Chap. 16 Dive
...IF IT'S HARD TO LIVE WITH, WHY NOT TRY TALKING...
...ABOUT YOUR-SELF?
EVEN IF IT'S JUST TO SHIMADA.
I CAN DO IT, IF YOU LIKE—
NO...
I'LL DO IT MYSELF.
I'LL TELL SHIMADA-KUN.

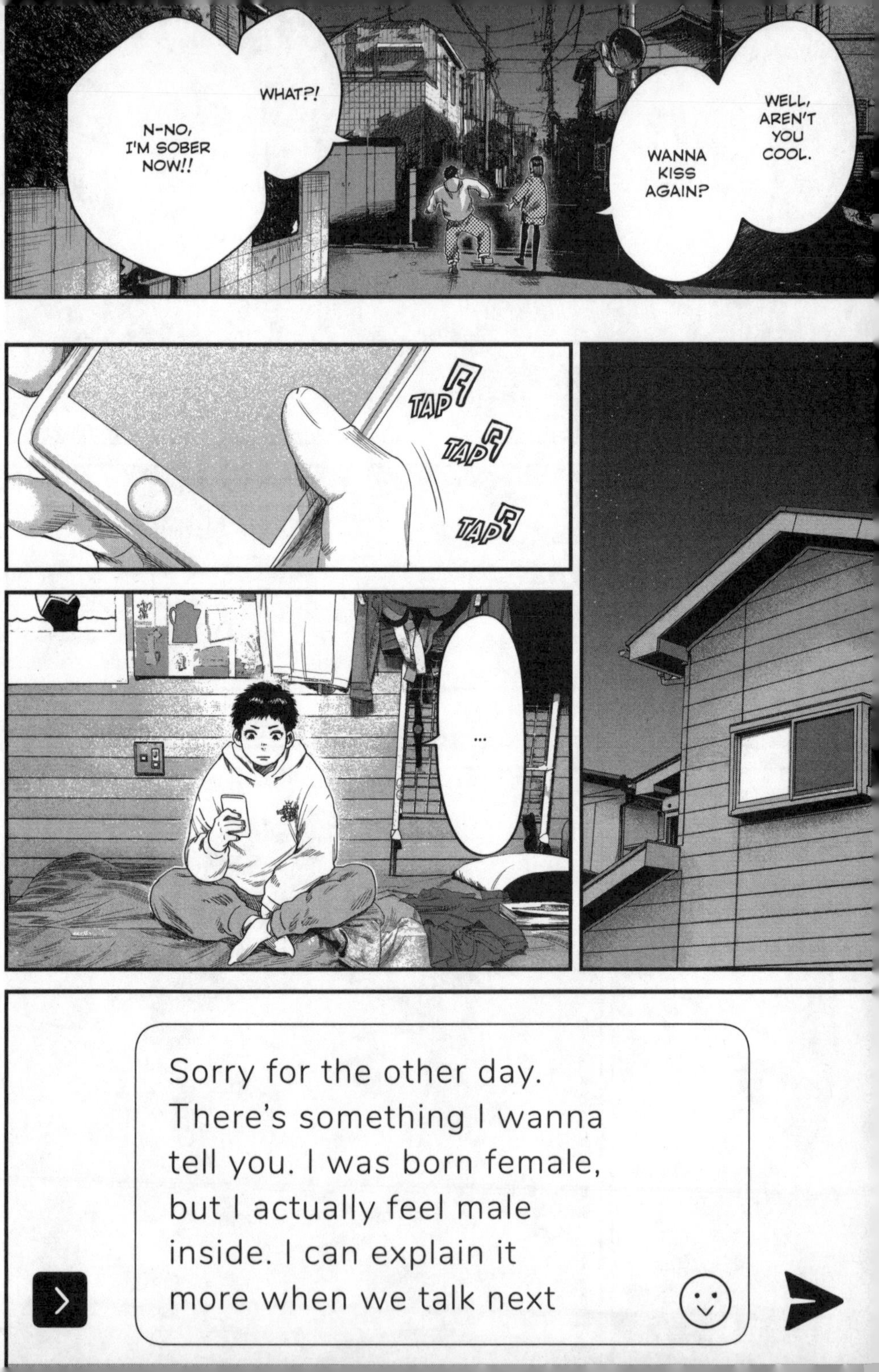
WELL, AREN'T YOU COOL.
WANNA KISS AGAIN?
WHAT?!
N-NO, I'M SOBER NOW!!
TAP
TAP
TAP
...
Sorry for the other day. There's something I wanna tell you. I was born female, but I actually feel male inside. I can explain it more when we talk next

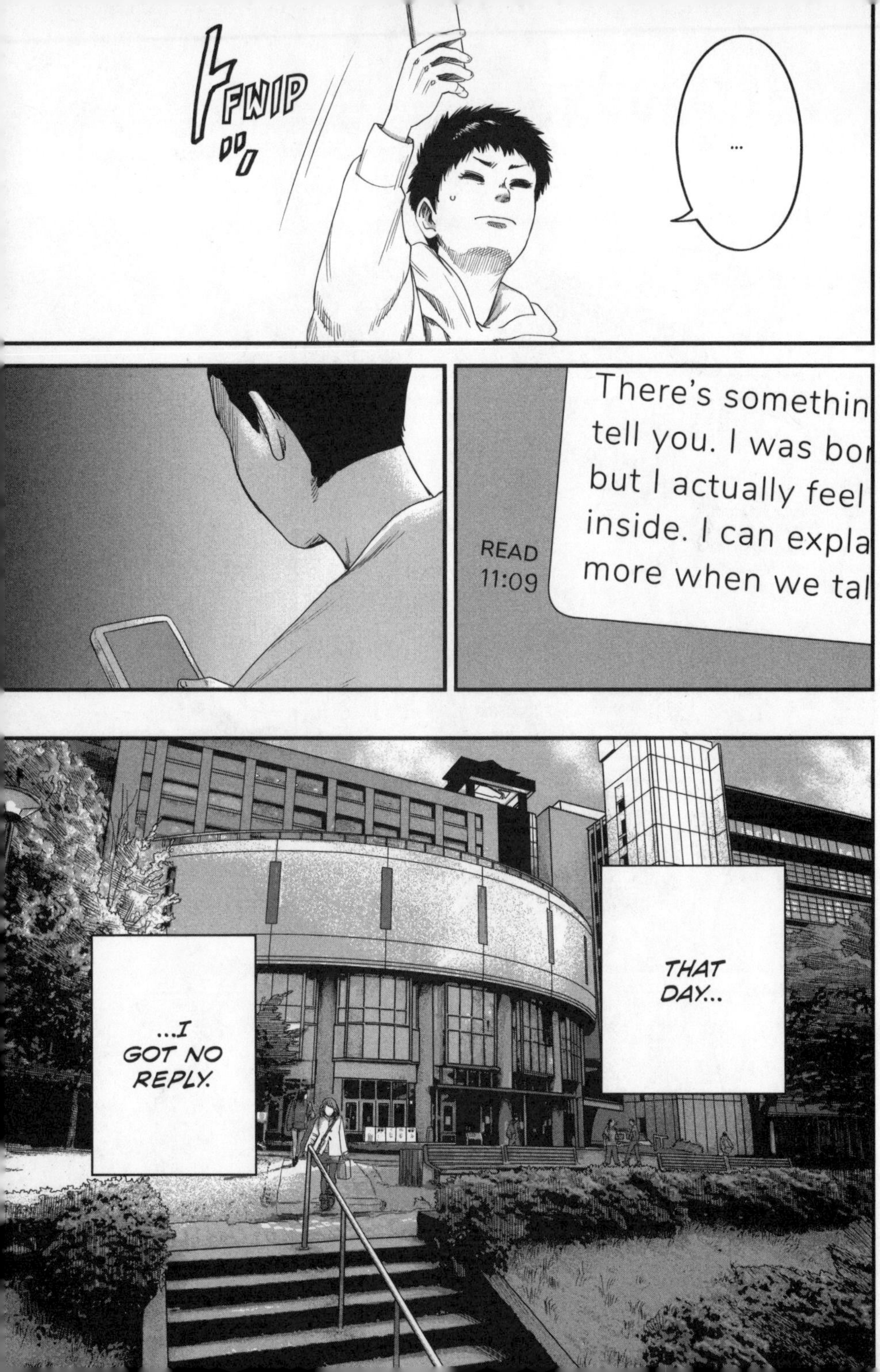
...
FWIP
READ
11:09
There's somethin
tell you. I was bor
but I actually feel
inside. I can expla
more when we tal
THAT DAY...
...I GOT NO REPLY.

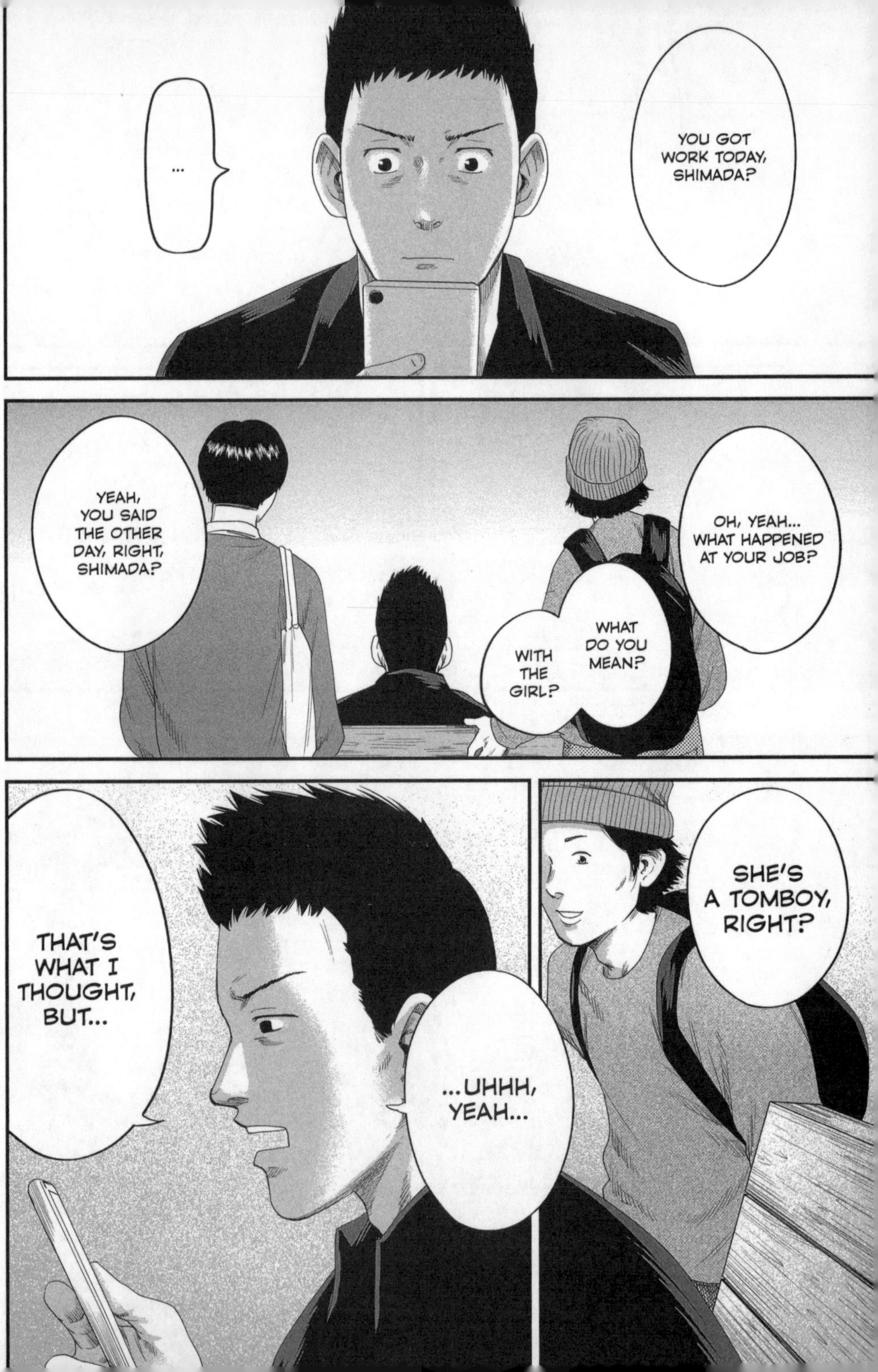
YOU GOT WORK TODAY, SHIMADA?
...
OH, YEAH... WHAT HAPPENED AT YOUR JOB?
WHAT DO YOU MEAN?
WITH THE GIRL?
YEAH, YOU SAID THE OTHER DAY, RIGHT, SHIMADA?
SHE'S A TOMBOY, RIGHT?
...UHHH, YEAH...
THAT'S WHAT I THOUGHT, BUT...

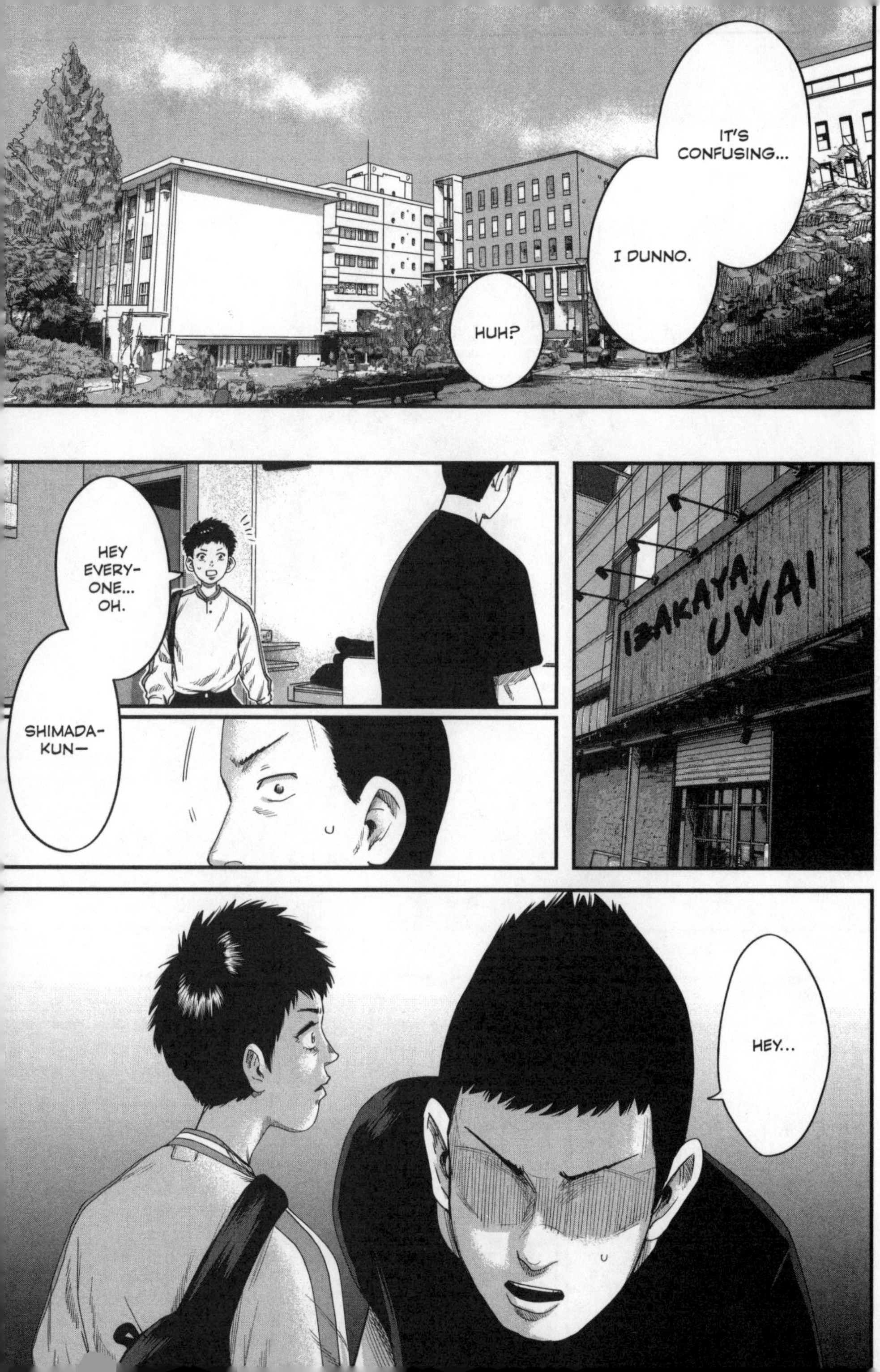
IT'S CONFUSING...
I DUNNO.
HUH?
IZAKAYA UWAI
HEY EVERY-ONE... OH.
SHIMADA-KUN—
HEY...

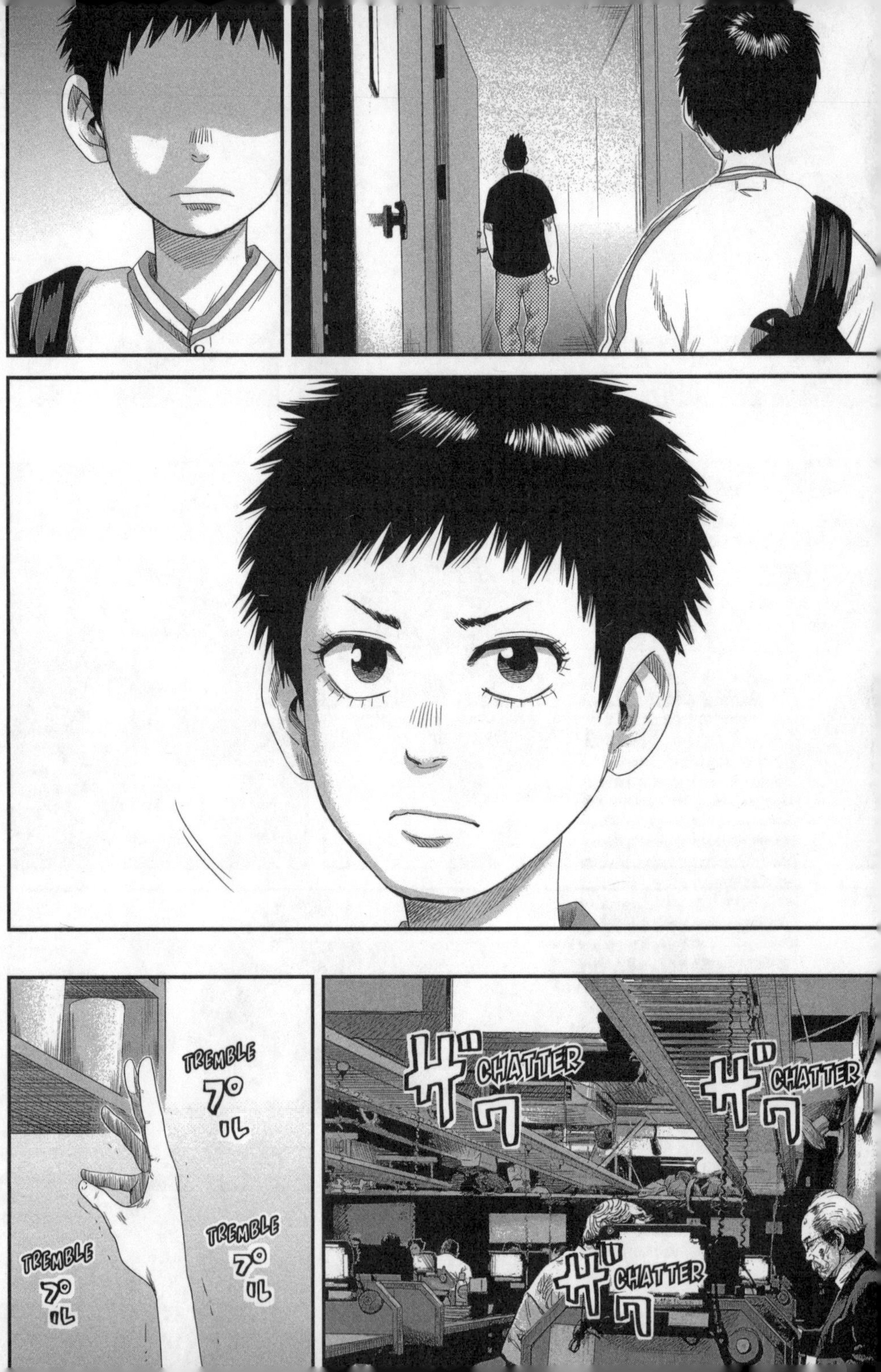
ザワ CHATTER
ザワ CHATTER
ザワ CHATTER
TREMBLE プル
TREMBLE プル
TREMBLE プル

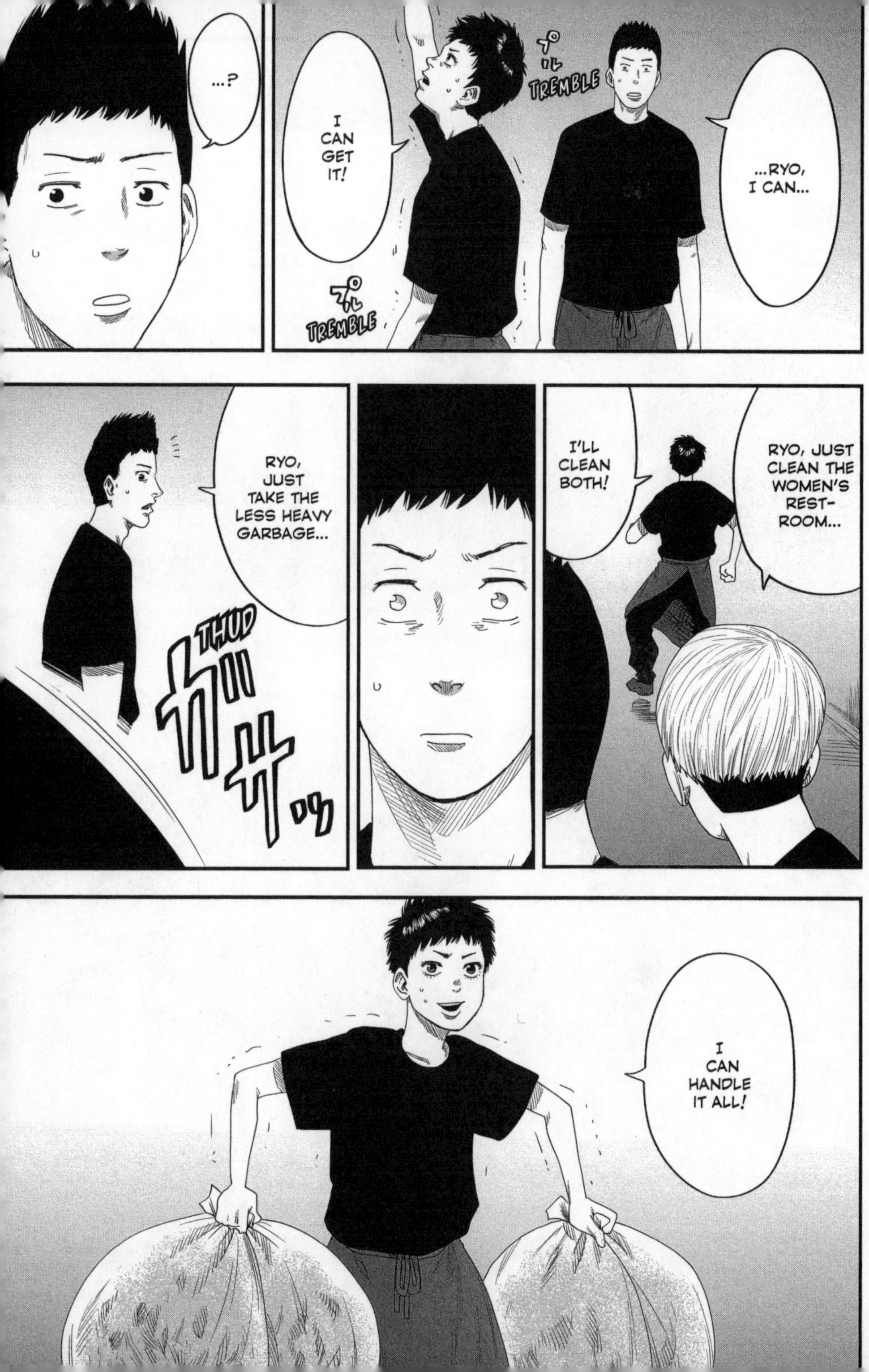
...RYO, I CAN...
TREMBLE
I CAN GET IT!
TREMBLE
...?
RYO, JUST CLEAN THE WOMEN'S REST-ROOM...
I'LL CLEAN BOTH!
RYO, JUST TAKE THE LESS HEAVY GARBAGE...
THUD
I CAN HANDLE IT ALL!

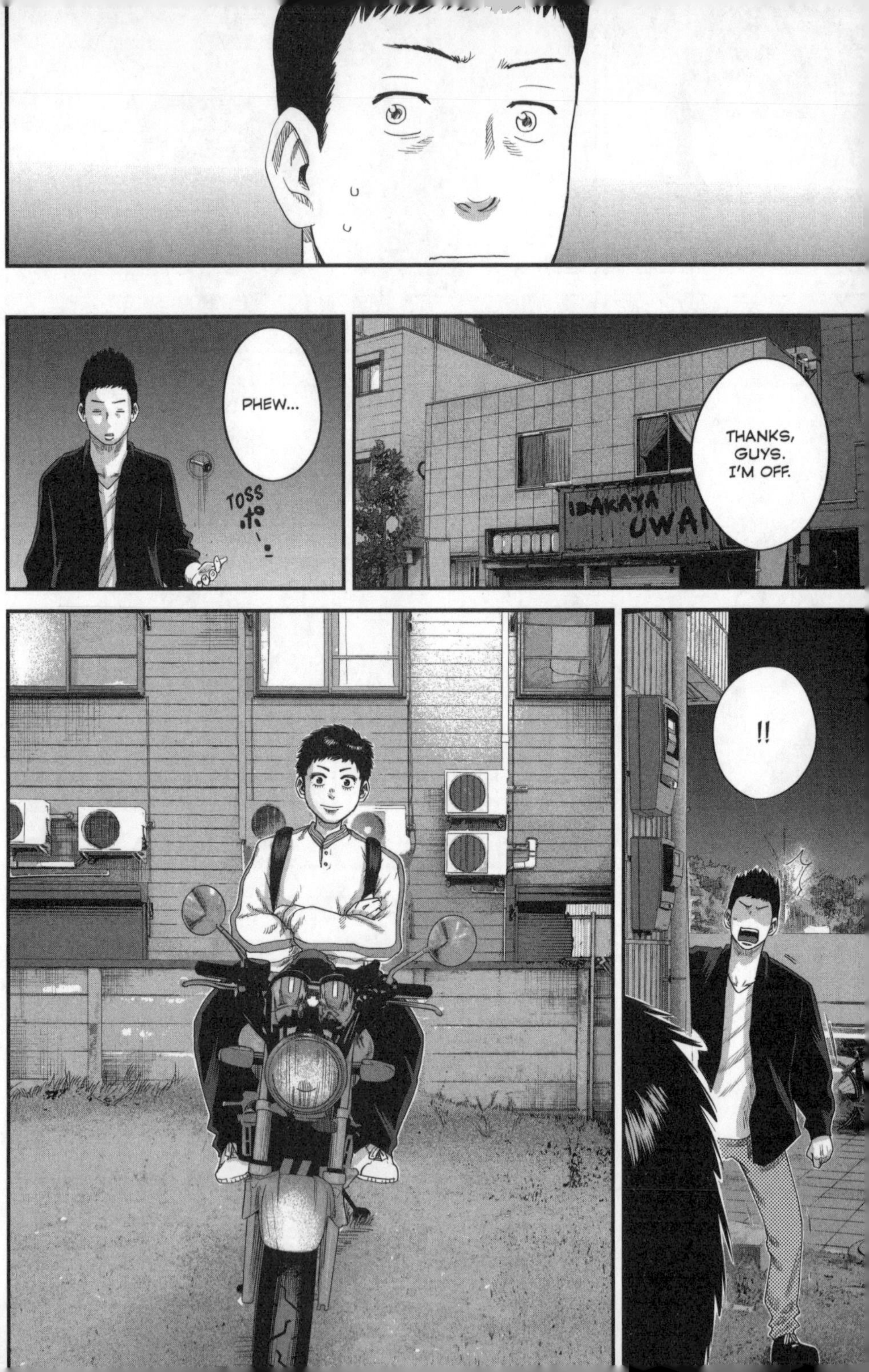
THANKS, GUYS. I'M OFF.
IZAKAYA UWAI
PHEW...
TOSS
!!

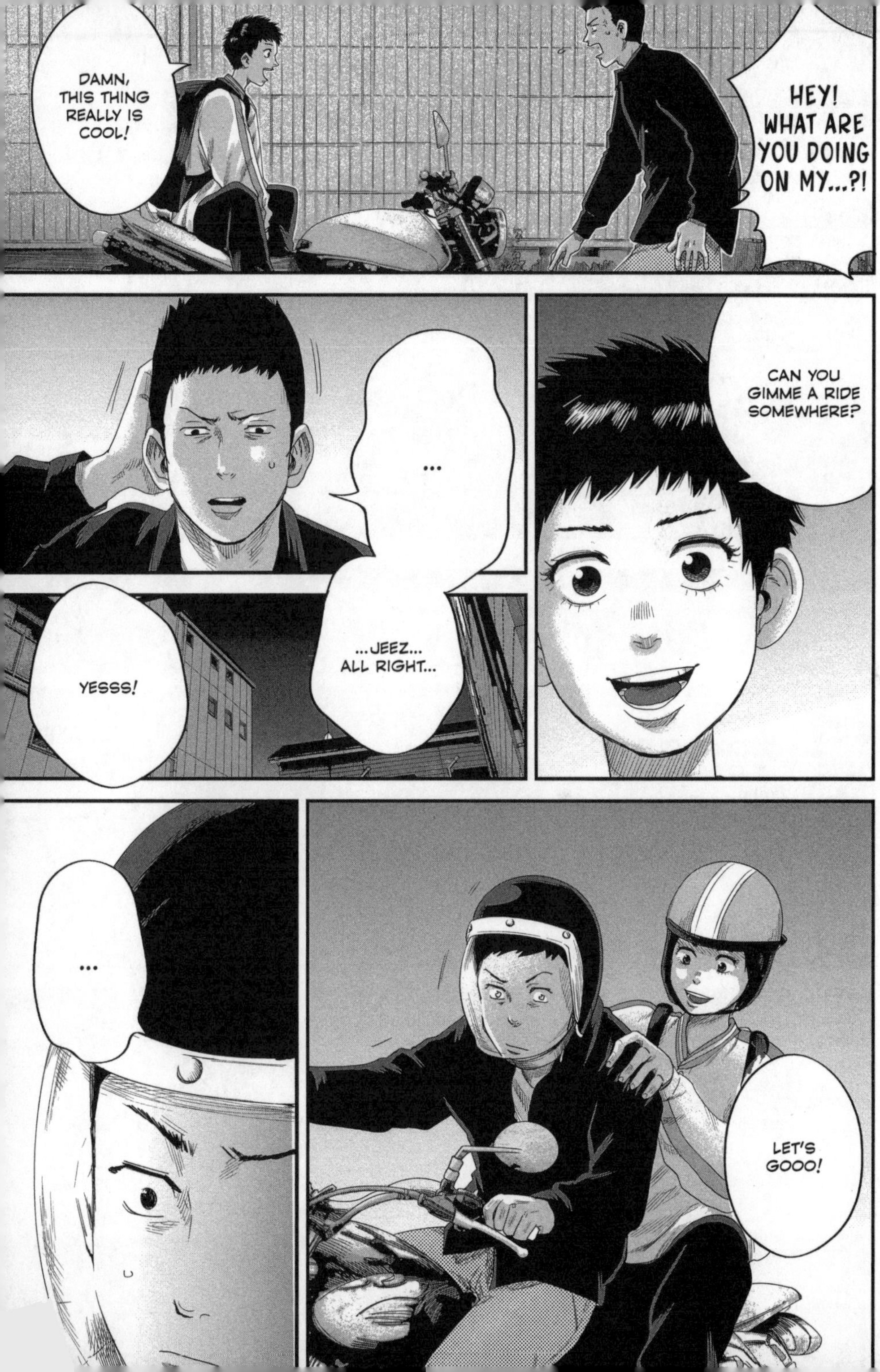

HEY! WHAT ARE YOU DOING ON MY...?!
DAMN, THIS THING REALLY IS COOL!
CAN YOU GIMME A RIDE SOMEWHERE?
...
...JEEZ... ALL RIGHT...
YESSS!
LET'S GOOO!
...

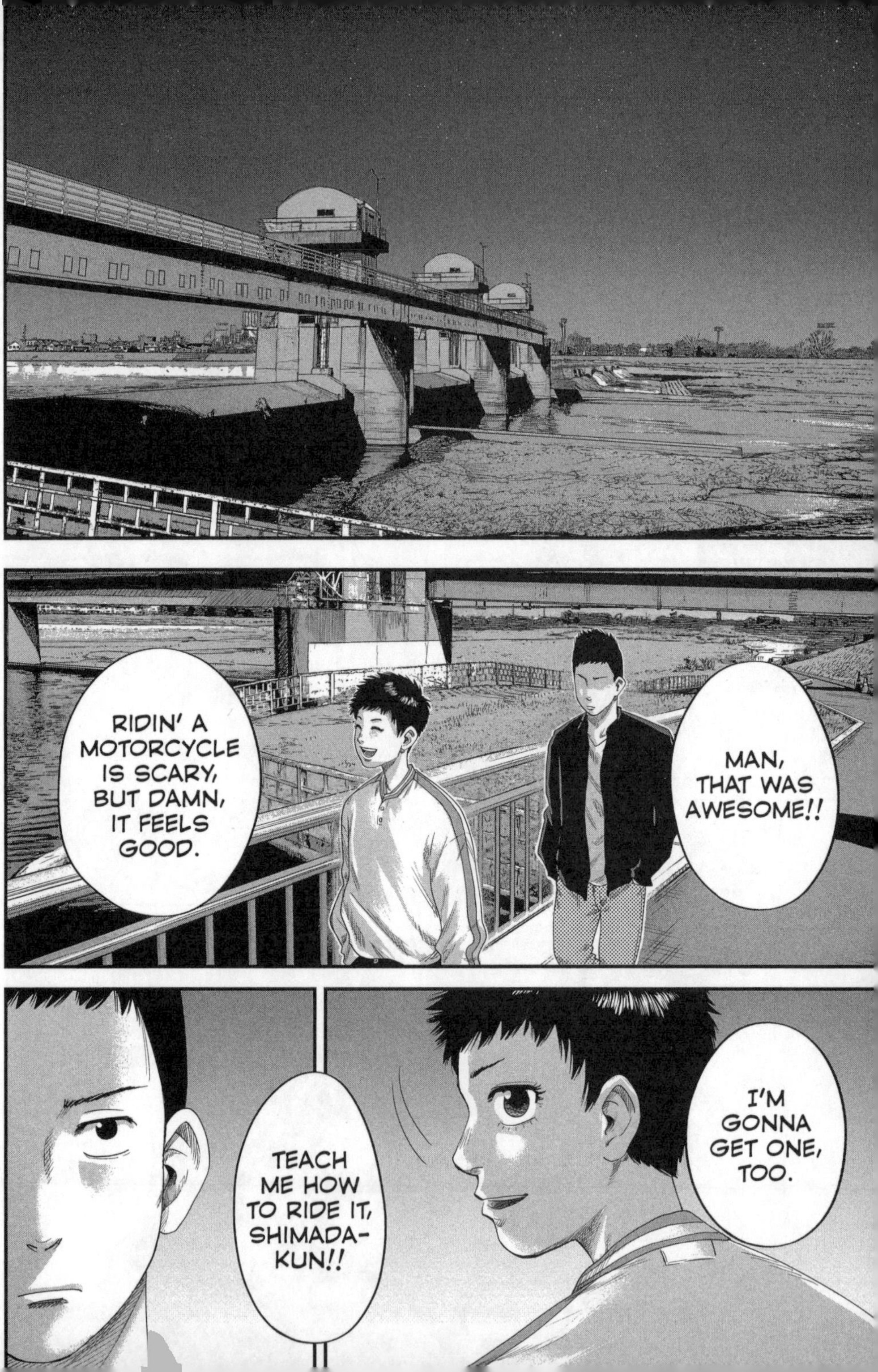
MAN, THAT WAS AWESOME!!
RIDIN' A MOTORCYCLE IS SCARY, BUT DAMN, IT FEELS GOOD.
I'M GONNA GET ONE, TOO.
TEACH ME HOW TO RIDE IT, SHIMADA-KUN!!

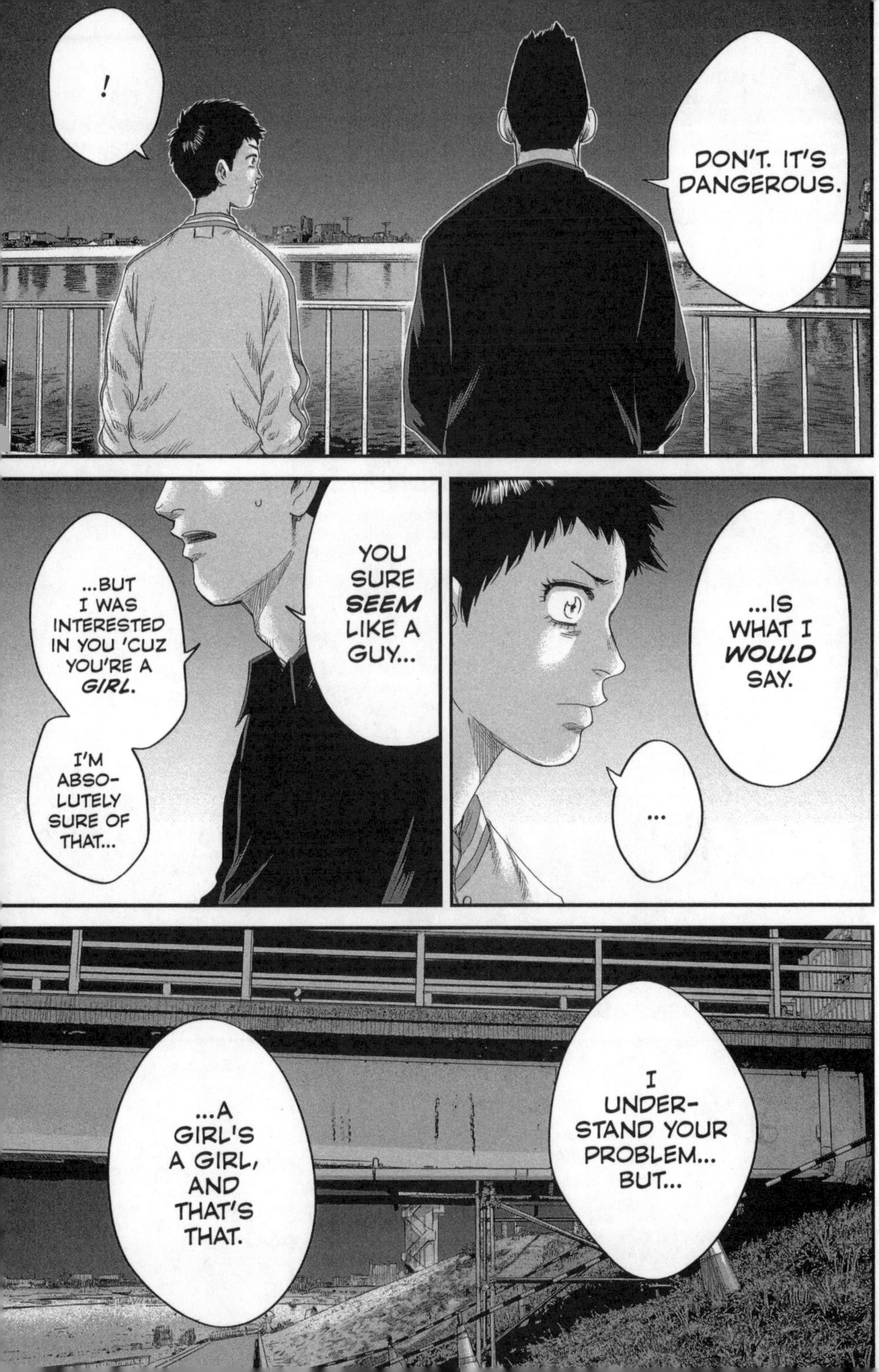
DON'T. IT'S DANGEROUS.
!
...IS WHAT I *WOULD* SAY.
...
YOU SURE *SEEM* LIKE A GUY...
...BUT I WAS INTERESTED IN YOU 'CUZ YOU'RE A *GIRL*.
I'M ABSOLUTELY SURE OF THAT...
I UNDERSTAND YOUR PROBLEM... BUT...
...A GIRL'S A GIRL, AND THAT'S THAT.

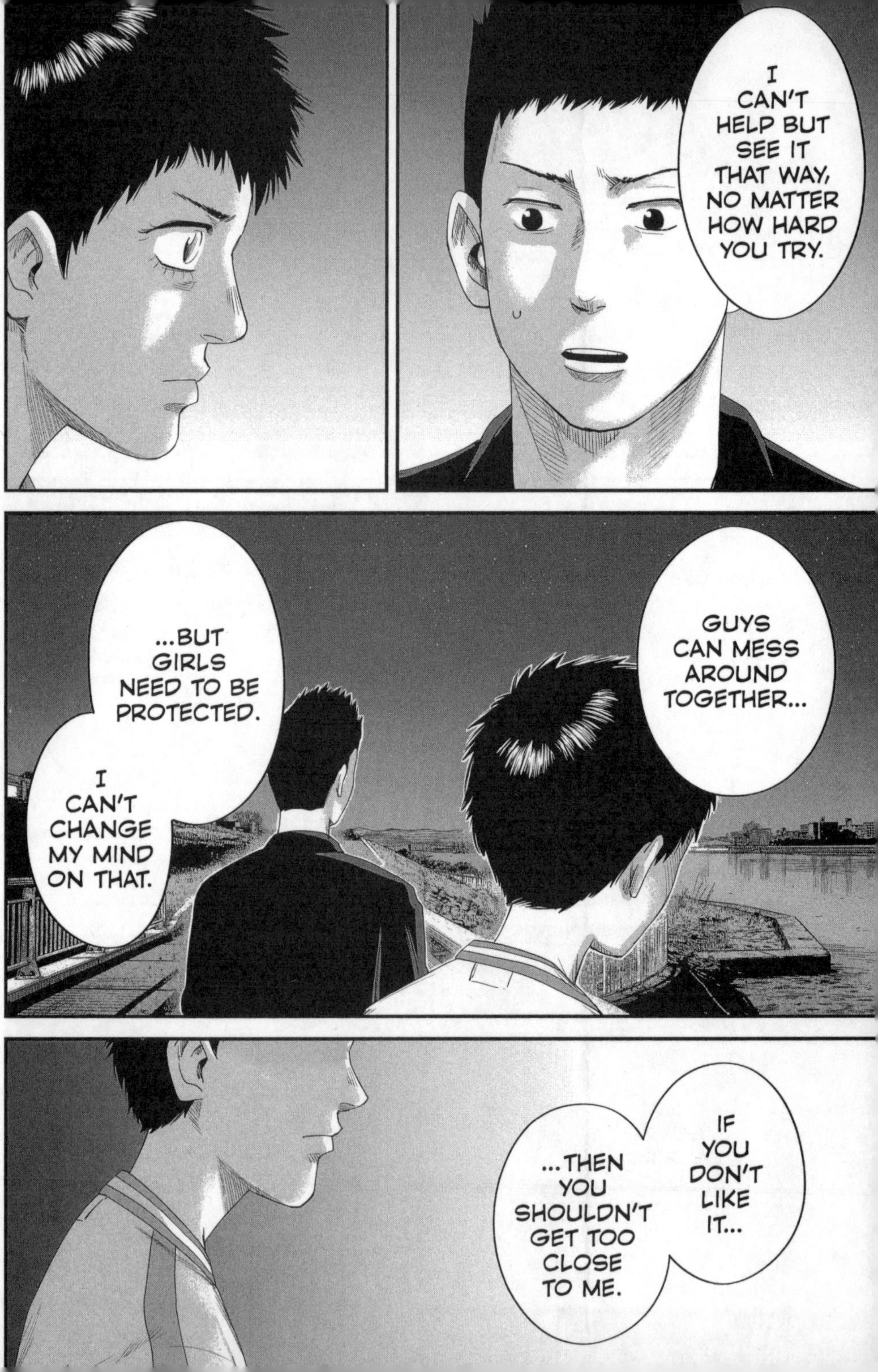
I CAN'T HELP BUT SEE IT THAT WAY, NO MATTER HOW HARD YOU TRY.
GUYS CAN MESS AROUND TOGETHER...
...BUT GIRLS NEED TO BE PROTECTED.
I CAN'T CHANGE MY MIND ON THAT.
IF YOU DON'T LIKE IT...
...THEN YOU SHOULDN'T GET TOO CLOSE TO ME.

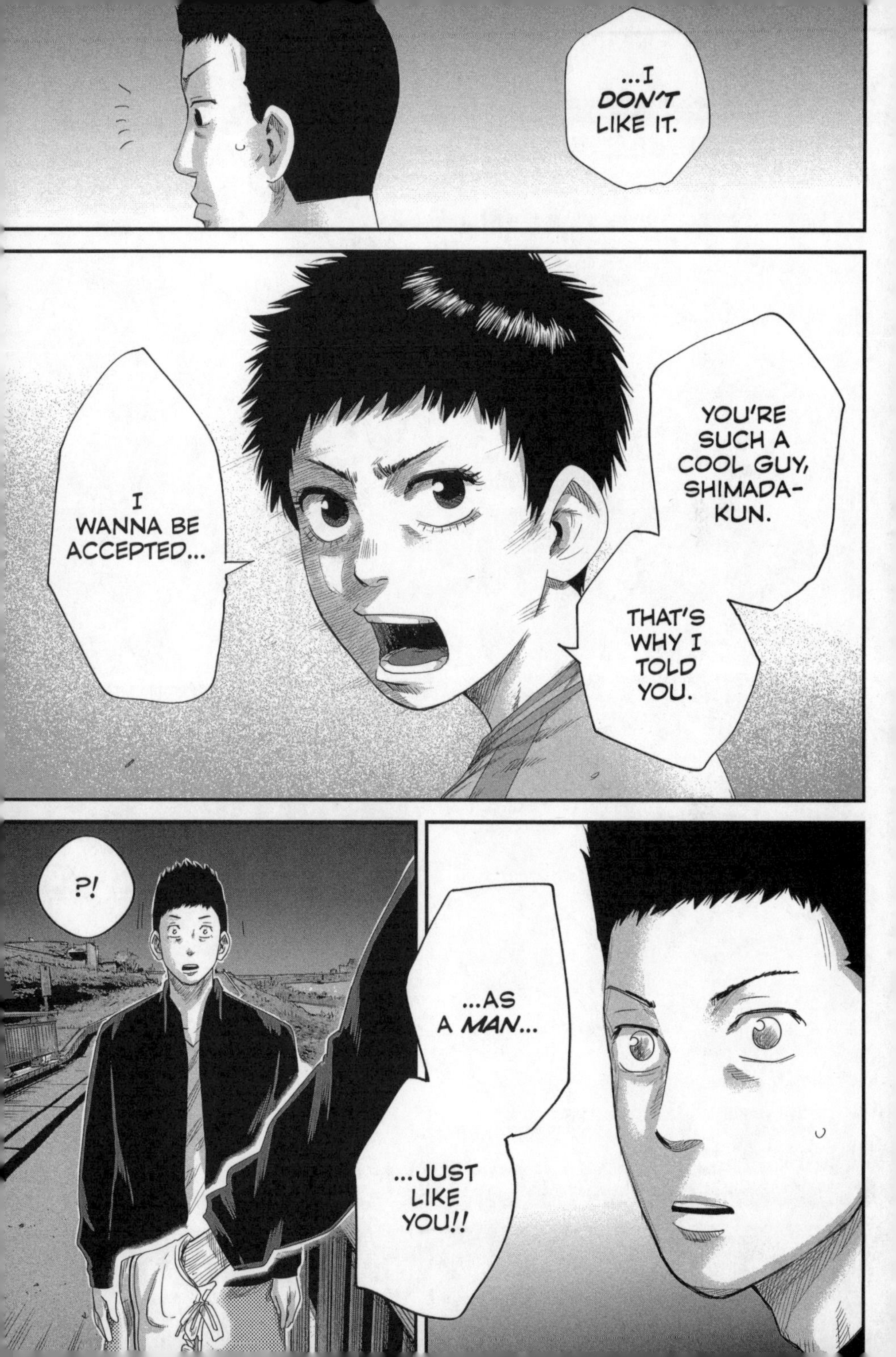
...I *DON'T* LIKE IT.
YOU'RE SUCH A COOL GUY, SHIMADA-KUN.
THAT'S WHY I TOLD YOU.
I WANNA BE ACCEPTED...
...AS A *MAN*...
...JUST LIKE YOU!!
?!

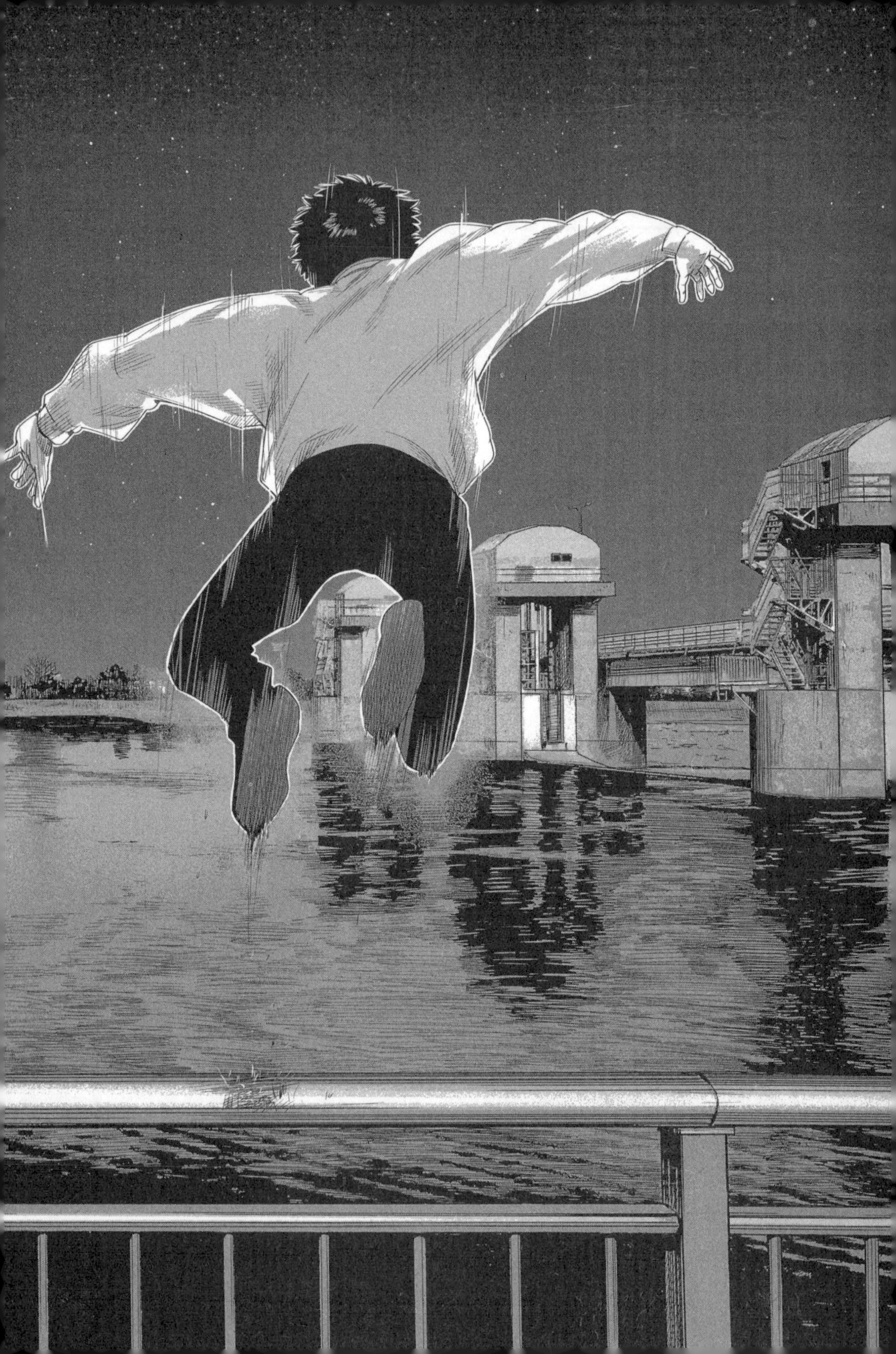

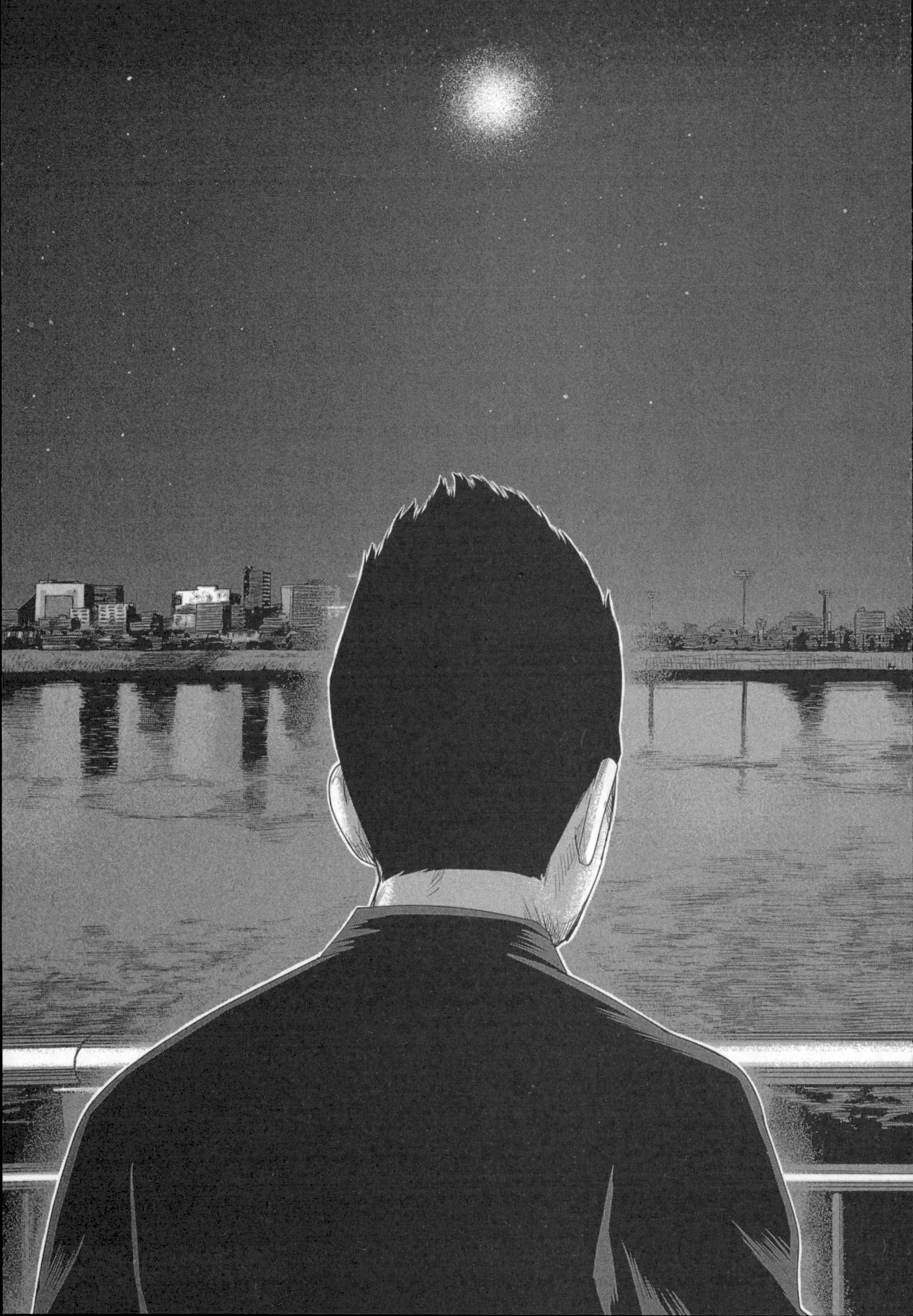

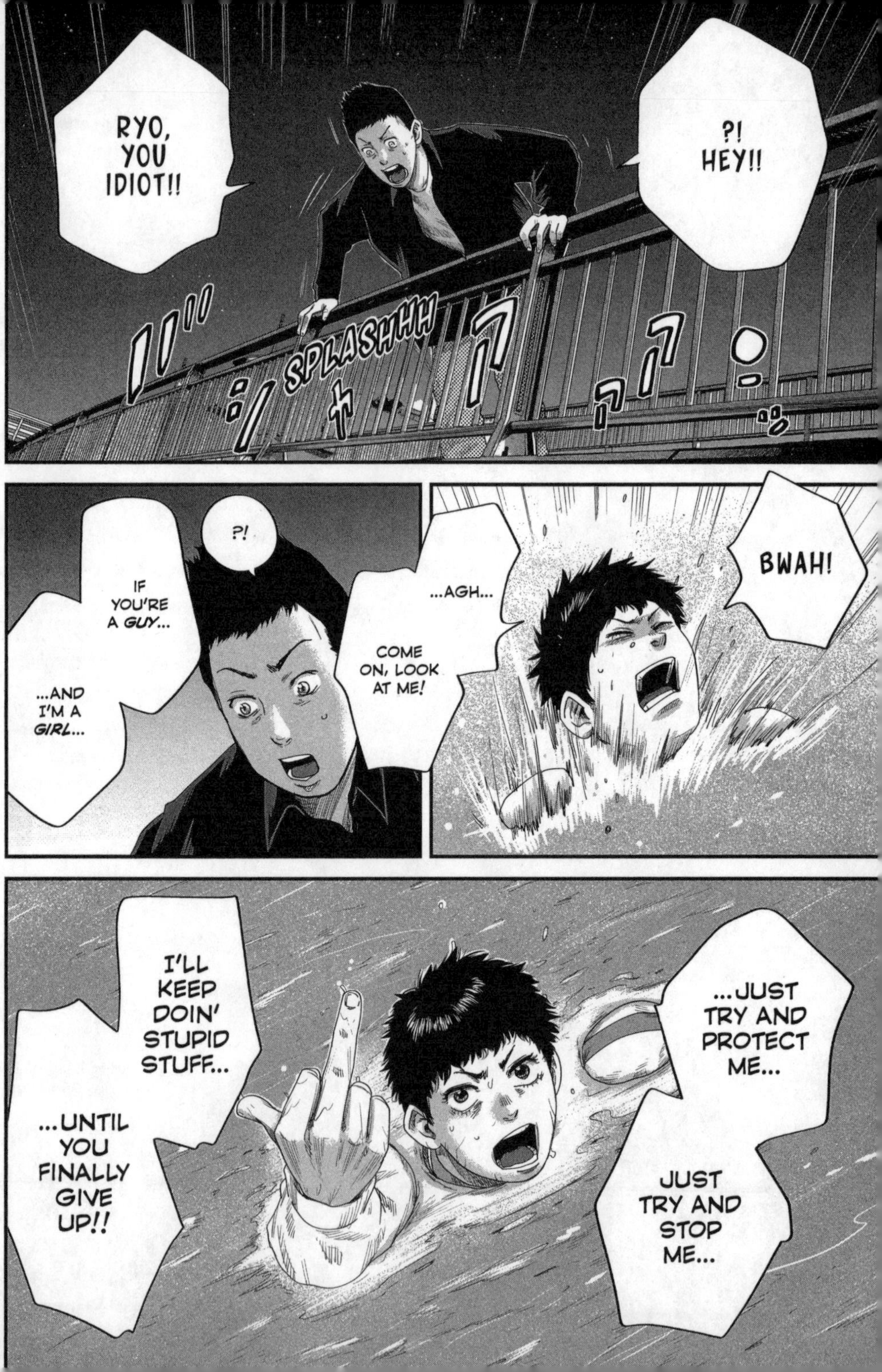
?! HEY!!
RYO, YOU IDIOT!!
SPLASHHH
BWAH!
...AGH...
COME ON, LOOK AT ME!
?!
IF YOU'RE A *GUY*...
...AND I'M A *GIRL*...
...JUST TRY AND PROTECT ME...
JUST TRY AND STOP ME...
I'LL KEEP DOIN' STUPID STUFF...
...UNTIL YOU FINALLY GIVE UP!!

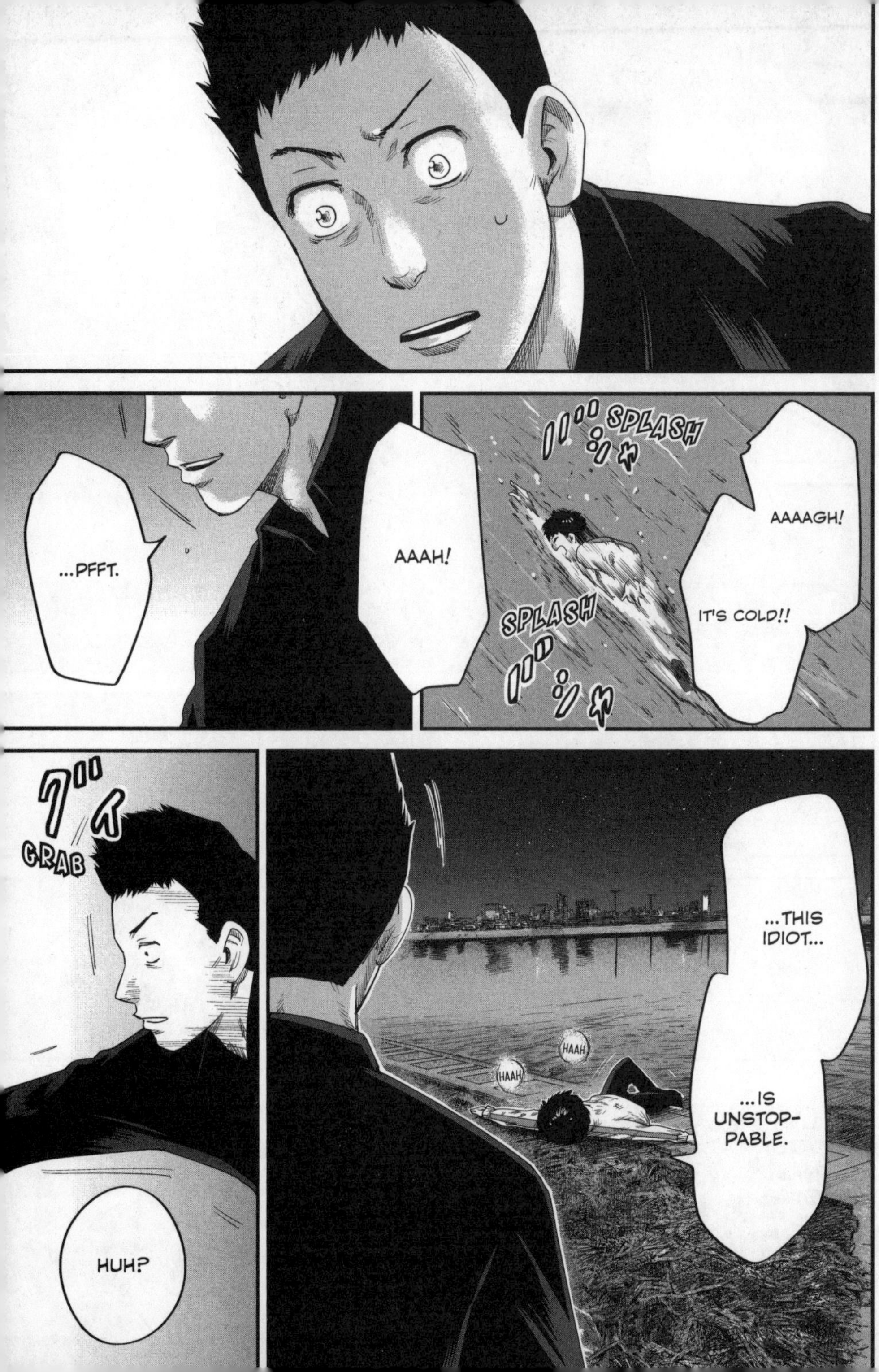
SPLASH
AAAAGH!
IT'S COLD!!
SPLASH
AAAH!
...PFFT.
...THIS IDIOT...
...IS UNSTOP-PABLE.
HAAH
HAAH
GRAB
HUH?

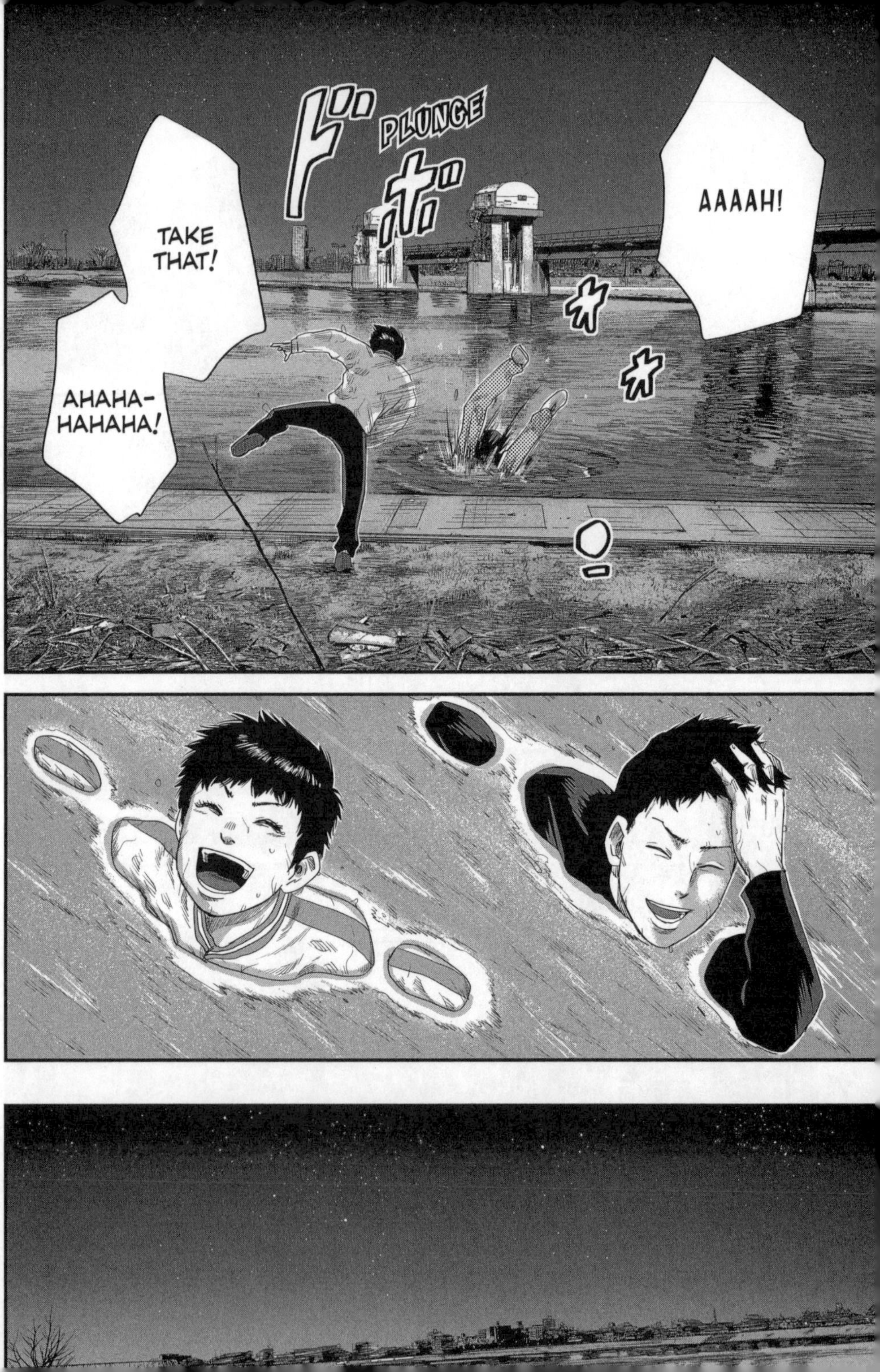
AAAAH!
PLUNGE
TAKE THAT!
AHAHA-HAHAHA!

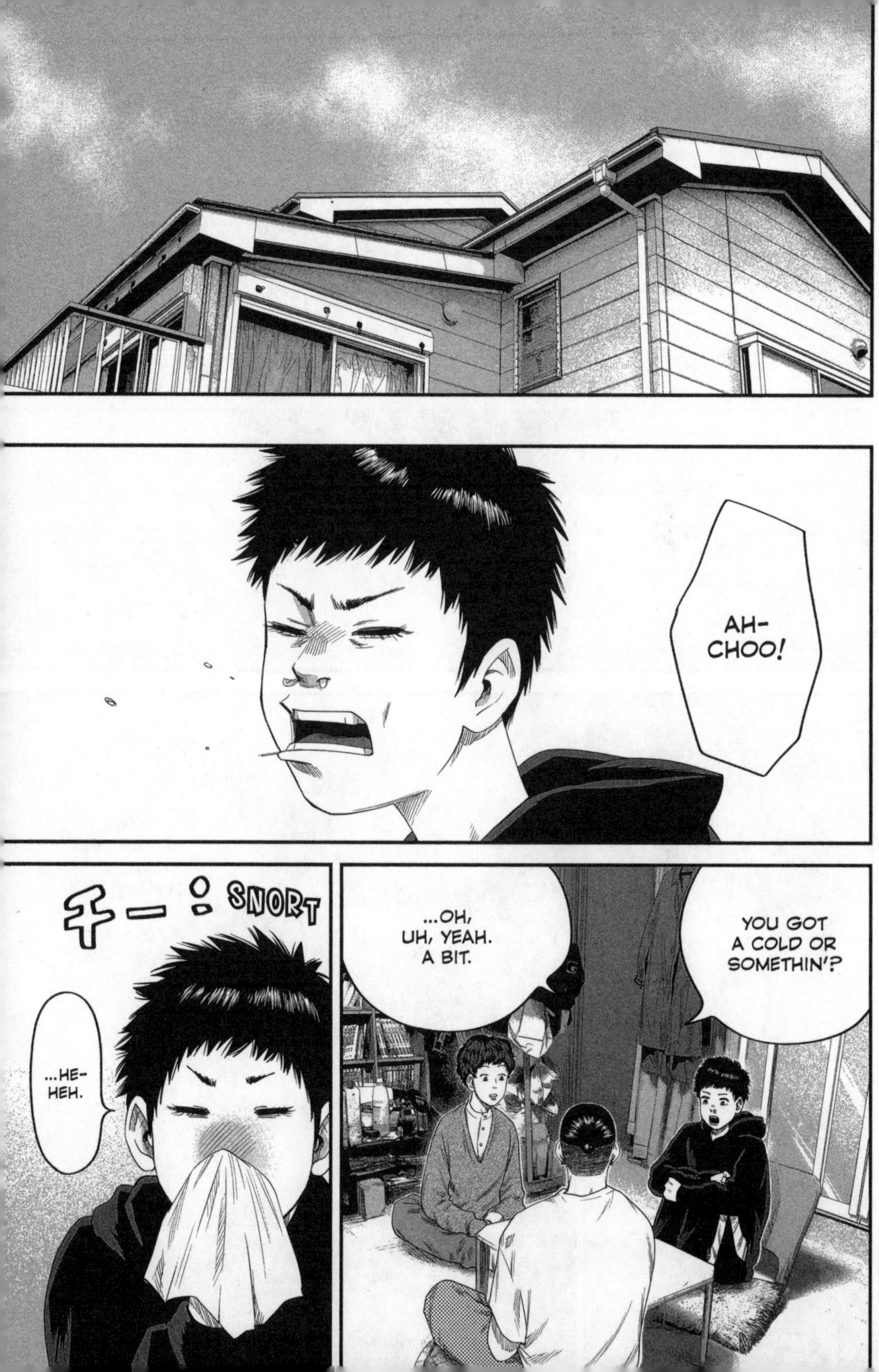
AH-CHOO!
YOU GOT A COLD OR SOMETHIN'?
...OH, UH, YEAH. A BIT.
チー SNORT
...HE-HEH.

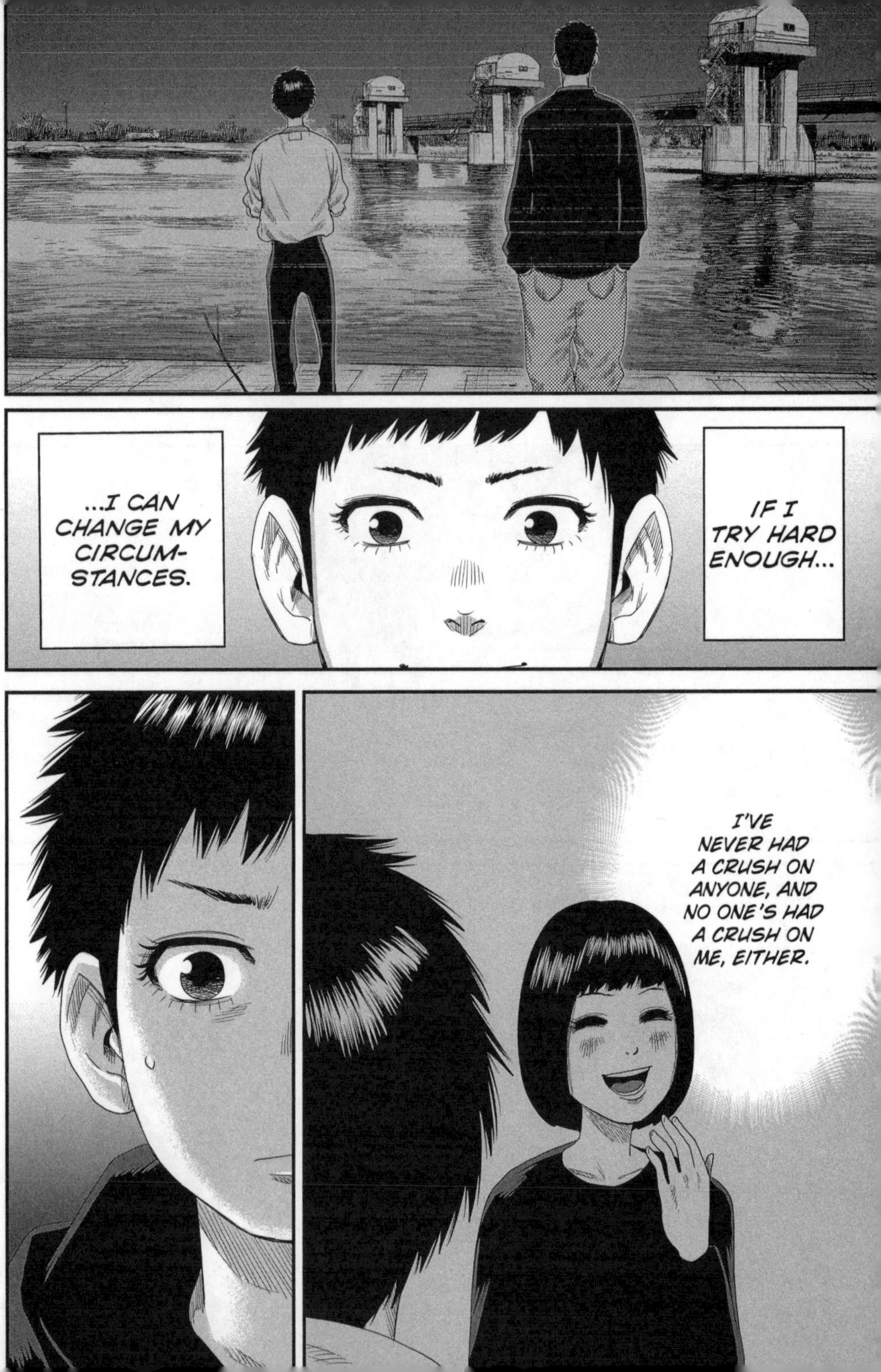
IF I TRY HARD ENOUGH...
...I CAN CHANGE MY CIRCUM-STANCES.
I'VE NEVER HAD A CRUSH ON ANYONE, AND NO ONE'S HAD A CRUSH ON ME, EITHER.

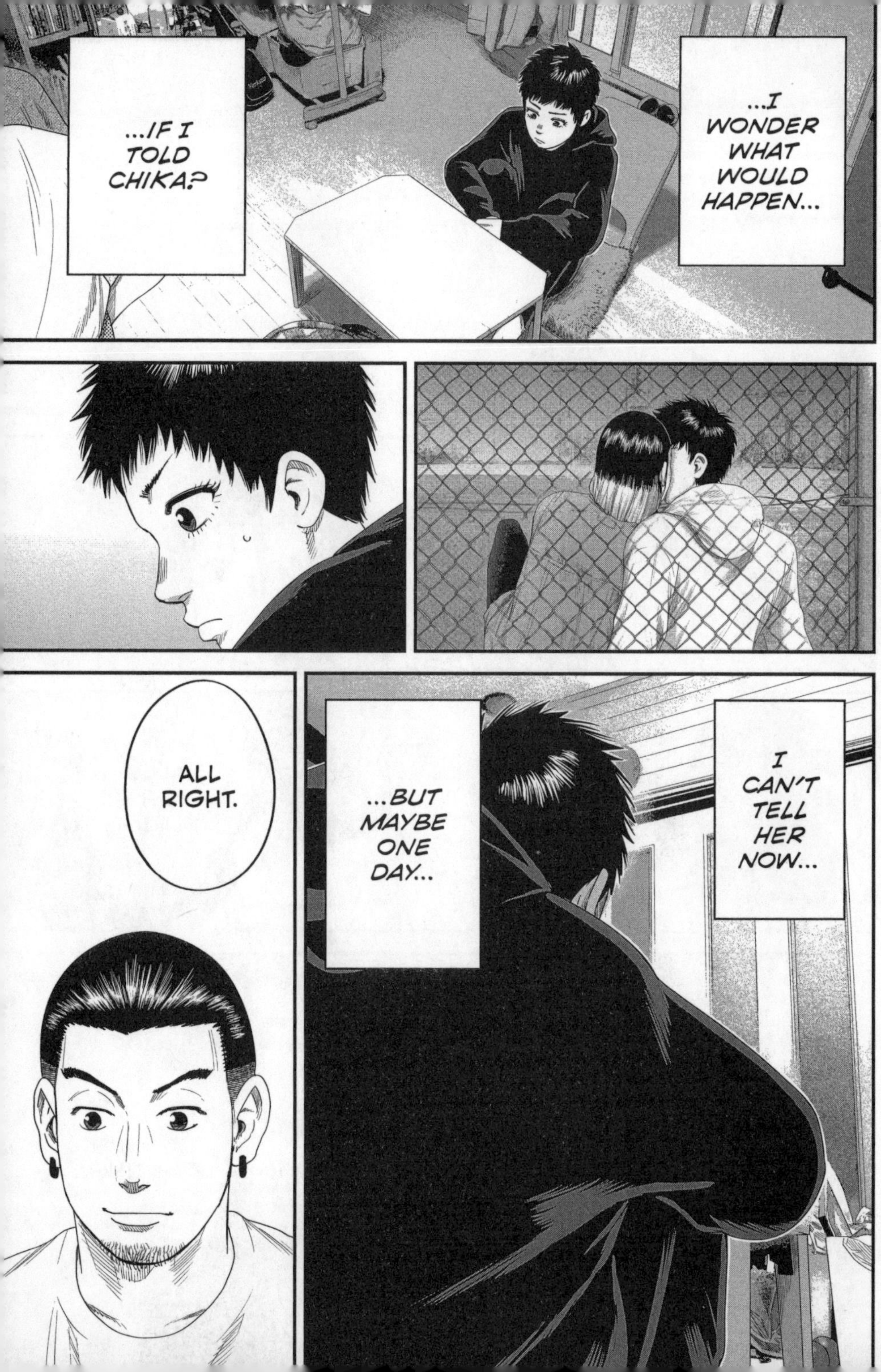
...I WONDER WHAT WOULD HAPPEN...
...IF I TOLD CHIKA?
I CAN'T TELL HER NOW...
...BUT MAYBE ONE DAY...
ALL RIGHT.

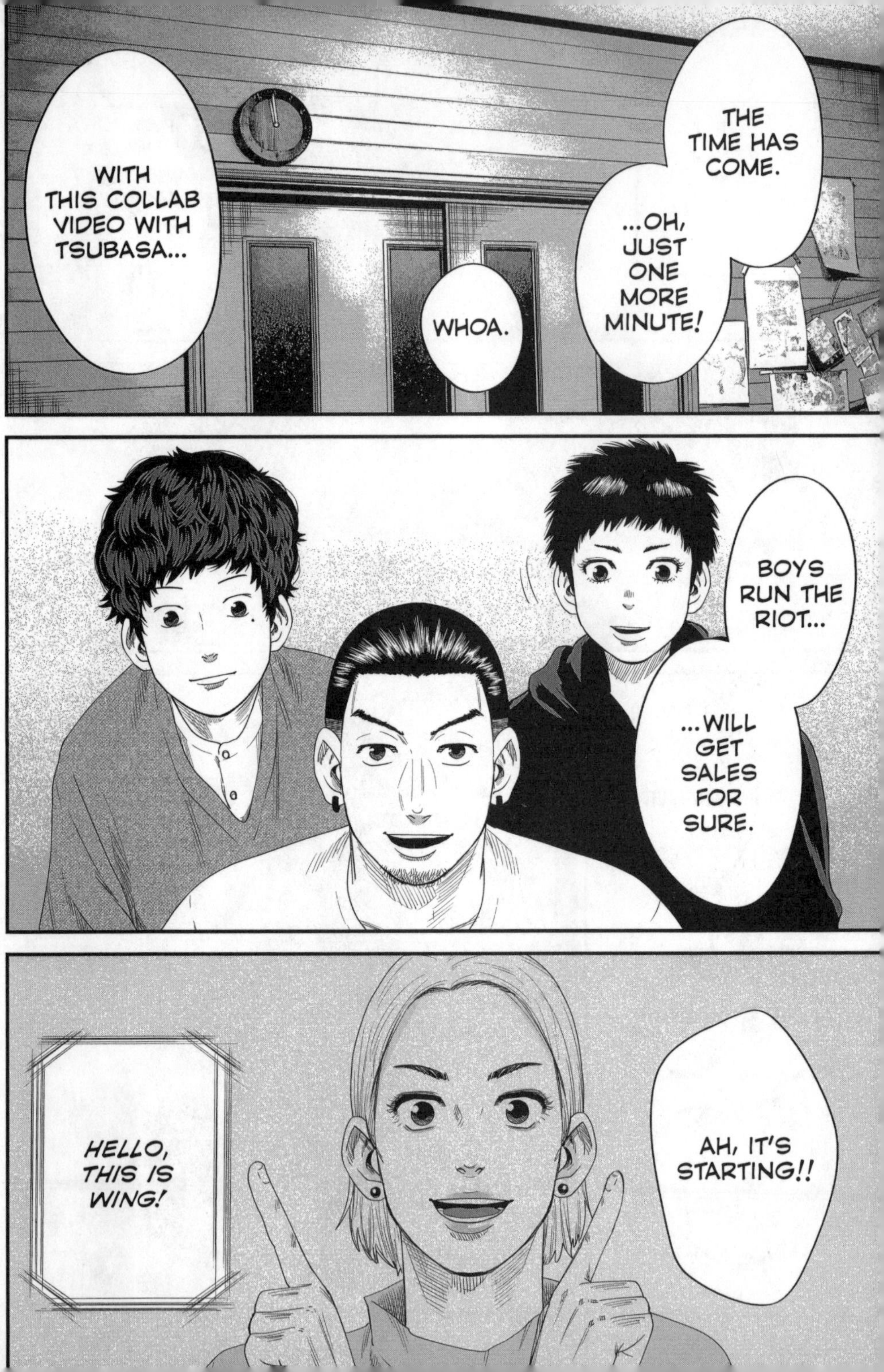
THE TIME HAS COME.
...OH, JUST ONE MORE MINUTE!
WHOA.
WITH THIS COLLAB VIDEO WITH TSUBASA...
BOYS RUN THE RIOT...
...WILL GET SALES FOR SURE.
AH, IT'S STARTING!!
HELLO, THIS IS WING!

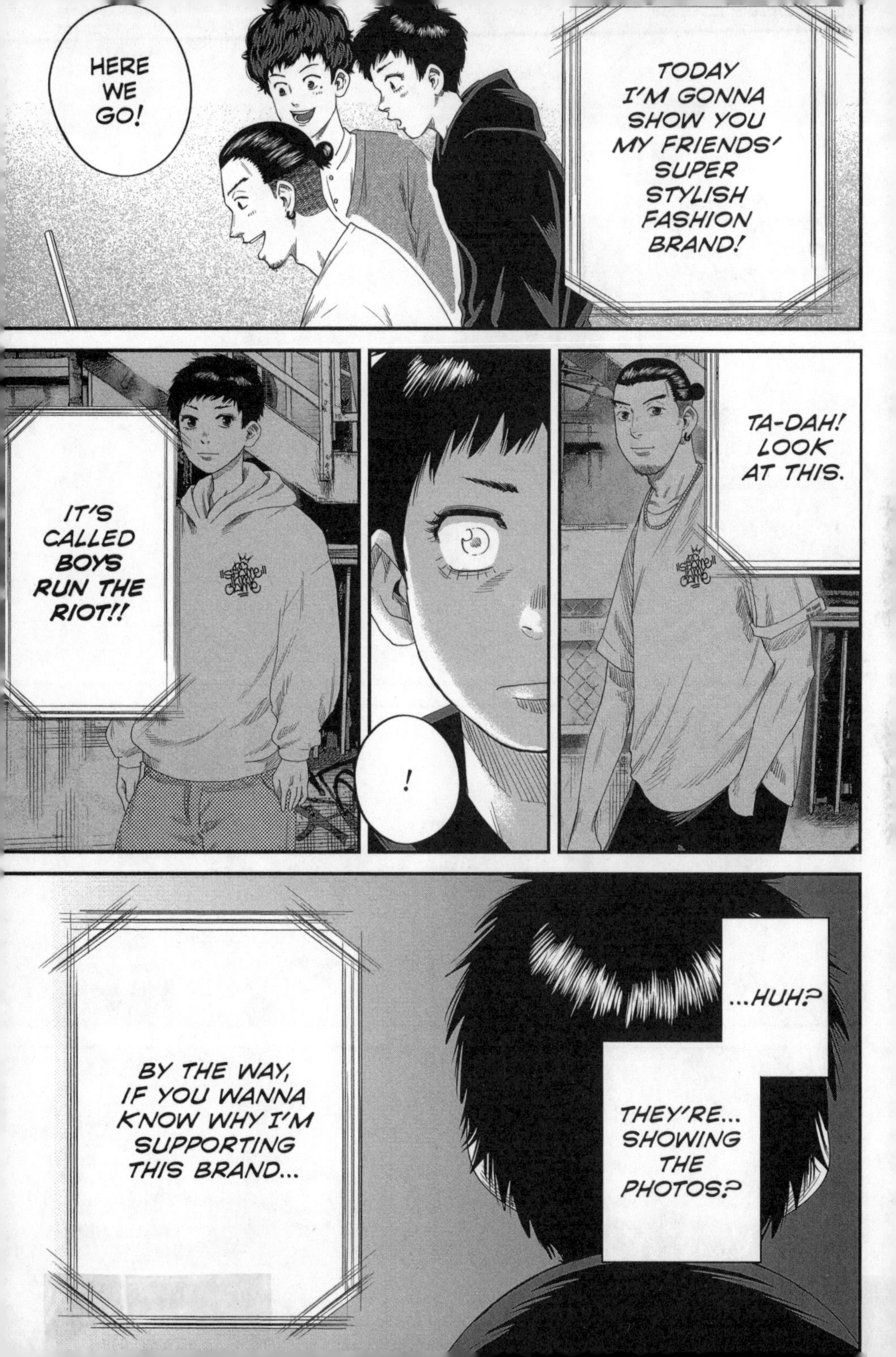
TODAY I'M GONNA SHOW YOU MY FRIENDS' SUPER STYLISH FASHION BRAND!
HERE WE GO!
TA-DAH! LOOK AT THIS.
!
IT'S CALLED BOYS RUN THE RIOT!!
...HUH?
THEY'RE... SHOWING THE PHOTOS?
BY THE WAY, IF YOU WANNA KNOW WHY I'M SUPPORTING THIS BRAND...

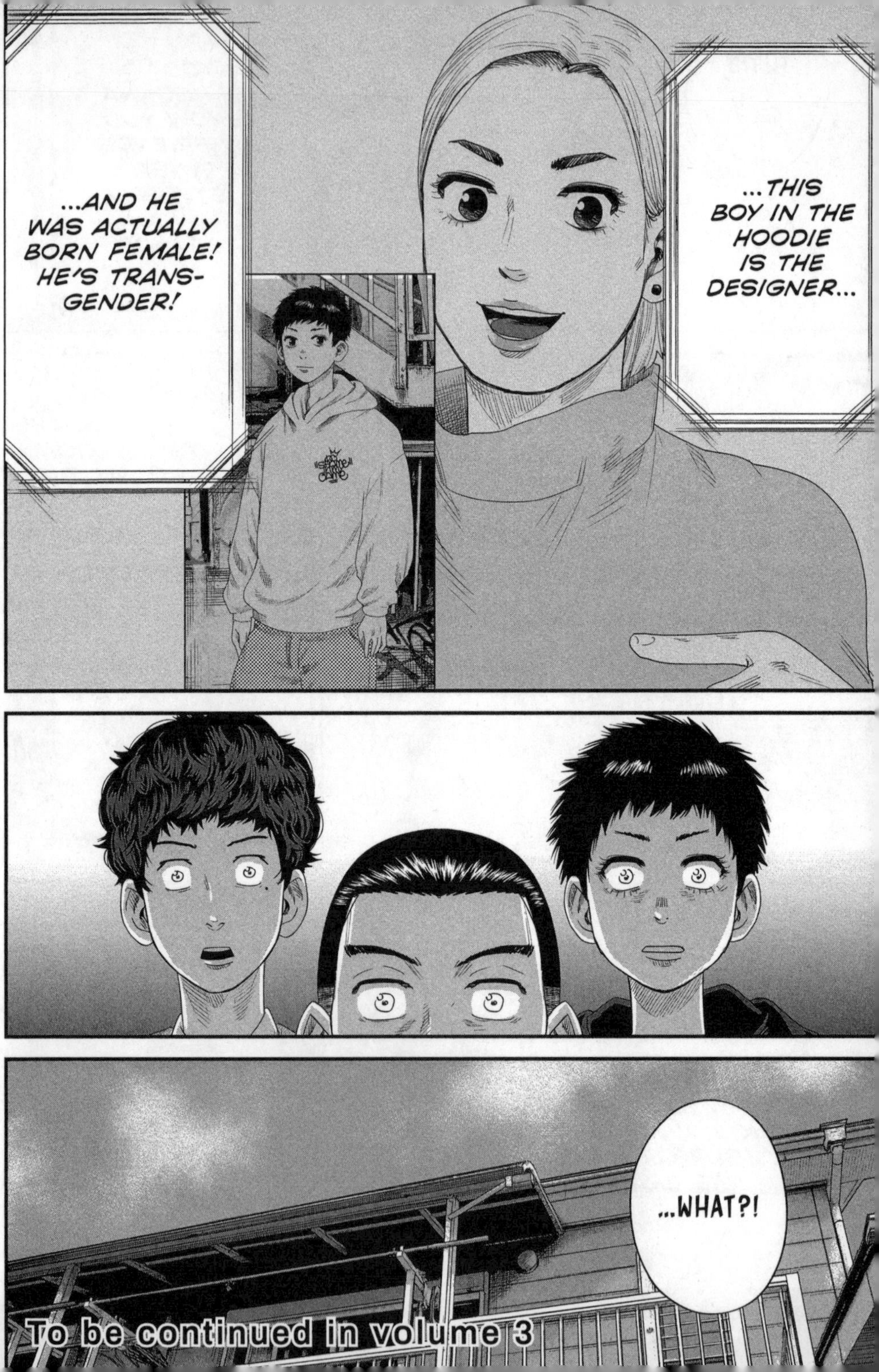
...THIS BOY IN THE HOODIE IS THE DESIGNER...
...AND HE WAS ACTUALLY BORN FEMALE! HE'S TRANS-GENDER!
...WHAT?!
To be continued in volume 3

STAFF

Igarashi
Ryuusei Terada
Taiga Miyahara
Pankue
Misaki Yoshimura

SPECIAL THANKS

SPECIAL VOLUME DESIGN

fake graphics – Akito Sumiyoshi

EDITORS

Hidemi Shiraki
Haruhito Uwai

SPECIAL VOLUME EDITORS

Tomohiro Ebitani
The Young Magazine editorial team

TRANSLATION NOTES

"IS HE GAY? A CROSSDRESSER?", page 3
In the original Japanese, this character is asking if Tsubasa is an *onee*. *Onee* literally means "big sister." It can be used for anyone assigned male at birth who acts or looks effeminate, so it can encompass effeminate gay men, crossdressers, drag queens, transgender women, and transfeminine people. Some people do not like being called *onee*, but some people do, and even self-identify as *onee*.

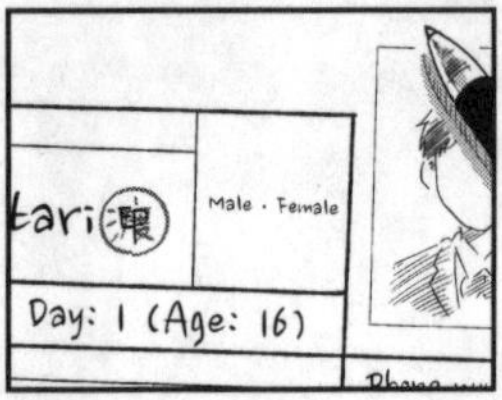
tari
Male · Female
Day: 1 (Age: 16)

SEAL, page 31
In Japan, individuals often sign official documents and paperwork with a personalized *inkan* (also sometimes referred to as a *hanko*), or stamp, rather than signing their name or initials in pen. The characters on an *inkan* usually include part, or all of, the characters of an individual's last name. Depending on what kind of document the person is signing, an individual may use one of the three common forms of *inkan*: a *jitsu-in* ("actual/true seal"), an official registered seal used for signing documents such as contracts (and is likely the kind of seal Ryo used here), a *ginko-in*, for bank transactions, or a mitome-i ("personal seal"), for everyday use, such as signing for parcels or packages. Here, Ryo's *inkan* bears the character for Ryo's last name, Watari, and the character *in* from the beginning of *inkan*.

"SO YOU WANT TO HAVE -KUN ADDED TO YOUR NAME AND STUFF?", page 35
-kun is an honorific often attached to the names of boys or younger men. As with most honorifics, though, there's some nuance to the exact use of *-kun*, and it can also be used in cases of superiors addressing or referring to juniors or subordinates, such as a teacher addressing a student, or, in this case, a boss addressing an employee.

***IZAKAYA*,** page 39
An *izakaya* is an informal Japanese bar that serves alcoholic drinks and snacks.

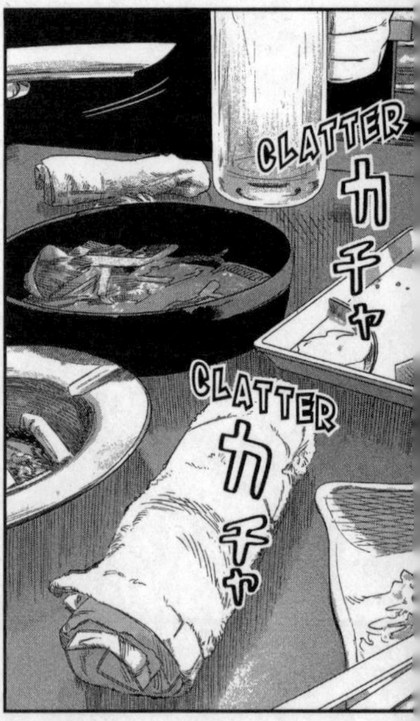
CLATTER
カチャ
CLATTER
カチャ

THE WORD-CHAIN GAME, page 51
Here Shimada is referring to the Japanese game *shiritori*. In *shiritori*, players take turns saying, or in this case, drawing, words, with one of the rules being that the next word a player says in the game must begin with the final syllable of the word before it. This can be seen more clearly in panel four, where the drawing for a car (*kuru**ma***) connects to a microphone (***ma**iku*).

LEMON SOUR, page 77
A sour is a type of carbonated, alcoholic cocktail that is very popular in Japan.

SHIMOKITAZAWA, page 79
A trendy area of Tokyo with a lot of secondhand vintage thrift stores, indie coffee shops, and live music.

"YOU DON'T SEEM LIKE A RYO-*KO* ANYWAY.", page 79
The kanji character for *ko*, meaning child, is often used at the end of female Japanese names.

HIGH SCHOOL BASEBALL, page 91
In the original Japanese, Shimada makes a reference to Koshien, the national high school baseball championship that runs every year across Japan, which is very famous.

BOYS RUN
ボーイズ・ラン・ザ・ライオット
THE RIOT

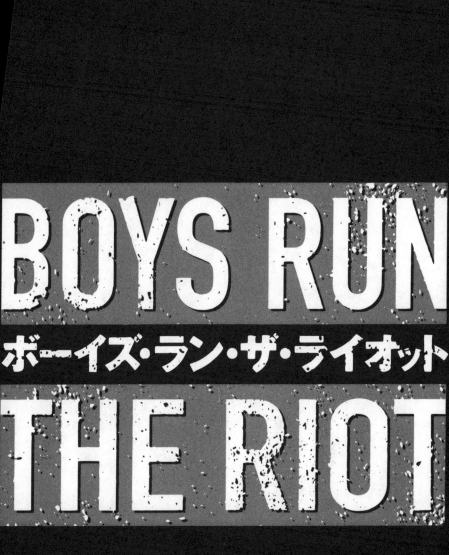

BOYS RUN THE RIOT VOLUME 2
ORIGINAL U.S. COVER SKETCH
BY AUTHOR KEITO GAKU

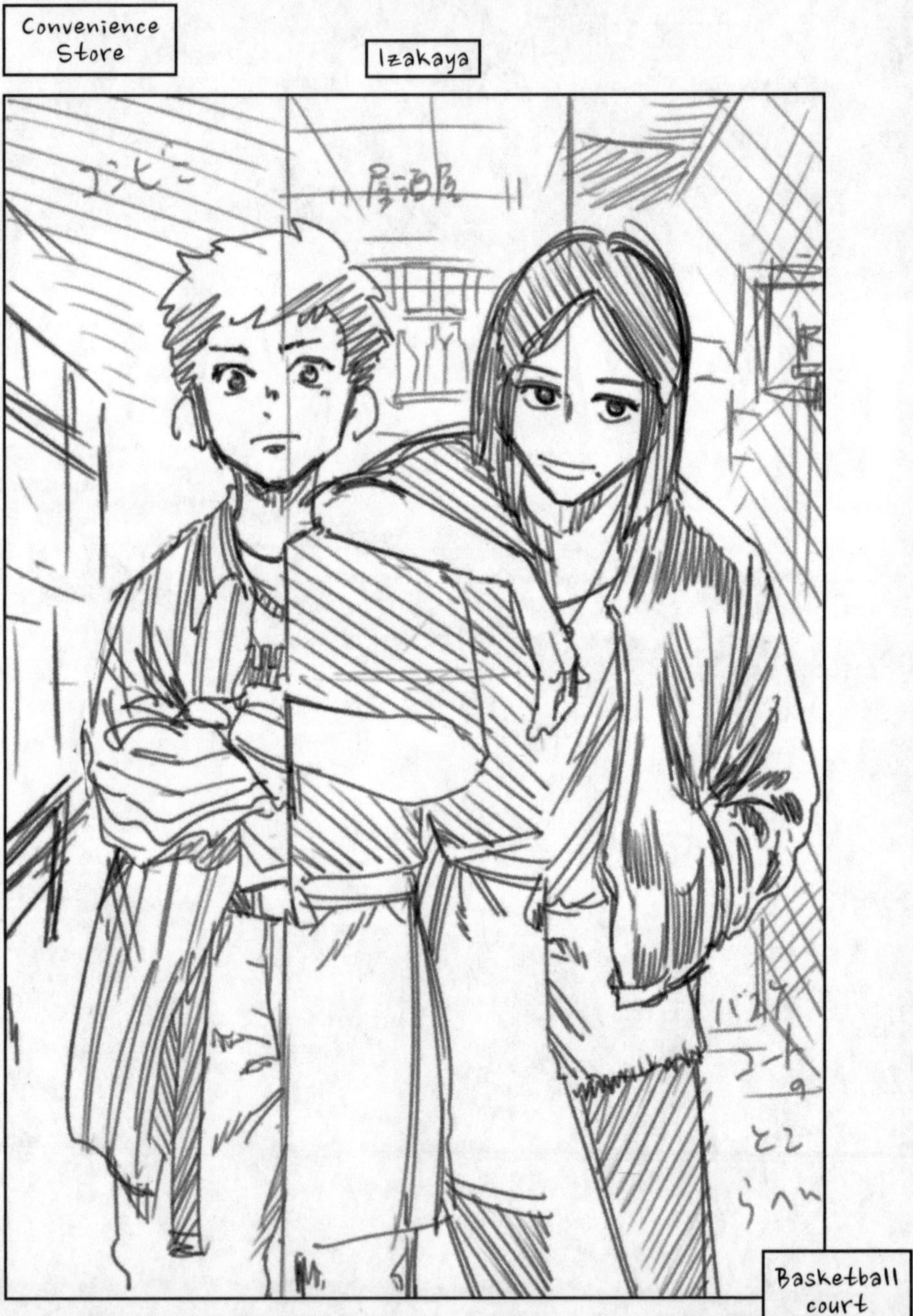
Convenience Store
Izakaya
Basketball court

ALTERNATE COVER SKETCH (UNUSED)

Pose 2

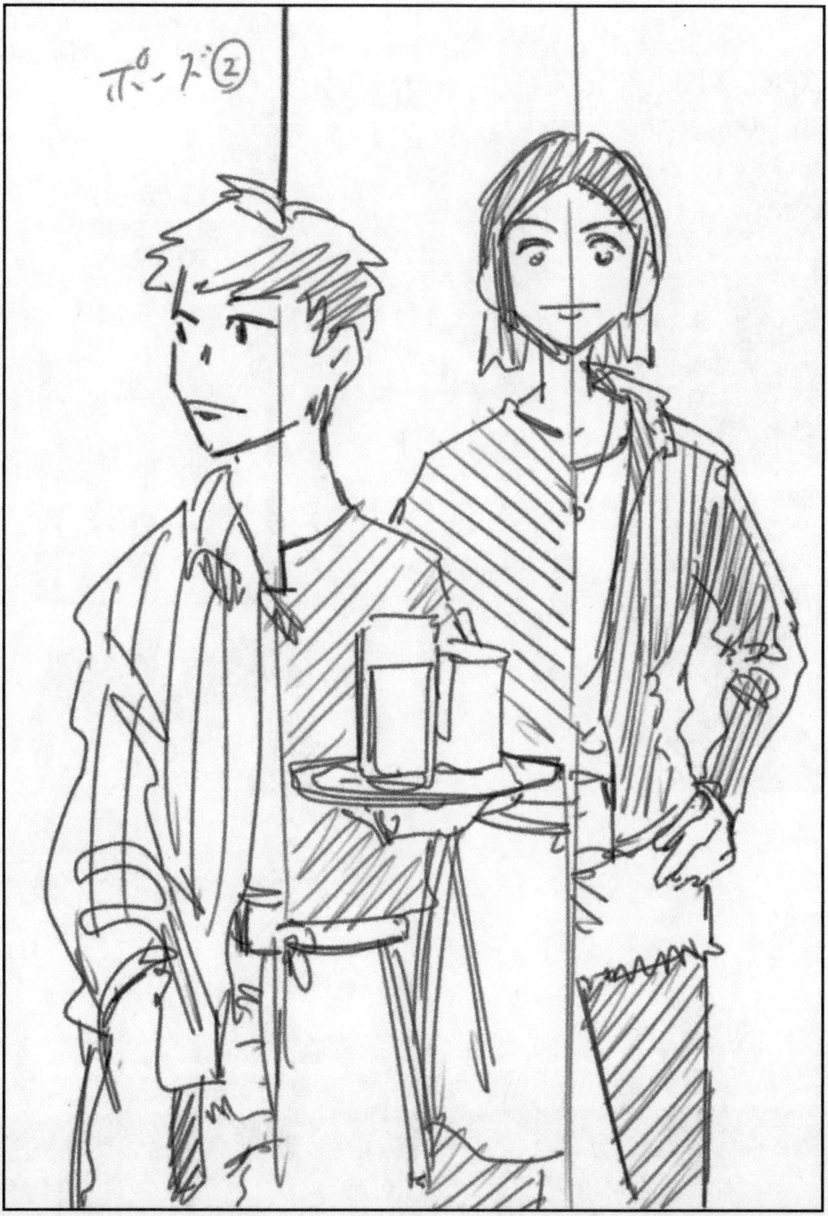
ポーズ②

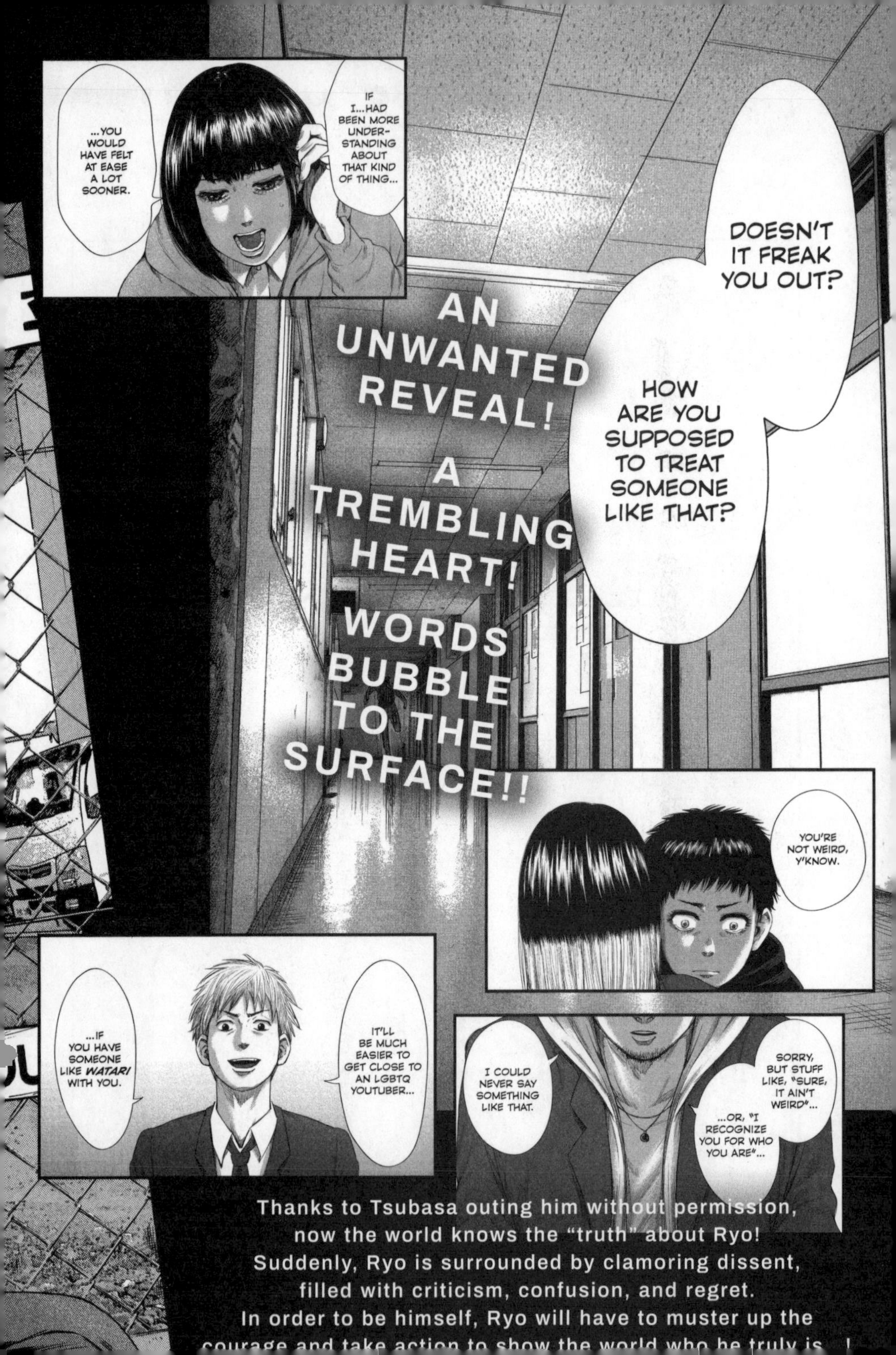
DOESN'T IT FREAK YOU OUT?
HOW ARE YOU SUPPOSED TO TREAT SOMEONE LIKE THAT?
AN UNWANTED REVEAL! A TREMBLING HEART! WORDS BUBBLE TO THE SURFACE!!
IF I...HAD BEEN MORE UNDER-STANDING ABOUT THAT KIND OF THING...
...YOU WOULD HAVE FELT AT EASE A LOT SOONER.
YOU'RE NOT WEIRD, Y'KNOW.
SORRY, BUT STUFF LIKE, "SURE, IT AIN'T WEIRD"...
...OR, "I RECOGNIZE YOU FOR WHO YOU ARE"...
I COULD NEVER SAY SOMETHING LIKE THAT.
IT'LL BE MUCH EASIER TO GET CLOSE TO AN LGBTQ YOUTUBER...
...IF YOU HAVE SOMEONE LIKE *WATARI* WITH YOU.
Thanks to Tsubasa outing him without permission, now the world knows the "truth" about Ryo! Suddenly, Ryo is surrounded by clamoring dissent, filled with criticism, confusion, and regret. In order to be himself, Ryo will have to muster up the courage and take action to show the world who he truly is...!

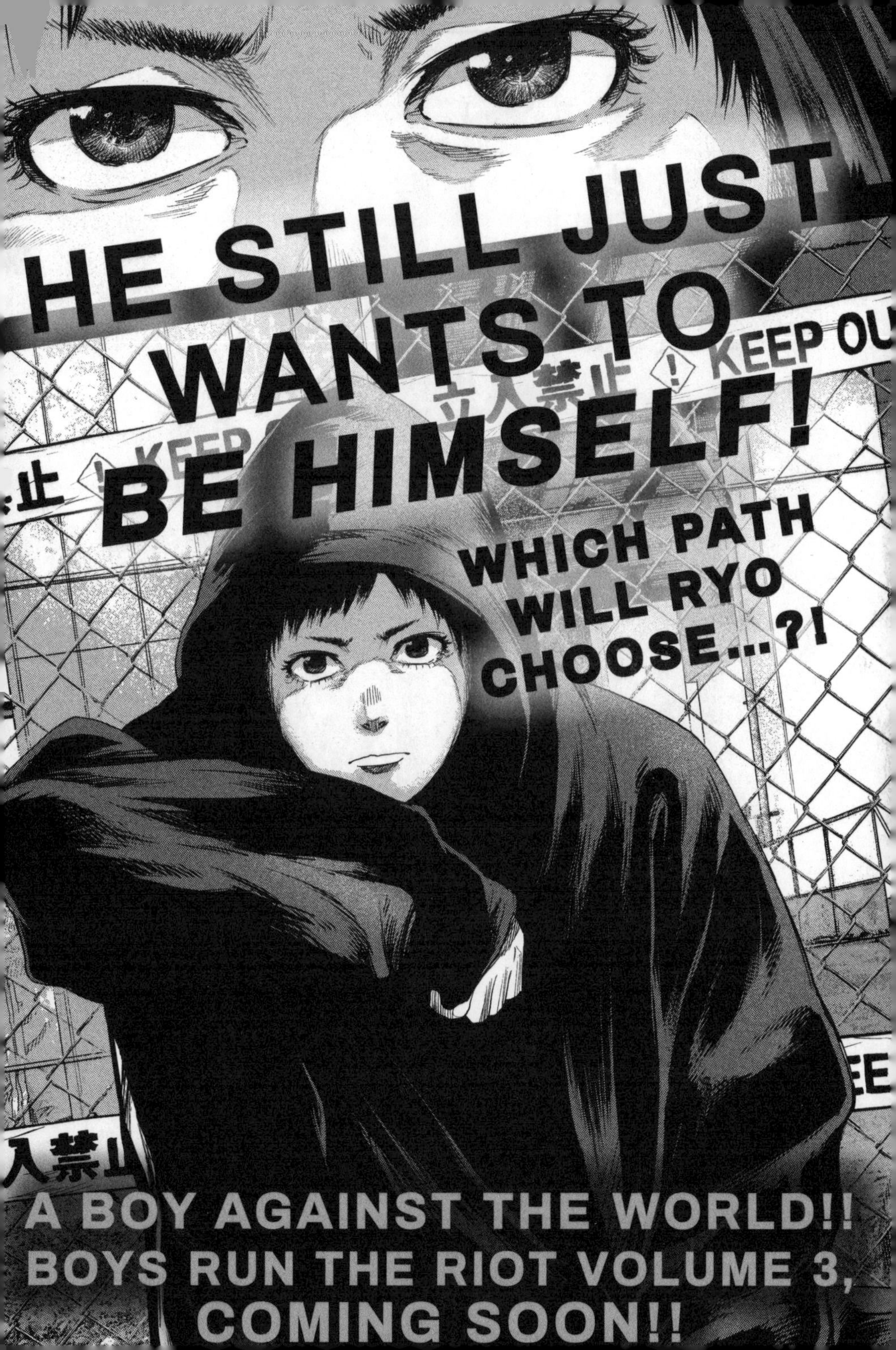
HE STILL JUST WANTS TO BE HIMSELF!
WHICH PATH WILL RYO CHOOSE...?!
KEEP OU
立入禁止
A BOY AGAINST THE WORLD!!
BOYS RUN THE RIOT VOLUME 3, COMING SOON!!

PERFECT WORLD

Rie Aruga

A TOUCHING NEW SERIES ABOUT LOVE AND COPING WITH DISABILITY

An office party reunites Tsugumi with her high school crush Itsuki. He's realized his dream of becoming an architect, but along the way, he experienced a spinal injury that put him in a wheelchair. Now Tsugumi's rekindled feelings will butt up against prejudices she never considered — and Itsuki will have to decide if he's ready to let someone into his heart...

"Depicts with great delicacy and courage the difficulties some with disabilities experience getting involved in romantic relationships... Rie Aruga refuses to romanticize, pushing her heroine to face the reality of disability. She invites her readers to the same tasks of empathy, knowledge and recognition."
—Slate.fr

"An important entry [in manga romance]... The emotional core of both plot and characters indicates thoughtfulness... [Aruga's] research is readily apparent in the text and artwork, making this feel like a real story."
—Anime News Network

The adorable new odd-
couple cat comedy manga
from the creator of the
beloved *Chi's Sweet Home*,
in full color!

Sue & Tai-chan

Konami Kanata

Sue is an aging housecat who's looking forward to living out her life in
peace... but her plans change when the mischievous black tomcat Tai-
chan enters the picture! Hey! Sue never signed up to be a catsitter!
Sue & Tai-chan is the latest from the reigning meow-narch of cute kitty
comics, Konami Kanata.

KC
KODANSHA
COMICS

Young characters and steampunk setting, like *Howl's Moving Castle* and *Battle Angel Alita*

Beyond the Clouds © 2018 Nicke / Ki-oon

A boy with a talent for machines and a mysterious girl whose wings he's fixed will take you beyond the clouds! In the tradition of the high-flying, resonant adventure stories of Studio Ghibli comes a gorgeous tale about the longing of young hearts for adventure and friendship!

THE WORLD OF CLAMP!

Cardcaptor Sakura
Collector's Edition

Cardcaptor Sakura:
Clear Card

Magic Knight Rayearth
25th Anniversary Box Set

Chobits

TSUBASA Omnibus

TSUBASA WoRLD CHRoNiCLE

xxxHOLiC Omnibus

xxxHOLiC Rei

CLOVER Collector's Edition

Kodansha Comics welcomes you to explore the expansive world of CLAMP, the all-female artist collective that has produced some of the most acclaimed manga of the century. Our growing catalog includes icons like *Cardcaptor Sakura* and *Magic Knight Rayearth*, each crafted with CLAMP's one-of-a-kind style and characters!

The beloved characters from *Cardcaptor Sakura* return in a brand new, reimagined fantasy adventure!

"[*Tsubasa*] takes readers on a fantastic ride that only gets more exhilarating with each successive chapter." —Anime News Network

In the Kingdom of Clow, an archaeological dig unleashes an incredible power, causing Princess Sakura to lose her memories. To save her, her childhood friend Syaoran must follow the orders of the Dimension Witch and travel alongside Kurogane, an unrivaled warrior; Fai, a powerful magician; and Mokona, a curiously strange creature, to retrieve Sakura's dispersed memories!

MAGIC ◉ KNIGHT RAYEARTH

25TH ANNIVERSARY EDITION

CLAMP

A BELOVED CLASSIC MAKES ITS STUNNING RETURN IN THIS GORGEOUS, LIMITED EDITION BOX SET!

This tale of three Tokyo teenagers who cross through a magical portal and become the champions of another world is a modern manga classic. The box set includes three volumes of manga covering the entire first series of *Magic Knight Rayearth*, plus the series's super-rare full-color art book companion, all printed at a larger size than ever before on premium paper, featuring a newly-revised translation and lettering, and exquisite foil-stamped covers.

A strictly limited edition, this will be gone in a flash!

KODANSHA COMICS

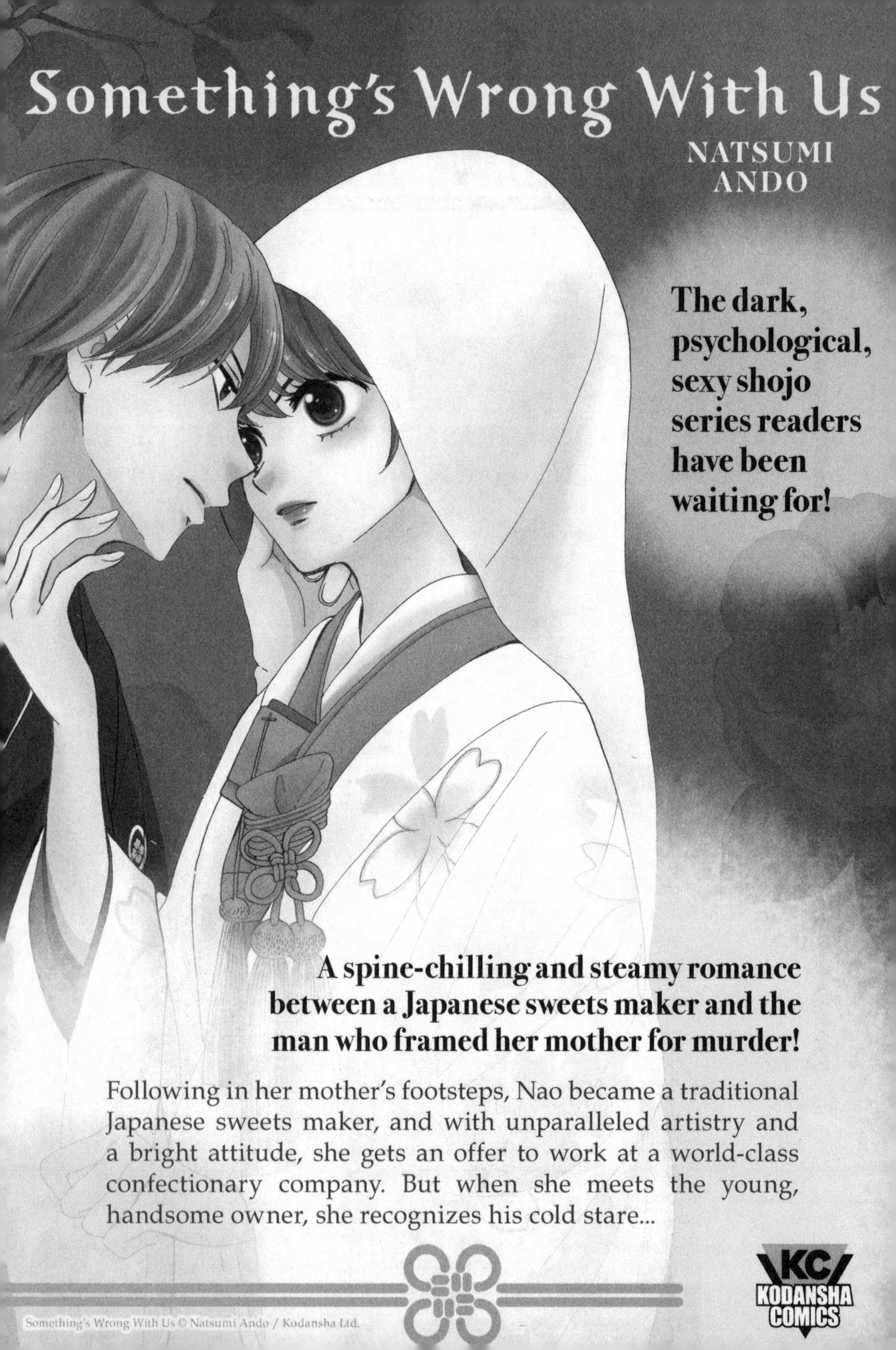
Something's Wrong With Us
NATSUMI ANDO
The dark, psychological, sexy shojo series readers have been waiting for!
A spine-chilling and steamy romance between a Japanese sweets maker and the man who framed her mother for murder!
Following in her mother's footsteps, Nao became a traditional Japanese sweets maker, and with unparalleled artistry and a bright attitude, she gets an offer to work at a world-class confectionary company. But when she meets the young, handsome owner, she recognizes his cold stare...
KC KODANSHA COMICS
Something's Wrong With Us © Natsumi Ando / Kodansha Ltd.

A SMART, NEW ROMANTIC COMEDY FOR FANS OF *SHORTCAKE CAKE* AND *TERRACE HOUSE!*

KC KODANSHA COMICS

A romance manga starring high school girl Meeko, who learns to live on her own in a boarding house whose living room is home to the odd (but handsome) Matsunaga-san. She begins to adjust to her new life away from her parents, but Meeko soon learns that no matter how far away from home she is, she's still a young girl at heart — especially when she finds herself falling for Matsunaga-san.

"Clever, sassy, and original....*xxxHOLiC* has the inherent hallmarks of a runaway hit."
—NewType magazine

Beautifully seductive artwork and uniquely Japanese depictions of the supernatural will hypnotize CLAMP fans!

xxxHOLiC OMNIBUS 1

CLAMP

xxxHOLiC © CLAMP ShigatsuTsuitachi CO.,LTD./Kodansha Ltd.
xxxHOLiC Rei © CLAMP ShigatsuTsuitachi CO.,LTD./Kodansha Ltd.

Kimihiro Watanuki is haunted by visions of ghosts and spirits. He seeks help from a mysterious woman named Yuko, who claims she can help. However, Watanuki must work for Yuko in order to pay for her aid. Soon Watanuki finds himself employed in Yuko's shop, where he sees things and meets customers that are stranger than anything he could have ever imagined.

KC KODANSHA COMICS

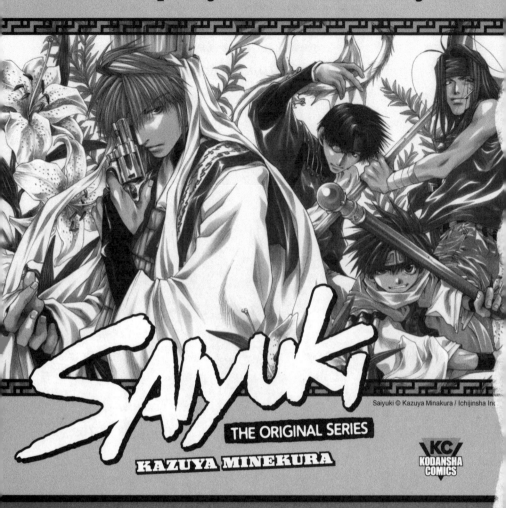

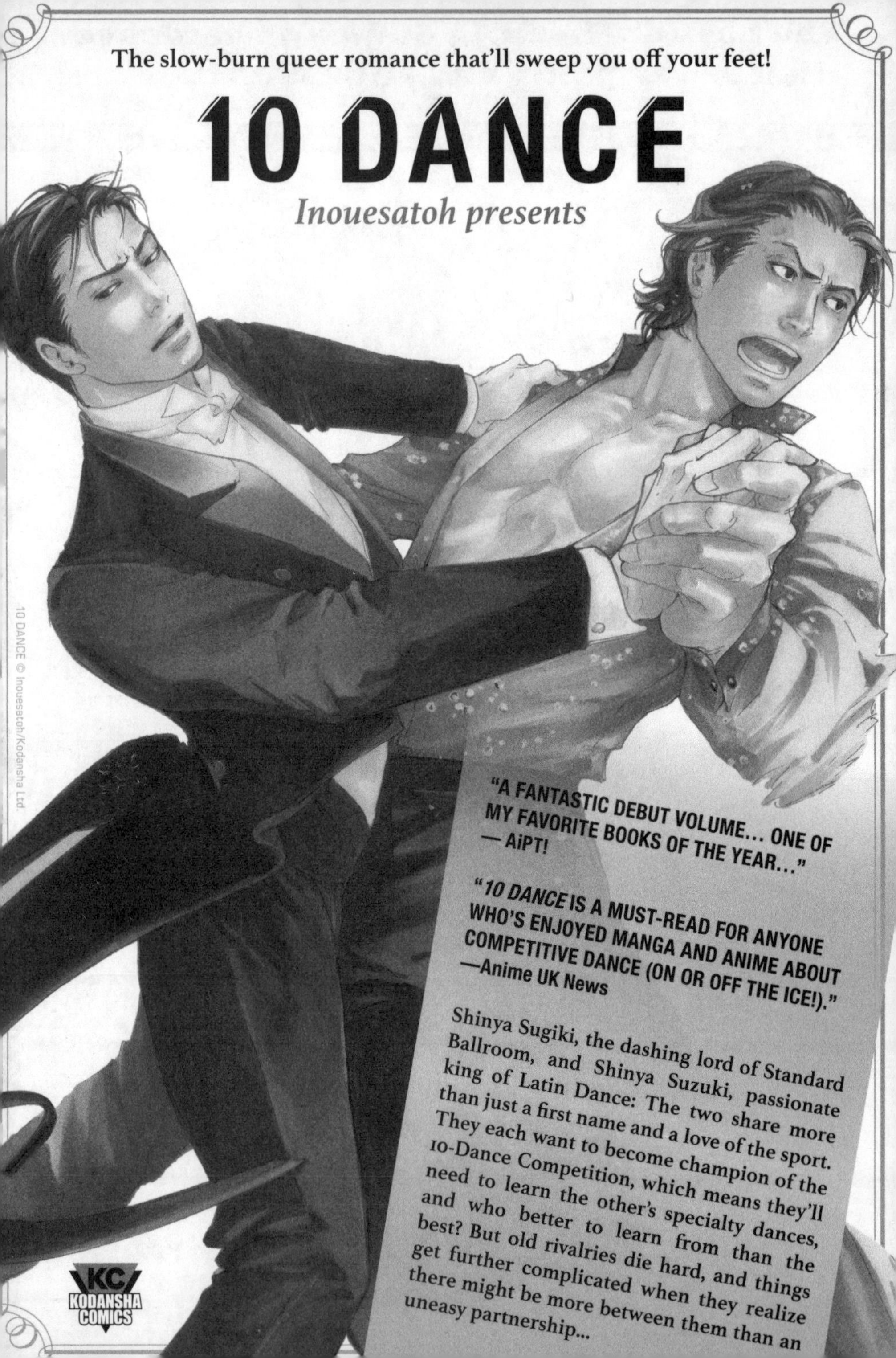

The slow-burn queer romance that'll sweep you off your feet!
10 DANCE
Inouesatoh presents
10 DANCE © Inouesatoh/Kodansha Ltd.
"A FANTASTIC DEBUT VOLUME… ONE OF MY FAVORITE BOOKS OF THE YEAR…"
— AiPT!
"10 DANCE IS A MUST-READ FOR ANYONE WHO'S ENJOYED MANGA AND ANIME ABOUT COMPETITIVE DANCE (ON OR OFF THE ICE!)."
—Anime UK News
Shinya Sugiki, the dashing lord of Standard Ballroom, and Shinya Suzuki, passionate king of Latin Dance: The two share more than just a first name and a love of the sport. They each want to become champion of the 10-Dance Competition, which means they'll need to learn the other's specialty dances, and who better to learn from than the best? But old rivalries die hard, and things get further complicated when they realize there might be more between them than an uneasy partnership…
KC
KODANSHA COMICS

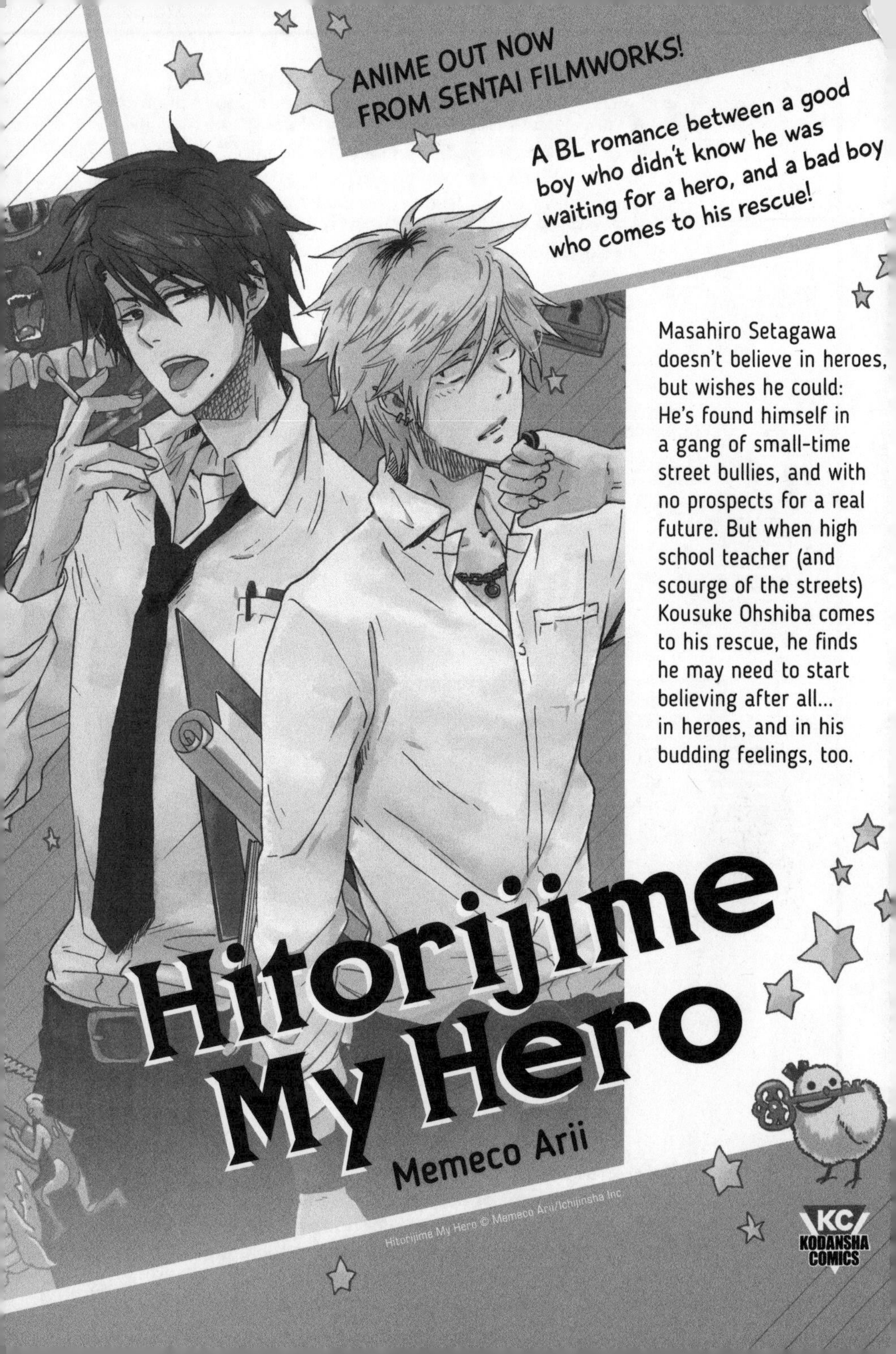
ANIME OUT NOW FROM SENTAI FILMWORKS!
A BL romance between a good boy who didn't know he was waiting for a hero, and a bad boy who comes to his rescue!
Masahiro Setagawa doesn't believe in heroes, but wishes he could: He's found himself in a gang of small-time street bullies, and with no prospects for a real future. But when high school teacher (and scourge of the streets) Kousuke Ohshiba comes to his rescue, he finds he may need to start believing after all... in heroes, and in his budding feelings, too.
Hitorijime My Hero
Memeco Arii
Hitorijime My Hero © Memeco Arii/Ichijinsha Inc.
KC KODANSHA COMICS

A Kodansha Comics Trade Paperback Original
Boys Run the Riot 2 copyright © 2020 Keito Gaku
English translation copyright © 2021 Keito Gaku

All rights reserved.

Published in the United States by Kodansha Comics, an imprint of Kodansha USA Publishing, LLC, New York.

Publication rights for this English edition arranged through Kodansha Ltd., Tokyo.

First published in Japan in 2020 by Kodansha Ltd., Tokyo as *Boys Run the Riot*, volume 2.

ISBN 978-1-64651-117-4

Printed in the United States of America.

www.kodansha.us

9 8 7 6 5 4 3 2
Translation: Leo McDonagh
Lettering: Ashley Caswell
Editing: Tiff Joshua TJ Ferentini
Kodansha Comics edition cover design by Phil Balsman

Publisher: Kiichiro Sugawara

Director of publishing services: Ben Applegate
Associate director of operations: Stephen Pakula
Publishing services managing editors: Alanna Ruse, Madison Salters
Assistant production managers: Emi Lotto, Angela Zurlo
Logo and character art ©Kodansha USA Publishing, LLC